BUILDING A *21*ST CENTURY SES

ENSURING LEADERSHIP EXCELLENCE IN OUR FEDERAL GOVERNMENT

★ A PUBLICATION OF THE NATIONAL ACADEMY OF PUBLIC ADMINISTRATION ★

Edited by Dr. Ronald P. Sanders

With Dr. Elaine S. Brenner and Frederick S. Richardson

A powerful (and unprecedented) collection of perspectives on the future of the Federal government's elite career executive corps, from some of our Nation's most respected public sector leaders.

NATIONAL ACADEMY OF
PUBLIC ADMINISTRATION

The National Academy of Public Administration (the Academy) is an independent, non-profit, and non-partisan organization established in 1967 to assist government leaders in building more effective, efficient, accountable, and transparent organizations. Chartered by Congress to provide non-partisan expert advice, the Academy's unique feature is its over 850 Fellows—including former cabinet officers, Members of Congress, governors, mayors, and state legislators, as well as prominent scholars, business executives, and public administrators. The Academy helps the Federal government address its critical management challenges through in-depth studies and analyses, advisory services and technical assistance, Congressional testimony, forums and conferences, and online stakeholder engagement. Under contracts with government agencies, some of which are directed by Congress, as well as grants from private foundations, the Academy provides insights on key public management issues, as well as advisory services to government agencies.

The opinions expressed in these writings are those of the authors and do not necessarily reflect the views of the Academy. To access Academy reports, please visit our website at www.napawash.org.

BUILDING A *21*ST CENTURY SES
ENSURING LEADERSHIP EXCELLENCE IN OUR FEDERAL GOVERNMENT

★ A PUBLICATION OF THE NATIONAL ACADEMY OF PUBLIC ADMINISTRATION ★

Edited by Dr. Ronald P. Sanders

With Dr. Elaine S. Brenner and Frederick S. Richardson

Contributors
(Listed in order of appearance):

The Honorable Beth Cobert
The Honorable Michèle Flournoy
The Honorable Christine H. Fox
Emelia S. Probasco
Robert Shea
General Michael V. Hayden (USAF, retired)
Ambassador Patrick F. Kennedy
The Honorable Sean O'Keefe
The Honorable Beth McGrath
Admiral Thad Allen (USCG, retired)
The Honorable Charles Rossotti
Professor Steven Kelman
Dr. Ronald P. Sanders
The Honorable David M. Walker
Professor Robert Tobias
Letitia Long
Dr. Reginald Wells
Robert Corsi
Dr. Suzanne Logan
The Honorable G. Edward DeSeve
The Honorable Robert F. Hale
Robert Goldenkoff
Stephen Shih
The Honorable Daniel Werfel

BUILDING A *21*ST CENTURY SES
ENSURING LEADERSHIP EXCELLENCE IN OUR FEDERAL GOVERNMENT

★ A PUBLICATION OF THE NATIONAL ACADEMY OF PUBLIC ADMINISTRATION ★

Edited by Dr. Ronald P. Sanders

With Dr. Elaine S. Brenner and Frederick S. Richardson

NATIONAL ACADEMY OF
PUBLIC ADMINISTRATION

Contents

Foreword

The over 7,000 dedicated public servants comprising the career United States Senior Executive Service (SES) are critical to the functioning of our federal government. Established as a government-wide executive corps by the Civil Service Reform Act of 1978, the SES of the 21st Century is at a critical juncture as it approaches its fortieth anniversary. Widely acknowledged challenges include:

- An ongoing retirement wave that could result in the loss of institutional knowledge at the very time when government's tasks have become more complex than ever;

- Limited inter-departmental and interagency mobility that reinforces government silos and makes solving enterprise-wide challenges more

- The need for new skills and competencies in order to lead and manage in a more virtual, networked, and globalized world; and

- A succession pool of up-and-coming GS-14s and 15s who may be less inclined to apply for and join the SES.

This book is based on a forum on the future of the SES sponsored by the Brookings Institution's Office of Executive Education and Booz Allen Hamilton, and it includes thoughtful chapters by many of the forum's participants, as well as a number of other commentators—all of whom are either current or former senior government leaders in their own right. This makes the book unique in bringing together the practical perspectives of leaders with substantial experience as (or with) members of the SES to offer their perspective on such fundamental issues as the proper institutional role of the SES and the most critical leadership qualities for the 21st century, as well as how to develop the next generation of senior government leaders and revitalize the SES for decades to come.

The National Academy of Public Administration (the Academy) is an independent, nonpartisan, nonprofit organization chartered by the U.S. Congress to offer trusted advice on public governance and management to governments at all levels. The book was edited by Academy Fellow (and Booz Allen Vice President) Dr. Ronald Sanders, with the critical assistance of his colleagues

Dr. Elaine Brenner and Fred Richardson, and he also offers his own introductory and concluding commentary, as well as a number of recommendations for reform, in each section of the book.

As Fellows of the Academy, we are pleased that our organization has been able to collaborate with Dr. Sanders and the contributors—most of whom are also Academy Fellows in their own right—to publish this important book. Although as individuals we do not necessarily endorse all the views expressed, we are pleased that the Academy can serve the American people by ensuring a wide variety of perspectives and ideas are presented.

In that regard, this book is dedicated to the senior career executives who have contributed so much to this nation and to those who will join and lead them in the future. Our hope is that this book not only educates, informs, enlightens, and inspires, but also spurs needed actions to reform and revitalize a critical component of the American Civil Service.

Rodney Slater

Janice Lachance

Linda Springer

Robert Shea

Acknowledgements

I would like to acknowledge the efforts of several individuals whose contributions helped make this book a reality. First and foremost, I would like to thank Elaine Brenner and Fred Richardson, two of my Booz Allen colleagues; this project was over two years in the works, and it is no exaggeration to say that without their tireless efforts, this volume simply would not have been possible...they did much of the dirty work that goes on behind the scenes in any effort like this: Proofing and editing (endlessly, so it seemed), gently but forcibly riding herd on our many very busy contributors, and perhaps most importantly, telling me—sometimes diplomatically, sometimes not—that something I'd written made no sense. Gayle Daniels, my faithful Executive Assistant, also lent a hand whenever we asked. Their assistance was too invaluable to measure, and I'll forever be grateful for what they did.

In addition to these individuals, two organizations deserve special recognition: The National Academy of Public Administration and Booz Allen Hamilton. Realizing early on the potential importance of the project, former Academy President Dan Blair took a chance on it without hesitation, and both he and his successor, Terry Gerton, have never wavered in their support for it. The same goes for their very capable and dedicated staff—most especially Joe Mitchell, Harrison Redoglia, Adam Darr, and Allison Brigati—who made good on that support; they were always there when we needed them, always ready to roll up their sleeves and work an issue, and always encouraging when we hit a snag.

Booz Allen was equally forthcoming, especially Executive Vice Presidents Jack Mayer and Betty Thompson, the firm's HR Director; sponsors of Booz Allen's innovative Fellows program (I was privileged to be the first to receive that designation), they and other senior company leaders were just as unwavering in their support as well, generously providing financial and other in-kind support as necessary, and more importantly, allowing me—as well as Elaine and Fred—to devote what turned out to be a considerable amount of time to the project. However, Booz Allen counts thousands of career Federal executives as its valued clients, and this book offers a way for it to express the firm's appreciation for the tough jobs that those career executives have.

A number of other individuals also deserve our thanks:

- First, the contributors themselves, whose commitment to the project—and to the career senior executive corps—was unequivocal, who took time from their more-than-busy schedules to author their individual chapters, each important in its own right, and who were always patient

- Secondly, the Academy Fellows who provided advice and input to this important project—the Honorable Rodney Slater, the Honorable Janice Lachance, the Honorable Linda Springer, and Robert Shea—for their wisdom, insights, and patience.

- Thirdly, Brookings Executive Education (BEE), and especially its Deputy Director Mary Ellen Joyce (herself an Academy Fellow). BEE and Mary Ellen were my partners in organizing the original Brookings symposium back in 2014 that led to this anthology, and they were always there for us, supportive right up until the very end.

- Fourth, Booz Allen's Grant McLaughlin and Hillary Komma, who helped with publicity; Gina Fisher, our meticulous editor; Michael Pacheco, who designed the cover, and Christopher Rogers, Miriam Langermann, and Dena Papazoglou, who provided research assistance. And thanks to the many others who contributed in small but important ways to the production of this anthology.

And last but certainly not least, on behalf of everyone who had a hand in this project, I want to personally thank the members of the Federal government's senior executive corps, past, present and future. Your selfless dedication and unflinching commitment to public service are too often unappreciated and unrecognized, but that makes what you do all the more remarkable, and I am proud to say I was one of you once. I just wish the American public knew all that you do on their behalf, but I hope that this book helps them begin to understand how important your role is in our way of governance.

Dr. Ronald Sanders

Editor Biographies

Ronald P. Sanders, DPA

Dr. Ronald P. Sanders is a Vice President and Fellow with Booz Allen, where he supports the firm's top clients deal with their most pressing organizational challenges. He joined the firm in 2010, after almost 39 years of Federal service, 21 of them as a decorated senior career executive. Over the course of his government career, he served as the Intelligence Community's first Chief Human Capital Officer; the Office of Personnel Management's first Associate Director for Human Capital Policy; the Internal Revenue Service's first Chief Human Resources Officer; and the Defense Department's Director of Civilian Personnel. He has also held faculty appointments with Syracuse University's Maxwell School, The George Washington University (where he received his doctorate in public administration), and the Brookings Institution. Dr. Sanders has received three Presidential Rank Awards from three different agencies, two Theodore Roosevelt Awards for Distinguished Public Service from OPM; the National Intelligence Distinguished Service Medal; and an Innovations in American Government Award from Harvard's Kennedy School. Elected a Fellow of the National Academy of Public Administration in 2006, his previous books include *Tackling Wicked Government Problems: A Practical Guide for Enterprise Leaders* (Brookings Institution Press, 2014).

Elaine S. Brenner, Ph.D.

Dr. Elaine S. Brenner has over 25 years of experience consulting with federal agencies on their executive development programs, workforce transformation strategies, and human capital initiatives. As a business leader in Booz Allen's Health market, she oversees organizational consulting projects designed to improve organizational performance, individual performance, and employee engagement. Her work with federal executives includes launching a first-of-its-kind, cross-agency senior executive development program designed to encourage cross-agency collaboration; creating and administering leadership assessments; establishing an SES coaching program; and designing enterprise leadership labs. Dr. Brenner holds a Ph.D. in Industrial/Organizational Psychology from The George Washington University and is certified to administer several commercially-available leadership assessment tools.

Frederick S. Richardson, MPAff

Mr. Frederick S. Richardson is a leadership and organizational development consultant at Booz Allen, where his clients have included the Office of the Secretary of Defense, the Federal Executive Institute, VA Learning University, OPM, NASA, EPA, the Securities & Exchange Commission, the US Forest Service, the Department of the Navy, and the Department of the Interior. Mr. Richardson is the manager of Booz Allen's Leadership Development Community of Practice and is also an adjunct instructor for the Booz Allen Learning & Development program. He holds a Master of Public Affairs from the University of Texas, a BA in English from Kenyon College, and is certified as a leadership coach by Georgetown University and the International Coach Federation.

Academy Foreword Author Biographies

The Honorable Rodney Slater

Slater was the 13ᵗʰ U.S. Secretary of Transportation from 1998-2001. During his services as Secretary, Slater's bipartisan and inclusive approach to problem solving earned him tremendous respect and admiration on both sides of the aisle, enabling him to have strong relationships with the White House, Congress, and business, labor and political leaders. Previous to his service as transportation secretary, Slater served as director of the Federal Highway Administration. Slater led Toyota's Safety Advisory Panel and was recently selected by National Highway Transportation Safety Administration to serve as the Independent Monitor of FCA. Slater was elected into the Academy Fellowship in 2006.

The Honorable Janice Lachance

Janice Lachance is President-Elect of the American Society for Public Administration. She served as Chief Executive Officer of the Special Libraries Association for over a decade, leading a comprehensive research effort to create a shared, evidence-based vision of the future role of the information professional operating in a global economy. Prior to her service at SLA, she was nominated by President Clinton and unanimously confirmed by the U.S. Senate to be the Director of the U.S. Office of Personnel Management, the federal government's independent human resources agency. A leader in her profession, an expert in governance, and a dedicated community volunteer, she is a Fellow of the American Society of Association Executives, a past Member of the Board of Directors of ASAE and The Center for Association Leadership, and former Chair of its CEO Advisory Board. Lachance is also a Fellow of the National Academy of Public Administration.

The Honorable Linda Springer

Springer served as the Director of the United States Office of Personnel Management from 2005 to 2008. Previously, Ms. Springer was Controller at the White House Office of Management and Budget and head of the Office of Federal Financial Management. She has been deeply involved in public service as a Fellow, National Academy of Public Administration; Principal, Partnership for Public Service; the President's Commission on White House Fellowships; Principal, U.S. Joint Financial Management Improvement

Program; the President's Council on Integrity and Efficiency; and the President's Management Council Executive Committee. She also led the Federal CFO, CHCO and Senior Real Property Officers Councils. Prior to her government service, Ms. Springer spent 25 years in the financial services industry in financial and executive management positions.

Robert Shea

Shea is a Principal at Grant Thornton LLP, an accounting and consulting firm. He is Past Chair of the National Academy of Public Administration and a member of the Commission on Evidence-based Policymaking. Before joining Grant Thornton, he was with the U.S. Office of Management and Budget as Associate Director for Administration and Government Performance, Associate Director for Management, and Counsel to the Controller. Previously, he served as Counsel to the Senate Committee on Governmental Affairs, Legislative Director in the Office of Representative Pete Sessions, and Special Assistant/Professional Staff Member for the House Committee on Government Reform and Oversight.

The Case for Change

Introduction: The Senior Executive Service…yesterday, today, and tomorrow

They number just over 7,000, yet their work affects every citizen of this country …and millions more across the globe. They are responsible for a Federal budget that exceeds $3.5 trillion annually, yet they represent an infinitesimally small fraction of the people and programs they oversee. Millions of people in and out of uniform—and in and out of government—depend on them for direction and leadership. They do glamorous things like landing robots on Mars and searching for a cure for AIDS. But they also do the mundane (but essential) work of government: collecting taxes, paying Medicare bills and Social Security pensions, building roads and bridges and dams, and processing the countless forms that fuel the engines of government.

They are members of the Federal government's Senior Executive Service (SES) and its progeny, archetypal bureaucrats who've dedicated a good part of their working lives to public service; largely invisible to the public, they are taken for granted—unless and until there's a scandal involving one of their own, and then they're demonized. Their official symbol is a stylized keystone; like its architectural equivalent, it is intended to underscore the institutional importance of the SES as a lynchpin in our system of government…even though the SES was never envisioned by the Founding Fathers.

Called on to lead the unbelievably complex organizations and programs that deliver public goods and services, the SES—and its excellence—is undeniably essential to effective governance. This book is about its members, the mandarins of our nation's career civil service. They are the senior career executives who operate at the interface between the deciding and the doing of government. And our premise in this anthology is simple: The competence of these career executives is vital to 21st century government; the efficacy of our public institutions—especially but not exclusively Federal ones— depends in no small part on their technical expertise and leadership skills.

And they are at risk.

Purpose and promise: The classical paradigm

Conceived almost four decades ago as part of the landmark Civil Service Reform Act (CSRA) of 1978,[1] the SES promised the Federal government's very best and brightest, developed and deployed to meet the challenges of modern day government. I would argue that it has largely fulfilled its promise, but the world today is far different than the world was back then, and one must ask whether the SES can continue to keep that promise as we approach the third decade of the 21st century.

The original premise of the SES was grounded in public administration's classic (but now largely passé) paradigm: the separation of policy and administration. Thus, the underlying purpose of the SES is described in its enabling statute in purely instrumental and apolitical terms: to "ensure that the executive management of the U.S. government is responsive to the nation's needs, policies, and goals."[2] That paradigm was also implicit throughout the CSRA more broadly, with its emphasis on bringing an unresponsive and poorly performing bureaucracy under control. Sound familiar?

In the case of the SES, the Act established a government-wide system for selecting, assigning, developing, rewarding, and managing the men and women who administer the thousands of Federal policies and programs that are vital to the nation.[3] In theory, the personnel rules that direct that system serve as a common and defining denominator binding them together. And the SES members who are products of that system are themselves portrayed in the law by a number of classical characteristics, things like efficiency, effectiveness, continuity, accountability, and compliance.

In that regard, the SES has historically served at the interface (or buffer?) between the political appointees at the top of a government agency and the front-line career civil servants who perform its mission. Indeed, given the almost-inevitably hierarchical structure of government, senior career executives tend to be positioned at the confluence of policy and execution.

[1] Civil Service Reform Act of 1978, 6 Pub. L. No. 95-454 § 601 et seq. (1978).

[2] Ibid.

[3] Carey, M. P. (2012). The Senior Executive Service: Background and options for reform. Washington, DC: Congressional Research Service. Retrieved from http://digitalcommons.ilr.cornell.edu/cgi/viewcontent.cgi?article=1942&context=key_workplace

That seems the very embodiment of the classical public administration paradigm. However, I would argue that this structural artifact notwithstanding, most senior executives find themselves—on any given day—somewhere along a continuum of deciding on one end and doing on the other, in an institutional role that includes but goes far beyond neutral competence and apolitical administration.

Taken together, these characteristics describe an SES that was supposed to be neutral, instrumental, and value free, dutifully implementing law and regulation without bias or partiality. Of course, as we will see in the pages that follow, there's far more to being a career executive than that, even though the Service's enabling statute only *implied* a larger, more crucial, more institutional role for career executives among the various other actors in our system of governance.

This may have been deliberate, even politically expedient, given the historical context of the CSRA (it was not exactly a celebration of the effectiveness of the civil service). Nevertheless, while the neutral instrumentality of the SES may have been reason enough for its creation back in 1979, this is only part of the story. When it comes to the challenges of 21st century government, one must ask whether the system—and the leaders it produces—is still up to it.

SES summit at Brookings

The SES will be 40 years old in about 2 years so, as far as government institutions go, it is still relatively nascent. But even as it approaches that modest milestone, it is no exaggeration to suggest that it is at risk. The well-publicized malfeasance of just a few of its members has put the entire senior executive corps squarely in the crosshairs of Congress and the public. And while those headlines will (hopefully) fade, the demographics won't. This year, more than 65 percent of current SES members will be retirement eligible,[4] and the best and brightest of their potential replacements—current GS-14s and 15s—no longer automatically aspire to its lofty but increasingly tarnished status.[5]

[4] Partnership for Public Service & McKinsey and Company. (2016). *A pivotal moment for the Senior Executive Service: Measures, aspirational practices and stories of success.* Washington, DC: Partnership for Public Service.
[5] Federal Daily. (2010, April 27). Senior Executive candidates worry about pay, work/family balance. *FCW.* Retrieved from https://fcw.com/Articles/2010/04/27/SES-survey-salary-benefits.aspx

However, beyond those immediate exigencies, what of the longer term future of the SES? Is today's senior career service—and today's senior career executive—ready for the challenges that the third decade of the 21st century will bring?

In November 2014, with that daunting question at the fore, over two dozen current and former senior government executives—senior career and appointed leaders who served both Republican and Democratic administrations—convened at the Brookings Institution for a day-long summit on the future of the SES. Sponsored by Brookings Executive Education[6] and Booz Allen Hamilton, the summit's proceedings were intended to serve as the beginnings of a blueprint for modernizing the SES while still remaining true to its original vision and values.

The summit was keynoted by then-Office of Management and Budget (OMB) Deputy Director (later Acting Office of Personnel Management Director), the Honorable Beth Cobert, and former OPM Director Katherine Archuleta. Participants included *Ambassador Patrick F. Kennedy*,[7] then-Under Secretary of State for Management; *Chris Mihm*, Government Accountability Office (GAO) Director for Strategic Issues; *Professor Don Kettl*, then-Dean of the University of Maryland's School of Public Policy; the *Honorable Sean O'Keefe*, former National Aeronautics and Space Administration (NASA) Administrator; *Admiral Thad Allen*, former Commandant of the Coast Guard; the *Honorable Robert F. Hale*, former U.S. Department of Defense (DOD) Comptroller; the *Honorable Scott Gould*, former U.S. Department of Veterans Affairs (VA) Deputy Secretary; and the Honorable Christine H. Fox, former Acting Deputy Secretary of Defense.

Other participants included the *Honorable Rafael Borras*, former U.S. Department of Homeland Security (DHS) Under Secretary for Management; the *Honorable Beth McGrath*, former DOD Deputy Chief Management Officer (DCMO); the *Honorable Daniel Werfel*, former OMB Comptroller and Acting Internal Revenue Service (IRS) Commissioner; the *Honorable Dan Blair*, President of the National Academy of Public Administration (the Academy); and Stephen Shih and Dr. Suzanne Logan of OPM. The event was hosted by *me* and *Mary Ellen Joyce*, Executive Director of Brookings Executive Education, and moderated by *Tim Clark*, Editor at Large for the Government Executive Media Group.

---

[6] All references to Brookings Executive Education are used with permission. In addition, all references to Nickerson, J. A., & Sanders, R. P. (Eds.). (2014). *Tackling wicked government problems: A practical guide for developing enterprise leaders.* Washington, DC: Brookings Institution Press are with the permission of the Brookings Institution Press.
[7] Individuals whose names are in italics are Academy Fellows.

Beginning a blueprint for reform

So what do these luminaries know about the SES? Wouldn't it better to ask career executives (or human capital policymakers or academics) how to build an SES for the 21st century, instead of their far more transient political bosses?

Certainly the vantage of career executives is valuable in that regard, but, with all due respect to their point of view, we thought it would be better to ask those who have had a chance to see SES members (in most cases, dozens of them) in action on the job—that is, appointees who have had to rely on their career executives for information, advice, and action. Thus, instead of asking the usual suspects what ails the system and how to improve it, we posed that question to those who had a unique and heretofore untapped perspective on the matter: those senior political appointees who, in our system of government, actually had the opportunity to *lead* members of the SES to achieve the program and policy goals of a particular administration.

After all, serving those administrations is the overarching purpose of the SES, its raison d'etre, and we felt no group had a better lens on that purpose than those who, in theory, had themselves been held accountable to a president and the public to accomplish those ends. To be sure, we had a few career executives, personnel experts, and academics among us; however, most of the symposium's participants were current and former sub-cabinet-level appointees, drawn more or less equally from Republican and Democratic administrations. We asked them to address five fundamental questions:

- What kinds of challenges are senior government executives likely to confront as they lead 21st century government?

- Given the original vision for the SES, what should the institutional role of career executives be in that government?

- What leadership competencies, both enduring and emerging, will be required of senior career executives in the future?

- How can the Federal government best identify and develop the next generation of SES members in the face of changing external and internal challenges, career patterns, and individual expectations?

- What can the Federal government do to sustain a viable, vital senior executive corps into the future, given the likelihood of continuing fiscal austerity and antipathy toward government?

We divided up our group of luminaries into five panels, one for each of these questions, with each panelist asked to prepare an abstract-length paper or short presentation to share with the symposium at large. The insights they provided, both individually and collectively, were remarkable.

For example, symposium participants unanimously agreed that the founding vision of the SES—that is, a mobile corps of career executives intended to provide senior leadership expertise across the whole-of-government, whenever and wherever it might be needed—was worth preserving and protecting...even though that vision was still largely unrealized. They also concluded that the SES needs to be modernized if it is to realize that vision in the second and third decades of the 21st century and beyond, with particular attention paid to developing a cadre of senior career executives able to effectively lead across the entire Federal enterprise and not just a single agency.

In that regard, executive mobility was a major topic of discussion. It remains one of the most important elements of the SES' original vision....and one of its biggest disappointments. With only a few exceptions—the U.S. Intelligence Community's (IC) civilian joint duty requirement for one—the senior executive corps remains organizationally and functionally stove-piped. Symposium participants (most of whom have held multiple leadership positions in and out of government) all argued that mobility added immeasurably to an executive's development, with many advocating that it should be mandatory like it is in the military, Senior Foreign Service (SFS), and IC.

Finally (and inevitably), summit participants also discussed the issue of SES accountability, termination, and expedited appeal rights, all stemming from then-recent VA legislation truncating those appeal rights. While those with private sector experience noted that at-will employment was the standard there, everyone agreed on the need for some due process protections for career senior executives, at the very least to guard against politicization. That said, most argued that with sufficient protections, greater SES accountability was a good thing, perhaps offset by increased salary potential—in other words, greater risk should entail greater reward. However, increased salary potential would require legislation; in the face of congressional and public antipathy, summit participants were pessimistic in this regard.

Of course, many of these ideas have been discussed before. What made this discussion different was the group doing the discussing. As I previously indicated, the summit's sponsors felt that theirs was a unique lens on the SES—not just its individual members, but the entire system. The experiences of these appointees in that regard, all selected because of their reputation for leadership excellence as well as their thoughtfulness, offered a priceless set of lessons learned for current senior career executives, those who aspire to be, and those who (like most of our summit participants) would lead them.

Building a 21st century SES: The book

Those lessons and the leaders who learned them were the genesis of this book. At the conclusion of the summit at Brookings, organizers and participants alike concluded that the thoughts and recommendations of the summit—

made all the more credible by the stature of those offering them—were just too valuable to leave to a few-page summary or a story or two in the media. Moreover, the recommendations, if they are to come to pass, will require bold action on the part of the new administration and the new Congress. The fact that they would have the backing of a group of senior political appointees who have served both political parties, four different presidents, and as many as eight administrations improves their chances of implementation immeasurably.

It did not take much to convince the venerable Academy (with a grant from Booz Allen)[8] to agree to sponsor the publication of an anthology that attempted to capture the insights revealed during the discussions the day of the summit…and since.

The result is this book, organized around the same five questions we asked of summit participants, plus the thoughts of several other notable leaders who couldn't attend the summit: the *Honorable Michèle Flournoy*, former Under Secretary of Defense for Policy; General Michael V. Hayden, former Director of the National Security Agency (NSA) and the Central Intelligence Agency (CIA); Letitia Long, former Director of the National Geospatial-Intelligence Agency (NGA); the *Honorable G. Edward DeSeve*, former OMB Comptroller and Acting Deputy Director for Management; and the *Honorable David M. Walker*, former Comptroller General of the United States.

We asked each of these luminary leaders to contribute a chapter to the anthology. Rather than a dry set of policy recommendations, we asked them to tell a story—about their careers, their defining moments as leaders of career executives, their own personal leadership philosophies, and, most of all, their own individual views on improving the SES. In so doing, our contributors provide what we believe is a unique perspective on the Federal government's senior executive corps. That is what this anthology is—a collection of personal observations and insights of experienced leaders who have had to depend on career executives to fulfill their responsibilities to the people and the President.

If that is what the book is, here is what it isn't. We do not pretend—nor do we contend—that this is a product of empirical research or a comprehensive analysis of policy options for the SES. That is not to say we refrain from making recommendations…we do, a total of 23 major ones in all. However, they are based on almost half a millennium of practical experience, most of which has involved working with senior career executives on some of the most significant challenges our government has ever faced: the Global War on Terrorism, the Challenger shuttle disaster, the transformation of the IRS (twice), sequestration and the great shutdown of 2014, the resurgence of Russia and China, and the explosion of technology. Those events, and many others less visible, provide the evidentiary basis for the conclusions and recommendations that follow.

---

[8] Booz Allen also donated my time to organize, edit, and write portions of the book.

Organization of the anthology

As noted, this book is organized around the same five themes we addressed during the SES summit, with a section devoted to each theme. Each section begins with an Introduction that lays out some of the issues associated with its topic, followed by a series of four or more chapters contributed by our individual authors, and ending with several pages of Concluding Commentary and Recommendations by me. As noted, the individual chapters represent the voices and views of each contributor—and, where applicable, with the approval of their organization—but they do not necessarily represent the views of the Academy or the Fellows that provided advice and input to this project. The same is true for the conclusions and recommendations; those are mine and mine alone, and those who agree (or disagree) should feel free to take it up with me.

With that backdrop, here is the actual architecture of the book: We begin, as we did at the summit, with a sampling of the various challenges, internal and external, that senior leaders in government (political appointees as well as career executives) will likely confront in the future...although in retrospect, most of those future challenges are already demanding our attention today. With that strategic context, we then examine the institutional role of the SES, as originally conceived in 1979 and as it has since come to pass; in so doing, we ask whether that original role (or roles) is still valid today and tomorrow, and, if so, how it can become a reality.

Next, we look at the leadership qualities that will define the successful career executive in the future—some emerging, some enduring—and consider how those qualities can be refreshed. Given those qualities (and others), we look at how we can best develop the next generation of career executives to master them, not just in a classroom but on the job. And finally, we consider how the Federal government can sustain a vital, viable senior executive corps with some of our most sweeping conclusions and recommendations.

Here is a section-by-section roadmap of the book.

Section 1: The Challenges of 21st Century Government. In her lead-off chapter, the Honorable Beth Cobert,*[9] former Acting Director of OPM, discusses the Federal government's imperative to develop, engage, and mobilize a senior executive corps capable of taking on tomorrow's whole-of-government challenges. She is followed by the Honorable Michèle Flournoy, former Under Secretary of Defense for Policy, who suggests that government leaders need to understand the complex, interdependent geopolitical environment, and in particular, how nation-states—and their senior leaders—exercise

---

[9] Those individuals identified by an asterisk authored their chapters in their official government capacity; as such, their contributions are considered works of the U.S. Government and are not subject to U.S. copyright laws (however, foreign copyright laws may apply).

power in that world. Flournoy also discusses the importance of developing career leaders and recounts her own successful Pentagon efforts in that regard.

In her chapter, the Honorable Christine H. Fox, former Acting Deputy Secretary of Defense, and her co-author Emelia S. Probasco describe the ubiquitous nature of high-technologies, especially two-edged technologies that can both benefit and imperil society, and how all senior government leaders—not just those who oversee technology programs—need to understand their implications. And finally, former senior OMB official Robert Shea discusses the challenges of leading government in today's hyper-partisan political environment, and he offers some lessons learned that may help career executives navigate it.

Section 2: Reexamining the Institutional Role of the SES. In a story drawn from his challenging days at the CIA, General Michael Hayden, former Director of the CIA and the NSA, talks about the need for career executives to have the courage to "speak truth to power," especially when lives are on the line…and the need for their senior leaders (like him) to have the courage to defend them when they do. The U.S. Department of State's (DOS) former Under Secretary for Management, career Ambassador Patrick F. Kennedy,* talks about integrating and managing State's two senior services—the SES and the SFS—and in so doing, he offers a model for the rest of government.

The Honorable Sean O'Keefe, former NASA Administrator and Deputy Director of OMB, discusses what may be one of the career executive's most important institutional roles, even though it happens only once every 4 years: maintaining continuity during presidential transition and "breaking in" a new set of political bosses. And finally, the Honorable Beth McGrath, former Deputy Chief Management Officer for DOD (a Senate-confirmed post), shares her story about serving as both a career executive and then a senior political appointee and the difficult road to reaching that all-too-rare milestone.

Section 3: Leadership Qualities for the 21st Century. Admiral Thad Allen, former Coast Guard Commandant, draws on his experience leading the Federal response to Hurricane Katrina and the Deepwater Horizon disasters to describe the qualities necessary to lead collaboratively in tomorrow's chaotic, complex, increasingly "co-produced" government. The Honorable Charles Rossotti, former Commissioner of the IRS, offers a case study on implementing the transformational 1998 IRS Restructuring and Reform Act,[10] including some of the controversial measures he took to integrate IRS executives with senior leaders he recruited from outside government.

---

[10] Internal Revenue Service Restructuring and Reform Act of 1998, Pub. L. No. 105–206, 112 Stat. 685 (1998).

Harvard Professor Steven Kelman, former Director of the Office of Federal Procurement Policy, and I share the results of an innovative research project we did together, and we make the case that senior government executives need to demonstrate courage and character in order to tackle many of the wicked, whole-of-government problems they will face. These are just the kind of characteristics agency Chief Operating Officers need to demonstrate every day, and in his chapter, former U.S. Comptroller General David Walker makes the case that those key positions should be reserved (or at least pre-ferred) for career executives; he also describes some of the developmental experiences they'll need to prepare themselves for those responsibilities. Finally, Professor Robert Tobias, former President of the National Treasury Employees Union and now on the faculty at American University, also explores how senior executives can learn to lead more collaboratively with their labor unions and, in so doing, see vastly improved levels of employee engagement.

Section 4: Developing the Next Generation of the SES. Letitia Long, former Director of the NGA and a longtime leader in the IC, makes the case that executive development programs should be based on a holistic talent management strategy linked to the organization's overall management framework—and start on day 1 of an employee's career. Dr. Reginald S. Wells,* Chief Human Capital Officer for the Social Security Administration, focuses on his agency's highly regarded SES Candidate Development Program as a model for grooming a leadership cadre capable of leading the Federal government through difficult times.

Robert Corsi,* former Deputy A-1 (Manpower and Personnel) for the U.S. Air Force and board member of the Senior Executives Association, shows how his agency has adapted the military's proven leadership development model to its civilian career executives, and he suggests that other agencies could do the same. Dr. Suzanne Logan,* Director of the Federal Executive Institute, addresses the essential role of the Institute in developing and delivering a lifelong "continuum of leadership learning" to current and future genera-tions of career executives. And finally, former OMB Comptroller and Acting Deputy Director for Management Ed DeSeve takes a different tack on senior executive development, suggesting that an agency's political and career lead-ers should undertake joint developmental activities, perhaps focusing on re-vising the agency's strategic plan, in part to set the agency's strategic direction as a team and, in so doing, build stronger relationships amongst those senior leaders.

Section 5: Revitalizing the Federal Senior Executive Corps. The Honorable Robert F. Hale, former Under Secretary and Comptroller for DOD, addresses the need for civil service reforms—especially those dealing with accountabil-ity and streamlined hiring practices—to enable SES members to lead more effectively; he also argues that more attention be paid to intangible rewards to motivate senior executives. For his part, Robert Goldenkoff,* Director of Strategic Issues at GAO, delves into the results of OPM's landmark 2015 SES Exit Survey to highlight some of the so-called "regrettable losses" occurring in the ranks of the government's top leaders; he also discusses the importance of understanding and addressing SES attrition from a risk management perspective and offers steps agencies can take to improve executive retention.

For his part, Stephen Shih,* OPM's Deputy Associate Director for SES policy (among other responsibilities), talks about what his agency is doing to confront the challenges that face the SES—and what more needs to be done. Finally, the Honorable Daniel Werfel, former Acting Commissioner of the IRS, applied many of the same principles to build and motivate an integrated team of executives from within and beyond the IRS when he was tapped to lead that agency through a particularly difficult period in its recent history.

A word about the recommendations

As noted, each section includes introductory and concluding commentary, along with a number of recommendations for consideration by policymakers in the White House and on Capitol Hill. These are mine and mine alone, and I take full responsibility for them. They represent my personal observations and opinions and do not necessarily reflect or represent the views of the National Academy of Public Administration, the contributors to this anthology, the Academy Fellows who wrote the anthology's Foreword, or Booz Allen.

The same applies to the words of the various contributors themselves. We are all responsible for our own views; by contributing to this anthology, none of us necessarily agrees with or endorses those of our fellow authors, nor does the Academy, as an independent, nonpartisan, nonprofit organization chartered by Congress, necessarily endorse those views.

Rather, the Academy and all who contributed to this work want it to serve as a way of presenting a wide variety of perspectives on this important topic to the American people, especially during a time of transition to a new administration.

In that regard, with only a few exceptions, the recommendations are administrative in nature…that is, they could be implemented by government regulation or executive order. And even those few that require legislation are relatively modest—more incremental than revolutionary.

In that regard, several who have reviewed the pre-publication manuscript have suggested the recommendations are not bold enough, that the SES (and its progeny) requires sweeping, 'blow it up and start over' changes. I disagree. It is clear that unless the composition of Congress changes dramatically, the chances of legislative action—especially constructive legislative action—are relatively low. As others have pointed out, legislative action these days is a bit of a crapshoot—just as likely to take a step or two backward as forward—so I have opted to back off from more radical statutory recommendations in favor of those that are just bureaucratically bold. That is a deliberate calculation on my part, and I take full responsibility for it.

As noted, there are several exceptions, recommendations that do require congressional action, but one of them deserves a bit of an explanation. That one—dealing with the controversial subject of SES adverse action appeals—can hardly be considered incremental. Indeed, many (including me) believe some of the legislative proposals that are afoot in that regard are truly revolutionary in nature, potentially changing the classic institutional role of the career executive...and not necessarily for the good. However, they are afoot, and my recommendation to pursue another "grand bargain" to achieve more foundational SES reforms is made somewhat guardedly. Given the likelihood of some legislative action to dilute SES adverse action appeals, we might as well try to get something positive for it. But the details of such a Hobson's choice are set forth in the book's final section.

A Senior Service for the 21ˢᵗ Century

This is not your grandfather's government…or your grandmother's, for that matter. Just think about how much our world has changed, just since the turn of the millennium some 17 years ago. From cell phones and video games to drones and GMOs, from artificial intelligence and artificial islands to ISIL and Anonymous—and more darkly, from San Bernardino and Sandy Hook to Brussels and Paris—a time traveler arriving from just Y2K would be bewildered and befuddled. Through it all, governments at all levels have struggled to keep pace. And the responsibility for doing so falls squarely on the shoulders of those who lead them, whether they are elected, appointed (by themselves or someone else), or selected.

What of our own government? On one hand, with its openness and transparency (especially these days, with a social media-fueled 24/7 news cycle), the Federal government is expected—often unrealistically so—to maintain some semblance of order and progress amidst all the chaos. And to its credit, it usually manages to do so…to the point that such unbelievably complex things as controlling air traffic, processing millions of Medicare and Medicaid claims, operating a carrier battle group, or building an International Space Station are taken for granted.

Dare I say it, American citizens are spoiled by the invisible hand of their government, so much so that when it does not meet their expectations (or when it breaks), they can become disenchanted and disaffected. Yet by definition, our national government, with its constitutional set of checks and balances, is not designed to change and adapt quickly, even as the society that surrounds it does. That is the paradox of our system of government; to those who don't understand the 'intelligent design' that is implicit in our founding documents, it can be frustrating. Therein lies the challenge for the Federal government's senior leaders—the political appointees and career executives who run our government's departments and agencies: getting the system to change when it was designed to resist it.

And that challenge is getting exponentially harder. Mind-blowing changes occur every day in science and technology, society and culture, demographics and geopolitics, the environment, and the global economy, and no single human being can keep track of them all, much less understand them (thank goodness for Google and Bing). Separately and together, they all affect our nation and government in unexpected and unpredictable ways…yet our citizens expect the leaders of our government—elected, appointed, and selected —to figure it all out. The fact that they do most of the time is remarkable.

Our focus in this book is on selected leaders…the members of the Senior Executive Service (SES) and its sister senior services who are selected (presumably on the basis of their qualifications), sometimes by political appointees and sometimes by their career colleagues, to lead the millions who serve our Federal government—service members in uniform, civil servants, government contractors, and the myriad others who do the people's work these days.

As we have argued, perhaps rhetorically, career executives occupy a unique and essential niche in our Federal system of government, yet the way government develops and deploys them—indeed, the way it treats them—has become problematic. The senior executive corps faces challenges from without and from within. While no one challenge is sufficient to put that corps at risk, if taken together (and allowed to fester), those various challenges form a perfect storm that is existential in nature.

Those challenges, and there are many, are not fleeting phenomena (there are plenty of those too); rather, they are endemic and enduring, and as such will have a profound influence on the composition and capabilities of a 21st century SES. Accordingly, in this first of our six sections, we examine the nature of those challenges, both internal and external…starting with the latter. We do so from the vantage of four senior leaders who have served at the very highest levels of our government and who have done so without losing sight of those who have served them.

Challenges from within and from without

As we have argued, the nature of our government is such that, perhaps like no other, it is shaped by forces and events from both within and without. To be sure, given our still-overwhelming "hard" military and economic power (something former Under Secretary of Defense Michèle Flournoy talks about in her chapter), as well as the Federal government's influence on our society and culture at large, the latter does some significant shaping of those trends and forces in its own right. And taken together, these internal and external forces represent the sorts of challenges a 21st century SES—and 21st century SES members—must confront. Insofar as those that are more internal in nature are largely dependent on what happens outside government, let us look to our four contributors to describe at least some of those external forces, reserving an examination of the internal forces for my Concluding Commentary and Recommendations.

- Beth Cobert, former Office of Personnel Management (OPM) Acting Director and former Office of Management and Budget (OMB) Deputy Director for Management sets the stage by focusing on the challenge of building a senior executive corps for the whole-of-government and not just a collection of individual agencies. That's certainly consistent with the founding but as yet largely unrealized vision of the SES, but former Acting Director Cobert does not rely on that as the basis for her thesis. Rather, she makes a compelling mission case for such an executive cadre and, in so doing, sets the overarching theme for this book. It is a case supported by the fact that nothing of national importance can be accomplished by a single agency acting alone. To borrow a phrase, it takes a village—of multiple Federal agencies, levels of government, nations and nongovernmental organizations, sometimes even all of the above—to do the important work of government. Former Acting Director Cobert describes some of the things her agency has done to begin to build such a cadre...as well as what still needs to be done in that regard.

- If there were any doubt about the need for a whole-of-government senior executive corps, Michèle Flournoy's chapter ought to dispel it. The chapter is based on a lengthy interview with the former Under Secretary of Defense for Policy under President Obama (now President of the Center for a New American Security, a DC-based think tank). Secretary Flournoy paints a graphic picture of a complex, chaotic world increasingly beset by competition and conflict. In that world, everything is connected to everything else, such that seemingly random events can have globe-spanning consequences. Flournoy makes the point that government leaders, political and career, are going to have to learn to navigate the "ship of state" in that turbulent world. Perhaps most importantly, Secretary Flournoy describes how she herself navigated the byzantine Pentagon bureaucracy to set up a program to help her career executives to do just that. Future political appointees should take note.

- Technology is one of the things that has brought us closer together, but as we have seen, it can also create tensions that drive us apart. Christine Fox, now with the Johns Hopkins University's Applied Physics Lab but former head of the Pentagon's Cost Analysis and Program Evaluation shop and Acting Deputy Secretary of Defense for Secretary Chuck Hagel, and her co-author Emelia S. Probasco, focus on the paradoxical, two-edged nature of many of today's emerging technologies…their undeniable promise to make life better, but also their potential to make it worse. Our reliance on information technology (IT), with its value and its vulnerabilities, is one of several examples Fox offers. She argues that government leaders—not just chief technology officers or chief scientists, but all government leaders—must know enough about those emerging technologies to understand how their promise can be leveraged (quickly, before obsolescence sets in) and their threats mitigated in these leaders' agencies… in other words, to strike a balance between promise and peril.[11]

- Finally, as challenging as today's organizational, geostrategic, and technological environments may be for the 21st century senior executive, they pale in comparison to the political environment. After all, this anthology is all about government and governance. Both are rooted in politics, and not the office or organizational kind. No, government—and by definition, government executives—operates in a partisan political world. No matter how many buffers and barriers may be erected to mitigate partisanship's most egregious effects, senior career executives must learn to deal with it.

Indeed, as Robert Shea, former OMB Deputy Associate Director for Management and now a Principal with the consulting firm Grant Thornton,[12] writes, today's political environment is worse than ever. It has become hyper-partisan. Senior career executives, once insulated from its most distasteful machinations, have two choices when faced with this environment's prospects: They can hope to avoid it by taking no risks whatsoever (possibly an abdication of their senior leadership responsibilities), or they can lean in to it and lead, come what may. Shea, a political appointee in the George W. Bush administration, tells a story about the latter, and he offers some valuable lessons worth learning in that regard.

---

[11] Fox and Probasco's chapter, read in conjunction with Cobert's and Flournoy's, suggests the need for a more liberal (that is, broader and more eclectic) education for our senior career executives to prepare them for the ongoing explosion of technology—something we consider in the book's fourth section.

[12] Mr. Shea is also a one of the four Academy Fellows who authored the foreword, but he recused himself from reviewing this section. He was also Chairman of the Academy's Board of Directors from 2014 to 2016.

CHAPTER 1.1:

Creating an Executive Corps for the Whole-of-Government

By the Honorable Beth Cobert, former Deputy Director for Management, U.S. Office of Management and Budget and former Acting Director, U.S. Office of Personnel Management

Introduction

When I joined the Obama administration as the Deputy Director for Management at the White House OMB, our team focused on making government more effective and efficient for citizens and businesses through our support of the President's Management Agenda. We looked across government and set up structures that encouraged collaboration and the exchange of best practices between agencies, within agencies, and even within teams. Instead of the focus on the day-to-day operations that comes with leading one organization or initiative, it was our job to take a whole-of-government, enterprise-wide view and encourage other senior executives around government, both political and career, to do the same.

Then, in the summer of 2015, I found myself in a different role. As Acting Director of OPM, I was at the center of the response to a serious cybersecurity intrusion against the U.S. government, a breach which resulted in the compromise of millions of personnel and background investigation records. As leaders at OPM tackled this unexpected challenge, I was able to practice some of what I had preached in my previous role. Here, I gained a more tangible understanding of the importance and impact of taking a whole-of-government approach to solve difficult problems.

We sought out the experts. Our team spent countless hours (and boxes of pizza) working to secure, monitor, and upgrade OPM's networks with help from technical experts from across the civilian government and the national security community. We consulted with privacy officials from OMB, the Federal Trade Commission, and across government. We collaborated closely with the U.S. Department of Defense (DOD) on a contract to provide identity theft protection and notify affected individuals securely by mail. We did not try to fix everything alone. We recognized that a whole-of-government problem warranted a whole-of-government solution.

OPM's challenge is not unique. Whether responding to a crisis like the Ebola outbreak in West Africa, revitalizing a community through a place-based initiative, or tackling Cross-Agency Priority Goals like improving mental health outcomes for veterans or reducing the Federal government's carbon footprint, leaders in the Federal government are faced with daunting challenges in increasingly complex and fast-moving times; those challenges more often than not require a multiagency response. Our leaders face challenges they cannot always anticipate and may not have seen before. And the American people rely on them to deliver results.

While no two challenges facing our leaders are identical, my experience in government so far has taught me that at least one theme applies to nearly every problem that government executives face: No complex problem can or should be solved alone. Modern leaders in the Federal government need to take a whole-of-government approach to tackling the challenges of tomorrow.

A whole-of-government approach

A whole-of-government approach can take many forms. It can mean collaborating across departments, levels of government, and even sectors to coordinate efforts and share data and best practices. It can mean breaking down silos to foster collaboration among the bureaus and subdivisions of a particular department. It can even mean fostering better collaboration *within a given* agency by encouraging senior line leaders to take ownership of key responsibilities like talent management and employee engagement.

The rest of this chapter describes some of the great work going on across the government to foster this approach. Then it outlines how the Obama administration took another major step forward by institutionalizing many of these best practices in December 2015 with its announcement of Executive Order (EO) 13714, *Strengthening the Senior Executive Service.*[13]

Interagency collaboration

Nearly every administration achievement, large or small, requires collaboration that draws on the talents, expertise, and resources of senior leaders in different parts of the government. For example, President Obama asked agencies to develop a tool that would allow aspiring college students and their families to make smarter choices about which schools met their needs.

The government had the data but lacked a central location to organize and present it in a way that was helpful to students. So leaders from the U.S. Department of Education, U.S. Department of the Treasury, and Council

---

[13] Exec. Order No. 13714, Strengthening the Senior Executive Service. (2015, December 15). Retrieved from https://www.whitehouse.gov/the-press-office/2015/12/15/executive-order-strengthening-senior-executive-service

of Economic Advisors enlisted the help of technical experts from the U.S. Digital Service and a unit of the General Services Administration (GSA) called 18F. The group discussed what data were available, what would be most helpful to students, and how to make the data user friendly. The result was a tool that allows students and families to search from nearly 2,000 columns of data on over 7,000 schools.

Whole-of-community collaboration

There are countless examples of Federal agencies working together to better serve the American people. Yet sometimes collaboration needs to expand beyond the confines of the Federal government. Place-based initiatives like President Obama's Promise Zones break down silos between agencies and levels of government and work across sectors to solve problems identified by the community. Designated communities are given priority access to Federal assistance and investments of staff and technical assistance. Federal agencies work together to streamline otherwise redundant and connected programs to maximize available resources. To help communities leverage these Federal resources, Federal staff are trained and embedded full time to support local leaders and help them coordinate across Federal, state, and local governments and the private sector.

While these programs are young, early results are promising. In Eastside San Antonio, for example, high school graduation and school attendance rates have increased, a new equity investment fund is growing local small businesses, and at-risk and formerly incarcerated youth are gaining access to new job skills in growing sectors like healthcare. This success should be instructive for Federal executives—by viewing the Federal government as a member of a broader community, we can tackle more complex problems and deliver better results to the American people than if we try to operate on our own.

Collaboration within organizations

A whole-of-government approach can also mean breaking down barriers within organizations. Like the government as a whole, many agencies are organized by program area and staffed by subject matter experts. If senior leadership focuses on fostering collaboration between the components of an organization, there is a real opportunity to break down silos and deliver results. To do so, senior executives need the right skills and vocabulary. Nowhere is this more apparent than in IT. All modern leaders should have a basic IT literacy so they can ask the right questions, hire the right talent, take advantage of the opportunities technology provides, and take necessary steps to mitigate the risks it creates.

This responsibility cannot be left to the agency's Chief Information Officer (CIO) alone. During the OMB-led government-wide "cyber-sprint" review of the Federal government's cybersecurity policies, procedures, and practices in the summer of 2015, agencies were asked to dramatically accelerate the implementation of multifactor authentication. Federal CIO Tony Scott enlisted the help of top agency leadership through the President's Management Council (PMC) to make swift and substantial changes within their agencies. Within a month, government-wide rates of dual-factor authentication rose dramatically. This progress came from senior leadership working as partners with their CIOs and IT experts to remove obstacles and implement these important security reforms.

But it does not stop at IT. In the spring of 2016, OPM launched a national Hiring Excellence Campaign, a series of events designed to foster collaboration between hiring managers and human resources (HR) professionals. HR professionals have unique expertise in the technical aspects of bringing on new staff. But every team is different, even within the same organization, and managers are best equipped to know what kind of distinctive skills and talents they need on their team. Rather than leaving the business of hiring to the HR team alone, hiring managers need to fully engage as true partners in the effort. This is particularly true at the highest levels of leadership. Only by breaking down these silos and working collaboratively can leaders attract and hire the best possible talent.

Strengthening the SES to support the whole-of-government

In a 2014 speech to the SES, President Obama reminded us that "[w]e need the best and brightest of the coming generations to serve. [T]hose of us who believe government can and must be a force for good…we've got to work hard to make sure that government works."[14] This year, more than 60 percent of the Federal government's SES members are eligible for retirement. While this potential loss of senior talent presents a challenge in knowledge transfer, it also provides an opportunity to recruit and develop new leaders and to make sure they have the skills, structures, and mindset necessary to embrace a whole-of-government approach.

The administration took a major step toward this goal when President Obama announced his EO on strengthening the SES in December 2015. The EO builds on the original intent of the SES, which was to create a cadre of expert managers and leaders capable of leading organizations and solving problems across the Federal government. The actions focus on making it easier to hire the most qualified senior executives, strengthen tools for developing talent within the SES, and improve accountability and recognition. At its core, the EO's recommendations highlight the importance of developing

[14] Obama, B. (2014, December 9). Remarks by the president to senior leaders of the Federal workforce. Retrieved from https://votesmart.org/public-statement/941830/remarks-by-the-president-to-senior-leaders-of-the-Federal-workforce#.V_VjD-IrLIU

leaders with the skills, experience, tools, and mindset to be enterprise-wide assets—that is, to take a whole-of-government approach to solving tough problems. Its recommendations aim to develop the capacity to cultivate the best possible leaders from within existing Federal leadership and recruit the best possible leaders from outside government. It also highlights the importance of senior government leaders taking full ownership over both of these efforts and making them a core part of their mission.

Developing our senior leaders through talent management

To cultivate senior executives who can provide the best enterprise leadership, we need a thoughtful and comprehensive approach to talent and succession management that helps us make decisions about how to best position our leaders for success. The EO requires agencies to establish their own processes to inform decisions about such things as SES hiring, career development, and executive rotations. The EO allows flexibility to tailor the processes to meet particular needs but builds on successful models currently employed at DOD and in the U.S. Intelligence Community (IC).

DOD uses a talent management system to track its senior executives. The system solicits input from executives and their supervisors on past and current assignments, rotations, and long-term plans. Rather than tracking each leader separately, DOD takes an organization-wide view. Which SES members have experience in resource management? Who has spent time in a different part of government? Who is nearing retirement? This information is independent of formal performance reviews and evaluations. Instead, it gives DOD agencies the information they need to make strategic decisions about which executives are ready for greater responsibilities or who might benefit from a rotation. The result is a better approach to executive talent management and succession planning that improves employee engagement and retention and helps make the most of the most precious resources in the organization—people.

This approach is working in agencies smaller than DOD as well. The GSA also takes an agency-wide view of its senior leaders. It tracks the developmental path of its senior executives and makes well-informed decisions to cultivate its leadership.

The common theme is a commitment from top agency leadership. In the Army, the Secretary plays an active role in talent management. At GSA, talent management of senior leadership is a major piece of the Deputy Administrator's job.

Developing talent through rotations

The EO also helps develop leaders with a whole-of-government mindset by requiring agencies to develop plans to facilitate rotations. As senior leaders, we work with our interagency colleagues every day. By spending time with other agencies, departments, components, and even non-Federal partners, our leaders are given the chance to learn new best practices, understand other processes, and build relationships that are critical to getting work done across the government.

Think about OPM's response to its cyber intrusion. Our work was made stronger by our interagency colleagues' knowledge and perspective, and the experience they gained at OPM made them more effective leaders when they returned to their home agencies. In the Promise Zones initiative, Federal staff went beyond the boundaries of the Federal government to share and acquire knowledge from state and local governments and the private sector. In these efforts, formal or informal rotations added value for both agencies and individuals. Rotations are a key element of talent management, and it is important that senior leaders take ownership of this process. In the IC, for example, you cannot join its equivalent of the SES unless you have completed a joint duty assignment (JDA) in another agency or organization. Employees starting at GS-11 are encouraged to take advantage of these opportunities, and senior leadership works to create an environment where employees are encouraged to do so. All rotational opportunities are advertised in a widely accessible, centralized location, and current senior career executives publicly list the JDAs they have completed. This environment sends a strong signal that leaving for a rotation does not take you off the track or impede your career progress; rather, it accelerates it.

The EO takes other steps to develop our senior leaders by setting a clear understanding that they are, as senior leaders, enterprise-wide leaders who are responsible for the success of their teams, their agencies, and the whole of the Federal government. This starts from day 1. The EO creates new formal onboarding programs based on best practices developed by OPM and the Office of Presidential Personnel that go beyond the traditional building floor plans and paperwork and invest in an extended inculcation process complete with mentoring and action-oriented activities. It continues by requiring annual professional development sessions. Every 3 years, senior executives receive a full 360-degree leadership assessment, where they receive feedback from multiple sources on areas including their ability to work collaboratively across the enterprise.

Recruiting the best talent

Our best recruiting tool has been and always will be our mission. Nowhere else can experienced and talented people have an impact at the scope and scale they can have as a senior executive in the Federal government. Whether it's keeping our roads safe, our water clean, or our economy strong, senior executives devote their lives to keeping America running. However, we must acknowledge that talented senior leaders could work in a lot of places, and the private sector has certain advantages with which it is hard for the public sector to compete. The EO addresses this by providing additional tools to make it easier to attract and hire the talent we will need for the future.

One step is making the hiring process a little simpler and more accessible to folks from the private sector and other parts of government who have the desire and the credentials but are intimidated by the cumbersome application process or unfamiliar terminology used to establish the Executive Core Qualifications (ECQ). Several agencies have moved to a resume-based application system. OPM is working to identify alternative application options that could reduce the burden on applicants and HR professionals while increasing the pool of qualified candidates from within government and the private sector.

This also means pay and recognition. Many potential applicants forgo significantly higher salaries to join the Federal government. While the public sector may not be able to fully compete financially with the private sector yet, we can make sure we do our best to remain competitive. The EO begins this process by taking steps to increase the starting pay for SES employees with the goal of arriving at a point where they make more than the General Schedule (GS) employees they supervise. It also increases the limit on aggregate spending on agency performance awards, so agencies have more discretion to reward top performers.

We work in an increasingly fast-paced and complex time when, paradoxically, trust in government's ability to solve problems is waning as the complexity of the problems we face is growing. To rise to the challenge, we must break down silos within our organizations, build bridges between departments and agencies, and embrace those in the private sector and state and local governments who share our commitment to making life better for the American people. Leaders in our SES are uniquely positioned to do so if they embrace a whole-of-government, enterprise-wide approach to solving problems. It is our collective responsibility to provide them with the tools necessary to enable this. The roadmap set out in President Obama's EO is clear. Attracting, cultivating, training, and rewarding our leaders is not a task to be delegated. It is a core responsibility of senior executive leadership and an important part of moving the government forward in the 21st century.

Executive Leadership in a Complex, Chaotic World

By the Honorable Michèle Flournoy, former Under Secretary for Policy, U.S. Department of Defense[15]

On tomorrow's complex leadership environment

It is very difficult to predict exactly what the world is going to look like in the future, but we can be confident that it will be an increasingly complex one, a very volatile environment in which the speed of unfolding events will continue to surprise us. Indeed, when you look back at our history, it's hard to find a time since World War II when the international environment has been this multifaceted, chaotic, and challenging for the United States, and it will only become more so in the future.

Senior leaders in government are going to face a world in which events directly affecting our nation's interests will occur simultaneously in multiple regions of the world. For example, we confront continuing turmoil in the Middle East, even as we see fundamental changes in the balance of power in Asia and a resurgent, more aggressive Russia. Bottom line: We're not going to have the luxury of focusing on one region or even one event at a time. Our attention is going to be pulled in multiple directions at any given point, with the economic, political, informational, and security dimensions of these events all intertwined.

China offers a case in point. The rise of China as a more powerful, wealthy, and confident player—certainly in the Asia-Pacific region but also globally— is a major phenomenon, and something that leaders in government—not just those in the national security business—will have to address. This is of particular concern because of early signs that China may not necessarily accept, as a given, the rules of international order that we and our allies architected after World War II; they are unilaterally changing or challenging that rules-based status quo in ways I think are concerning. I don't think

---

[15] Editor's Note: I had the opportunity (and the privilege) to interview Ms. Flournoy about the challenges—primarily geopolitical but also organizational and individual—that Federal executives would likely face in the second and third decades of the 21st century. Her observations on these subjects as well as her thoughts on leadership in general are set forth below as edited excerpts from that interview.

anybody believes China will necessarily become a military adversary, but there will clearly be both cooperative elements in our relationship—in areas like trade and climate change mitigation—and competitive areas, as we are already seeing in the cyber and maritime domains. China is just one example of the kind of very complex challenges future U.S. leaders are going to have to manage in creative and effective ways.

All this means we are going to have to invest in—and learn how to leverage —the full range of instruments of power, both hard and soft power, to achieve our national interests. Historically, those on the soft side of the equation tend to be grossly under-resourced—for example, we have more military band members than Foreign Service Officers (FSO). And if you added up all of those FSOs, they would number less than one brigade. I'm all for a strong military, but I also think we need other ways of projecting power—diplomatic, economic, developmental, and so forth—if we are to meet these complex geopolitical challenges.

On leading the whole-of-government

It's hard to think of a challenge that is unidimensional. It's hard to think of a challenge in which the Federal government would respond with only one instrument or element of national power…only one tool in our toolkit. In the national security arena, we have learned that our nation is at its most effective when it responds to complex challenges with a combination of tools—diplomatic, military, economic, political, etc.—and we will need senior executives in government who understand the full range of tools, for use both within and beyond their own purview, and how to integrate their use in effective strategies.

For example, there are many examples in history where diplomacy was much more effective when coupled with some element of coercive threat behind it—whether the threat of sanctions or the use of force, even if it is simply a military deployment that communicates our resolve. These are all mechanisms for advancing our foreign policy objectives, and learning how to best integrate them will be critical to being effective.

To compound this challenge, it is clear that some of the most effective of those tools will not be under the exclusive control of the U.S. government. For example, many of the most effective means of influencing international affairs are now largely in the domain of the private sector. Look at the information domain. The U.S. doesn't control social media or the Internet, but friends and adversaries alike leverage it. ISIS today is putting out 90,000 messages per day on social media.

How does the U.S. government deal with that? How do we as a nation deal with that, given that these instruments of power are beyond our control? So even as there will be challenges with integrating the suite of tools available to the government, there will also be challenges in how we leverage and respond to the tools the Federal government doesn't control.

Thus, you have this panoply of complex geopolitical developments—like the rise of China, the decline of Russia (even as it becomes more aggressive), the collapse of the old order in the Middle East, and the spawning of violent extremist organizations finding fertile soil there—that is made even more challenging by two-edged technologies like the global communications architecture. Events that happen in one locale are known around the world in seconds, and decision makers are expected to respond to them immediately, before they can truly understand what has happened. They are being asked to address events literally as they are happening, and as if the events are fully understood.

Contrast that with earlier periods of history, when nations had the luxury of time to reflect before responding. President Eisenhower, for example, established what he called a planning board in the National Security Council (NSC). It was far more influential than the part of the NSC that dealt with the crisis of the moment, largely because the board had time to respond to issues and to do so in a way that was strategic and proactive.

It's more than just the proliferation of communications technology…it's the proliferation and acquisition of any technology—by both state and non-state actors alike—that could have some sort of military application. Take unmanned aerial vehicles, commonly known as drones. Until fairly recently, we were the unrivaled leader in developing autonomous or semi-autonomous systems and using them for both military and non-military purposes. Now at least 75 countries either have military-grade drones or are in the process of acquiring them. We've seen them acquired and used by non-state actors, like Hezbollah, and now the technology is even available to individuals like you and me. Now we live in a world in which everybody is using drones for a range of benign and nefarious purposes. That is quite a different world than the one in which we operated previously. So, I think the proliferation of technology is a key challenge for us.

Thus, one of the biggest challenges for leaders in government (and not just ours!) is to remain focused on strategic considerations, but that's easier said than done. How do you keep the initiative? How do you push proactively for your priorities when you are literally being bombarded daily with an information flow concerning crisis events around the world? That's a far different environment than the one many U.S. presidents and their leadership teams had to deal with in the past.

On leading in an interconnected world

There is no longer a bright line between the national security domain and the domestic one, nor are there neat dividing lines between the work of national security agencies and that of domestic agencies. Who would have thought

OPM would become the subject of conversations between the presidents of the United States and China?

The cyber threat really is illustrative, in the sense that organizations and governments are only as cybersecure as their weakest link. Our national security agencies may have developed very good cyber defenses and feel confident that they are adequately protecting classified information, yet they can still be very vulnerable to attacks that come through the back door. The same is true when you look at the amount of our critical infrastructure that is owned and operated by the private sector—whether it's our electrical power grid or our financial markets, energy production and distribution, or nuclear power plants.

The list is long. Our critical infrastructure is now all plugged into and connected by the Internet, but most of it lacks the kind of cybersecurity necessary to prevent a large-scale catastrophic attack. But that's just the extreme example of a world that is interconnected, and I believe it will require leaders who are able to think and act outside of their traditional bureaucratic stovepipes. It will require leaders who can work horizontally, across organizational boundaries.

And in that interconnected world, government leaders need to engage critical stakeholders to get them involved, get their buy-in, and get them aligned with where we're trying to go, even when we don't have the authority to compel them to follow. Most of us were brought up as leaders to think vertically and hierarchically. There was always that implicit power relationship, and suddenly you have to deal with peers—individuals, organizations, nations—who can just say no. The leadership skills we need include not only those classic ones like visioning, directing, and empowering but also new, emerging ones—skills like the ability to work horizontally to coalesce and align broader communities. Those skills will be key.

A few examples come to mind. For example, when we were working on the range of issues associated with Afghanistan and Pakistan, we found that, on one hand, the U.S. Department of State (DOS) had the authority to do what needed to be done but had no money and, on the other hand, DOD had the money and a critical mission to accomplish but no authority. We had to figure out ways to marry DOS' authority and DOD's financial resources and mission requirements. While it was initially like pulling teeth, we eventually made a lot of progress as two departments working in unison.

Frankly, the biggest challenge was getting Congress to let us collaborate in such a way as to pool our respective authorities and funding, with joint approval—between the ambassadors on the ground and the Office of the Secretary of Defense here in Washington—on the exercise of those authorities. The various congressional committees involved jealously guarded their jurisdictions and were reluctant to let us work in a more integrated manner.

Another example of working collaboratively with critical stakeholders to get their buy-in actually involved President Obama and the treatment of sequestration under the Budget Control Act.[16] That process forced us to fundamentally rethink our national security priorities. What are we going to protect? Where are we going to manage risk? And rather than the President just ordering it, he realized he was going to have to bring everybody along with him. So he set up a series of intense 3–4 hour meetings at the White House and personally attended at least three of them, which is a lot of presidential time.

We had all of the service chiefs, all of the service secretaries, all of the combatant commanders, the Chairman and the Vice Chairman of the Joint Chiefs, the Secretary of Defense—the whole national security leadership team. And we had a very frank give-and-take discussion of our defense priorities. Everybody involved had their say, had multiple bites of the apple, and we ultimately reached a consensus. Even if there was something they didn't like in that consensus, they "slapped the table" because they had a chance to debate it, had a chance to express their concerns to the President, and, at the end of the day, bought into the compromise.

For me it was very educational to see how a leader could pull together a broad set of stakeholders even when he didn't have to—he could have just issued an order. In so doing, President Obama was far more effective in getting the buy-in necessary for implementation of some hard decisions.

Leadership skills for the 21st century

In addition to this ability to collaborate and win stakeholder buy-in, there are some other leadership skills I believe are going to be vital in the future. For example, listening is one of the most important and undervalued leadership skills. First, when you listen, you can actually learn. There are a lot of people in government who may have more expertise than you do as a leader, and listening is the highest form of respect, even if you ultimately decide to go a different way. If someone feels you've truly listened to them, it goes a long way toward winning them over. At least they respect the fact that you gave them a fair shake as you made your decision.

We also need leaders who are willing to foster tolerance for dissent and create an organizational climate in which people don't shoot the messenger —an environment where someone can speak up when they really think the group is heading in the wrong direction or they have a strongly felt difference of opinion. Staff members need to feel safe to speak up before you've made the decision as opposed to after. Again, getting a diversity of perspectives and a full range of views almost always produces a better decision in the end. Even if it's not where you end up, being aware of those

---

[16] Budget Control Act of 2011, Pub. L. No. 112-25 § 354, 125 Stat. 240 (2011).

different perspectives may add a little risk mitigation to your solution…and that will make it more effective.

Future leaders should understand that sometimes the most powerful thing they can do as leaders is to invest in their human capital. So often in government, your only real resource is your people, and yet too often we appointees are so focused on the relatively short-term result that we end up chewing up our career staffs and spitting them out. We don't take time for or invest in their professional development. We don't take time for or invest in their training. We don't take time to recognize or reward them, even if it may not be monetary. We need to hold up success and celebrate people who do good work.

When I became Under Secretary of Defense for Policy, I had very mission-driven staff who wanted to serve the Secretary as best they could. But they were exhausted; they hadn't had a break. They never knew when they would get a break, and they were beaten down. So I launched a human capital strategy that really focused on taking better care of our people, in ways large and small, and it was like watering plants in the desert. The flowers bloomed. After a few months even Secretary Gates asked, "What is going on down there? Something's different. I'm getting a different quality of work out of your organization." So again, I think that investment in our human capital—in this case, my career staff—can be the most powerful thing you do to improve performance. It doesn't necessarily take a lot of money. There are lots of things you can do short of offering bonuses.

On the role of a political appointee

I think part of being a political appointee is about stewardship. You should leave the institution you're leading better off than when you found it. Self-ishly, you want the organization to perform its best while you're there. You want to get the most out of that situation, but my experience was that getting the most out of my career staff was not about making the days longer or demanding that my people work harder. It was actually trying to work smarter, starting with understanding where we were wasting time. One of the first things I did when I was appointed was run a contest for my staff to identify the 10 dumbest administrative burdens they had to deal with every day. I got 250 entries, and we were immediately able to address dozens of them.

I also borrowed a page from the business literature and conducted a series of town hall meetings with my career staff. In my first one, I put "work-life balance" up on the screen as one of my priorities, and the group responded with laughter. It was as if they thought I had intended it to be a joke! I said, "This isn't a joke. I'm serious; we are going to try it." The staff was reluctant. They said they couldn't reduce their hours because the mission demands were just too great.

So I took two talented managers, who happened to manage the two busiest offices in the policy directorate—the Middle East and the Southeast Asia desks—and I said, "We are going to do an experiment." They met with their teams and asked each person to suggest one thing that would help them achieve a better work-life balance. It was actually very simple. For example, one person said, "I have a new baby, and if I could get home a little earlier 2 days a week, that would make all the difference in the world." Another person said, "I have elderly parents. If I can occasionally get a predictable 2-hour window off during the work week, I could take my mother to the doctor." Whatever it was, it became the manager's job to ensure the team flexed and cross-covered to enable each person to do that one thing that would improve their work-life balance.

As an added benefit, people learned about one another, and it fostered a greater depth of communication and understanding among the staff. The people started to see each other more as human beings with needs beyond the workplace. In truth, not only did morale go up but also the quality of the output from theses office went up. Once we piloted it with the two highest tempo offices, we rolled it out across the organization. People were still working long hours and were still working very hard. But they gained a modicum of control and greater predictability for the highest priorities in their lives. It made a big difference.

On developing good career executives and managers

Really, organizational performance is about making sure you develop good managers and leaders. In my office—and I am sure this is true in almost every other part of government—we take really great technicians and action officers at the GS-13, GS-14, or GS-15 level and promote them into the SES. They suddenly get thrown into the deep end of the pool, with little if any preparation. They are expected to direct the office despite having zero training and zero help in understanding what managing other people really requires.

It is a totally different skill set, yet we offer no preparation. In our case (and I suspect this, too, is typical), we had very little money for training. But I wanted to have the most talented senior executives in the organization, so we created our own (voluntary) management development program. We designed it by asking our most seasoned, highest performing leaders what lessons were most important for new executives to learn. We then had these seasoned, high-performing leaders teach our newest execs, all subject matter experts of the highest order, how they, too, could become good leaders. This was a small effort that had a very big impact on the organization.

As a general matter, we're going to need a different way of thinking about how we develop leaders and how we define what a civil service career looks like. Are we going to let future civil servants take time away from government service to get private sector experience and then come back? Are we going to allow for a greater variety of experiences to enable senior executives and aspiring senior executives to hone their skills as professionals and then bring them back to government service? We can think of it as a series of off-ramps and on-ramps rather than "once you're off, you're off and you can't ever come back."

On what appointees should expect from career executives

When it comes to members of the SES, I expect integrity and institutional knowledge. I expect them to be full partners in leading the organization. For example, if they had seen previous Under Secretaries try and fail at something five times before, I wanted them to tell me before I tried it a sixth time. I also wanted them to share ideas on how to do things differently so I actually had a chance of succeeding. In addition, I wanted them to share their institutional knowledge and to partner together to help make us successful.

When you come into a position as a new political appointee (in my case, as an Under Secretary of Defense), the career senior executives will know the organization and the people far better than you ever will during your tenure. I expected my career executives to guide the political appointees who were new to the Pentagon in terms of how business actually gets done, especially when it comes to executing policy. In my experience, making DOD policy is not the end of the process, it's just the beginning. Effective implementation is more important than the policy itself, and that's where career executives can really add value. They know the system; as an appointee, I wanted to create a partnership that leveraged that knowledge to enable me to get through the learning curve faster and be more effective.

However, the other part of the deal is that you have to create a climate where that sort of courageous candor is truly valued and rewarded. When some-body is courageous, they shouldn't get their head chopped off for it. The first time someone is punished for showing courage will be the last time anyone in the organization is courageous. You create a climate conducive to that sort of courage by clearly and explicitly articulating your expectations of what good career executive leadership should look like, how you are going to work together, and what your values are as a team and as an organization.

One step I took to create that kind of collaborative climate was to collect 360-degree feedback on all of our leaders, starting with me and including my executives, managers, and front-line supervisors (that in itself took some courage on all of our parts!). We got feedback, which included how others saw us as leaders, and all of us put together individual leadership develop-ment plans to work on the areas where we needed to improve.

We followed that up with some surveys to see how we were doing. If the 360-degree feedback indicated that a particular executive had some leadership issues, we provided that executive with some professional coaching and mentoring; after 3 months, we did pulse surveys of the executive's organization to assess progress. It isn't very complicated; it just takes focused attention from senior leadership to set the tone.

Bottom line: I think we have a tendency to invest in new systems, hardware, equipment, and tools. That's very important, but we also need to invest in our people. Dollar for dollar, investments in human capital probably provide more relative return than almost anything else you can do to improve organizational performance.

CHAPTER I.3:
Leading at the Edge of Technology

By the Honorable Christine H. Fox, former Acting Deputy Secretary of U.S. Department of Defense; and Emelia S. Probasco, Special Assistant, Policy and Analysis, Johns Hopkins University Applied Physics Laboratory

Introduction

Today's senior government leaders stand at the friction point of technical innovation and societal norms. Depending on their role, those leaders must be able to understand, regulate, and/or employ the technologies shaping global competition and conflict; as a consequence, they have the opportunity to truly shape the future of the nation. For example, how senior government leaders choose to invest precious research and development dollars, and what they choose to buy and not buy, will have significant impacts on society, not to mention the prosperity and security of the nation. Thus, opportunities are so great, and yet the dangers are so murky and dark.

How can a government leader stay prepared for the technological challenges that the 21st century holds? The pace, pervasiveness, and diversity of technological change hold promise for everything from defense to education to trade, and yet the onslaught seems almost insurmountable. Few if any government executives could possibly be prepared for the full gamut of changes. Complicating the matter further is the fact that technological change—in and of itself —will not shape our opportunities and challenges. Rather, it is the complex and constantly evolving relationship between society and technology that will determine our future.

So where do we start? Listing and examining every technological breakthrough or advancement would be pointless. The list would be too long and would be out of date before printing (as if anyone printed anything anymore!). It is even difficult to take any "old" technologies off the table—even vinyl is making a comeback in the music world. However, it is necessary to at least frame the choices government leaders will have to make. To do so, we first examine trends in technology and the evolving societal expectations those trends engender.

However, as pointless as it would be to list every new technology, listing all the dangers and risks associated with these technologies would be even worse. Nevertheless, with technology trends in mind, we examine those technologies that are, or could be, exploited by adversaries to do the nation and our citizens harm.

Thus, while it is clear that there are dangers that come with any given technology, those dangers are usually offset by just as many opportunities. If we can mitigate the former while taking advantage of the latter, there is every reason to hope for a better future. That is the challenge for all leaders, but especially those in government; as a consequence, we conclude with an investigation of the friction points those leaders must be able to navigate, and we propose a framework for them to do so.

Technology trends, attitudes, and expectations

Think about how your own attitudes toward and expectations of technology have changed recently. Take for example your attitude toward your mobile phone. Do you expect to be able to figure out how to use it intuitively? Do you expect it to help you with everyday tasks, like sending emails, navigating to a new restaurant, or alerting you when you are about to be late to a meeting? Those expectations are important indicators of trend lines in technology, if for no other reason than the consumer electronics industry wants to meet (or anticipate) and exceed our expectations and desires. Furthermore, the expectations that are developing as a consequence of our interaction with consumer technologies shape our expectations of how government will both employ and regulate technologies. It is thus worth taking a close look at the forces that might shape future technologies.

Fading technology

It's a little ironic that while we have put technology front and center in this paper, we want it to fade into the background in our everyday lives—invisible yet ever present. Think about the evolution of computers. They went from behemoths housed in specialized facilities to desktops in our homes to lap-sized, then pocket-sized, and now wrist-sized devices. With advances in miniaturization, voice recognition, bioengineering, and wireless communication, computing power seems poised to follow a trend line that either takes it into our bodies or just into the ether. The recent advances in brain computer interfaces and the explosion of the Internet of Things make this seem possible to an extreme. The expectation is that technology will not be clunky but rather a seamless part of our otherwise human existence.

Productivity and quality of life

That technology should be an invisible part of our lives is also indicative of another expectation: that its purpose is to improve productivity and with it, the quality of our lives. Technologies that free us from the mundane and mindless are popular, like the Roomba (no one likes vacuuming), Siri (a virtual personal assistant to find that phone number for you), and data-enabled services like Amazon's Subscribe and Save (you'll never forget diapers again). Typing is even becoming a bother, slowly eliminated by advances in voice recognition, so we can interact with technology the way we interact with humans. How exciting!

The expectation and desire that technology might improve our quality of life is more exciting and compelling than the fear that the technology might go wrong in same way. Take for example autonomous vehicles, a technology the public still remains wary of generally. While drivers may not yet be ready for fully autonomous vehicles, they still have a strong desire to improve safety and reduce commuter fatigue, so car companies have designed increasingly more assistive technologies that—should they satisfy customers and interact well—will walk consumers down the path toward driverless vehicles.[17]

The attitude that technology should be used to improve our standard of living goes beyond productivity. While using science to improve health is by no means new, the trend of applying science and technology to the human body for both repair and enhancement is achieving new breakthroughs… and precipitating new questions. The social debates and norms regarding cosmetic surgery have been around for decades, but new debates—ranging from the use of health trackers and a GPS to augment physical performance to the eligibility of a runner with prosthetic legs to compete in the Olympics—are pushing us into new territory. At the fringes today are movements of "biohackers" and "grinders" who experiment with implantable technology,[18] with the brain becoming as much a target of improvement as the body.

Individualization and customization

In addition to improving our quality of life, we have also come to expect technology to be able to specifically address the needs of a particular individual, vice the generalizable population. In the health setting, personalized medicine is a good example of how technologies that harness and leverage big data, genomics, and synthetic biology can be used to improve health not only generally but also specifically—person by person. But mass customization is a technological trend that goes far beyond the medical setting. Consumers expect to be able to customize everything from their shoes to their cars, and advances in manufacturing, especially additive manufacturing, seem poised to continue this trend toward ever greater, and ever more accessible, individual customization.

[17] Stephens, R., & Kolodge, K. (2016). Building consumer trust in technology. Retrieved from http://www.jdpower.com/sites/default/files/jdp_ces_2016_final_for_distribution.pdf
[18] 1919 Loria, K. (2014, August 19). 6 Strange body hacks that are actually useful [Web log post]. Retrieved from http://www.businessinsider.com/strange-body-hacks-that-are-actually-useful-2014-8

Even the technologies that deliver us information are becoming customized. Tailored news is not new. The Pentagon's Early Bird—a news clipping service for the DOD—was started during the Cold War, and tailored RSS news feeds have existed in some form since the early 2000s. But algorithms and deep machine learning stand to continue the trend by actually forecasting and presenting only the news that might interest the reader, without prompting. That few readers understand these algorithms (much less know that their news feeds may be subject to them) is an example of impenetrable technology, but it also raises a serious concern about such tailored information creating separate societies of people who live in information bubbles.

It is important to note that the technological trends we have described both evolve and reflect public attitudes and expectations. Public attitudes and norms do not entirely lead technology, but neither does technology entirely lead public attitudes and norms. It is the interplay between the two that shapes the future of both, and it is that interplay that governments—and government leaders—can and should shape. But leading at the intersection of society and technology is by no means easy, especially because of the pace of change, which is the final trend we will discuss.

Speed

Like the other trends, the dizzying speed of technological change has been with us for some time. For both hardware and software, frequent updates and upgrades are expected. Rapid technological evolution is a boon in many cases and an accepted part of life, as mobile phone owners well know. But the pace of change is also stressing. The need to learn or relearn new skills poses challenges to workers and consumers alike. But when technologies that moderate personal and professional interactions change quickly (as everything from social media to drones is prone to do), government leaders must react quickly before the friction between the speed of technological change and the speed of societal change becomes disruptive.

Technology and international competition

Global access to technology is another factor government leaders must consider, especially when that technology may pose a threat to U.S. national and global security and stability. Our framework for dealing with these threats was largely formed against the backdrop of a two-state competition: the United States and the Soviet Union. However, the availability of information on how to develop and acquire these capabilities today has significantly complicated our national security landscape. We now face a growing number of serious threats from a growing number of potential state and non-state adversaries. The following are some examples.

Cyber

In improving our productivity and quality of life, nothing has been as influential as the Internet. We are dependent on it for connectivity, communication, and commerce. The Internet has given us "smart" everything—smart phones, smart cars, and, soon, smart cities. And sophisticated networks are enabling new, autonomous systems that hold the promise of yet another technological step forward. But each of these developments, as exciting as they are, also exposes a new attack surface for those who mean to do us harm. Identify theft, human trafficking, and terrorist recruiting are all enabled by our integrally connected world. If something is connected to a network, it is vulnerable to a cyber attack or exploitation.

Government leaders have to operate at the intersection of these trends and threats. Tensions between an individual's right to privacy and the need to protect ourselves have been with us since 9/11, but more and more of these challenges are emerging. For example, what policies are necessary to ensure that as technology makes our cities better places for our people to live, we also build in cybersecurity from the ground up to protect them? How do we best make our power grid and financial sector resilient? And how do we protect our intellectual property when hackers are so adept at gaining access? Can we establish agreed-upon norms in the cyber arena? The tension between capabilities people want and increasingly need and the vulnerabilities these new capabilities introduce will pose tough challenges for government leaders.

Biology

Another area already posing complex choices for governments and government leaders is synthetic biology. As mentioned previously, advancements in bio-technology offer great promise, but they also pose significant ethical dilemmas and new risks from potential adversaries. For example, gene-editing techniques like CRISPR-Cas9, cloning, and designer vaccines are all incredible breakthroughs that offer new hope for millions in the prevention and treatment of diseases and disabilities. Genetic engineering is already an integral component of our food supply. But what of the risks? Biological threats— to people or our food supply—are truly existential. What steps can be taken now to leverage these incredible advances in biology for the benefit of society and out of the hands of potential adversaries? What is the potential for international norms in the area of synthetic biology? How can government leaders and policymakers keep pace with or, better yet, get ahead of these new bio-technologies?

Space

It is hard to imagine a faster moving technology domain than space. Once the sole purview of the National Aeronautics and Space Administration, DOD, and National Reconnaissance Office, it is now within reach of the commercial sector, which is taking full advantage. According to *Fortune* magazine, the commercial space business has grown six-fold in the last 5 years and now includes more than 800 companies that provide everything from launch capacity and space-based Internet to high-resolution earth imaging. Small commercial satellites offer the potential to plug new people and markets into the global web-based marketplace. And the promise of real-time satellite imagery will generate high-resolution visual data for both individual companies and governments alike. As a result, space is increasingly crowded, and the capabilities space systems provide are increasingly available to a large number of people—no longer the exclusive domain of governments and militaries.

But space is not only congested; it is also increasingly contested. General John Hyten, Commander, U.S. Space Command, has said publicly that Russia and China have ongoing counter-space development programs, including laser weapons and microsatellites. He charges that we have to be ready for that. Thus, government leaders will face difficult choices in the area of space policy in the future. How do we protect our military and commercial satellite capabilities? How do we encourage the obvious economic benefits of the commercial satellite explosion while maintaining unfettered access to space for national security purposes? What are the right policies for an extreme domain that is increasingly important and increasingly threatened?

Leading with and through technological change

Technology gives today's leaders many opportunities and diverse challenges. While the changes may sometimes feel overwhelming, giving up is not an option. But then again, neither is chasing down technological omnipotence. How can one lead? What are the key questions? What is a good approach when confronting technological change?

We would recommend a simple but effective framework summed up as follows: Be practical, be thoughtful, and think broadly. Like three points in a triangle, these considerations will pull at one another and shape decisions that can most benefit society and our security.

Beware of unintended consequences

This means asking deceptively simple questions: Is the technology safe for humans? How could it affect children? Will it improve the lives of the elderly or be used to exploit them? While the questions are simple, the answers are less so. The speed of technological development may stress and push leaders to make quick decisions with non-obvious, unintended consequences. The complexity of new technologies, especially synthetic biology and autonomous systems, will make understanding the implications of any decision more difficult. But difficult decisions are the purview of leaders. Pausing amid the speed of technological change to consider the unintended is essential, especially when it comes to law and policy, which may not have kept pace with the latest iteration of a rapidly evolving technology.

Consider the sociocultural implications

While policy and law must be considered, so too must public norms. Those public norms evolve differently depending on public perception and sometimes even fear—in some cases, well-founded and in others misplaced. Government leaders are responsible for understanding, helping inform, and being sensitive to public perceptions and norms regarding new technologies, even as those perceptions and norms continuously evolve. The commercial market alone is neither best positioned nor responsible for the heavy duty of educating the public about—and potentially safeguarding it from—the next leap in technology.

Connect the dots

Finally, given that technology is advancing by leaps today and into the foreseeable future, no individual leader or organization will be able to grasp all of the implications of all of those changes alone. It is important to survey the diversity of trends and their relative speeds. Knowing all that is happening might not be reasonable or feasible, but developing and accessing a diverse network of colleagues with varied backgrounds and expertise will certainly help—in understanding both the technologies and how they might intersect with society. Government leaders should seek to have this broad perspective not only so they can manage and regulate the technologies that currently exist but also because they may be in a position to help U.S. researchers and companies lead the world in the next technological revolution.

Unfettered technological development—made in the absence of societal regulation and government intervention—is a good plot device for another science fiction dystopia. Likewise, totalitarian rule over technological innovation (or its use) presents its own kind of dystopia. Government leaders have the opportunity and responsibility to understand, foster, and intervene in technological changes for the good of the nation.

From Partisan to Partner: Getting Things Done in Washington

By Robert Shea, former Associate Director for Management, U.S. Office of Management and Budget

Introduction: Bridging the partisan divide

Partisanship is not new. Fierce disagreement about policy is part of our national fabric. Our country was formed from disagreements so strong that bonds with our sovereign had to be broken. Even after that, though, partisanship has sometimes resulted in violence. Take, for example, the day in 1856 when Congressman Preston Brooks (D-SC) beat Senator Charles Sumner (R-MA) with a cane so badly Senator Sumner almost died. It's bad today, but partisanship has been worse. However, it need not get in the way of progress or collaboration. A little personal outreach can bridge gaps thought impassable. It happens, even today.

If you viewed the most damning statements from our political leaders, you would wonder why anything gets done at all. Before leaving on a congressional recess, Senator Mitch McConnell (R-KY) said in a floor speech, "Senate Democrats are now trying to make it impossible to get the basic work of government accomplished with some filibuster summer sequel." He continued, "Democrats are again reverting to their dysfunctional ways because they believe it suits them politically."[19]

Not to be outdone, Senator Harry Reid (D-NV) took to the floor in response. He said, "Mr. President, I assume my Republican friend feels that if you say just the opposite of what is valid and true, some people will believe it. You talk about a logic-free zone…boy, we got one in the last half hour here." He continued his verbal assault: "This is what Democrats and the American people have come to expect from Republicans—promises not kept, commitments not honored, and work not done."[20]

This is the tone of rhetoric in our nation's most deliberative legislative body. There's a contest going on for who can be nastiest. And it shows no sign of abatement.

---

[19] Gun Violence Epidemic, 162 Cong. Rec. H4981 (2016). Retrieved from https://www.gpo.gov/fdsys/pkg/CREC-2016-07-14/html/CREC-2016-07-14-pt1-PgH4981.htm
[20] Ibid.

Nor is it a recent phenomenon. My very first job in Washington was with the House Subcommittee on National Security, International Affairs, and Criminal Justice of the Committee on Government Reform and Oversight. The Committee was conducting an investigation of the siege and death of the Branch Davidian cult at its compound in Waco, Texas. After 51 days surrounding the compound, authorities assaulted the home with tanks in an attempt to flush out the residents, injecting tear gas in mass quantities. There were genuine questions about whether law enforcement employed the right tactics to save the almost 90 lives then under the influence of Branch Davidian leader David Koresh. But as a young staffer, I saw firsthand that the temptation to score partisan points by politicians on both sides of the aisle was too great.

In its final report on the Waco investigation, Republicans concluded that "[i]n light of [then] Attorney General Janet Reno's ultimate responsibility for the disastrous assault and its resulting deaths the President should have accepted [her offer of resignation]."[21] Then-Congressman Charles Schumer (D-NY) reacted bluntly and crudely, saying, "This Waco report striptease is highly irresponsible. It is pure politics being danced on the graves of dead Federal agents."[22] There were more thoughtful questions and important issues discussed in the final report. But the experience gave me a crash course in the use of oversight to gain partisan political advantage, regardless of the facts.

An endless capacity to screw up

When you're a cog in the House's oversight machine, as I was then, you are in receipt of a steady stream of audits and investigations of government mismanagement or malfeasance. Though I am an optimist about government's potential to do good, its capacity to screw up is seemingly endless. At one point, the Government Accountability Office presented me with a report showing an increase in the number of agencies reporting annual tallies of "improper payments," payments made in the wrong amount or to the wrong person. Counting just the 17 programs that reported such numbers at the time, the total amount of money paid improperly was $19.1 billion.[23]

---

[21] Committee on Government Reform and Oversight, Committee on the Judiciary. (1996). Investigation into the activities of Federal law enforcement agencies toward the Branch Davidians: Thirteenth report (Report No. 104-749). Washington, DC: U.S. Government Publishing Office.
[22] McCaleb, I. C. (1996, July 11). GOP Waco findings skewer Reno, ATF. United Press International. Retrieved from http://www.upi.com/Archives/1996/07/11/GOP-Waco-findings-skewer-Reno-ATF/2411837057600
[23] U.S. Government Accountability Office. Financial management: Improper payments reported in fiscal year 1999 financial statements (Report No. GAO/AIMD-00-261R). (2000, July 27). Washington, DC: Government Accountability Office.

Improper payments are a serious issue. The complexity of government programs, combined with the temptation by some to defraud them, makes

it really difficult to get all payments right. But agencies could do a lot more to limit improper payments and ensure the right people get the right amounts. Back then, the issue wasn't getting a lot of attention. That is, until it landed in the *Washington Post*.

Of the $19.1 billion paid improperly, the Post reported, "In many cases, the government never recovers the lost money." It continued, "[Senator Fred] Thompson said that, of the 24 largest cabinet departments and agencies, only nine reported estimates of overpayments. There is no overall requirement that they do so."[24] After a stream of enacted laws—the Improper Payments Information Act of 2002,[25] the Improper Payments Elimination and Recovery Act of 2010,[26] ate the Improper Payments Elimination and Recovery Improvement Act of 2012[27]—improper payments remain a problem. The tally of improper payments today is almost $140 billion annually. That's partly because more programs are measuring the extent of the problem more accurately. But it is clear that better analytics and more effective prevention could save taxpayers tens of billions of dollars at least.

This is a story of good oversight highlighting an issue that needs attention. But it also underscores a reality in Washington: If it's not covered by the media, it must not be important. The glare of the press gets the attention of policymakers...and it can also make policymakers go out of their way to get the attention of the press, by whatever means possible.

As a congressional staffer, I was on the giving end of oversight. Not until I joined the staff of OMB did I "enjoy" being on its receiving end. At OMB, I was among the earnest ones churning out directives aimed at addressing long-standing management challenges. If a story on our initiatives appeared on the Internet, my vanity caused me to peruse the comments section. I never got used to the unfair, sometimes partisan criticism. People are mean, and while it sometimes hurt, I tried not to take it personally; I also tried not to let the vitriol get in the way of making sound management policy, but it was sometimes challenging.

PART-ing ways

I experienced that up close and personal in leading OMB's Performance Improvement Initiative. I invested much of my time while at OMB on that effort, with particular attention paid to something called the Program

[24] Barr, S. (1999, November 6). Improper payments cost U.S. big; GAO report cites $19.1 billion in errors at just 9 agencies. The Washington Post. Retrieved from https://www.highbeam.com/doc/1P2-621786.html
[25] Improper Payments Information Act of 2002, Pub. L. No. 107–300, 116 Stat. 2350 (2002).
[26] Improper Payments Elimination and Recovery Act of 2010, Pub. L. 111-204, July 22, 2010.
[27] Improper Payments Elimination and Recovery Improvement Act of 2012, Pub. L. No. 12–248, 126 Stat. 2390 (2013).

Assessment Rating Tool (PART), which was designed to assess and improve the performance of government programs. With PART, career staff at OMB worked with program staff at agencies to arrive at an objective evaluation of a program's performance and, where appropriate, agree on steps to improve it. And as hard as we worked to make PART transparent and fair, some saw partisan ulterior motives.

Early in the process of evaluating programs with this new tool, the left-leaning watchdog organization OMB Watch wrote of the tool, "Under the guise of a neutral scientific tool, PART evaluates programs using questionable criteria, some of which conflict directly with programs' authorizing statutes." The biting critique continued, "After conducting these problem-ridden assessments, OMB then uses the PART scores to justify changes in program budgets."[28] The implication of course, was that we were using PART to get rid of programs the Bush administration didn't like. Later posts by OMB Watch were increasingly critical: "Despite failing to produce any meaningful results for the public interest, PART and performance rhetoric are being pushed in a number of policy proposals. Uncritical acceptance of the PART is a recipe for disaster."[29] Problem-ridden assessments. Recipe for disaster. Seriously.

We at OMB worked diligently to address criticism of the tool and its application. At one point, we developed a new website, ExpectMore.gov, to make the effort even more transparent than it already was. However, OMB Watch didn't see it that way. When the site launched, OMB Watch wrote:

> This year OMB has simultaneously made PART data more and less accessible. OMB has increased the PART's exposure and simplified the data by launching a new website with a user-friendly, searchable database format that displays less information. In doing this, OMB has removed the comprehensive information that the White House once published.[30]

A bigger person might have let the criticism wash off him like water off a duck's back. Not me. I found the author of the blog post, Adam Hughes, and asked him to meet me to discuss his concerns. My proposition to him was that before lobbing criticism grenades over the Internet, he could at least do me the courtesy of a phone call or email. We met. We discussed OMB Watch's concerns, some of which were legitimate. We made adjustments to improve navigation on ExpectMore.gov. Hughes was kind enough to applaud the responsiveness in a subsequent blog post.

That began my unexpectedly constructive relationship with the folks at OMB Watch. Their hearts were in the right place (the same place mine was), trying

[28] Center for Effective Government. (2005, May 31). House considers CDBG but avoids attacking PART [Web log post]. Retrieved from http://www.foreffectivegov.org/node/2453
[29] Hughes, A., & Shull, J. R. (2005). PART backgrounder (OMB Watch). Washington, DC: Office of Management and Budget. Retrieved from http://www.foreffectivegov.org/sites/default/files/regs/2005/performance/PARTbackgrounder.pdf
[30] Center for Effective Government. (2006, February 6). Initial analysis of the President's 2007 budget [Web log post]. Retrieved from http://www.foreffectivegov.org/node/2769

to get greater transparency into Federal spending. So when I was asked by the Bush administration to lead negotiations over the Federal Funding Accountability and Transparency Act of 2006,[31] OMB Watch became an unexpected ally. In our discussions with it over the bill, OMB Watch made the case for more transparency. While many of my executive branch colleagues insisted there was no need for it, that all the information being requested was already available, it wasn't; my erstwhile critics convinced me that there was a need for additional transparency.

The Transparency Act, sponsored by then-Senators Tom Coburn (R-OK) and Barack Obama (D-IL), required almost immediate posting of data on all financial transactions, including all grants and contracts. While procurement information was available, it wasn't easy to access. Information on grants was also public but badly delayed. That's why Congress and President Bush eventually agreed the law was necessary and enacted it. OMB Watch and other liberal transparency advocates joined with their political opposites, conservatives also interested in greater transparency (like me), to push for the Act's passage. Though there were last-minute attempts to block it, the bill eventually passed. Partisanship tried but didn't get in the way of this legislative feat.

Strange bedfellows

While a strange bedfellow of the Bush administration's OMB, OMB Watch was a strong partner in the enactment of the Transparency Act; however, it was an even stronger partner in its implementation. Accomplishing anything in government is difficult. Accomplishing something requiring the willing participation of every Federal agency is exceedingly more difficult. It was critical to ensure all stakeholders in the Transparency Act, including Federal agencies, both parties in Congress, and outside groups like OMB Watch, were on board with our implementation plans and progress. Endless meetings and consultations kept interested parties abreast of what was going well and what was going wrong. They knew the decisions we were making and the basis for them. Nonetheless, progress was tough.

During the Transparency Act's implementation, OMB Watch launched its own website that essentially accomplished all of the things the new law required, and it dawned on those of us working hard to meet the law's deadlines that we could just take over OMB Watch's site and call it a day. There was a lot more to it, of course. New policies were issued that included agreed-upon data elements and new and accelerated reporting procedures. But the fact that we could leverage what OMB Watch had already accomplished represented unprecedented cooperation among former antagonists. USAspending.gov, as imperfect as it was, launched on time and under

[31] Federal Funding Accountability and Transparency Act of 2006, Pub. L. No. 09–282, 120 Stat. 1186 (2006).

budget. At the time, it was the most comprehensive source of timely transaction data around, and the Washington Post even wrote an article about the partnership that produced it:

> *Robert Shea is a Republican insider with a head for business and a yen for Federal program performance standards. Gary Bass is a government watchdog with a mean bite who wants openness and knows how to get it. Official antagonists, political opposites, brought together by a wild, crazy idea: Federal budget transparency.*[32]

Of OMB Watch, I said in the article, "They were very cooperative and supportive when they recognized we were trying to do the right thing." OMB Watch's Gary Bass said, "Normally, we come to bury Caesar, not praise him, but they are doing something that's very cool, that's very innovative in government."[33]

It's a little self-indulgent to share these quotes. But it underscores media attention that can result from an unusual event: partisan opponents coming together as partners to achieve a common purpose. It can happen. And it happens a lot more than people know because otherwise absolutely nothing would get done in government.

From partisan to partner: Some takeaways

That's certainly a real danger these days, as partisan rancor seems to be the rule rather than the exception. However, behind the headlines (and the headline seeking), senior leaders who are truly committed to the public interest—in the executive branch, Congress, even in stakeholder groups—can get things done. The following are some lessons I've learned that seem to overcome what appears to be insurmountable partisanship.

- When criticized unfairly, contact the critic. It's easy to criticize someone you don't know. It's harder when the critic sees that you're sincerely trying to do the right thing. Getting to know your critic, understanding their point of view, and meeting them halfway will diminish criticism in the future.

- Communicate often with allies but, more importantly, with opponents as well. Staying in touch with allies makes sense; you want to ensure you have supporters when you need them. And though it may seem hard, staying in touch with your opponents will ensure they at least know and understand your point of view (even if they don't agree with it) and have open access to you when they need it or want it.

- Consult and collaborate with both allies and opponents on major initiatives of common purpose. In pretty much any policy field, even the most

---

[32] Williamson, E. (2007, December 13). OMB offers an easy way to follow the money. The Washington Post. Retrieved from http://www.highbeam.com/doc/1P2-11441162.html?refid=easy_hf
[33] Ibid.

divided partisans have some common ground. When you find it, collaborating with partisan opponents makes for a pretty potent team.

- Congress and the media can be allies if properly courted; outreach to them is essential. When you're in government, appointees typically impose strict policies against contact or collaboration between Congress and the media. Ignore them. That's right, just ignore them. Get to know your congressional stakeholders and those in the media covering you. This will pay enormous dividends when you need them most.

- Be transparent in reporting progress or slippage. No initiative will go as planned. Repeat: No initiative will go as planned. Keep stakeholders apprised of progress, but, more importantly, let them know about the hurdles you're facing and how you're dealing with them; this will dampen criticism that the initiative is failing. Such collaboration could also uncover solutions you might not otherwise have considered.

Partisanship need not get in the way of progress. There are myriad partnerships flourishing today between Republicans and Democrats, but they don't make the headlines. Outreach, transparency, and communication go a long way toward forging the bonds one needs to get things done in Washington.

Concluding Commentary and Recommendations

Introduction: Challenges from within

A never-ending supply of whole-of-government/whole-of-nation challenges; esoteric, two-edged technologies, many of which were once the stuff of science fiction; a chaotic and interconnected world that seems to be repeating Cold War history; the evils of political hyper-partisanship and the temptation to turn turtle in the face of it...all of these (and more) represent the sorts of external challenges that senior career executives must be prepared to face. That's daunting stuff, and our four contributors have only scratched the surface.

However, there's more...a series of challenges that come more from within government than without. These, too, will shape the nature of career executive leadership in the second and third decades of the 21st century. And taken together, they, too, provide evidence of an SES at some institutional risk. I have identified six such challenges (my list is by no means exhaustive) and examine them below, but I don't mean to dwell on the bad news. To the contrary, the Obama administration provided some temporary relief—in the form of EO 13714[34]—and I summarize it at the end of this section.

However, as important as that issuance may be, I would argue that it only goes so far, and that much more remains to be done. But that is the focus of the rest of this anthology.

Challenge 1: The retirement bulge

The SES (and its sister senior services) suffer from a retirement bulge. This is not a new phenomenon. The average executive's age and years of service have always been higher than the rest of the Federal workforce, but both have crept up over the last 10 years. This is due in part to the natural "graying" of the civil service, but also due in part to hiring freezes that have kept the number of new hires—especially millennial new hires— disproportionately low compared to the overall U.S. labor force.[35]

---

[34] Exec. Order No. 13714, Strengthening the Senior Executive Service. (2015, December 15). Retrieved from https://www.whitehouse.gov/the-press-office/2015/12/15/executive-order-strengthening-senior-executive-service
[35] Kim, A. (2015, April). The Federal government's worsening millennial talent gap. Retrieved from http://republic3-0.com/Federal-government-millennials-talent-gap

Statistics, especially workforce statistics, can often be misleading, but not in this case. Today, about 65 percent of career senior executive corps members are eligible to retire. If current trends continue over the next 5 to 10 years, that number will increase to 85 percent.[36]Those figures are alarming, but while many have been predicting a so-called retirement tsunami for at least the last decade, this really hasn't happened. SES retirements remain about on par with the rest of the Federal workforce, affected as much by external forces like the economy and the world situation as internal ones like morale.

I would posit several reasons for the relative inelasticity of SES retirements, a couple of which may soon change for the worse (or better, depending on your point of view). First, retirement eligibility doesn't matter as much as retirement propensity...that is, when an employee is most likely to take advantage of his or her eligibility to retire without penalty. That propensity may vary by grade level and occupation but, the last time I took an official look, the typical senior executive waited as much as 3 years or more beyond initial retirement eligibility to actually depart. So historically, a high percentage of retirement-eligible executives is worth noting but not necessarily worth losing sleep over.

An executive's decision to postpone retirement is also influenced by such immediate things as personal career stability and morale. We know that attrition—the decision to stay or go—depends in large part on the relationship between an employee and his or her immediate supervisor. Senior executives are no different, except that many have political appointees for bosses; based on my personal experience, that means SES attrition may be more likely to correlate to the movement of those political appointees. To put it bluntly, if you get one you like and get along with, you'll stay and support them; however, if during the mythical get-acquainted period (see the discussion in Section 2) you find you're incompatible from a personal, policy, or even political standpoint, you'll move on...after a suitable transition period. The fact that so many senior executive corps members are retirement

Definition of Terms: SES

As discussed in the pages that follow, the original SES, established under Title 5 of the United States Code (U.S.C.), is not the Federal government's only senior service. There are no less than six others (and maybe more), each agency-specific, and together, they may number as many as 12,000 senior career officials; however, those various progeny all have much in common with the Title 5 SES and face many of the same challenges. Thus, I use terms like SES members and senior career executives more or less interchangeably, as well as the collective term senior *Federal* services, to connote the *entire* senior executive corps, regardless of the particular senior service.

---

[36] Partnership for Public Service & McKinsey and Company. (2016). A pivotal moment for the Senior Executive Service: Measures, aspirational practices and stories of success. Washington, DC: Partnership for Public Service.

eligible is a challenge, maybe not of tsunami proportions, but enough to worry about—especially given that this has turned out to be a turbulent presidential transition.

Challenge 2: Transition turbulence

If you buy my hypothesis that SES retirements may roughly correspond to the comings and goings of the appointees they work for, then a disproportionate number of those retirement-eligible career executives are likely to consider leaving during a presidential transition, especially given the natural desire of a new administration to bring in its own team.[37]

And then there's transition fatigue. I'll confess to that myself. In my case, I was fully 5 years past retirement eligibility (under the grandfathered Civil Service Retirement System) before I pulled the plug. I'd intended to retire after the George W. Bush administration left office, for many of the reasons cited above, but I agreed to stay on at the request of Denny Blair, President Obama's choice for Director of National Intelligence. However, Admiral Blair's transition and tenure were turbulent, and when he resigned a year in, I just didn't want to go through the suspense and turmoil again. It was not about Jim Clapper, Blair's replacement; it was about transition fatigue.

Bottom line: I expect an unusually large number of SES retirements over the several months after the 2016 presidential election, especially around the time the get-acquainted periods begin to expire in the summer and fall of 2017. It won't come all at once, and it may only achieve mini-tsunami status, but the executive brain drain—the loss of technical expertise, institutional memory, and just plain solid leadership—will have potentially significant impact.

Challenge 3: Accountability...code for diminished appeal rights

Another factor that may drive high SES attrition is the ongoing debate over SES adverse action appeal rights. Partly in response to the U.S. Department of Veterans Affairs' (VA) 2015 wait-time scandal, Congress passed legislation significantly truncating those appeal rights (at least for VA executives) in order to make it easier for the VA Secretary to hold the SES members involved "more accountable"—a euphemism for making it easier to fire them. However, the legislation fell short of its objective. First, the Merit Systems Protection Board (MSPB), which remained responsible for adjudicating adverse action appeals by VA career executives, sustained several appeals, reversing VA's termination orders. And to make matters more interesting, one appeal made

---

[37] This is not intended as an editorial comment on any particular candidate; rather, when it comes to presidential transitions, career senior executives commonly refer to the transfer of power from one political party to another (for example, Republican to Democrat) as a *hostile takeover* and from one administration to another of the same party as a *friendly takeover*. As I have noted, however, that doesn't necessarily mean one is more or less friendly or hostile; in fact, and as discussed in Section 2, career executives will loyally serve the government of the day in either case.

its way to Federal court, where the U.S. Department of Justice under President Obama declined to contest it, citing constitutional flaws in the original VA legislation.

Don't think for a moment that that ended the matter. As I discuss at length in Section 5, that initial piece of legislation has spawned a number of bills, all of which are designed to curtail SES adverse action appeal rights. In some cases, they're limited to VA executives; in other instances, they apply to the entire SES. Some (like the Senior Executives Association [SEA]) are arguing that the bills are borderline unconstitutional and would essentially leave career SES members in an employment-at-will status; that is, subject to summary discharge, with little if any due process.

That concern is arguable. None of the bills, passed or proposed, eliminates advance notice of an adverse action, the executive's right to reply to that notice and to be represented by counsel, or the requirement that the final decision be made by an agency official other than the one who first initiated the action. That constitutes due process, and none of the legislative proposals so far tampers with it. Interestingly, all of those bills also provide for some appeal to MSPB, albeit on an expedited basis, even though third-party review is not a due process requirement.

That is not to minimize the seriousness of the situation. As we've noted, greater executive accountability is code for making it easier to fire someone. If placed in irresponsible hands, the adverse action authorities in play or already in place could wreak havoc in the senior executive corps. And what's so disturbing in all the debate on this issue is the relative absence of regard or respect—from either Congress or the administration—for the SES *as an institution*…an institution whose members are the buffer between politics and administration and, as such, are the most susceptible to partisan purges, especially during transition. Indeed, one can argue that SES members need more, not fewer, protections. To be sure, some elected and appointed officials have come to the SES' institutional defense, but not nearly enough, and that is mightily disappointing.

Bottom line: The impact of those bills on SES morale—and thus SES attrition —may be as or more important than their procedural and legal implications. And in that regard, just the fact that some in Congress seem intent on vitiating those appeal rights, not just for VA (that's bad enough!) but for the entire senior executive corps, may be enough to convince retirement-eligible senior executives that it's time to go…especially before a new appointee shows up and the get-acquainted clock starts ticking!

Challenge 4: A problematic succession pool

The good news is that if all of these factors drive higher than usual SES attrition, senior executive positions that have been encumbered for years will now become vacant…and those GS-14s and 15s whose promotion prospects had been blocked may now have an opportunity to progress. At least in theory. However, there are disturbing signs that those GS-14s and 15s, the most likely succession pool for vacant executive positions, may be wondering whether it's all worth it.

Survey after survey of those likely candidates suggest that the SES is no longer seen as the ultimate culmination of a civil servant's career,[38] and this should not come as a surprise. With some exception, the image of the SES has taken a beating, and that has undoubtedly made many would-be candidates question their aspirations. For example, scandals (real and imagined) involving individual executives have put the SES in a harsh light, with a few bad apples prompting more sweeping, systemic reactions from Capitol Hill that range from ugly accusations and hearings to pay freezes and attempts to diminish SES adverse action appeal rights.

We've already talked about the potential impact of so-called accountability measures on SES retention, which will unquestionably make aspirants think twice. But that's not all. Years of executive pay and bonus freezes have made salary compression within the SES—already a perennial issue—even more acute. While those freezes are beginning to thaw a bit (last year, the Obama administration allowed agencies to fund SES performance bonuses at 7.5 percent,[39] still short of the statutory maximum but at least a start), they've left the spread between pay at Executive Level (EX) III, where most executives reside, and the EX II salary cap at a mere $14,700—$170,400 and $185,100 respectively.[40] That's hardly enough to enable agencies to recognize individual differences in SES performance, expertise, or positional responsibility, and it may not be enough to overcome the misgivings that many GS-15s may have about the SES.

Challenge 5: Exacerbated by pay compression

The situation is even more challenging at the boundary layer between GS-15 and SES, and pay compression here directly affects the senior executive pipeline. Even though across-the-board GS pay increases have been curtailed in recent years, they've increased more on a percentage basis than SES salaries, so the difference between the top steps of the GS-15 salary range and EX III is now only a few thousand dollars (for Washington, DC, it's just $8,400…the difference between $160,300 and $170,400).[41] That hardly makes all the additional headaches that come with an SES promotion worth the extra money. To be sure, money is not the only motivator—it may not even

---

[38] Federal Daily. (2010, April 27). Senior Executive candidates worry about pay, work/family balance. FCW. Retrieved from https://fcw.com/Articles/2010/04/27/SES-survey-salary-benefits.aspx
[39] U.S. Office of Personnel Management. Pay & leave salaries & wages—2016 executive & senior level employee pay tables. Retrieved from https://www.opm.gov/policy-data-oversight/pay-leave/salaries-wages/2016/executive-senior-level
[40] Ibid.
[41] Ibid.

crack the top five reasons someone would covet a promotion to the SES—
but it surely has some effect.

To make matters worse, SES salaries can start as low as $148,700; as a result,
many new senior executives are paid far less than the GS-14s and 15s who
work for them. That has always been a matter of agency discretion. As noted,
since 2004 the SES has had an open salary 'band' that ranges from that minimum all the way to EX II; thus, an agency can place a new executive anywhere
in that range,[42] and the fact that most have not is disappointing. That inequity
has been rectified to some extent by President Obama's recent SES Executive
Order, which encourages agencies to set new SES starting salaries at or above
that of their subordinates,[43] but the fact is that GS-15 to SES pay compression
is still problematic.

So if you're a GS-15 who is thinking about applying for an SES vacancy,
you might think twice. The surveys tell us as much, but my own personal
experience gives life to those numbers. I'm a fairly regular speaker at the
Federal Executive Institute's (FEI) flagship, *Leadership for a Democratic Society*,
a course designed to prepare new senior executives and SES candidates.
I've made it a practice to poll the participants (typically numbering 60–70
per 4-week class) on their composition as well as their aspirations, and the
results of this informal polling have been disappointing. First, usually fewer
than 10 members of any given class are actually in the SES, and about the
same number are in formal SES Candidate Development Programs (CDPs).
And if that's not bad enough, when I ask the rest to raise their hands if they
aspire to the SES, less than half of those remaining do so. I know that's not a
very scientific sample, but it's worrisome nevertheless.

Challenge 6: Depressing diversity

So one must wonder: When the current generation of senior executives
moves on and their vacancies are posted, will the best and brightest GS-15s
apply? Note the caveat…there will always be applicants for SES positions,
but the question is whether those candidates will be ready. That's especially
problematic when it comes to the best and brightest female and minority
SES candidates.

Historically, the SES has remained stubbornly white male in complexion,
despite the best efforts of a succession of OPM Directors, both Republican
and Democrat. And its sister senior services have fared no better.[44] Across

---

[42] Assuming a "certified" SES appraisal system; see Performance Appraisal, 5 U.S.C. 43 § 4301
et seq. (2006).

[43] Exec. Order No. 13714, Strengthening the Senior Executive Service. (2015, December 15).
Retrieved from https://www.whitehouse.gov/the-press-office/2015/12/15/executive-order-
strengthening-senior-executive-service

[44] Office of the Director of National Intelligence. (2016, June 10). *ODNI releases first public report on
intelligence community workforce demographics, seeking diverse talent pool* [Press release]. Retrieved
from https://www.dni.gov/index.php/newsroom/press-releases/215-press-releases-
2016/1387-odni-releases-first-public-report-on-intelligence-community-workforce-demograph-
ics,-seeking-diverse-talent-pool..

the board, women and minorities remain significantly underrepresented in the senior executive corps writ large compared to the U.S. civilian labor force. While some will argue that that's too high a bar, the corps is only slightly better when compared with the so-called "relevant" civilian labor force,[45] the fact is that the diversity needle hasn't moved much, and no one is quite sure why. To be sure, diversity declines as GS grade level increases, so the composition of the GS-15 candidate pool is part of the problem but, even so, women and minorities are selected for the SES in numbers that are disproportionately low when compared to that pool as well.

Part of the issue is that SES diversity (or lack thereof) is the product of hundreds of individual SES selections. While precise statistics are not available, most successful SES selectees come from the immediate organization that has the vacancy—despite the fact that the competition for those vacancies is supposed to be full and open to all applicant sources. And when you draw from a GS-15 candidate pool that lacks diversity, it should be no surprise when the SES cadre does too. The fact is that each vacancy announcement attracts dozens, in some cases hundreds, of applicants, and paper screens and panel interviews are simply not discriminating enough (in a legal sense) to identify a heretofore unknown candidate who, regardless of paper qualifications or interview performance, is likely to beat out a local candidate who is already familiar to the selecting officials…and who is often an heir apparent to the job anyway.

It is quite understandable then that many potential senior executive candidates, especially women and minority candidates, may view SES vacancy announcements posted in USA Jobs a bit like playing the lottery. Of the dozens of vacancies posted at any given time, candidates' perceptions are that only a small fraction of those vacancies are real—that is, where the selecting official doesn't already have someone in mind. The evidence of this is anecdotal rather than empirical and is based on personal conversations I've had with dozens and dozens of potential SES candidates, especially women and minorities, but their perceptions have become reality. Their conventional wisdom is that the vast majority of SES vacancy announcements are posted just to fulfill OPM's full-and-open competition requirement and aren't really serious candidate searches.

More SES CDPs aren't the answer either. They are supposed to be part of the solution, preparing an SES pipeline in advance of a vacancy so that when one occurs, an agency can noncompetitively promote a CDP graduate straight away. However, CDP selection rates are low—less than one in four SES vacancies is filled from an ever-increasing pool of several hundred graduates government-wide. So while the composition of that pool may be more representative from a diversity standpoint, it really doesn't matter. The fact is that there are highly qualified female and minority SES candidates

---

[45] For example, see Equal Employment Opportunity Commission Management Directive 715 (https://www.eeoc.gov/Federal/directives/715instruct/section2.html)

out there, but many lack opportunities in their immediate organizations and don't bother to play the USA Jobs lottery for opportunities elsewhere. The challenge is that they need to be found and connected to those SES vacancies that are real, something we explore in Section 4.

A perfect storm…and a temporary lull

Most of these issues—a retirement bulge, a disaffected succession pool, pay compression and inversion, a stubborn lack of diversity—are not new. Others, like the scandal-born debate over SES accountability and appeal rights, are of more recent vintage. Are any of these existential threats to the continued viability of the SES? Separately, no. But taken together, they represent a perfect storm that may indeed threaten the continued viability of the SES and its various sister senior services (more on those later), especially given the tectonic whole-of-government challenges outlined by our contributors to this section.

The good news: Some help is on the way. After meeting with a 3,000-strong sampling of career executives in the sixth year of his administration, President Obama issued EO 13714—aptly entitled *Strengthening the Senior Executive Service*—on December 15, 2015.[46] It directs a number of administrative actions designed to deal with many of the problems we've addressed above… at least for the moment. Thus, among other things, the EO:

- Loosens up SES bonus spending, allowing agencies to increase their performance bonus pools to up to 7.5 percent of SES (or equivalent) payroll, up from a 4-year cap of 5 percent—but below the 10 percent maximum established by law;

- Encourages agencies to set the salary of someone newly promoted to the SES at a level that exceeds the salaries (including applicable locality adjustments) of their subordinate GS employees;

- Mandates that OPM evaluate and allow alternatives to the requirement that new SES selectees submit lengthy essays to a qualifications review board as evidence that they meet Executive Core Qualifications (ECQs);

- Requires agency heads to streamline their career SES hiring processes to make them more efficient, more effective, and less burdensome for applicants;

- Requires most agencies to submit a 2-year plan to OPM to increase the number of career executives on rotational assignments, with a government-wide goal of having at least 15 percent of the senior executive corps on a rotational assignment of 120 days or more each year;

---

[46] Exec. Order No. 13714, Strengthening the Senior Executive Service. (2015, December 15). Retrieved from https://www.whitehouse.gov/the-press-office/2015/12/15/executive-order-strengthening-senior-executive-service

- Directs agencies to establish an annual SES talent management and succession planning process to assess the development needs of their executives, and to inform decisions about hiring, career development, and executive reassignments and rotations;

- Holds agency Deputy Secretaries (and equivalents) accountable for conducting quarterly reviews of SES recruitment efforts, including the quantity, quality, source, and diversity of candidates, as well as hiring timeliness;

- Directs senior executives to plan for at least one developmental activity each year and at least one leadership assessment that includes employee feedback (for example, 360-degree input) every three years; non-career SES members are also required to receive such an assessment during their first two years on the job and every three years thereafter; and

- Orders each agency to establish a formal executive onboarding program (based on an OPM framework) that provides new SES members—especially those who are new to government—critical support during their first year.

To oversee the implementation of these various initiatives, the EO also establishes a subcommittee of the President's Management Council (PMC, (comprising department Deputy Secretaries and executive agency equivalents) to oversee SES matters. It also directs the agencies that have statutory authority to establish their own independent SES—such as the Federal Bureau of Investigation/Drug Enforcement Administration SES, Senior Foreign Service, Defense Intelligence SES, or Senior National Intelligence Service—to determine the extent to which they will implement the EO's requirements.

Make no mistake: The EO helps. But it took seven years for the Obama administration to address these issues (indeed, it took six years for the President to even meet *en masse* with career executives, something his predecessors did early in their administrations). And even then, it stops short of proposing any sweeping legislative reforms. As far as legislation goes, the Obama administration apparently calculated that either a Republican Congress would be unresponsive or, in an election year, a vengeful few would try to make matters worse with "gotcha" legislation.

It's hard to take issue with that calculation, at least for now. But in my opinion, more is needed, and the time to start shaping a 21st century SES is now.

RECOMMENDATION 1.1: START WITH A WHOLE-OF-GOVERNMENT EXECUTIVE TALENT MANAGEMENT STRATEGY

Introduction: Leading yesterday's government…not tomorrow's

As important as the senior executive corps is to the functioning of government, the actual development and deployment of its individual members has been left up to individual agencies, and the effectiveness of their efforts in that regard has been uneven at best. To be sure, OPM has established a government-wide policy framework to regulate those efforts; however, by necessity, that framework sets minimum requirements and standards—for example, for the certification of agency SES CDPs or performance management systems—which only serve to establish a lowest common denominator for each agency. OPM also offers some products and services to support that framework, most notably the FEI and its leadership and management development centers, but those have limited capacity and only scratch the surface when it comes to building a *whole-of-government* executive corps for the 21st century.

For the most part, agencies are left to their own devices when it comes to the management of their executive talent; they make the day-to-day decisions—to develop, promote, reward, assign—that operationalize that framework. This means agencies' separate career executive cadres reflect their individual missions and cultures…their leadership DNA. There's nothing wrong with this model per se, but for the purposes of our discussion, it has two significant (and interrelated) problems. First, it makes the original vision of the SES hard to realize; and second, it inevitably produces executives who will find it increasingly difficult to deal with the sorts of whole-of-government/whole-of-nation challenges that Beth Cobert and others—including myself—argue are the norm of 21st century government.

Bottom line: I would assert that as currently configured, the SES writ large—that is, the sum total of the rules, system(s), and leaders it produces—is not up to that new normal, and we need a serious, long-term strategy to reimagine[47] and reinvent it.

Leading the SES back to the future

That strategy should start with the original vision of the SES—not because we owe any great deference to that vision, but rather because (as we argue in the pages that follow) it turns out that that vision got it right. It was just before its time, premature, proffered at a time when government and governance were much simpler. We—at the very least, all of the individuals who contributed to this book—believe the Federal government does in fact need a corps of mobile career leaders with whole-of-government experience and an enterprise perspective now more than ever. And it will take a concerted, sustained effort to achieve it.

To that end, this book offers 23 formal recommendations (summarized in Section 6) that could form the basis for this "back to the future" strategy to reinvent the SES as it was originally intended. Summarized below and detailed in the sections that follow, the formal recommendations are not intended to be exhaustive, nor are they all necessarily new. Indeed, for the

---

[47] Partnership for Public Service & Booz Allen Hamilton. (2014). *Building the enterprise: A new civil service framework*. Washington, DC: Partnership for Public Service.

record, they are intended to build on the EO issued by President Obama, the considerable efforts of former Acting OPM Director Beth Cobert (and her predecessors Katherine Archuleta, John Berry, Linda Springer, and Kay Coles James), and those in Congress who are taking a serious look at SES reforms; collectively, these efforts provide real impetus for real reform...more now than in recent memory.

Undoubtedly, some will take strong exception to this assertion. But, as I explain below, I believe extant circumstances have opened the door for another grand bargain like the one that led to the last round of substantive SES reform in 2004, led by then-OPM Director Kay Coles James—this time, one that will ensure that the Federal government's senior executive corps is ready for the 21st century—and I believe we must take advantage of it.

In that regard, one final point: I must acknowledge that the recommendations that follow are not offered or advertised as the product of consensus among the contributors, especially those who did so in an official capacity. They are mine and mine alone, and I take full responsibility for them.

The beginnings of a strategy

The first set of recommendations (discussed in this section) is foundational, beginning with the instant one: If we want a senior executive corps that can effectively address whole-of-government challenges, we need an executive talent management strategy and system specifically designed to do so. And if we want career executives to embrace those foundational elements, we also need a governance structure that engages and empowers them to be accountable for their own destiny—not just as individual leaders, but also as a corps.

Reexamining the institutional role of the SES. In that regard, the second set of recommendations (at the conclusion of Section 2) is also foundational, focusing on the overarching institutional role of the SES. The law describes that role in purely instrumental terms, but there's far more to it than that. From a normative standpoint, that role is grounded in a set of fundamental core values, almost all implicit but that nonetheless serve a vital, if largely invisible, function in our system of government. Those values—and the roles that personify them—should be made explicit, and the FEI should be charged with inculcating those core values in new career executives...in other words, with teaching them what it really means to be a member of the SES. And because living those core values may sometimes place career executives at odds with their political superiors or Congress, I also recommend that agencies be required to identify someone—like State's Director General of the Foreign Service—to 'run interference' for these executives.

Leadership qualities for the 21st century. As previously noted, Section 3 considers some of the leadership qualities that will be required of the 21st century senior executive. In so doing, it becomes apparent that the competencies that compose the current ECQs could stand to be refreshed—and not just today, but continuously, constantly looking forward to the competencies that will make an executive successful in the future.

It also becomes clear that the ECQs themselves, now over two decades old, could stand revision, and we offer three additions. First, we need to put the unique qualities associated with leading in the public service back in the ECQ model. Second, we need to add *character*—and a due diligence process to assess it—to the list of attributes that are essential to senior career leadership. Finally, we need to identify the unique competencies that are required to lead the whole-of-government and combine them, perhaps to establish a sixth ECQ called *Leading the Federal Enterprise.*

Developing the next generation of the SES. If those are the qualities a 21st century executive will require, how do we ensure the next generation of SES will be able to demonstrate them? That is the focus of Section 4 and its set of recommendations, starting with a whole-of-government succession plan to guide that effort. In addition, I believe interagency experience will be essential to the SES of the future, and I recommend that (along with a complementary ECQ) one or more mobility assignments become a prerequisite for promotion, at least for certain key SES positions.

Further, to help prospective candidates meet that and other requirements, OPM should strengthen agency CDP programs and, building off of the new executive development and rotational programs sponsored by the White House and the PMC, resurrect the government-wide one it piloted in 2005. Finally, OPM should establish an internal headhunting capability to find and place talented SES candidates and CDP graduates (especially minority and women candidates). And when it comes to assessing and actually selecting SES candidates, OPM should take a more decentralized approach, setting common standards but giving agencies more flexibility in terms of how they meet those standards.

Revitalizing the Federal senior executive corps. Section 5 discusses how to sustain a viable senior executive corps, and it provides our most sweeping recommendations. First, OMB and OPM should propose a common *federated* framework for the Federal government's several senior services, as well as a common, four-level (or tiered) structure of salary bands and rank, to facilitate interagency mobility and movement among them. In addition, the PMC should establish an Enterprise Executive Resources Board (EERB) to coordinate that movement, as well as to oversee government-wide executive talent management more generally. To further enable interagency mobility, OPM should also establish a master interchange agreement that would ease movement between and among all of the government's various senior services.

Last but not least, I offer some recommendations on enhancing executive accountability, proposing that SES members facing demotion or removal be judged by a jury of their peers rather than a tribunal of lawyers...and that that judgment be based on a standard that acknowledges that they have a special responsibility as leaders.

RECOMMENDATION 1.2: ESTABLISH A PERMANENT MECHANISM TO ENGAGE CAREER EXECUTIVES

These recommendations are certainly not intended as the final word in the matter or the only ones that could prepare the SES for the 21st century. Rather, they are intended to light a fuse, to make the case for further reform, and, above all, to elevate and expand the conversation. There are two perspectives to this, and the contributors to this book represent the first: As senior political appointees and career officials who have served both Republican and Democratic presidents with distinction, they represent a strong, bipartisan force for reform...and I suspect they are not alone in that regard. However, the second perspective may be of even greater import: that of career executives themselves.

It should go without saying that career executives should have a say—indeed, a substantial one—in the policies and programs that affect them. In that regard, many, perhaps even most, support various degrees of reform, even those dealing with greater SES accountability; however, they have no institutional voice to express their views, individual and collective. For example, when OPM or OMB proposes a change to SES policies, each typically solicits input from individual agencies; that input is officially provided by the agency's chief human capital officer or, in some cases (if the matter is significant enough), its chief operating officer...usually the Deputy Secretary or equivalent. However, once again, those agencies are left to their own devices when it comes to how they go about preparing that input, and they may or may not actually consult with their executive cadres when they do.

The voice of career executives

As an alternative to that "official" input, OPM and OMB also reach out to the Senior Executives Association (SEA), which was founded by career executives to represent the interests of the larger senior executive corps. SEA provides input on an ad hoc basis, when asked or as matters of concern and controversy emerge from the administration or Congress.

SEA also provides formal input to administration proposals via its membership on the National Council on Federal Labor-Management Relations. As should be apparent from its title, the Council was originally created as a forum for senior government officials—it's co-chaired by the OPM Director and OMB's Deputy Director for Management—to consult with Federal employee unions. After some back-and-forth debate, the Council was eventually expanded to include management associations like SEA. However, SEA is one voice among many at that table, and there is every opportunity for its voice to be drowned out by those organizations representing far larger constituencies.

In my opinion, neither avenue is optimal when it comes to engaging the senior executive corps, especially when it comes to considering views on a reform agenda. Thus, while SEA tries to speak for career executives, historically only about half of the SES are dues-paying members. In that regard, I should note that I served as a member of SEA's 12-person Board of Directors from 1991 to 2002,[48] all of us elected (and re-elected) by our peers. While that sounds good, like our national elections, voter turnout always lags total membership by a substantial margin; I can tell you that while we tried our very best to be the voice of the entire corps, all of us worried about whether we really had its pulse.

Until recently, the only other way for career executives to express their views on a particular OPM or agency SES policy was to vote with their feet (in other words, depart for greener pastures). More recently, SES views have been captured by various surveys—most notably the annual Federal Employee Viewpoint Survey, which measures general levels of job satisfaction for the entire workforce, or a specialized survey like OPM's recent SES Exit Survey[49] —but as with all surveys, these are fairly blunt instruments. They can capture a civil servant's state of mind at any given point in time but only in response to the various questions asked.

A mechanism for self-governance

No, when it comes to real engagement, something more sustained and substantial is necessary; to its credit, the Obama administration set a potentially effective precedent in that regard. As a precursor to EO 13714, the President established an SES Advisory Committee comprising some 25 members, most of whom were career executives from across government, to make recommendations regarding changes (mostly administrative in nature) which would strengthen the SES. The Advisory Committee divided up into subcommittees covering various topics of interest—things like mobility and development, or compensation—and spent several months talking to lots of current and former executives (including me), political appointees, and other subject matter experts before making those recommendations to OPM, OMB, and the White House.

---

[48] I resigned from the SEA Board when I became Associate Director of OPM because my responsibilities in that position included SES policy and continued board membership would have represented a potential conflict of interest.
[49] U.S. Office of Personnel Management. (2015). Senior Executive Service exit survey results: April 2015. Washington, DC: Office of Personnel Management. Retrieved from https://www. opm.gov/policy-data-oversight/senior-executive-service/reference-materials/ses-exit-survey-resultspdf.pdf

How those on the Advisory Committee were chosen and how their many recommendations were prioritized, triaged, and finally adjudicated remain a mystery. But the fact that an administration (especially one that took so long to reach out to senior executives) actually asked a sampling of career executives for substantive, sustained input is notable—and worth replicating.

I would go even further. While the SES Advisory Committee is a start, I believe it needs to be institutionalized, with respected senior career executives who represent the 25 executive departments and agencies, nominated and named by their peers and their agency heads to serve a set term on the body. And while I would not disturb existing communications channels—through SEA, the National Council on Federal Labor-Management Relations, or the various Chief Officers Councils—I would look to this body to provide a measure of self-governance for the entire senior Federal service, including the original SES and its sister senior services.

A senior executive advisory board

As far its responsibilities are concerned, I would give this senior executive advisory board a seat at the table where the Federal government's management decisions are made: the PMC. And I would also give it purview, in whole or in part, over several of the recommendations made in the pages that follow, including membership (and co-chairmanship) of the EERB suggested in Section 5, participation in a master government-wide SES succession plan, SES slot allocations, and even the certification of agency SES CDPs.

However, in my view, this board should not just focus on senior executive management policies and strategies. Rather, it should embody the very best leaders in the senior executive corps and thus should have a broad say in government *management*—human capital, financial management, IT, acquisition, etc.—just as the founders of the SES intended. Interestingly, there is precedent here as well. Few will remember the old President's Council on Management Improvement, a forebear of the PMC established by President Reagan. While it had a similar charter, it featured substantial career executive involvement. It may be time to go back to that future as well.

Reexamining the Institutional Role of the SES

Back to the Future

A leadership corps before its time. As originally conceived in the Civil Service Reform Act (CSRA) of 1978,[50] the institutional role of the Senior Executive Service (SES) was described in the blandest of terms:

> *"It is the purpose of this subchapter to establish a Senior Executive Service to ensure that the executive management of the Government of the United States is responsive to the needs, policies, and goals of the Nation and otherwise is of the highest quality."*

Who would have thought that that modest language was intended to engender a nonpartisan corps of seasoned, savvy executives to serve in the Federal government's top career posts? Modeled in part after the British senior civil service, members of the SES were supposed to bring senior *leadership* experience gained in multiple agencies and disciplines—the civilian equivalent of a general officer in the military—to bear on the nation's toughest problems as these executives moved from one challenge to the next.

However, the original vision has remained elusive and, according to some (including many SES members), that reality is dispositive of the matter. They say that the facts speak for themselves: That original vision—of a "mobile corps of generalist leaders"—has never been realized because it just doesn't fit the federated, largely decentralized structure of today's Federal government. Moreover, there is just too much inertia—cultural and functional, organizational and operational, historical and even political—to overcome. As a consequence, some believe we should simply accept today's agency-centric reality and quit trying to force it.

Should we concede that point? Should policymakers at the Office of Management and Budget (OMB) and the Office of Personnel Management (OPM) abandon all attempts to impose an alternative on an executive corps (and an executive branch) that seems to neither need nor want it? President Obama's recent Executive Order (EO)[51] says otherwise, and Beth Cobert's OPM

---

[50] Civil Service Reform Act of 1978, 6 Pub. L. No. 95-454 § 601 et seq. (1978).
[51] Exec. Order No. 13714, Strengthening the Senior Executive Service. (2015, December 15). Retrieved from https://www.whitehouse.gov/the-press-office/2015/12/15/executive-order-strengthening-senior-executive-service

valiantly tried to achieve the SES' original vision without resorting to potentially risky legislation, but the question remains: Is that original vision still relevant?

I believe the answer is yes, that the original vision was just before its time. At the birth of the SES in 1979, the world was much less chaotic and complex, more placid and predictable...at least in relative terms. And the various problems that faced our nation then could more or less fit into their neat bureaucratic boxes, where government technocrats could go about solving them. In that bygone world, deep functional, technical, and organizational specialization was a good thing, and narrow, agency-centric, or functionally specific career paths were the norm. Today, we refer to those specialized career paths as stovepipes—or, as we used to say wryly in the U.S. Intelligence Community (IC), "cylinders of excellence"—but they've proven remarkably resistant to change.

Thus, the original vision for the SES may have been a solution to a problem that did not yet exist—that is, the emergence of challenges that require whole-of-government or even whole-of-nation solutions and, correspondingly, a need for a whole-of-government executive corps to conceive and execute them. That is certainly the case today...and it will be even more so in the future. As a consequence, I would still contend that the original notion of a mobile corps of "super" public servants (my friend James Pinkerton once referred to them fondly as Samurai bureaucrats) will be far more relevant in the coming years than at the inception of the SES. And as a consequence, the way the Federal government manages its executive resources may literally be forced back into the future.

But before we go back to that future, it is worth attempting to validate that vision—and perhaps more importantly, the institutional role of the SES that it implied—against today's reality, to make sure it is worth what may be a difficult journey.

A Balkanized senior executive corps

As I have suggested, the grand (if largely implied) vision of the SES and the ensuing reality are two very different things. Many have argued that the institutional role, conceived more than 35 years ago, is obsolete; it has been replaced by a far more practical, utilitarian reality.

For example, statistics show that, with only a few exceptions, the vast majority of SES members are not mobile—organizationally, functionally, or geographically—either before or after they enter the SES. Most remain in a single agency or department for their entire career, and typically in the same functional or occupational specialty. Moreover, unlike their counterparts in the Foreign Service (FS) or the U.S. military, few members of the senior executive corps serve as generalist leaders...and, for the most part, their politically appointed bosses like it that way. Their appointed leaders see them as specialized agency assets rather than enterprise ones, providing deep institutional memory, functional and technical expertise, and long-tenured continuity that to the impatient, short-time appointee are seen as just too valuable to the agency's (and the appointee's) performance to be redeployed…or developed as a long-term, corporate investment.

Thus, today's SES can be characterized by stove-piping in the extreme, with each department and agency a relative island, and executive mobility among them further exacerbated by the fact that instead of the single senior service originally envisioned by its architects, we have seen the proliferation of many senior services—both formal and informal. Some, like the Central Intelligence Agency's (CIA) Senior Intelligence Service or the Federal Aviation Administration's Executive System, have been specifically carved out by law because of the specialized missions of their parent agencies, and they coexist separate and apart from the original SES. Others are less formally defined, existing within the overarching SES but as separate clans and tribes, some organizational in nature (the Internal Revenue Service [IRS], the Department of Defense [DOD], the Department of Homeland Security [DHS]), others functionally defined around professional communities like human resources, procurement, and information technology (IT).

Institutional roles…and role models

This differentiation is to be expected (indeed, given the complexities of today's world, desired!), so long as the senior executives who occupy and operate in those spaces are bound together, if not by common policies, missions, or experiences, then perhaps by the common ethos that is implicit in their institutional role. But what exactly is that role? And is it, in all of its various dimensions, still relevant…not just today, but on into the future?

To answer these questions, we asked four accomplished senior leaders—a senior military officer, a career ambassador, a very senior political appointee, and a senior career civil servant turned appointee—to look back at some of their own experiences. Each is a role model, perhaps even an archetype, by biography and background, and each may represent a different aspect of a career executive's institutional role.

- General Mike Hayden (USAF, retired), a career Air Force Intelligence Officer who ultimately rose to the rank of four-star general, led the National Security Agency (NSA) and the CIA, each with hundreds of career executives in their own separate senior services. As a military officer and an intelligence officer, he was double-duty bound to speak truth to power, regardless of the personal or professional consequences, and he asked no less of those senior civilian executives whom he led. In his chapter, he underscores the importance of that truth-speaking, of the courage to tell it like it is (or in the case of intelligence, the analyst's best take on that reality) to policy- and decision makers, not as they wish it would be. He also addresses the role of the senior leader in creating a culture conducive to that core value, where it may have life-and-death consequences.

- Ambassador Patrick Kennedy, a career Senior Foreign Service (SFS) Officer, is the personification of the neutral competence that is expected of the career senior executive, offering selfless service to the government of the day. In Pat's case, that service has encompassed nine Secretaries of State in eight presidential administrations (both Democratic and Republican), all while residing in some of the U.S. Department of State's (DOS) most senior positions, including Under Secretary for Management. It has also meant serving presidentially appointed ambassadors—both political appointees and career Foreign Service Officers (FSO)—all over the globe and often in harm's way. In that capacity, Pat personifies the geographic mobility expected and envisioned (but rarely demanded) of the SES and the generalist leadership skills that come with it. And in Pat's case, that's significant, as he manages two senior services at State—the 'regular' title 5 SES and the SFS—and in so doing, presides over a possible model for the rest of government.

- The Honorable Sean O'Keefe, former National Aeronautics and Space Administration (NASA) Administrator, Navy Secretary, and OMB Deputy Director, whose numerous career accomplishments have spanned public service, academia, and the private sector, addresses head-on the transient and sometimes tendentious relationship between senior career executives and political appointees. The interdependency between the two groups is especially critical during times of presidential transition—perhaps the most important of a career executive's institutional responsibilities—and as such, he offers suggestions for bridging the divide so everyone can work together as one team. Sean's lessons learned are particularly relevant in an election year, but they also play out every day in the halls of government, and they are worth noting by both career and political leaders.

- Finally, for her part, the Honorable Beth McGrath typifies the classic Federal career civil servant, coming to government early in her professional career and working her way up through the ranks from a GS-7 to a Senate-confirmed political appointment as the DOD's Deputy Chief Management Officer (DCMO). Unfortunately, that career path is anomalous these days —in my opinion, far too few senior career executives are tapped for political appointment—and so, too, is her mobility. Beth moved around quite a bit, but maybe not quite as envisioned by the architects of the SES; in her case, her mobility was functional and geographic if not organizational (at least if you define DOD as the organization; her entire civil service career was in DOD). Along the way, she had to not only demonstrate functional expertise as an acquisition professional but also learn and apply an enterprise perspective…that is, the ability of a leader to rise above his or her own parochial organizational interests to focus on the greater good. That, too, is implied in the institutional vision that grounds the SES, and it emerges as one of our predominant themes in this book.

The contributors to this section offer a unique point of view on the institutional role of the SES, not only in the words they've written but also in the career paths they've followed—the senior military officer, the career ambassador, the cabinet-level political appointee, and the senior career civil servant. However, taken together, they personify a common set of institutional roles and values that I believe the architects of the SES originally envisioned… and all of the qualities we would want from those who lead our government.

Their stories are set forth in the pages that follow, and they provide a basis for explicating and examining those sometimes paradoxical roles, which I do in my Concluding Commentary and Recommendations. But the bottom line up front: Without exception, these four authors, as well as the other contributors to this anthology, all believe that the institutional roles that career executives play in our system of government are (and will be) no less valid today and tomorrow than they were when the SES was first conceived. Taken together, those roles make it abundantly clear just how critical the SES and its various progeny are to the functioning of our government. As we shall discuss at the end of this section, the fact that those roles remain largely unwritten and unrealized does not necessarily mean they should be treated as merely aspirational. But more to come on this…

CHAPTER 2.I:

Courage, Integrity, and Accountability at the CIA

By General Michael V. Hayden (USAF, retired), former Director of the Central Intelligence Agency, Principal Deputy Director of National Intelligence, and Director of the National Security Agency

Introduction

Throughout my career, I have had the privilege of working with literally hundreds of senior civilian leaders—members of the Defense Intelligence Senior Executive Service when I was Director of NSA; executives of the IC's Senior National Intelligence Service, which I helped create as Principal Deputy Director of National Intelligence; and finally, executives of the CIA's Senior Intelligence Service when I was Director of CIA—through some of our nation's most challenging times.

The challenges facing our nation may have changed over time, but they are certainly no less difficult today. Thus, while those of us who were on the front lines of the Cold War may have confronted a world more dangerous than today's, none of us have lived and led in a world more complicated or immediate.

What does that mean for senior leaders in government? What special traits will be required for success in the future? Over the course of my career in public service, I have had the opportunity to see senior civilian *officers* (yes, that's how we see them in the IC, as officers, with all that that label connotes) at their very best, more often than not in high-stakes, life-or-death situations, and I've had a chance to reflect on what makes them successful.

A different kind of leadership challenge

In my "second life," the one beyond government, I am often asked to speak publicly about global threats. I usually begin by reminding the audience that, as bad as things seem to be, I have actually seen the world more dangerous than it is today. I remind them of the Cuban Missile Crisis, of Soviet and American armor facing off at Checkpoint Charlie in Berlin, and of the U.S. going to DEFCON 3 during the October 1973 war in the Middle East.

So, we have seen it more dangerous, *but* we have never seen it more complicated, nor have we ever seen it more immediate. And by immediate, I don't mean that we just get to see it on the evening news. I mean that events in faraway places have concrete, fast-arriving, and often unanticipated impacts on our own space. I also suggest that this reflects an entirely new flavor of threat, with the empowerment and interconnectedness of modern technology allowing groups and gangs and even individuals to create the kind of evil effects we formerly associated only with malevolent nation-states. Frankly, and here I am probably not surprising anyone, our Federal bureaucracy is ill equipped to handle the agile, multiple, omnidirectional, and nuanced dangers of the modern age.

When discussing national security issues at the highest levels of government, we more often than not don't even have the right people in the room. Our national security structure was hardwired in 1947, as we harvested the l essons of the last great war of the industrial age and organized ourselves to deal with a repeat of that same kind of conflict. So it is no surprise that the industrial age's power ministries—departments like DOD and State and agencies like CIA—are often ill-equipped to handle today's security issues.

But the challenge is even more fundamental. Bureaucracies were developed to handle the complexities of the *industrial* era. Their layered hierarchies were created to break work down into manageable chunks and to make complex efforts synchronized and controllable, their results stable and predictable. Controlled. Stable. Predictable. Not exactly a formula for the speed and agility and adaptability we need for the kinds of dangers we now face. The world is now networked, and networks routinely beat hierarchies. However, as badly needed as it might be, I don't expect a major restructuring of our government anytime soon. We will make incremental changes, to be sure, but we are going to be stuck with legacy organizational structures and philosophies for a long time. That puts an incredible (and often unfair) burden on senior government executives who have to lead in such an environment: Create results for the greater good even in the face of flawed and outdated structures and processes.

As a young military officer, I was told that success in a career of service was defined (up to a certain point) by doing things right; in other words, it was about efficiency. Beyond that point though—typically defined by a measure of seniority—achievement was better defined by doing the right things; in other words, it was about effectiveness and final outcomes. It was about true leadership. Today's world has made that even truer, and that puts a great premium on courage…and above all on a wisdom to see larger issues in their true context. We each have to find those qualities—wisdom and courage—within ourselves. Reflecting on my own time in government, it's clear to me, at least in retrospect, when I most acted with those virtues and when I didn't.[52] Three instances—think of them as leadership case studies—come to mind.

Wisdom to see and speak the truth

In 2007 the CIA Inspector General (IG) finished his review of the rendition and detention of Khalid el-Masri, a German citizen who had been detained by Macedonian authorities on New Year's Eve 2003 because his passport appeared suspect and his name matched a terrorist associated with the 9/11 Hamburg cell. A few weeks later he was turned over to CIA and taken to a black site for interrogation based on the analytic judgment of a senior officer in the al Qa'ida cell in the Agency's Counterterrorism Center.

El-Masri was the wrong man. He had a clouded past, but he was not the Khalid el-Masri we were pursuing. The passport checked out, and it wasn't long before interrogators knew that this was a dry hole, intelligence wise. He was released in late May of 2003.

There were lots of issues here. One was the time (weeks to months) it took to release el-Masri once CIA knew his true identity. Another was the manner of release: dropped on a road in the Balkans with no apology and little compensation. Finally, there was the public relations disaster (and later diplomatic storm) when el-Masri predictably went public with his story of confinement and claims of abuse. But none of those formed the core issue in the IG report. *The* issue there was the IG's recommendation that I form an official Accountability Board (a kind of professional jury used by the Agency to determine personal responsibility when things go bad) to judge the behavior of the senior analyst who had launched this chain of events.

I declined, and that declination later became part of the Senate Select Committee on Intelligence's (SSCI) partisan December 2014 report on detentions and interrogations,[53] the one that characterized CIA as a rogue and unaccountable agency. Actually, it was a pretty easy call. The analyst was among the best al Qa'ida watchers we had. She had been doing this since well before 9/11, and her knowledge was encyclopedic. So I'm not sure whom I would have gotten to second guess her judgment. I certainly was not prepared to do so.

But there was a bigger question, and it had to do with the nature of intelligence and the near absolute inappropriateness of applying a law enforcement mentality to its conduct, although that is now the reflexive habit of American public discussion. We make much in American courts about our willingness

---

[52] Hayden, M. V. (2016). *Playing to the edge: American intelligence in the age of terror.* New York, NY: Penguin Press.

[53] Senate Select Committee on Intelligence. (2014). *Committee study of the CIA's Detention and Interrogation Program. Findings and conclusions.* Retrieved from https://web.archive.org/web/20141209165504/http://www.intelligence.senate.gov/study2014/sscistudy1.pdf

to let the guilty go free to protect the innocent. Benjamin Franklin summarized it: "It is better 100 guilty persons should escape than that one innocent person should suffer." But that is a process of assigning guilt and meting out punishment *after* an evil has been done, with time not a factor, and with beyond a reasonable doubt being the appropriate standard of proof.

None of that applies to intelligence, where the evil is pending, time is always critical, and the objective is to enable action even in the face of continued doubt. Absent clear malfeasance, if I would have disciplined an analyst for a false positive (thinking someone was a terrorist when he wasn't), the institution would have digested the lesson in the most perverse way: That is, that the most important thing is to avoid false positives (you'll be punished for those) even if it means a few true positives slip through (bad things might happen, but probably not to you).

What might be admirable for a judicial system is unconscionable for an intelligence agency charged with protecting the American public. My job was to create circumstances where we got more of both the positives and the negatives right…and not to incentivize one at the expense of the other. And the one message I could not afford to send to our analysts was, "Take hard jobs and make tough choices, but if you f*** up, we're coming after you." After all, we still wanted to get the *other* Khalid el-Masri.

I suppose I could have had that wrong. But it seems so clear to me—as much now as it did then—and I'm glad I closed the matter out then and there. Others could whine and opine. But only I could just act and move on—if I would have the courage do so. So it took two kinds of courage. Courage on the part of the analyst to make a tough judgment call. And courage on the part of her leadership to protect her willingness to do so. Some may be tempted to chalk that episode up as less about wisdom or courage and more about my protecting my own tribe. Which is what the Democrats on the Senate Intelligence Committee pretty much accused me of in 2015.

Admittedly, the instinct to defend my institution and its people made that call easier, but it was still the right call. And there are plenty of times when the *right* answer cuts across the grain of the home culture.

Doing the right thing…even if it is distasteful

Take balancing security and liberty. Lord knows that intelligence has its issues with the press. In June 2008 a reporter for the *New York Times* was finishing a piece highlighting a CIA analyst-turned-interrogator who had great success with Khalid Sheikh Mohammed. It was an interesting story, but the *Times* was insisting on using the true name of the CIA officer. He wasn't under cover, but we believed that the use of his name would invade his privacy and might jeopardize his safety. Besides, he had refused to be interviewed for the story, so this looked like one of those "we can talk with you or we can talk about you" conundrums that public officials often face.

Two days before the *Times* was going to publish the story, Defense Secretary Bob Gates retired me from the Air Force after 39 years of service; this is a very big deal in the military, and I was entertaining the Hayden family clan who had arrived from Pittsburgh, Chicago, and other points under a large tent in my backyard at Bolling Air Force Base. I broke away from the party to call the *Times'* managing editor, and our conversation went like this: "[Your reporter] is a good enough writer that he can do the story without naming names," I told the editor. "You don't need to do this." I guess I didn't show enough fire. The editor later described my effort as "doing it out of respect for [the officer] and his family's concerns more than a concern the CIA had." Probably true, but hardly disqualifying. Later, after the *Times* put the officer's name out there, its public editor said that doing so did not put him in any greater danger than the scores of others involved in counterterrorism whom the media had identified.

Let me rephrase that in an unkind way: The media does this all the time. What's one more, one way or another? The reporter who wrote the story is actually a very conscientious correspondent, but some writers are hopelessly driven by an agenda, personal or otherwise. Other reporters are not so much agenda driven as simply following the general trend in coverage of American espionage, which is to say that they take the story to the darkest corner of the room. And there always seems to be a quotable official from some nongovernmental organization or think tank or even a disgruntled agency "former" eager to show them the way.

Then there is the choice of terms. Routinely labeling activities or documents as "torture" flights or memos buries the very point of contention in a casually used but defining adjective. The same could be said of "domestic surveillance" or "assassinations." They are useful catchphrases, but they are not always accurate and often oversimplify complex issues. They are conclusions masquerading as narrative. I would also argue that some of what claims to be journalism isn't about keeping the public informed, but rather about keeping the public titillated—espionage porn, if you will.

When intelligence officials see unarguably classified information in the press, we are required to file what is called a crimes report. In 10 years working at the highest levels of the IC, I probably directed, participated in, or was at least aware of scores of such reports. In all that time, I saw one case make it to a courtroom: the leak of Valerie Plame's identity as a CIA officer—and that was about perjury rather than unauthorized disclosure. Since I left government, though, investigations have become more robust. So robust, in fact, that even I have been uncomfortable with some of them. It's not that real secrets haven't been revealed. They have. Sources have been compromised, and journalists, of all people, should understand the need to protect sources and relationships. But the investigations have been very aggressive, and the acquisition of journalists' communications records has been broad, invasive, secret, and—one suspects—unnecessary.

I have always been uncomfortable with the government's reliance in these cases on the Espionage Act,[54] a blunt World War I statute designed to punish aiding the enemy. It's sometimes a tough fit. The leak case against a former NSA employee brought under that Act collapsed of its own over-reach in 2011. In a subsequent case, former CIA case officer Jeffrey Sterling was accused of leaking details of CIA covert action against Iran's nuclear program. I was long out of government when a jury finally rendered a guilty verdict, but when the case first began during my tenure as CIA Director, the U.S. Department of Justice (DOJ) had asked me, "How much classified information are you prepared to reveal at trial to get a conviction of Sterling?"

By then unauthorized leaks had become so routine that I decided to break with tradition (which was to be cautious) and simply told DOJ, "Whatever it takes. Just tell us what you need." The cumulative effect of previous, cautious, and individually correct decisions to guard against further disclosures at trial had fostered a climate of impunity on the part of those revealing legitimate secrets. Note that there was no claim to whistleblower status here, either. Failed, clumsy, or even stupid covert actions aren't a crime.

Much later, as this case was being contested in 2015, I was interviewed by *60 Minutes*. Jim Risen, the *New York Times* reporter who had written the story, seemed to be facing jail time if he did not expose Sterling as his source. I still had strong feelings about the case. As National Security Advisor in the George W. Bush administration, Condi Rice had convinced the *Times* to scotch the story, but Risen put it in his 2006 book, *State of War*, anyway.[55]

So I wasn't sympathetic at all to what Risen had done or what he had written. It was irresponsible and caused real harm to the safety of the nation, and I said so. But I also said that redressing this particular harm by compelling Risen to reveal his source might cause even greater damage to American freedoms if it chilled a free press. I think I surprised the national TV audience when I said that if I had to choose, I was willing to sacrifice secrets, but not the First Amendment. This time the big picture was really big, beyond my narrow portfolio as an intelligence officer. But to me as a citizen, the First Amendment remained sacred, even when it was being abused at the expense of legitimate intelligence activities.

Leadership as a disruptive force

I would like to think I always got the big picture right and acted boldly on it, but of course I didn't. While I was at NSA, I aggressively hired from the outside to create cross-currents within our own culture. I was being intentionally disruptive (and it was the right decision), and I'd do it all over again...just more so. My new Chief Financial Officer came from an investment firm. We

---

[54] Espionage Act of 1917, 18 U.S.C. § 792 *et seq.* (1917).
[55] Risen, J. (2006). *State of war: The secret history of the CIA and the Bush administration.* New York, NY: Free Press.

got our new IG via an advertisement in the *Wall Street Journal*. We created the position of Senior Acquisition Authority and filled it with a Navy official with 35 years of acquisition experience. The Chief Information Officer came from the Federal Trade Commission (and NASA). The Chief of Legislative Affairs had been an executive assistant on the Hill for 5 years. Working through a member of the NSA Advisory Board who was a Hollywood Academy Award winner, we recruited our new Chief of Research from the R&D department at Disney Imagineering.

At the time, though, I didn't think there was sufficient expertise in the private sector to delegate mission responsibility to newcomers from the outside, so I didn't do so. Wrong decision (or maybe insufficient courage). In any event, I missed an opportunity since American industry was already breaking new ground in what came to be called the cyber domain. Only later, as I learned more, did the strong parallels became apparent. I was broadly right, and I had been bold, but I hadn't been bold enough. I should have known better and been even more willing to be disruptive.

I also know now that I was too cautious during my first year at NSA. We knew that IT was a problem; no one could even explain the system to me. But NSA was a national treasure and my first task had been to do no harm. I moved slowly. I studied things.

Then 10 months in, the Agency's IT network collapsed. At that moment, satellites and earth-bound collection points around the world were still intercepting communications, their vast take—telephone calls, faxes, radio signals—still pouring into memory buffers. But once in hand, the data froze. We couldn't move the data. Nobody could access the data. Nobody could analyze the data. For all intents and purposes, NSA was brain-dead. The blackout gave me clarity: *No course of action I could set out on would be as dangerous to the Agency as standing still.* From the outside looking in, I think that applies to a lot of today's situations.

So that's my offering to today's government executives, even as they labor mightily to make a difference in largely outmoded institutions. Work hard to get the big picture—the really big picture—right. Work to achieve the broadest possible perspective. And then act, even in the face of opposition, personal or organizational risk, indifference, or just plain inertia. No need to be vindictive or arrogant about it. In fact, true humility is a real enabler of change. But act you must. Boldly. The times and your oath require it of you.

Serving State: Two Executive Corps, One Mission

By Ambassador Patrick F. Kennedy, former Under Secretary for Management, U.S. Department of State, and former Deputy Director of Office of the Director of National Intelligence.

Introduction

I have been introduced by colleagues as someone who became a DOS FSO before they were even born. I can only acknowledge that I have been at the Department for 43 years (the last eight in a presidential appointment as Under Secretary for Management), and I have seen a lot of changes over that time—an expanding foreign policy mission, shrinking resources, major advancements in technology, and the growth of the interagency presence in foreign affairs both at the headquarters level and overseas. I have also had the privilege of serving eight presidential administrations and 14 Secretaries of State, all of whom brought different foreign policy priorities and leadership styles to the Department. And as the longest serving Under Secretary at State, I've always been mindful of my obligation to serve the current administration to the very best that I can. However, in so doing, I've learned some lessons along the way.

As background, the Department is the nation's oldest and most senior cabinet agency, established in 1789 by Congress as the lead U.S. agency for the conduct of American diplomacy. State is America's first line of defense in a complex and often dangerous world.

Department of State Mission Statement

The Department's mission is to shape and sustain a peaceful, prosperous, just, and democratic world and foster conditions for stability and progress for the benefit of the American people and people everywhere. This mission is shared with the USAID, ensuring we have a common path forward in partnership as we invest in the shared security and prosperity that will ultimately better prepare us for the challenges of tomorrow.

This mission requires an extensive global presence, maintaining diplomatic relations with 195 countries through a network of more than 280 embassies, consulates, and other missions in 170 countries. In addition to its Washington, DC, headquarters, the Department also operates in 38 cities throughout the United States; we have 27 passport agencies, 5 logistic support offices for overseas operations, 20 security offices, 2 data centers, and more.

However, physical infrastructure notwithstanding, what makes American diplomacy work is the people who give their lives (figuratively, and unfortunately, sometimes literally) to that mission. State has two main types of American employees—members of the FS and members of the civil service (General Schedule [GS])—who work collaboratively to achieve the goals and implement the initiatives of American foreign policy. There are approximately 25,000 American citizens employed directly by State—around 14,000 FS and 11,000 GS—plus around 48,600 foreign national staff, mainly hired from the local population of any given host country.

Given the Department's overseas mission, much of the focus is on our efforts abroad and, to be sure, there is a unique FS culture, partly because of the constant rotation and the tendency to form a close-knit community when sent abroad. However, an essential truth that I constantly espouse is that we are all one team—whether FS, civil service, or foreign national. Day in and day out, we depend on *all* of the Department's employees to represent the U.S. government in the course of carrying out our foreign policy mission.

Two senior executive corps...but one team and one mission

In keeping with State's integrated FS/GS workforce, the civil service and FS have comparable senior-level corps to lead the Department. Whereas the CSRA of 1978 established the SES, the Foreign Service Act of 1980[56] established the SFS. The SFS was established to correspond to both the SES and to the higher ranks of the military. The four ranks of the SFS are Counselor, Minister Counselor, Career Minister, and Career Ambassador, which correspond to one-star to four-star military officers, respectively.

We currently have 996 SFS Officers and 210 SES members, with approximately 170 of the latter career senior executives (the remaining 40 are non-career SES). Our two senior services have two very different—but ultimately complementary—roles.

We look to our SFS Officers to lead overseas. At State, SFS Officers carry out our diplomatic and consular missions on the front lines—at our embassies and consulates in 170 countries. They are ambassadors and deputy chiefs of mission, and they run political, economic, public diplomacy, management, security, and consular sections. In Washington, DC, they bring their overseas experience to our headquarters work—from developing foreign policy to countering terrorism to improving management.

[56] Foreign Service Act of 1980, Pub. L. No. 96-465, 94 Stat. 2071 (1980).

In that regard, the Department's civil service corps, most of whose members are headquartered in Washington, DC, and in our offices around the United States, is involved in virtually every policy and management area, including democracy and human rights, trade and environmental issues, and security and consular responsibilities. They lead teams who innovate new ways to work and mentor the next generations of both civil service and FS personnel. And inasmuch as most FS employees rotate to different posts every 1 to 3 years (much like our military counterparts), the Department's career civil service provides a critical and essential continuity, technical expertise, and institutional knowledge for our mission.

The SFS and SES were intended to be counterparts at State, but there are differences. The FS, like the military, is an "up or out" system. FS personnel must be promoted within certain timeframes or they are retired from the Service. FS personnel must also spend a good deal of their career serving abroad; while this is attractive to many, it can be stressful to be separated from extended family and to live in environments that do not have the same amenities as in the United States—in some places, having clean drinking water is even an issue. These days, FS personnel must often spend some time at our most challenging and dangerous posts, such as Iraq and Afghanistan, where immediate family members cannot join. The civil service has the advantage of greater job stability, and there is no limit on how long you can work, but there are far fewer opportunities for those who wish to undertake a foreign assignment, and the opportunities for advancement are dependent on a specific job opening at the next higher grade.

These days, as our national security demands more of both our SFS and SES, the historical boundaries between our two senior services are blurring. We must more closely integrate our two senior cadres to accomplish our complex, multifaceted missions. Today and going forward, State will need to rely more and more on its SES and SFS ranks to work as a seamless team.

Within my office, there are 11 bureaus and several offices; each week I hold a meeting with all the assistant secretaries and office directors. There are eight FS, seven civil service, and one political appointee on my team, all gathering together to hash out the security, training, medical, consular, and other management issues that the Department must address. Each and every one of their units is critical to the success of the others, and their leadership must constantly innovate together, bridge disagreements, and find the best way forward in an era of ever-shrinking resources and ever-greater foreign policy challenges.

Career leadership in foreign policy

While there has been much unrest, along with many global hot spots, during my tenure, it seems the world is becoming even more challenging with each passing day. For example, I am concerned about the small but determined terrorist groups that find our system of values an anathema; as a consequence, perhaps the most critical issue facing the Department is the fight against terrorism—the threat against the United States, our allies, and other nation-states by groups such as ISIL and Boko Haram. These threats are fed and fueled by internal conflicts that tear states apart, such as in Syria, Libya, and Yemen, but with global ramifications. If unrest and terrorism persist, in 10 to 20 years they will be complicated by the results of global warming— higher sea levels threatening coastal areas, as well as areas of increased aridity that will lead to food insecurity and strife.

Each of these whole-of-nation challenges, as well as many we may not even be able to anticipate, requires sustained career leadership from the DOS, and that will come from our career SFS Officers and SES executives working collaboratively and seamlessly together, along with our military and civilian colleagues in DOD, the IC, and other Federal agencies, not to mention other countries and international organizations. Our embassies and consulates overseas provide the platform for 30 other U.S. government agencies to carry out their foreign policy missions, from DOD and myriad law enforcement agencies to the U.S. Departments of Commerce and Agriculture and the Centers for Disease Control and Prevention. The maintenance of that platform, which every other U.S. government agency operating overseas draws upon, is the responsibility of the DOS.

Leading State: Core principles

I believe that, as a general matter, the State Department has always had a history of strong leadership, from its senior career personnel to its political appointees. But it was not until March 2014 that we actually developed and published 10 leadership principles for the Department. Several Department bureaus had developed leadership tenets that espoused State's core values, and the Department was able to build on these efforts to create this overarching set of principles. These tenets have even been published in our *Foreign Affairs Manual* as "Leadership and Management Principles for Department Employees." They represent and reflect our core values; they affirm the fundamental philosophy that day in and day out, all Department employees represent the U.S. government in the course of carrying out their mission, and they apply to everyone, regardless of rank or employment status—civil service, FS, foreign national staff, or contractors—in recognition of the fact that we're all one team. These principles take up several pages in the *Foreign Affairs Manual* but, boiled down, they are:

1. Model Integrity
2. Plan Strategically
3. Be Decisive and Take Responsibility
4. Communicate
5. Learn and Innovate Constantly

6. Be Self-Aware
7. Collaborate
8. Value and Develop People
9. Manage Conflict
10. Foster Resilience.

Although I subscribe to and try to embody all 10 principles, I have found 2 of them to be absolutely critical: modeling integrity and fostering resilience. First and foremost, one cannot lead without integrity. I have found this to be true as an entry-level staffer and no less true as an Under Secretary. You must always hold yourself and others to the highest standards of conduct, performance, and ethics, especially when faced with difficult situations. Unfortunately, we have had senior leaders whose lack of integrity rendered the offices they managed ineffective and deprived the Department of the necessary contributions they were being called upon to make. Bottom line: You must always take responsibility for yourself, your resources, your decisions, and your actions, but never take responsibility for the accomplishments of others.

Leadership integrity is especially important when dealing with the Department's political leadership. In fact, I consider it to be central to my role as a senior career FSO. One must always set out—forthrightly and succinctly—the regulations that govern in a particular situation. I once tried over a period of months to provide context and history to a new boss, who in the end did not want to give context and precedent their due. I moved on and was very impressed a number of years later when he told me he wished he had listened more to the information I had tried to share with him.

Fostering resilience is second on my leadership priority list, and it can be a challenge for even the strongest person. By resiliency, I mean persisting in the face of adversity, managing the pressure, and staying flexible while embracing new challenges and new techniques and learning from them all to accomplish the mission. And sometimes it takes years to accomplish that mission. For example, in 2008, when it became clear that we would remain in Iraq and Afghanistan for the foreseeable future, we identified the need for a special security training center to train our Diplomatic Security Service special agents, as well as State and other U.S. government personnel about to be deployed to our highest threat posts.

We began seeking a suitable site and quickly found the perfect one on the Eastern Shore of Maryland; however, while our project enjoyed the initial support of many stakeholders, by early 2009 strong opposition from the local community shelved this site. We expanded our site search and soon found an accommodating military training base in Virginia that was willing to share some of its facilities, and we also found some adjacent local government-owned property to round out our requirements. Our training activities were compatible with their training, and we were warmly received by the community. We began site environmental studies in 2010 and by 2012 found that the site would work, but once again various roadblocks began to emerge: fiscal constraints, lobbying from those with alternative (but unsuitable) sites, calls for more studies…so we stopped, started again, stopped again.

In late 2015, we were ordered to conduct yet another study. It would have been easy to become discouraged and give it up; at this point, a core team of State staff had been working to get this security training center up and running for 6 years. In spite of the delays and the frustrations, they persisted. Finally, in early 2016, we got the full go ahead, and the project is now underway. And while our staffing in Iraq and Afghanistan is not what it once was, security challenges at other dangerous posts around the world mean that the security training center is more important to our mission today than it was when we began this journey. The persistence of the project team—their doggedness in answering every question, crunching the data over and over, patiently addressing the concerns of opponents and supporters alike, and maintaining an underlying belief in ultimate success—was an inspiration to me.

Four decades of leadership lessons learned

So what have I learned in 40+ years?

First, teamwork is paramount. Nothing at State is ever accomplished by one person; we have a very collaborative working environment. This doesn't happen by accident; fostering this team-first environment may be one of the most important responsibilities of senior leaders in the Department, SFS and SES alike. When you achieve success, it is great to be able to share it with a team. If you fail, you have each other to lean on, and to rally to try again. This is important at all levels of the Department, from the front lines to the "seventh floor," and I believe it starts with the senior career personnel who are the Department's institutional fabric.

Second, you must protect your staff. State operates in a fishbowl, with lots of people who are quick to give us advice…or second guess what we do. But no matter the heat of the moment, a leader cannot allow his or her staff to be abused by others, even if they made a mistake. And if they have erred, this should result in a private discussion between you and your staff, not a public airing. Once the private airing has taken place, let it go and move on. This too doesn't happen by accident; rather, it is one of the most important institutional roles we career leaders have—it must be learned, and it must be passed on from one leadership generation to another. When I was Executive Director of the Secretariat and responsible for all logistical elements of the Secretary of State's travel, we always said that if the Secretary of State didn't see it, it never happened. Fix the error, find an alternative, and move on.

Third, personal relationships will always have leadership value. I praise many of our technological advances (although I still don't tweet), but, for a leader, there is still no substitute for personal relationships when it comes to getting things done, especially when they're tricky or complicated. When the State Department was talking over all the logistical, security, and medical responsibilities in Iraq, it was the tight working relationships that we had developed with our DOD counterparts over the years that made the transition a success.

Fourth, never forget where you came from. I am now a Senate-confirmed Under Secretary with direct, day-to-day access to some of our government's most important officials, but I was once an entry-level employee who needed someone to listen to me, advise me, and mentor me. My mentors helped me learn the way around a large, complex, and sometimes imposing bureaucracy and understand its traditions and rules. Some of these (like "corridor reputation"—how you are perceived by others) are unwritten and only passed along through relationships. It is critical to have strong mentors to encourage and retain talent, to pass on our experience to the next generation, and to develop our upcoming leaders. As a senior, it is payback time. You are where you are because of those who taught you. Mentoring is one of a senior's most critical institutional roles; because of its impact on generations of State employees and executives who may follow us, this is our enduring legacy as leaders.

Fifth, your staff have opinions and they want to express them. As a leader, you never have to take your staff's advice—but you are foolish if you don't ask them for that advice and hear it out. Otherwise you demean them, and no one who feels unvalued will ever give you the 110-percent effort that you will need to get the job done. In the crush of responding to crises and accomplishing the mission, we leaders need to remember to take the time to actively listen to and value those who work for us. I have been responsible for setting up major diplomatic meetings, such as Wye River and Dayton, and I went into the first meetings convinced that I had the right game plan. But I came out of those meetings, and every other similar one, absolutely convinced that the changes and improvements voiced by my colleagues made for a significantly better result.

Sixth, if it's a mission impossible, tell them. As a leader, you never send your staff out to do an impossible task, unless you tell them up front that it is impossible. Give them the resources and support their needs. They will still try, and some will use the impossible nature of the endeavor as a personal challenge, but they know they won't be faulted if they can't pull it off. And they just might come up with a miracle. For example, when Haiti was hit by the massive earthquake in 2010, the Department was charged with evacuating over 16,000 U.S. citizens, a seemingly impossible task in a country that had long suffered poverty, political instability, and poor infrastructure. Communications were down, the airport was closed, and public services were in shambles. I wondered how in the world we would carry out such a major undertaking.

Two of my bureaus, Consular Affairs and Diplomatic Security, marshalled their manpower and resources and partnered with the regional bureau. Our newly constructed U.S. embassy in Port-au-Prince became the command center for earthquake response. Diplomatic Security got part of the airport open with DOD assistance, and my Consular colleagues organized the process to locate our citizens, ensure their travel documents were in order, and arrange their travel from Haiti. State could not have done this alone—we worked closely with the U.S. Coast Guard, DOD, DHS, and the U.S. Department of Health and Human Services to evacuate all those thousands of U.S. citizens and their family members from Haiti. Together, we made the impossible possible. That takes leadership—not the command and control kind, but the kind that stresses teamwork, leverages personal and professional relationships, and, above all else, helps staff believe they can do almost anything.

CHAPTER 2.3:
Transition Turbulence and Shared Leadership

By the Honorable Sean O'Keefe, former NASA Administrator, Secretary of the Navy, and Deputy Director of the U.S. Office of Management and Budget

Introduction

Presidential transition. It comes around more often than the 7-year cicadas or the onslaught of locusts, but to senior career executives, it is ubiquitous in daily tasks and conversation every bit as much as the natural cyclic events. Indeed, the transition of national government leadership always brings with it high elements of angst and skepticism among senior career executives, as the new team loyal to the new President begins to slowly populate the senior ranks of government...not just those appointees requiring Senate confirmation but also the scores of others who will be part of the attendant staffs, all aspiring participants in the tasks of governing and administration. The 2017 transition has been the first turnover of executive power from one party to the other since 2009, and it has been acutely felt by those who serve the government.

The turbulence of transition

Transitions are always about change, and that means they are challenging regardless of how seamless these events may appear to those outside government. And although it is part of the natural order of things, change (and the uncertainty that comes with it) is one of the most difficult things for humans to come to grips with. While most political campaigns and prevailing public sentiments suggest the desire for electoral change, there is rarely a tolerance for it when it occurs, largely because it may not be the change most citizens had in mind. We're often advocates for change in situations or circumstances we don't like, but rarely does that advocacy coalesce around visions and specifics of altered conditions that we want to see come to pass.

Change for its own sake—without defining what comes after—is often unsatisfying and almost always unsettling. This can be particularly true in presidential campaigns. Is a candidate in favor of some specific change, or is he or she merely against what currently exists? Unfortunately, the default option for many candidates is either advocacy for ambiguous policy positions or opposition to someone or something that presently dominates, both of which are often lacking in detail or specifics.

Among the notable exceptions to this persistent political phenomenon is the rhetorical flourish from public officials, editorial contributors, and the general public about career civil servants in general. It seems this is the one thing upon which most politicians agree. Intentionally derisive terms like "bureaucracy" and "bureaucrats" amply serve to be at once both descriptive and denigrating.

Stereotypes and bureaucratic baggage

In the former descriptive instance, bureaucracy is meant to describe a process-driven, hierarchical government organization populated by position descriptions rather than people. In the latter denigrating instance, it's a catch-all word used to brand government employees as dull, clock-watching apparatchiks who lean on shovels for most if not all of their short workday. And there is just enough evidence, sometimes barely enough, that each of us derives from experience or natural bias to validate these labels. When you hear the term, you immediately conjure up an image of a bureaucrat. Pretty rough stuff for those who faithfully serve the public.

But when the public view is shaped by those who seek public office or write scathing editorials about the process of governance, the composite view is that every experience with public servants is the equivalent of a trip to the stereotypical Department of Motor Vehicles. No one misses the point. Our fractious body politic can reach near-unanimous consent when it hears that the elixir to our problem is to change the way government is run…and to hold those who work for it more "accountable."

The stark reality is that public service is hard, and given the broad range of constituencies government is designed to serve, achieving consensus around change is even harder. But more often than not, the public servants who administer the status quo are among the least resistant to change once they are offered the opportunity to be part of the solution. Indeed, a "bureaucrat" in its finest instance is described by National Academy of Public Administration (the Academy) Fellow Jeff Neal as a person who knows how government works and how to make it work better.

But that subtlety is hard to weave into the political rhetoric. It is particularly hard when the overwhelming temptation of opinion shapers and public officials is to pander to the popular bias that bureaucrats, like obstinate mules, are set in their ways, impossible to manage, and even harder to change. Running against Washington is a surefire crowd pleaser. Among the few in Congress who rise to the defense of public servants, Congressman Steny Hoyer, the House Minority Whip, has observed, "nothing makes me angry like hearing a member on the floor of the House use 'bureaucrat' as an epithet."[57] But Congressman Hoyer is often pretty lonely expressing this view.

It's no mystery that newly elected public officials and those who continue in public office come to this negative view. It's an easy political argument to advance and is universally well accepted. And it's not a new habit. Syracuse University's commencement speaker in 1957, a first-term U.S. Senator from Massachusetts, lamented that serving the public had become an "abused and neglected profession." John F. Kennedy's speech that day was dedicated to the challenging task of trying to persuade the new graduates to consider the noble calling of public service. He observed that it is a mother's dream for her child to grow up to be the President, but it's a blemish on the family name if her children become politicians or associated with the politics of public policy. Clearly, the commencement speech that day formed the outlines of his inauguration speech just a few years later when he issued the call, uncharacteristic of a politician, that we ask not what our country can do for us but what we can do for our country. It's high minded, and not part of the election campaign playbook, but a worthy notion to remind us all that service is the responsibility of citizenship.

A two-way mirror

The current public perception of public service is, in part, why many new presidential appointees (as well as non-career SES members and so-called Schedule C's) arrive in senior leadership positions with the view that the career public servants serving with them are bureaucrats unless or until proven otherwise. Indeed, to these newly arrived champions of the public good, committed to cure all ills and right all wrongs, career civil servants are guardians of inertia to be managed and overcome. And more often than not, the mindset knows no partisan boundaries.

And by the same token, this is also what career executives think the incoming team thinks of them. As such, the career professionals often have an equally derisive view of the new administration. Hence, the use of the equally derogative term "politicals," which conjures up the classic *National Lampoon* definition of the word "politics," which is derived from the Greek word "poly" meaning many, and "tics," which are blood-sucking leeches.

The more polished term used by career denizens of public institutions is "political appointee," which suggests some mysterious institutional process residing in the White House. But to the public servants who stand like Horiatis at the Bridge, the arriving crop of politicals is often viewed as an odd collection of campaign hacks, uninformed and misguided neophytes with no clue how to make or manage public policy, or arrogant egotists who believe that if only government were managed like some other benchmark

---

[57] Clark, C. S. (2016, February 23). Hoyer to union: Lawmakers shouldn't use "bureaucrat as an epithet." *Government Executive*. Retrieved from http://www.govexec.com/oversight/2016/02/hoyer-union-lawmakers-shouldnt-use-bureaucrat-epithet/126147

enterprise, all would be right with the world. And equally, there is just enough evidence of these descriptive traits to make the typecast seem perfectly fitting.

These tensions have always been present, and for just the stereotypical reasons mentioned. But to make matters even more difficult, this is a particularly anxious time we are embarking on. It is worth noting that, for the first time in our history (or at least the history of presidential polling), less than half of the American people believed that *either* one of the 2016 leading presidential candidates was trustworthy. As such, President-elect Trump[58] most likely won't arrive with the public confidence that he will do much of what he said. To be sure, this predicament is partly attributable to the personas of the candidates themselves. But another part of the equation is the reality that the public has a low opinion of government in general, and politics in particular—the same condition Kennedy lamented in the late 1950s. In essence, the public view is that the best remedy is a pox on all of the houses.

Finding common ground...and common language

Therein lies the potential common ground between senior career executives and those appointed to serve, as well as a basis for a shared objective. Whether appointee or career civil servant, the reality is that most serve because they feel it is important. And indeed it is. The trick is to have both contingents realize they are in this together. Both must deal with the American electorate's lack of trust and faith in the institutions these officials serve. And perhaps most starkly, as government officials, both career and appointed leaders are responsible for implementing existing policy and programs regardless of their origin or legacy unless or until changed. The success or failure of the public enterprise is thus a shared interdependence.

The President's appointees presumably know where the policy decision levers are—indeed, the one element every one of them will have in common is the appointment order parchment specifying that each serves "during the pleasure of the President of the United States for the time being." Conversely, their senior career counterparts know how the implementation engine rooms work by virtue of experience that comes with status. Thus, it takes both working together to turn the wheels of government. An appointee had better have a strong working relationship with those who know how the machine functions. And, by the same token, career executives need to elicit and enlist the support of appointees who are willing to drive decisions in the administration. Both are essential.

Given the institutional baggage that both carry, this is easier said than done. So where to begin?

Begin with common language. The 41st President, George H.W. Bush, made a regular habit of assembling all of the career members of the SES and appointed officials (or at least as many as could fit) at Constitution Hall in Washington,

---

[58] Editor's Note: This chapter was written prior to the 2016 Presidential election.

DC. Regardless of how they got to their positions, he considered them all to be an essential part of his team. This set the proverbial "tone at the top" that was unmistakable. President Bush articulated the view that public executives —appointed and career—are public servants, regardless of whether that service is for a season, a year, a term, or a career. He struck the tone of dependency on each other without ever having to dwell on it. If the President feels this way, it's harder for others to act otherwise, but there will be a few.

Absent the President's imprimatur, the next best thing is for the agency head or the next rung of appointee to articulate this principle of shared interdependence. If none of the appointees step up, then it is incumbent upon the most senior career executives to make the case to the civil service staff that the success of the administration, and of government as a whole, will be dependent on the performance of the whole team.

One team, one fight

As a second guiding principle, appointed agency leaders need to take full advantage of the legislation (and the grounding vision) that created the SES. That means providing SES members the opportunity to sit at the table when it comes to major decisions; to lead in different capacities; and to be active, engaged, and, above all, contributing members of the agency or department senior leadership team.

Regrettably, the SES mobility and rotation authorities of that enabling legislation (the CSRA of 1978) have taken on a negative connotation—that an SES reassignment is retribution at best, demotion and exile at worst, and definitely not career enhancing. The reality is that senior leaders are significantly more valuable to the institution when they develop a broader set of leadership experiences—and this often accrues greater benefit and standing to the individuals themselves. It also avoids institutional stagnation as "silos of excellence" are built to preserve the *status quo*. It's hardly a cure-all, but deliberate, managed executive mobility yields the benefit of developing leaders and building teams within an administration. An early understanding (and application) of this by both career executives and the appointees they serve can provide the foundation for the teamwork that is so critical to effective governance, to the benefit of all concerned.

Similarly, President Obama's EO to strengthen the SES signed in late 2015 provides a required framework for executive development and mobility as an essential element to achieve advancement. The EO reflects the clear intent expressed in 1978 to establish the identity of the SES cohort as a mobile one. And it surely reflects the modern, progressive strategies employed by just about every major corporation to develop future leaders and adopt continuous succession planning practices. If implemented by the incoming administration as a conscious effort to accomplish near-term leadership placements, this renewed emphasis on mobility could be seen as evidence of commitment to it as a pathway for advancement.

The adoption of a more aggressive commitment to executive development shouldn't stop at the senior executive level. At every advancing grade in the GS, there is the mid-tier pool of those most likely to be considered for senior executive appointments in the short years ahead. While the civil service rules require the consent of individuals participating at these levels, the same strategy of mobility as a means to address near-term staffing deficiencies can yield mid- to long-term career development opportunities. The requirement that there be consent of the willing actually becomes a means to build a cohort of advocates who assume collateral duty as missionaries to convert the skeptical and incredulous career force colleagues. Not a hint of a downside in any of this.

Along with a career development commitment, the new administration needs to embrace a proactive strategy to retain the people who want to serve and encourage those who simply want to mark time to leave when they can. There are several options on how to effect this outcome. One approach is to declare a 1-year open season of financial inducements to help the growing contingent of more than a quarter of all SES members who are eligible to retire make a decision sooner. For those who elect to stay, they should be asked to agree to a fixed-term contract, renewable thereafter at the invitation of the leadership with a retention incentive. Absent such an invitation, they agree that their eligibility to move on will be exercised. This approach provides ample opportunity for professionals to make an informed decision on when to move on after they are eligible. Concurrently, it also opens new opportunities for GS aspirants to refresh the leadership ranks. At present, few mid-grade public servants think they'll ever see room for growth to SES or find such appointments particularly desirable.

Perhaps most difficult, but essential to achieve—it is incumbent upon the incoming presidential appointees in the new administration to declare a cease-fire in the jihadist campaign against bureaucrats. Whether he likes it or not, the new President will come to understand that he will be held accountable to the public for the conduct of the far-flung enterprise known as the Federal government. Risk-averse behavior is a natural reaction when people see public floggings for every real or perceived incident and the leadership of the institution fails to step up to support the rights of the persecuted. It's tough for leadership to encourage and expect creative, innovative solutions to public challenges if the likely reaction is to blithely expect success and severely penalize failure.

The most common, shopworn strategy is to back into a practice of incident management by responding to each emerging episode of contaminated water supplies, backlogged veterans medical cases, or agency-sponsored conferences in resort destinations as another outrageous example of bureaucratic ineptitude to be excoriated and legislated against. Alternatively, a more sober approach is to reach agreement with Congress to take a holiday from legislating new punitive measures and adopt an accountability policy. Using *existing* legal authorities, the administration can keep a scorecard on every incident response and adopt a National Collegiate Athletic Association (NCAA) practice of self-reporting. It's perhaps the only NCAA compliance practice with merit and is surely worth emulating. If the responses or penalties are collectively found to be deficient by Congress, they'll have at it with new punitive legislation. But that inevitable reaction will be minimized if the administration can be responsive to public service delivery needs by demonstrating a clear distinction between penalizing deviant, unethical, or stupid behavior and correcting institutional failure.

Perhaps most important is for the new administration to ask for a cease-fire from the legislative efforts to penalize the SES ranks. A comprehensive review needs to be undertaken to vent the anxiety on both sides of this ledger, but the piecemeal tactics underway presently are sure to be more destructive. There's nothing easy about this task, but the mere act of making this part of the new agenda will be a demonstrated commitment to career public servants. Besides, it's worth a shot. The present condition is unsatisfying to the affected and the public alike.

None of these observations are new and none are novel ideas for improvement. The operative issue is to help arrive at the awareness that both appointees and career executives need each other—and to understand that reality as soon as possible, early in the transition. The faster that enduring truth is arrived at, the sooner the new administration can get on with its agenda and all public servants can do what they signed up for.

Kennedy was right. For all its challenges, abuse, travails, setbacks, and conflicts, public service is still the noblest of professions.

CHAPTER 2.4:
Leading the Defense Enterprise

By the Honorable Beth McGrath, former Deputy Chief Management Officer, U.S. Department of Defense

Introduction

Members of the SES provide a vital link between presidential appointees and the rest of the Federal workforce, operating and overseeing nearly every government activity across the executive branch. As such, SES members translate policy and direction into consistent and effective government, sustaining the broader corporate interests within and between administrations. This linkage between political leaders and the front-line Federal workforce is crucial. In fact, most SES members start as front-line Federal workers. And occasionally, they even progress from the SES to a political appointment, as happened in my case. Regardless of the journey one takes, there are lessons to draw from the steps along the pathway.

The need for leaders of high caliber is even more critical today as the range of Federal missions has grown more and more diverse and complex. For SES leaders to be able to effectively manage agencies and their major programs, they must possess the right blend of skills and experience, including an aptitude for collaboration, professional development, and mentorship in tactical acumen and strategy, and what some of us in government refer to as "enterprise" thinking—or keeping the goals, needs, and interests of the whole-of-the-department (and even the whole-of-government) in mind while addressing specific mission, business, and management challenges. This blend will vary for each executive and agency; however, the overall components are the same. It may be instructive to examine how these skills and aptitudes were both developed and deployed in different stages of my career.

In my view, there is no substitute for doing the work, no better classroom than the day-to-day challenge of meeting government and taxpayer needs, implementing change, and seeking to improve office or agency performance. My own journey offers insight into how these skills and aptitudes can be acquired, and how the building blocks of my career as a Federal employee prepared me for the challenges of leadership, first in an SES role and later as a Senate-confirmed appointee. While my experience may be uniquely mine, it shares common elements with many who have traveled the SES pathway. In particular, I've found that certain key factors—developing the ability to collaborate well; having mentors who both supported and challenged me; seeking out professional training and executive development; and cultivating a range of experiences in different aspects of government, all the way from the organization to the enterprise levels—enabled me to be successful as a member of SES and later as a political appointee.

The art of executive leadership in government

The early stages of one's career are arguably when skills and experience are acquired most rapidly. That was certainly true in my case, most especially with regard to the art of executive leadership in government—an essential skill that one starts to learn in one's first professional role and continues to practice and perfect for the rest of one's career.

My introduction to executive leadership came early in my civilian service with the U.S. Navy. I joined the DOD because of the array of opportunities it afforded and because I deeply supported the mission to keep our nation safe. I began my career as a logistics intern at the GS-7 level in the Naval Sea Systems Command. In addition to completing the required functional classroom training for my internship, I had the instructive experience of seeing—and learning—firsthand how all of the parts of the Navy worked as a team to successfully execute its complex, critical mission. I saw it at bases in the field, on ships, in headquarters elements, and in working with industry.

Through diverse assignments, like serving on a logistics overhaul team for Navy ships during their periodic maintenance "downtime" to working with military and civilian logistics experts to write policy that governed such ordinary but vital things like repair part replenishment, I learned the value of collaboration and communication—two essential executive leadership competencies that confirmed for me that there is no substitute for experience. For example, I saw up close and personal how the successful execution of military operations depended on an interconnected ecosystem of people, capabilities, and equipment—all welded together by collaboration. And I came to realize that the difficult, sometimes dirty work we performed at the overhaul site, for instance, was tied directly to the operational readiness of the Navy ships we serviced…in other words, the mission.

Like any good junior staff member, I worked hard to support the job that needed doing—it was its own reward. What I didn't appreciate then was how valuable this front-line, real-world operational experience would be to me in subsequent jobs. Years later, as a senior executive, my responsibilities often required me to apply those experiences to read the subtle signs of whether an entire program was stable and performing well.

When the executive knows whether and how decisions are actually implemented on the ground, where policy and practice work together (or not, as the case may be), then the executive is better able to lead and direct. Even when an SES member "grows up" in disciplines other than the ones he or she ends up leading as an executive, it is essential to strive for an informed perspective and understand the importance of drawing on the real-world experiences of those around—and below—them.

Make-or-break mentoring

When I graduated from my intern program as a GS-11, I served as the logistics manager for an international torpedo defense program that partnered with the United Kingdom (UK). It was here that another essential element of my career—cultivating and learning from committed mentors—became evident. I was given plenty of growth opportunities (although I may not have called them that at the time!), thanks in part to some important mentors and a strong sense of camaraderie on my teams. With the torpedo program, the program manager and chief engineer in particular were incredible mentors for me during my time with them, as well as for many years afterward.

And it wasn't just me they helped—they both felt it was one of their key responsibilities to actively assist the professional growth of our team. They were always willing to share their knowledge and experiences in order to help me, and the team, become successful. I also forged a good relationship with the program executive officer, an SES member and also the most senior official in the organization. That relationship later grew into full-fledged mentorship as I moved into more senior roles. Each of these executives unselfishly offered their mentorship, a lesson I carried forward as a mentor to others later in my career.

My mentors also invested in me through professional development and training, helping me select a program appropriate for my work track. Such programs seem harder to come by in today's government, but they are there and can help polish a promising worker's abilities. In my case, I attended a comprehensive 6-month training program for potential leaders of major acquisition programs at the Defense Systems Management College. With a doctrine of "train as you fight," the College taught us to analyze complex acquisition case studies representing contemporary acquisition program challenges and dilemmas, apply a broad cross-section of knowledge of the acquisition environment and experience, and deepen our understanding of acquisition principles and practices through peer and instructor mentoring and coaching. I later found these are foundational skills for managing in DOD, and they provided a depth of knowledge I drew upon, and enhanced, throughout my career.

As part of the international torpedo defense program for 8 years, I was exposed to a broad range of government issues in both the U.S. and the UK, and I played many roles, including acquisition manager and business financial manager, for this major defense acquisition program. From these experiences, I acquired acumen in a range of business areas, including in contracts, acquisition, financial management, and foreign military sales. Building blocks, all.

Mentorship also played an important role as I moved on to the Defense Finance and Accounting Service (DFAS). There I had the responsibility of shutting down programs and handling the difficult personnel matters that come with these decisions. I succeeded in part because, once again, I sought out and found committed, unselfish, attentive mentors who knew that I was up for the challenge, even if I wasn't so sure myself!

Their confidence (and mine) grew from being able to watch me work and adapt over a period of time. While *Merriam Webster* defines a mentor as "someone who teaches or gives help and advice to a less experienced and often younger person," I also worked for leaders who went beyond that— who deliberately put me in situations in which I had little or no experience. Think of it as tough-love mentoring. There were times when I felt I wasn't ready for an assignment but was expected to do it anyway—as if the operating principle of my mentors was "give her something hard to do, and if she doesn't quit, we'll keep her." Well, I didn't quit.

It was only by challenging me, and by putting me in situations where I was forced to lead, that I grew into the leader my mentors thought I could be. They believed in me and invested their time—a service I tried to repay by similarly challenging and mentoring my own staff as I grew in my own career. My agency at the time (DFAS) also invested in my leadership development by providing me with professional executive coaching. These sessions were focused on honing my skills related to people, relationships, and organizational and behavioral changes—proficiencies I needed while at DFAS and that I leveraged for many years afterward. I made my transition to SES while at DFAS, partly due to my achievements and my demonstration of the requisite competencies, but also from the assistance of demanding mentors who helped prepare me for the opportunity when it arose. In addition to the value of collaboration, my mentors stressed the importance of speaking truth to power and driving results through transparency; these principles made their way to the center of my leadership philosophy.

Learning to "think" enterprise

My mandate at DFAS also introduced me the world of IT and the value of holistically understanding and optimizing end-to-end processes. This allowed me to both deepen my expertise in acquisition and program management and also begin to acquire and sharpen my enterprise perspective to assess performance across the entire organization. I discovered that the world was *actually* bigger than the organization in which I lived. DFAS serves the entire DOD, providing pay and financial products and services in support of DOD's mission.

These services are vital—after all, we're talking about people's paychecks—
and their successful execution required a uniquely broad, enterprise-wide
perspective because nearly *every* policy we promulgated, every process we
established, and every system decision we made crossed multiple organization and functional boundaries. "Good of the whole" was our catchphrase;
leading change and leading people (two Executive Core Qualifications [ECQ])
were expected, but leading from an enterprise perspective turned out to be a
critical skill for me, as it involved combining strategic vision with tactical
acumen and executing a plan that featured both.

The next stop on my path was the Office of the Secretary of Defense, where I
focused on broad-scale business systems transformation, initially as part of
the Office of the Under Secretary/Comptroller and then for the Under Secretary for Acquisition, Technology and Logistics. This position required that I
apply my growing enterprise perspective to an even larger set of issues, and
I brought the full sum of my experience to bear on my assignments. My main
task was to transform DOD's multibillion-dollar suite of business systems
from an approach that strongly valued the *status quo* and was short term and
risk adverse to one that was more strategic and enterprise-wide in nature.
Managing this transition required focusing not on the success of a single
mission or program but instead on making many programs work optimally
together.

Finally, I was appointed the DCMO, where I was charged with optimizing
the *entire* business environment across the DOD. My portfolio included not
only IT but also organizational performance management, business process
reengineering, and acquisition oversight—literally everything that had anything to do with DOD business operations. Every issue required enterprise
thinking and relied heavily on collaboration, so I had to create a forum for
enterprise-wide governance that was critical to obtaining organizational
buy-in and achieving outcomes.

As part of this role, I also instituted an investment review process for the
$7 billion business IT portfolio—leveraging data and transparency to move
away from "thinking at the 'eaches'" to having a broader, more strategic
focus on the total enterprise. This process created an environment that illu-
minated how and where we spent our money, which, in turn, allowed us to
reduce the overall IT footprint and make sound investments for the future.
This job was *all* about the enterprise, and it required me to apply each ECQ
every single day, but in an even broader, more holistic, systemic way.

Across the divide: From SES to appointee

My role as DOD's DCMO was also notable because, for the first time in
my career, I became a political appointee via presidential appointment with
Senate confirmation. I found that this new status could change the views
of those around me; I was perceived by some as being more devoted to the

political goals of the administration (although I served two, one Republican and one Democratic), but my experience and my core leadership values were unaltered.

I was still committed to the fundamentals of good government, as I had been under both Republican and Democratic administrations previously. I was still devoted to achieving operational efficiencies and effectiveness and creating an agile and transparent government. I was still focused on making decisions based on facts. And I still knew that much of my success depended on maintaining strong relationships with stakeholders inside and outside the government. In sum, I felt the job to be a natural extension of the journey I'd been on all along.

Whether as a staff member supporting a senior executive, a member of the SES supporting political appointees and senior military leaders, or a political appointee serving an administration, I saw it as my duty to ensure the leaders I served had the best information in front of them to make decisions. Given my long association with the DOD, I was familiar with the wealth of resources the Department had at its disposal to collect and analyze that information.

When I became a political appointee, I knew what was available and what to expect, and therefore depended on senior career staff (GS, SES, and military alike) to navigate the Department swiftly and with precision. I can't imagine achieving as much as we did in that time without the knowledge and the core skills of that supporting executive cast. My experience highlights just how essential an institution the SES is: Members possess deep experience and historical knowledge of the agencies they serve, providing essential guidance and context to the revolving set of political appointees who lead agencies on a short-term basis. In my view, government wouldn't work without them.

My path differed from other political appointees who, in the main, come from outside government. Many have worked on presidential or congressional election campaigns that produced the appointments; others come directly from academia or industry. Depth of knowledge about the organizations they are appointed to lead can vary considerably. Whether or not it's true, there is a perception that political appointees put political interests first, ahead of more traditional institutional priorities. But I didn't encounter problems remaining nonpartisan in my appointed role, nor did transitioning to a political appointment distract from my objective views of the DOD's institutional needs.

Being an appointee was not a barrier to getting things done. In fact, it expanded my network in a way that enhanced that ability. With any mission challenge, I found that while the method of implementation could vary depending on the administration, the fundamentals of good government—efficiency, effectiveness, customer orientation, stewardship of taxpayer dollars—stayed consistent. It pleases me to say that I saw administrations from both sides of the political spectrum throw their weight behind initiatives that fostered those values. What is true across every administration is the value and importance of good people and effective leadership.

It's *not* a small world after all

In theory, one of the main tenets of the SES is the ability to deploy across government; however, while I spent my entire Federal career inside the DOD, DOD's breadth meant that I didn't stay in one organizational "home." Having access to this range of experiences was critical to developing the executive (and enterprise) mindset I put to use later in my career.

With more than 3 million military and civilian personnel and a global mandate, DOD offered a plethora of opportunities for me to serve in multiple disciplines at many organizations. Logistics, financial management, IT, systems architecture, contracting, and acquisition were all part of my path. In some ways, I had just as many opportunities inside the DOD as I would have had across other parts of the executive branch. However it may be acquired, that breadth of experience—not just at multiple levels but also in multiple organizations and functions—is essential.

Another way SES members can gain an enterprise perspective is by representing their department at interagency forums, such as those administered by OMB or the National Security Council. I had the opportunity to work with other agencies, both informally and formally, through such mechanisms as the President's Management Council (which drives government-wide management reform initiatives), the Performance Improvement Council (which collaborates to improve the performance of Federal programs), and the Performance Accountability Council (established to achieve specific reforms to security clearance programs).

These assignments also gave me the chance to expand my strategic aperture beyond the DOD and redefine my enterprise perspective. Each venue has a particular focus, but all share the goal of identifying and adopting best practices government-wide. Each also aims to design and develop interagency tools, processes, and technologies that accelerate the achievement of management priorities. These forums provide the unique opportunity to identify needed changes to government-wide policy—to update and modernize the rules by which all agencies play. It can be a thankless grind to get a new regulation or EO through the bureaucracy, but it can pay off with government-wide impact and consistent, cross-agency efforts that implement change and improve performance.

Looking and leaning forward

I am proud to say I spent 25 years in the Federal civil service, 10 as a career member of the SES, before I accepted a Senate-confirmed political appointment as the first DCMO for DOD. Through my service, I had access to training and development programs, as well as on-the-job experiences, that allowed me to develop skills critical to my executive responsibilities and gave me insight into how senior executives at other Federal agencies were tackling problems I was also encountering. I also benefitted from the network the SES provided me.

None of this is to say the system is perfect. It changed over the span of my career and needs to continue to evolve with the times. As we look to the future, it is clear the SES will continue to play a vital role in the high-level management of the Federal government. It will be essential, however, to adapt to the realities of the modern work environment—mobile workforces, ever-evolving technologies, the changing government-contractor mix—to ensure the senior executive corps stays relevant and effective. The value of the institutional knowledge the SES collectively possesses will only grow as the government workforce becomes increasingly fractured and resources stay scarce.

Trends suggest that younger professionals don't expect to spend their whole career in one field, let alone one organization, meaning that younger workers may rotate in and out of the Federal government without acquiring deep expertise in public administration. And the challenges the Federal budget has faced in the recent past may well assert themselves in the future, constraining the government from hiring new employees or offering competitive salaries to draw top talent. It will take a dedicated effort to monitor the makeup of the SES cadre going forward, to see how these factors affect the executive corps and its pipeline, and to make adjustments to ensure its sustained viability.

With all of these possibilities in play, the knowledge and leadership of SES members will become even more unique and valuable. As I stated in the beginning of this chapter, I believe that for SES leaders to effectively manage agencies and their major programs, they must possess the right blend of skills and experience and have the benefit of focused professional development. These qualities, coupled with an aptitude for collaboration, tactical and strategic acumen gained through strong mentorship, and enterprise thinking, are what's needed to effectively foster the institutional role of career executives.

The journey to achieving a broader perspective and experience base must be deliberate, and it can't be rotation for rotation's sake. Additionally, potential SES members must have strong multidimensional backgrounds, and leaders must work deliberately to cultivate them early in their careers. And finally, training and professional development must continue throughout a career to complement and leverage the experience-based learning that comes on the job.

Just as every journey begins with one step, every journey's steps can lead down many paths. What is critical is that future leaders have sufficient tools and direction to navigate their own journey, at their own pace and in their own direction, in order to reach their goals.

Concluding Commentary and Recommendations

Introduction: SES redux

From a normative standpoint, one can argue that the institutional role of the SES, as articulated (and implied) by its enabling statute, remains as vital and viable today as it was at the inception of the corps in 1979. Certainly there are a great many commentators and policymakers, including all of our contributors, who believe that—as do I. But what exactly does that role comprise? While much has been said and written about it (including much in this anthology), career executives have been expected to come to it instinctively, or by osmosis.

That role, in all of its various dimensions, has never been fully explicated, nor has it been deliberately inculcated and operationalized in the senior executive corps. And that is problematic. For instance, I was once facilitating a group of 25 top-level DOD senior executives (two- and three-star flag officer equivalents) as part of the Department's premier residential leadership development program. On a whim, I asked, "What does it mean to be a career executive in DOD?" No answer, just lap-looking…and this from a normally quite gregarious group. So I asked, "Okay, so what does it mean to be a member of the SES writ large?" Again, no answer…just more fidgeting in their chairs. I offered some thoughts on those two questions, some of which are repeated below, and, after some prompting, they began to get it. But what I found most troubling was that these executives, all with at least 5 years of SES time, had apparently never been asked to reflect on those critical questions.

Even more problematic, most of the class comprised former senior military officers—products of the "leave-no-colonel-behind" phenomenon that Bob Corsi discusses in our next section—who should have brought that military *ethos* with them. What some of them did bring was a stated reluctance to question authority…or even recognize that otherwise legitimate authorities may at times conflict. I found this just as troubling. Now, I can't say that this is characteristic of the entire Federal senior executive corps. But anecdotally, I personally know hundreds of SES members, and I've talked and taught leadership to them across the entire Federal landscape—from DOD and the IC to IRS, the Securities and Exchange Commission, DHS, and even OPM's orientation for new members of the SES—and I've found this lack of clarity around their institutional role to be more common than not.

And as I said, that's problematic. There are lots of official rules that tell an executive what not to do: ethics rules, prohibited personnel practices, merit system principles, and so forth—the list is almost endless. But as any career executive knows, those long lists of rules and regulations are often rife with uncertainty, inconsistency, and even potential paradox; and while they certainly tell SES members what they *cannot* do, those legions of rules are less useful when it comes to some of the difficult moral-ethical choices SES members have to make…in other words, when they have to decide the *right* thing to do. Just read Mike Hayden's chapter (or the one Steve Kelman and I wrote).

In sum, this notion of doing the right thing goes to the very heart of the career executive's institutional role. There's obviously more to it than that, but the answer isn't in the legislation that created and codified the SES, which reads like a government job description—mechanical, instrumental, *administrative*, and not exactly something that inspires. But there is something inspirational between the lines of that enabling legislation: an institutional role that, while more implied than expressed, is unique to the SES and underscores its essentiality to our system of governance.

Five core dimensions

What exactly is that role? What are its various dimensions? Before we can decide if the role is still valid, we must first understand it. To that end, I would like to examine five of the dimensions here. Note that these five are not meant to be exhaustive; rather, they represent those that in my personal experience (and that of at least some of our contributors) are paramount, but I am sure others could add to the list.

Nevertheless, a better understanding of that institutional role is necessary but insufficient. I would argue that the institutional role of the SES must be made not only more explicit but also more permanent if it is to serve as the foundation for a 21st century SES. Indeed, I would suggest that uncertainty and ambiguity in that regard may have something to do with at least some of the controversy surrounding the SES today, as politicians both elected and appointed attempt to reform a senior executive system they (and their staffs) know little about. Unfamiliar with the real raison d'etre of the SES, they may inadvertently misconstrue what are legitimate institutional actions of a career executive—for example, complying with the literal wording of a statute no matter how odious the result—and call for greater accountability 'to the will of the people.'

Upon reflecting on the institutional role of the SES, something even more interesting becomes apparent. In many respects, the role is almost by definition paradoxical, grounded in a set of core dimensions that may at times conflict and compete—for example, when an executive's mandate to serve the public interest butts up against his or her obligation to serve the government of the day—and are thus not so easily reconciled. Perhaps that is what makes the career Federal executive's role so challenging…and so critical. But to validate and fulfill that role, not just now but in the future, one must first understand it.

So what exactly does it mean to be a career executive?

First, commitment to the Constitution and the rule of law

If there is a seminal value that grounds the SES, it is this commitment. And as an institutional role, it may be *primus inter pares* ("first among equals"). It seems rather obvious; after all, all executives, like all Federal civil servants, take an oath of office when they're appointed to the SES (or at least they're supposed to). To some, that oath may become simply words to be repeated in order to check a box. However, to most SES members I know, the oath represents something else, something quite profound. Similar to the words that bind the allegiance of military officers, the oath is the DNA of the career executive. The core values implicit in its words—drawn from the Constitution, the Bill of Rights, and the Declaration of Independence—should guide the behavior of SES members.

When he was IRS Commissioner (and my boss), Charles Rossotti once observed to me that the oath represented a fundamental difference between leaders and leadership in the public sector and the private. Rossotti, who came to be IRS Commissioner after founding American Management Systems (AMS), once one of the top-tier IT consulting firms in the U.S., believed that those words set Federal senior executives apart from the ones he had led at AMS, and he insisted on administering the oath to those of us who joined his senior leadership team, even though most had taken it at least once before. Even IRS executives who were simply realigned to that leadership team retook the oath. To Rossotti—and because of him, to us—it was a reminder of our commitment to a higher purpose…in that instance, to not only the oft-criticized but no less critical mission of the IRS but also to the public service generally.

The Oath of Office

I do solemnly swear that I will support and defend the Constitution of the United States against all enemies, foreign and domestic; that I will bear true faith and allegiance to the same; that I take this obligation freely, without any mental reservation or purpose of evasion; and that I will well and faithfully discharge the duties of the office on which I am about to enter. So help me God.

5 U.S.C. §3331

Mike Hayden, in his career as a military officer and the leader of hundreds of civilian career executives at NSA and CIA, offers another example. Hollywood stereotypes notwithstanding, nothing was more important to him or his career executives than ensuring that every action they took or recommended was within the limits of the Constitution and the law, even if neither of those artifacts ever contemplated some of the life-or-death situations he and his executives faced.

Thus, when it comes to the institutional roles of the SES, commitment to the Constitution and the rule of law remains as valid and vital today as it did four decades ago. That fundamental topic used to be a core element of the Federal Executive Institute's (FEI) flagship, *Leadership for a Democratic Society* (attendees had to read such seminal Supreme Court decisions as Marbury v. Madison)[59]; however, the topic, once supplanted by more "modern" material, seems to be making its way back into the curriculum. We discuss this further in Section 4.

Second, serving the public interest

If the Constitution and the rule of law serve as the legal foundation for senior executive leadership, the ideas and ideals of public service are its moral-ethical compass. However, determining the direction of its needle—that is, what may or may not be in the public interest—is not always obvious or easy. Indeed, as Steve Kelman and I point out in our chapter in the next section, Federal executives often have to weigh conflicting and competing interests (as well as conflicting and competing values), each equally legitimate, in setting and implementing public policy.

And when executives do weigh those competing interests, whether by design or default, the end result is by definition in the public interest. Again, think about the biographies of our contributors—those in this section, as well as the rest of this anthology; each personifies "public servant" in his or her own unique way, and each had to define the public interest in that very personal and professional context throughout his or her career.

I certainly had to. I once lied to a reporter—deliberately—to protect something I believed to be in the public interest, even though I had to violate my own personal values to do so. But to tell the truth, to acknowledge as fact a rumor the reporter had picked up would have caused great harm to a large number of DOD employees, something I felt morally bound to avoid. Harm was not what the reporter intended in pressing for the truth (he was just doing his job, after all), but harm still would have been the result had the rumor been acknowledged and reported as fact. So I lied in the public interest but not my own…one of my several defining moments as a career executive.

Of course, senior career executives have always been called upon to make difficult decisions, but I would argue that what makes the government exec-

---

[59] Marbury v. Madison, 5 U.S. 137 (1803).

utive's decisions harder is that often the competing values at stake—such things as efficiency versus effectiveness, equity versus equality, privacy versus security—are all in the public interest, each one no less important than the next, and SES members must make judgment calls that weigh and ultimately decide among them. Moreover, unless a miracle happens, and laws and regulations suddenly become clear and unambiguous, this institutional role would also seem to be as valid in the 21st century as it was in the 20th or the 19th…perhaps more so.

And there's still another dimension to this institutional role: a cultural one. The values and behaviors associated with public service and the public interest are not just supposed to be part of a career executive's individual *ethos* as a leader; rather, I would argue that career leaders are also responsible for ensuring that those same core values and behaviors—that same public service mindset—are also part of their *organization's* culture and thus inculcated and reinforced in those whom they lead.

We see this in almost every one of our contributors' chapters. It is well documented that leaders shape (and are in turn shaped by) an *organization's* culture, and this too would seem to be an essential part of the SES member's institutional role: to create and sustain an *ethos* of public service by modeling, instilling, and reinforcing it in the agencies and people they lead.

This is easier said than done, especially insofar as SES members are not examined or evaluated for this proclivity. As essential and seemingly obvious as this aspect of an executive's institutional role may be, it is not even mentioned in the Service's enabling statute; at best, it is taken for granted and at worst it is seen as unimportant. Nor is it even mentioned in any of the ECQs that every SES member is supposed to meet. Indeed, there is almost nothing of "the public interest" expressed or implied in any of the ECQs. Instead, they are generic, applicable equally to executives in either the public or private sector, and this too is problematic in my view (more on this in our next section).

In this regard, effective leadership is part skill set and part mindset, and the competencies that make up the ECQ "admissions test" for the SES are almost exclusively of the first sort. Yet a public service mindset—in this case, a commitment to public service and the public interest—may be far more important to the SES of the 21st century, as executive governance becomes even more complex. So I would contend that we need to make the assessment of that mindset part of the test for selection to and retention in the SES.

Third, neutral competence in service to the government of the day

Neutral competence would also seem to be a core institutional role of the SES, an integral part of its *ethos*. As we noted at the outset, members of the SES operate at the interface between the deciding and the doing of government; as career civil servants, they are duty bound to serve those elected or appointed to lead them without reservation or regard for their own personal politics. Like their commitment to the rule of law and the public interest, neutral competence should also be embedded in the SES member's leadership DNA. In theory as well as in practice, that neutral competence can and should be relied upon; indeed, it should be taken for granted by those elected and appointed as leaders, as well as the citizens those leaders serve.

That has certainly been the case with Pat Kennedy. As many as 14 Secretaries of State, appointed by both Republican and Democratic presidents, took his nonpartisan commitment to serving their respective administrations and the Department—in many cases as a direct report to them—for granted. They relied upon it. Beth McGrath offers another example, as a career executive who was appointed to a Senate-confirmed position twice, once by a Republican administration, and then again by a Democratic president—no doubt because each trusted her neutral competence.

But, as in most aspects of the career executive's role, this is not as easy as it would seem, for allegiance (or obedience) to one's political superiors is not unfettered. Career executives are explicitly bounded by other elements of their role, such things as the rule of law or the public interest, or those institutional tenets of the department in which they serve. And there are times when these various interests—of an administration, of a government institution, of the public, even of an individual executive—may seem to conflict. In those most difficult circumstances, the career executive must try to reconcile them or, failing that, make difficult choices among them.

Here again, I have had some personal experience in that regard. I was once told by a political appointee to "sign or resign"...that is, sign a particular memorandum approving an agency's request on a personnel matter or resign my position. The problem, of course, was that I strongly disagreed with the merits of that request. It wasn't exactly illegal or contrary to regulation, but I felt it violated their spirit, and I was not comfortable agreeing to it. I did have a bit of leverage—the controversial request had become widely known, many others shared my view that it lacked merit, and it would have set a bad precedent—and as a consequence, the appointee did not want to sign it himself.

So with some trepidation, I refused, and the appointee elevated the matter to our superior...who promptly sided with me. And while that provided some momentary satisfaction, this was a classic Pyrrhic victory (a no-win situation), something I'd anticipated going in; I'd won the battle but was in danger of losing the war with an appointee who would have made my life miserable out of revenge. Thank goodness he failed, though not for lack of trying, but that's another story...

It is always problematic to serve more than one master, even more so to have to decide which one to ignore. Should one ignore an administration elected by the people and the officials appointed to act on its behalf? They and their wishes (orders!) are often direct and unambiguous, and ignoring them can have immediate personal consequences. Or should one ignore the law or your own personal or professional definition convictions? These are often more abstruse and abstract, the consequences of ignoring them less immediate, tangible, or predictable. In that regard, I believe career executives may be morally and duty bound—even legally obligated—to speak truth to power, to tell it like it is to the political appointees they serve, regardless of the personal or professional consequences; however, they often do so at some personal and professional risk.

That may be the ultimate expression of neutral competence. But as Steve Kelman and I found in research we derived from the results reported in the next section, the courage to do so is not a universal quality of senior government executives.[60] Perhaps it should be…something we argue in Section 3.

Of course, it also takes finesse. This, too, is part of neutral competence… speaking truth to power in a way that will most likely be heard. This requires a certain amount of bureaucratic jujitsu, an organizational art practiced and perfected by some of the most seasoned career executives. Thus, when a new (or even an experienced) appointee proposes something that's been tried before without success, he or she is expecting to hear all sorts of reasons why not from career executives. And just like Newton's third law of motion, a "no" is likely to elicit an equal and opposite reaction. Neither serves the government of the day. Nor does the classic "yes, Minister" response, regardless of the merits. But there's plenty of room between "just say no" and "yes, Minister," and that's what makes life interesting.

Fourth, taking a whole-of-government perspective

One could argue that a whole-of-government perspective is implicit in the Service's original vision, but it remains the most elusive among the various dimensions of the career executive's institutional role. As we have already noted, there is little argument that the SES was intended to provide a corps of career executives who would ply their leadership skills across the whole-of-government. Implicit in that vision is the idea that its members would also bring with their tradecraft a government-wide mindset (that is, an enterprise perspective) as opposed to a narrow, parochial, agency-centric one.

I believe that mindset is a natural byproduct of mobility—by definition, senior executives who move from organization to organization learn to adapt to and lead in a variety of organizational settings, and along the way, they are likely to shed an agency-centric bias in favor of a more ecumenical, enterprise view. The absence of mobility, an unfortunate characteristic of today's senior executive corps, has just the opposite effect, breeding insularity and parochialism.

[60] Kelman, S., Sanders, R., & Pandit, G. (2016, May). "Tell it like it is": Decision making, groupthink, and decisiveness among U.S. Federal subcabinet executives. Governance. doi:10.1111/gove.12200

We examine the various benefits and risks of SES mobility, as well as the administrative and cultural barriers to it, in subsequent sections, but here I wish to start with the proposition that this enterprise perspective is one of the potentially most important—and least developed—of the various institutional roles we expect of the SES, especially in an era of connected, collaborative government. Thus, if mobility is a necessary prerequisite and purveyor of this perspective, then it is also one of the most nascent.

That is certainly not the case in some of the SES' sister services, most of which take mobility of their senior executives for granted. We all know the important part that mobility plays in developing senior military leaders as well as career ambassadors (the biographies of Mike Hayden and Pat Kennedy, both typical of their professions, are more than enough evidence), and my own multiagency career path is far more like theirs than the vast majority of my SES peers.

Interestingly, Beth McGrath is the only one of our four contributors to this section who actually refers to an enterprise perspective, in her case the product of both geographic and organizational mobility within a single cabinet department—albeit the vast DOD, which is an enterprise unto itself. But even that sort of mobility, and the enterprise perspective that comes with it, is too rare among SES members.

A whole-of-government mindset certainly qualifies as an integral aspect of the career senior executive's institutional role, even though it remains more aspirational than actual.

Fifth, continuity and institutional memory

This, too, is one of the career executive service's most important—and most paradoxical—roles; in this instance, continuity has nothing to do with contingency plans and emergency management. Rather, it has to do with institutional (or corporate) memory. As Sean O'Keefe observes, almost without exception political appointees cite this as one of the most valuable commodities and contributions of their career executives…no wonder, given appointees' comparatively short tenure. And according to O'Keefe, it's even more important during presidential transition.

Almost by definition, every new administration—and virtually every new appointee—enters office with a mandate (real or imagined), a set of program and policy goals, and a relatively short time horizon. In other words, they're in a hurry; stereotypically, they see their career staffs as personifying the *status quo*, and they fully expect their agenda to encounter some institutional resistance from them.

That's not necessarily a bad thing. Indeed, one can argue that a civil service, senior and otherwise, is simply another aspect of our government's hallowed system of checks and balances, implied if not expressly enumerated in the

Constitution as a squealing, squeaking brake against arbitrary and precipitous executive action.

But in the extreme, this institutional continuity can become stereotypical… the picture of the entrenched bureaucrat ignoring the will of those we elect or appoint as their agents. And often, those elected and appointed officials harbor the same stereotype. As O'Keefe discusses in his chapter, stereotypes about senior career executives and political appointees alike, as well as the bureaucratic baggage that comes with them, are the norm.

As we've noted, new appointees typically view the career executives they find waiting for them with some suspicion, or at least a healthy skepticism; this is especially the case when presidential transition represents a "hostile takeover" by a different political party, but it can occur any time a new appointee arrives on the scene. Indeed, my own personal political purge (yes, I've had one of those, too) occurred in the middle of an administration, long after I had proved my worth to my department's new senior political leadership, and it was driven by jealousy rather than any policy differences.

But by definition, continuity implies that career executives serve the pejorative *status quo*. To be sure, there are some in our ranks who deserve the indictment. After all, the *status quo* is familiar and comfortable, and many a bureaucrat feels that he or she has an obligation to counterbalance the opposing stereotype: that of the political appointee determined to bend the law to suit the partisan political designs of a particular administration. However, all too often, that accusation is levied against a career executive who is merely trying to do his or her statutory duty, interpreting and administering the law as best as he or she can. After all, adhering to that rule of law is the cornerstone of the civil servant, no matter how unclear or unfair the law may be—and as citizens, the vast majority of us would have it no other way.

But therein lies yet another paradox of the career executive's institutional role. By definition, SES members are supposed to lead change. That's what the very first ECQ says. That means it is also part of a career executive's institutional role to always look for and find ways to make government work better. However, as we have argued, there is a concurrent responsibility to preserve and serve as an agency's institutional memory…the voice (and sometimes the conscience) of the *status quo*. A paradox? To be sure, but this is true of all of the institutional dimensions we describe above.

As I said at the outset, these five characteristics are by no means intended to be exhaustive. Rather, I offer them in the hope that they may begin to provide a better understanding of the career executive's institutional role. However, while that understanding is necessary, it is insufficient by itself. The institutional role of the SES must be made not only more explicit but also more permanent if it is to serve as the foundation for a 21st century SES.

Indeed, I would suggest that uncertainty and ambiguity in that regard may have something to do with at least some of the controversy surrounding the SES today, as politicians both elected and appointed attempt to reform a senior executive system they (and their staffs) know little about. Unfamiliar with the real raison d'etre of the SES, they may inadvertently misconstrue what are legitimate institutional actions of a career executive—for example, complying with the literal wording of a statute no matter how odious the result—and call for greater accountability 'to the will of the people.'

Upon reflecting on the institutional role of the SES, something even more interesting becomes apparent. In many respects, the role is almost by definition paradoxical, grounded in a set of core dimensions that may at times conflict and compete—for example, when an executive's mandate to serve the public interest may go against his or her obligation to serve the government of the day—and are thus not so easily reconciled. Perhaps that is what makes the career Federal executive's role so challenging…and so critical. But to validate and fulfill that role, not just now but in the future, one must first understand it.

RECOMMENDATION 2.1: FRAME AND FORMALIZE THE INSTITUTIONAL ROLE OF THE SES

Introduction: Laying the foundation

Whatever the institutional role of the SES, it is certain that to fulfill it, career executives must understand it, internalize it, and ultimately master it. However, such mastery is problematic in two respects. First, these institutional roles are not codified anywhere; many of them may be implicit in the original vision of the SES, but, as we have seen, even that vision has had to be inferred from otherwise sterile statutory language. So how does a new member of the SES come to know them, except perhaps by high-stakes trial and error (or osmosis)? Second, and in that same vein, where and how does a career executive learn to master the various dimensions of that institutional role? Few executive development programs, in government and otherwise, even examine what that role is, much less its various dimensions and their practical applications.

Before the various dimensions of career executive leadership can be learned and mastered, they must be institutionalized. In other words, they must be made not only more explicit but also more permanent if they are to serve as the foundation for a 21st century SES. Indeed, I would suggest that the uncertainty and ambiguity that currently attends that role may have something to do with some of the controversy surrounding the SES today, leaving its members—as well as their political leaders and overseers—no clear guide to what career executives are expected to do. And the only way to correct that deficiency may be to codify those expectations in law and/or government-wide regulation.

Guiding principles

Legislation would undoubtedly be a risky proposition these days, given what many perceive to be congressional attacks on the very viability of the SES. Thus, even a well-intentioned piece of legislation may attract amendments that make the situation worse. Nonetheless, if we want a strong institutional foundation, it may also be worth the risk of discussion and debate between the new administration and the new Congress.

After all, the current incremental approach to SES reform (such as is playing out in the congressional response to the Veterans Affairs wait-time scandal, as well as with EO 13714) is just as risky, inasmuch as it comes without the benefit of a serious conversation among leaders and legislators about the nature (and the future) of the SES. Better the risks that come with that broader debate—perhaps guided by a blue ribbon commission convened by the Academy (see my final recommendation in Section 6)—than the slow death of the corps by piecemeal papercuts.

A better option may be to articulate the institutional role of the SES, in all of its various intangible dimensions, in something like the Code of Federal Regulations (CFR). That too would benefit from the serious deliberations of a commission or Academy panel, with the result translated into regulations drafted by OPM, published in the Federal Register for public comment, and issued by the agency in 5 CFR Part 317 as part of the general regulatory framework for the SES.

Bottom line: While the regulatory option may not have the force of law, the content of those regulations would still be subject to public debate and discussion (including Congress, the administration, and other stakeholders) but exempt from the whims of the legislative process—as regulations governing the senior career service should be. But either way, something more explicit is needed.

RECOMMENDATION 2.2: TEACH CAREER EXECUTIVES WHAT IT REALLY MEANS TO BE ONE

Introduction: Learning and understanding the institutional role

I believe that codifying the institutional role of the career executive is necessary, but it is not sufficient. Career executives are not likely to learn and understand that role, as complex and potentially paradoxical as it may be, simply because it is codified in law or regulation; they need to be taught it, reflect on its tenets in the classroom, and eventually internalize and apply those tenets in everything they do. That requires a specialized, specially designed executive development curriculum and a faculty that has been there and done that when it comes to confronting the kinds of leadership challenges that may be unique to the SES and its progeny. Moreover, that understanding is not likely to be fully internalized during a one-time learning experience; it must be part of the continuum of leadership learning advocated by Suzanne Logan (see Section 4).

But where do career executives go to understand their institutional role? It used to be that FEI was the place where a new SES member went to learn what it meant to be one. At the risk of dating myself, when I went to FEI a little over 30 years ago, a substantial part of the curriculum was devoted to this subject. For example, we actually studied constitutional law—we even read a bevy of landmark Supreme Court decisions and discussed the legal and practical limits of administrative authority.

As new executives, that meant understanding the limits on *our* authority. I confess I'd never contemplated those limits, nor did I have any desire to do so…at least before I had to reflect upon them at FEI. But I can honestly say that that part of FEI's curriculum had a profound effect on me and my fellow new executives (indeed, it still does!), and it engendered lots of late-night discussions over what our newfound role meant to us collectively.

Fast-forward to today. At best, the Constitution and the limits of administrative authority are electives in FEI's flagship, *Leadership for a Democratic Society*; unless it happens by accident, there is nothing in the syllabus to suggest that students learn—from role models and case studies and even simulations —and reflect upon what it really means to lead at the most senior levels of government. In fairness, there's plenty on leadership in general, and students get plenty of time to think about their own individual strengths and weaknesses as leaders…that's a good thing, but less of the curriculum is focused on what that may mean to lead *in government*.

Indoctrination and inculcation

As far as FEI is concerned, it may be that it has chosen to compete with other more general executive education programs—like those offered by Harvard, the University of North Carolina, or the Center for Creative Leadership—and in so doing, it has inadvertently de-emphasized the essential "public-ness" of the career executive's role.

And as it competes with those top-tier executive education programs, FEI may have diluted its ultimate differentiator, something that could make its curriculum (once again) unique: an exclusive and intensive focus on what it means to be a career executive *in the Federal government*. This includes the sometimes-paradoxical institutional roles discussed above, as well as the legal and ethical foundations, the core values and ethos, and the emerging competencies that may be unique to government.

Bottom line: There is something special about being a senior career executive in government, but that special something has to be learned and practiced.

That learning can be deliberate—as part of a formal executive development curriculum specifically designed to explore it, complemented by focused mentoring or coaching on the job—or it can happen by accident, literally on the street. And if it's the latter, there is no guarantee that new or developing executives will learn the "right" way to lead in government.

One of the ways to bring more certainty to the matter is to refocus FEI on what was once its core mission: teaching career Federal executives what it means to be one, not only when they first become SES members, but periodically thereafter…at various milestones in their careers, and with their peers.

That is an essential element of the continuum of leadership learning posited by FEI Director Suzanne Logan in the next section, and the good news here is that, as of this writing, Dr. Logan's FEI has begun to do so. For example, it has sponsored a series of Enterprise Leadership Labs that are designed specifically for those top-of-the-heap, "most senior" senior career executives who have agency-wide or whole-of-government responsibilities. I applaud that and would advocate even more offerings of this sort.[61] Let other non-governmental executive education programs teach general leadership and management skills; have FEI teach those that are unique to government.

RECOMMENDATION 2.3: APPOINT CAREER DIRECTORS GENERAL AS STEWARDS OF THE SES' INSTITUTIONAL ROLE

Introduction: Perception and the reality of getting acquainted

You can codify a senior executive's institutional role, and you can teach and reflect upon it in the classroom and even with a coach or mentor, but none of those may prepare SES members for the reality of on-the-ground government.

As we have noted, career executives are often called upon to reconcile such relatively vague mandates as the public interest (or even a purposely ambiguous statute or regulation) with the unambiguous and potentially conflicting orders of a political superior, especially one who has come to office with a partisan agenda. And there will be times when those conflicting mandates are irreconcilable. What happens to the institutional role then? Especially when a career executive makes a difficult "right versus right" choice and suffers the consequences? Who protects and preserves that executive's institutional role (and the career executive!) when things get personal?

That happened to me early on in my SES career, as part of my first presidential transition in the Pentagon. I had been a direct report to an appointee in the previous administration and, as the organization's most senior career execu-tive, I had assumed that person's position on an "Acting" basis during the changeover. For various reasons not relevant here, that political position went without a new occupant for well over a year; however, the White House

[61] Truth in advertising: My Booz Allen team has designed and delivered the first two of these Enterprise Leadership Labs.

eventually got around to appointing someone, and, without getting too personal, let's just say that within a month, it became clear that the Pentagon wasn't big enough for the both of us. So the 120-day get acquainted period[62] notwithstanding, that appointee abolished my job and reassigned me to a lesser position in the same organization. Now, it wasn't quite as blatant as that—I was given the opportunity to "waive" the 120-day period—but it was clear my reassignment was only a matter of time.

The Pentagon's Godfather...and an offer I couldn't refuse

I was most fortunate to have someone I could turn to for relief…in this case, the legendary David O. Cooke, otherwise known as Doc. His was a relatively obscure position on the Department's organization chart—the DOD Director of Administration and Management—but that title notwithstanding, he was unquestionably the most senior career executive in the Federal government's largest department. Known as the Mayor of the Pentagon (or, more darkly, the Godfather), Doc saw it as his duty to protect the SES, both the individuals and the institution, from the vagaries of politics and political appointees; however, he also saw himself as an honest broker for those same appointees. After all, they represented the President, and they were entitled to deference in their decisions, including those that involved career executives.

That was a fine line to be sure, but a necessary one and, in my case, a lifeline. When I was told my job had been abolished (via a notice in a plain brown en-velope left on my office chair), I went to him incensed and ready to fight. However, Doc calmed me down and pointed out that if I stood on my "get acquainted" rights, I would just be postponing the inevitable and would likely make life in my new position even more miserable than it was going to be. But he also suggested that I had some leverage—after all, a fight would be messy and reflect poorly on the new appointee—so with my proxy, he ne-gotiated a reassignment that took me willingly out of that organization (and DOD) altogether and on a path that opened up all sorts of new opportunities for me. It was also my first interagency mobility assignment, and the rest, as they say, is history.

Now you can argue that justice was not served, and that the appointee got away with something, but upon reflection, I don't think so. Rather, I think this was a case of "that's just life in the SES," something that probably happens all the time. However, if not for Doc's honest broker influence with career executives on one hand and our political masters on the other (not to men-tion his network across the government), that little episode could have been my career Waterloo. Instead, it became one of my defining moments as a career senior executive.

---

[62] Reassignment and Transfer within the Senior Executive Service, 5 U.S.C. § 3395 (e).

The trials and tribulations of transition

Examples like mine can occur at any time, but the odds increase during presidential transition. Thus, career SES role models like Pat Kennedy and Beth McGrath notwithstanding, it is likely that a new political appointee may initially view long-tenured, "holdover" career executives with some suspicion, particularly those who may have been selected by a predecessor administration of a different political party. In such cases, there is a natural tendency for that career executive—in service to the government of another day—to have developed a strong affinity for it, and it is easy to assume that it may be difficult for that executive to set aside that affinity (sometimes, literally overnight) and loyally serve another political master, especially one with a dramatically different policy or program agenda.

That's the reason for the law's mandatory 120-day period for new political appointees to get acquainted with their career executives.[63] It prohibits an appointee from acting on those natural suspicions, at least immediately; however, it is not difficult for that appointee to wait that period out or even circumvent it altogether (I have personally seen the latter happen to SES colleagues, much like it did to me).

Nevertheless, while it is not unreasonable to assume that a new administration —or a new political appointee—may want to handpick their career leadership team, it would just seem to make good sense for them to give the benefit of the doubt to the career executives who are there to welcome them, and to assume that they can faithfully fulfill their duty to serve the government of the day. And by taking advantage of these executives' resident expertise, an appointee and an administration can hit the ground running rather than wait months to consider, select, and onboard new career executives. Of course, all this presumes that the career executives are able to set aside their own personal political views and serve the new appointee or administration with nonpartisan, neutral competence. If our career executive contributors are representative of SES members generally, they have clearly demonstrated their ability to do just that.

In that regard, one worries about Executive Order 13714's SES rotational requirements.[64] It is too easy, too tempting to use the "musical chairs" of those annual rotational assignments to periodically purge career executives who, through no fault of their performance or politics, may have run afoul of an appointee or simply proved to be incompatible. In such cases, an involuntary rotational assignment can be a career killer, unless there is a mechanism to place executives faced with those circumstances in a comparable position without prejudice.

---

[63] Ibid.
[64] Exec. Order 13714, § 3(a)(iv) and (v).

Directors General in each department

Doc Cooke was that mechanism in DOD. Now, the Department didn't create Doc, nor did it officially vest him with the responsibility to preserve and protect the institutional role of its hundreds of SES members. However, that is what he did, and in so doing, he managed to strike a delicate balance between the public interest and the law on one hand and obedient service to the government of the day on the other. Unfortunately, icons like Doc Cooke are few and far between these days. I'm not sure why, but I would argue that we need to formally establish and vest our most senior, most respected career executives with the kind of role and responsibilities he had.

The State Department has done so, and its model may be worth emulating. The Department long ago established the position of Director General (DG) to serve as an advocate and champion for its Foreign Service Officers (FSOs). The senior executive (typically a career ambassador) who serves in that post doesn't control the assignments of FSOs or set personnel policies for them, but he or she does advocate and represent their collective interests...in effect, playing the same Godfather/Godmother role that Doc Cooke played in

DOD. Senior career officers and executives in State were even more fortunate to also have had Pat Kennedy, a career FSO himself, as one of the longest serving Under Secretaries in the Department's history.

So the institutional role of the SFS is amply protected in State—officially via the DG and unofficially through Ambassador Kennedy—and I would argue that every department and agency needs to formally establish (or designate) an equivalent to balance the interests of career executives and rank-and-file civil servants on one hand with the agendas and objectives of their political leaders on the other. I would even call them DGs, with respected career SES members officially assigned to a position formally established in that regard. Or they could assume such responsibilities on a collateral, "other duties as assigned" basis (indeed, it's often an unofficial responsibility of the individual holding an agency's most senior career position, like the IRS' Deputy Commissioner).

Bottom line: I believe that DG role needs to be formally sanctioned and recognized—indeed, institutionalized in its own right—as one of the foundations of a 21st century SES. That role will figure prominently in many of the other recommendations that follow.

Leadership Qualities for the 21st Century

The DNA of Senior Leadership

Able to leap tall buildings in a single bound. What kinds of specific leadership qualities will career senior executives require, especially in light of the institutional roles they are expected to play? Given the daunting challenges facing those executives, one would presume that those qualities have changed dramatically over the last several years and, if anything, that the pace of that change will likely accelerate over the next decade. But, if past is prologue, the Federal government may not be able to keep pace.

These days, leadership qualities are typically described in terms of competencies; that is, the knowledge, skills, abilities, and attributes required for a particular position…in this case, a member of the SES. In effect, those competencies represent their leadership DNA, and many of them would seem to be intuitive. However, if they are to be used to make differentiating personnel decisions—who gets promoted, who gets a high performance rating and bonus, who gets admitted to an SES Candidate Development Program (CDP)—they must be *validated* against the specific requirements of the job.[65]

Those competencies must also reflect the reality of 21st century government. Thus, for members of the SES and those who aspire to be members, these competencies take on added significance. Twenty-two of them have been validated for career executives and managers by the Office of Personnel Management (OPM) and make up its leadership competency model.[66] Even

Executive Core Qualifications

- **Leading People:** Conflict Management, Leveraging Diversity, Developing Others, Team Building

- **Results Driven:** Accountability, Customer Service, Decisiveness, Entrepreneurship, Problem Solving, Technical Credibility

- **Business Acumen:** Financial Management, Human Capital Management, Technology Management

- **Building Coalitions:** Partnering, Political Savvy, Influencing-Negotiating

---

[65] Validation is an analytic methodology that attempts to empirically demonstrate the relationship between the competency and leadership success.

[66] U.S. Office of Personnel Management. Senior Executive Service executive core qualifications. Retrieved from https://www.opm.gov/policy-dat

more importantly for the purpose of our discussion, they have been clustered into five Executive Core Qualifications (ECQ) that serve as the admissions test for entry into the SES.

Those same ECQs also serve as the foundation for most Federal leadership development programs, at the agency level as well as government-wide. They have also become the basis for OPM's most recent (2013) SES performance evaluation framework, now the standard report card for all senior executives.[67]

Enduring versus emerging leadership qualities

Here's the problem. Those five ECQs have remained largely static since the inception of the SES almost 40 years ago. And many of the competencies that underlie them have been around for years. The implicit assumption behind the OPM competency model and the ECQs is that the qualifications required to become and remain a member of the SES are the same now as they were decades ago.

To be sure, some of those leadership competencies are enduring, as relevant to today's senior executive as they were in 1978…or for that matter, a senior civil servant serving the British Empire in the 1800s or even the Ming Dynasty a millennium ago. Moreover, as we have suggested, the institutional roles of the SES—for example, serving the public's interest, as well as the government of the day—remain as valid today as they did when the Civil Service Reform Act (CSRA) of 1978[68] created the SES.

Those enduring leadership qualities notwithstanding, the world has changed dramatically since the late 1970s…and for that matter, even the 1990s! And as contributors like Beth Cobert, Michèle Flournoy, and Christine Fox (along with her co-author Emelia S. Probasco) point out in Section 1, the pace of change—in technology, government, geopolitical affairs—is accelerating rapidly. Thus, it strains credulity to suggest that the ECQs, and the leadership competencies that compose them, are static, in whole or even in part.

Yet that's precisely what OPM found when it revisited the ECQs in 2005. Truth in advertising: I started that review when I was OPM's Associate Director (SES policy fell under my purview), but I left to be Chief Human Capital Officer for the U.S. Intelligence Community (IC) before the review was completed. When the review was finished, OPM concluded that the same ECQs established years before remained just as *valid* when it came to leading 21st century government.

Part of the problem is methodological. Technically, the way OPM (or any organization) validates leadership competencies is to look at today's successful leaders and examine in depth what makes them so. The downside of that

[67] U.S. Office of Personnel Management, Chief Human Capital Officers Council. Senior Executive Service performance appraisal system. Retrieved from https://chcoc.gov/content/senior-executive-service-performance-appraisal-system
[68] Civil Service Reform Act of 1978, 6 Pub. L. No. 95-454 § 601 et seq. (1978).

approach should be obvious: The leadership competencies that make a Federal senior executive successful today may bear no relationship to those that may mean the difference between success and failure tomorrow. Indeed, there may be cases where today's essential competencies may actually be counterproductive.

The good news is that there are ways to validate *future* leadership competencies—in the words of hockey great Wayne Gretzky, "to skate where the puck is going to be"—and the Concluding Commentary at the end of this section provides a number of examples of both.

Overview of the chapters

With that hypothesis in mind, we asked a number of former senior government leaders to comment on the leadership qualities and attributes that may be required of a 21st century Federal executive.

- Former U.S. Coast Guard Commandant Admiral Thad Allen, who, among other things, led the Federal government's response to two historic disasters —Hurricane Katrina and the Deepwater Horizon oil spill—looks at those experiences to conclude that tomorrow's senior executive needs to be able to manage the pressure of crisis, particularly given the complexities associated with a government that is co-produced; that is, where the delivery of almost every public good or service, especially but not exclusively in a crisis, is dependent on a network of agencies, companies, and nongovernmental organizations (NGOs). Federal leaders don't often enjoy formal authority over those networks, so Admiral Allen argues that they must learn to achieve *unity of effort* among them without having unity of command—not just in *extremis* but in any whole-of-government challenge.

- Former Internal Revenue Service (IRS) Commissioner Charles Rossotti, who presided over the Agency's historic restructuring and reform in the late 1990s, asserts that tomorrow's career senior executives need to do more than just lead change (as the ECQ requires); they must increasingly take it to the next level—to be able to lead a *large-scale* organizational transformation of the sort IRS went through in the 1990s and the kind the U.S. Department of Homeland Security (DHS), U.S. Department of Veterans Affairs (VA), and IC have gone through since. At the same time, he believes career executives also have to keep their subordinates and employees focused on their mission through the almost constant turbulence such a transformation engenders.

- Harvard Professor Steve Kelman, a former senior Office of Management and Budget (OMB) official in the Clinton administration, and I share the results of a study we did on the decision-making practices of Federal senior executives (in our case, at the sub-cabinet level). We started out looking at how those executives made complex decisions—for example, whether they sought multiple points of view, encouraged debate and dissent, and withheld judgment until all the facts were in—but we found something surprising and critically relevant to executive decision makers, both political and career…that is, that in their most difficult decisions, the most effective government leaders relied less on a lot of input and more on reflection and, ultimately, courage to do the right thing. In other words, we found that leadership success may come down to courage and character. Maybe that's not so surprising after all.

- David M. Walker, former U.S. Comptroller General and now Senior Strategic Advisor at PricewaterhouseCoopers (PwC), reflects on his experiences leading large-scale change at the agency level and the competencies senior executives need to possess to drive such transformations. He goes on to describe his experience designating and fully empowering career senior executives to serve as chief operating officers (COO) and full partners of his in driving those transformations.

- Bob Tobias, a Professor at American University, is the former President of the National Treasury Employees Union, and in that latter capacity sat right beside Commissioner Rossotti as his labor union partner during the 1990s IRS transformation. Drawing from that experience, Bob posits that a career executive's ability to lead collaboratively—in dealing with an agency's union as well as its workforce—will be one of the quintessential leadership skills in the 21st century. In that regard, he looks at disappointing Federal Employee Viewpoint Survey (FEVS) results across the Federal government, especially when it comes to employee engagement, and he suggests that a more *collaborative* approach to leadership would help those scores improve. In such cases, executives demonstrate the courage to be authentic, share their positional power, and collaborate not just to get along, but to get things done—especially with those who may have interests or objectives that are in conflict with them.

Note the technical distinction here. Each of these contributors addresses leadership qualities and attributes; their insights are based on observation and anecdote, but the qualities they describe have not all been validated in a technical or legal sense. However, I would argue that those qualities should enjoy a certain amount of face validity, given the stature of the leaders who have observed and/or practiced them and, as such, should be first-tier candidates for further, more detailed examination. I expand upon that, as well as other issues that relate to the qualities required of the 21st century senior executive, in the Concluding Commentary and Recommendations that follow these chapters.

Confronting Complexity

By Admiral Thad Allen, former Commandant, U.S. Coast Guard

Introduction: Leading in a co-produced government

In my view, being able to manage complexity is one of the critical leadership qualities of the 21st century. It is an idea that is simple in concept but difficult in application as situations become complex and begin to challenge existing rules, regulations, standard operating procedures, authorities, and legal limits on the use of government funds.

For example, traditional inherently governmental functions—the determination and delivery of a benefit or the provision of services from fighting forest fires to fishery conservation—are being co-produced by the private and non-profit sectors. These sectors are challenging government roles in deploying and operating space-based technologies, acquiring and analyzing large amounts of data, and providing healthcare for veterans. In recent years, we have seen large, complex programs or crises where the government does not solely own the means of production to fix the problem.

These situations are triggering a demand to rethink the role of government and government oversight. Two specific examples include the capping of the Macondo well following the loss of the Deepwater Horizon drilling rig and cyber threats to the structure and operation of the Internet and connected networks. In fact, we are living in an interconnected world that is challenging every aspect of Federal government operation and every department and agency. Despite connectivity, departments, for the most part, continue to operate under separate chains of command with separate authorities and responsibilities.

No part of government is immune from an unexpected problem beyond its ability to immediately solve, as we recently learned in the compromise of security background investigation data at OPM and intrusions into sensitive military networks. These challenges are juxtaposed against an increasingly demanding public that has greater access to technology and information and can exercise its revocable "public license to operate" for any leader or organization. This is a hard lesson learned from the delivery of medical care for veterans to local policing practices.

Confronting complexity

The call to government leadership in our time (or any time for that matter) is the ability to develop, evolve, and deploy new competencies and capabilities to address the challenges of a rapidly changing external environment. It is the opportunity of our time. We need to seize it.

At the heart of this challenge are two concepts that we must grasp, redefine in the context of our time, and employ to improve the operation of government. These concepts are (1) the need to confront complexity as both a risk aggravator and an opportunity and (2) to recognize that any significant government performance or outcome is necessarily co-produced by multiple actors from inside and outside government.

Leaders—whether political or career—who will be effective in deploying these concepts must be capable of challenging existing assumptions regarding organizational structure, governing frameworks, and presumed constraints associated with titles, roles, and position descriptions that inhibit innovation. They must lead across boundaries. They must reject the notion that inevitable "wicked problems" and "black swans" are too hard to tackle. They must accept the challenge to create the art of the possible where none appears to exist. Finally, they must accept that technology has now enabled the public to participate in virtually any aspect of government operations through Internet access, social media, and mobile devices.

From on-scene phone cameras to private drones, any major public undertaking is in public view, and privacy and civil liberties are constant considerations. This sociological equivalent of climate change has fundamentally altered the conditions and social contract under which the public license to operate is issued and overseen.

Complexity is not a new or novel concept, but it is taking on new meaning in a world of accelerating technological change, market globalization, and climate change. While these factors have been present throughout history, it is the speed of change and the conflation of effects that challenge our generation. *New York Times* columnist Tom Friedman addressed globalization in his 2005 book, *The World Is Flat: A Brief History of the 21st Century*.

Ten years later, in an address at the Coast Guard Academy, Mr. Friedman described this complex, conflated world as "fast." We need to also understand that there is a distinction between what is complex and what is complicated. While the terms appear to be synonymous, there is a difference between a problem that is complicated and one that is complex, a distinction made by Glen Woodbury, Director of the Center for Homeland Defense and Security at the Naval Post Graduate School. Treating patients for viral diseases can be complicated. Managing the source, transmission, and consequences of a global health threat like the Ebola virus is complex.

Complexity becomes a risk aggravator when its effects cannot be managed within existing policies, procedures, doctrine, legal authorities, or contractual relationships. This in turn becomes a leadership challenge because multiple entities must generally co-produce the needed outcomes. We will not see a complex problem in our lifetime where the needed outcome will not be co-produced. Government is constrained by authorizing legislation, limits on the use of appropriated funds, and ponderous acquisition regulations that are the sum of all real or perceived market failures. The private sector may have no legal authority to act autonomously outside government contract provisions and can be limited in activities beyond traditional corporate responsibility and philanthropic efforts. Similarly, not-for-profit organizations are constrained by both resources and mission scope.

Maritime operations and counterterrorism: A case study

In 1976, President Jimmy Carter signed Presidential Directive 1 (PD 1), *Establishment of Presidential Review and Directive Series/NSC*. PDs replaced the National Security Decision Memoranda (NSDM) used by Presidents Nixon and Ford. Among the PDs signed in the following year was PD 27, *Procedures for Dealing with Non-Military Incidents*, to ensure "that the government's decisions are reached expeditiously and the views of all concerned departments and agencies, as well as considerations of both domestic law and foreign policy, are brought together in reaching a decision…" This PD guided the U.S. response to maritime incidents that could adversely affect our foreign affairs and became the underpinning for the Coast Guard's close coordination with the U.S. Department of State and U.S. Department of Justice for nearly four decades of U.S. maritime operations against maritime drug interdiction, illegal fishing, and human trafficking.

Specific guidance related to post-9/11 maritime operations was issued by President George W. Bush in National Security Presidential Directive 41 (Homeland Security Presidential Directive 13) in 2004. Included was the requirement for the National Strategy for Maritime Security and associated supporting plans. One of those plans, Maritime Operational Threat Response (MOTR), signed in 2006, ambitiously expanded interagency coordination by bringing together additional departments, including the U.S. Department of Defense (DOD), and was set up to be used against all maritime threats (e.g., maritime terrorism). The MOTR Plan represents lessons learned from nearly four decades of interagency coordination of a whole-of-government response to countless maritime events under the original PD 27 direction.

Following the highly successful interagency coordination that underpinned the U.S. response to the capture of the MAERSK ALABAMA by Somali pirates in April 2009, the Global MOTR Coordination Center was established at Coast Guard Headquarters in February 2010. The Center is now recognized by Washington, DC, agencies as the Executive Secretariat for the MOTR Plan. Born out of an operational and political mistake at sea, MOTR epitomizes the quiet evolution of good government by committed public servants who subordinate organizational parochial interests to co-produce the right outcomes for the nation.

Throughout the course of my career I have had the opportunity to address complex problems of an increasing scale. The MOTR journey has been my personal exemplar to mature my tradecraft as a senior government leader. I offer my personal thanks to Scott Genovese, Director of the Global MOTR Coordination Center, for his help in presenting this gold standard of interagency co-production of outcomes.

Lessons learned from Hurricane Katrina

I recently went back to the Gulf Coast for the 10th anniversary of Hurricanes Katrina and Rita. I didn't rush the trip and took several days to retrace my steps and visit the areas that were most affected. The trip included a round-table discussion with President Obama, Federal Emergency Management Agency (FEMA) Administrator Craig Fugate, and others on how New Orleans had recovered thus far. I believe the general consensus was that much has been done but much remains to be done.

Ten years earlier, on Labor Day, September 5, I received a call from DHS Secretary Michael Chertoff. He asked me to go to New Orleans and assist FEMA Administrator Michael Brown to improve the Federal response. The previous week had been wrenching for the city and trying for FEMA, with well-publicized incidents at the Super Dome and Convention Center and the media framing the response as inadequate, poorly organized, and unresponsive to local needs. As I flew to Baton Rouge and on to New Orleans on September 6, 2005, I was perplexed at how the situation had become so problematic. The answer was revealed as I flew into a makeshift landing zone near the Convention Center. Eight days after the storm's landfall, New Orleans remained flooded. Repairs to the levees and drainage canal walls had to be completed to pump water out of the city, and most of the city was without electricity, sewage, and potable water.

The response in New Orleans had been narrowly framed as a response to the hurricane and associated flooding from levee and drainage canal failures. In actuality, something far more complex had occurred. Rather, I believe that what happened in New Orleans was the equivalent of a weapon of mass destruction used on the city without criminal intent that resulted in a loss of continuity of government.

The implications of not understanding this complexity resulted in resources being poured into the city for a week, yet not under the control of local authorities that had legal responsibility for the response. In the absence of a coherent, unified command structure, which existed in Mississippi, external resources were self-deployed and reporting back to their respective chains of command rather than a central coordinating structure. There was an overriding need at the outset to understand the scale of the event, suspend assumptions regarding how we deal with a natural disaster, and delve deeper into the real problems that needed to be addressed.

The response was ultimately stabilized when we were able to re-establish the elements needed for civil authorities to meet their responsibilities. We did that by providing access, logistics, security, administrative support, and communications that allowed local law enforcement officials to go house to house and account for every dwelling and remaining survivors, as well as the difficult task of recovering remains. This task required a unified Federal effort in support of—not in lieu of—local authorities. We were able to organize and lead inter-reliant organizations focused on a common goal: "reach every structure, save who still needed to be saved or evacuated, and begin the difficult process of the recovery of remains with dignity."[69]

While these operations were conducted, private sector contractors under the direction of the Federal government repaired levees and removed debris to allow access to every part of the city. Mobilization of the industrial base in disaster response is a critical component of Federal efforts. In the end, we created a structure that unified the efforts of diverse entities and co-produced the needed outcomes for the city. I believe that had the enormously complex nature of the problem in New Orleans been fully understood by those responsible for the response on August 29th and 30th, we might have seen different outcomes in that first week.

Lessons learned from Deepwater Horizon

The complexity I encountered as the National Incident Commander for the response to the Deepwater Horizon oil rig explosion and subsequent oil spill was far different from Hurricane Katrina. While Katrina was devastating, the physical impacts were bounded: from Southwest Alabama to South Central Louisiana and inland. The central political issue in Katrina revolved around the respective roles of Federal, state, and local government entities and creating unity of effort to co-produce outcomes.

The response to the well blowout was more physically and politically complex. I wrote in 2014:

> *While there was clear Federal jurisdiction over the event and the location (state jurisdiction ends at three nautical miles), five states were simultaneously threatened by an uncontrolled discharge from a well with no human*

---

[69] Sanders, R. P., & Nickerson, J. (2014). *Tackling wicked government problems: A practical guide for developing enterprise leaders.* Washington, DC: Brookings Institution Press.

access, for an indefinite period of time, under varying wind, sea, and tidal conditions, and with no precedent for controlling the well, other than drilling a relief well.[70]

In addition, state and local leaders demanded a greater role in the response similar to the authorities they had in a natural disaster, where the law and response doctrine call for an integrated, Federally led response. Finally, the states affected or at risk were led by Republican governors, and the event occurred just prior to mid-term elections in President Obama's first term. Every meeting with leaders, from local Louisiana parishes and the White House to BP and commercial fishermen, had political overtones.

Co-producing the outcomes needed to address this unprecedented event required a deconstruction of the problem into executable segments and a laser-like focus on those tasks. The response involved three segments of effort that were executed in parallel. The first and highest priority was to control the well and stop the discharge. The damaged wellhead on the seabed was over 5,000 feet below the ocean surface. The ultimate solution was to seal the damaged well with cement and also drill a relief well near the oil reservoir another 12,000 feet below the ocean floor. In total, the relief well would need to be over 17,000 feet in vertical depth from the surface drill rig. These drilling operations were complex and required the deployment of massive amounts of equipment.

While the relief wells were being drilled, a series of attempts to seal or control the oil discharging from the well were attempted. A cap was fitted over the wellhead that allowed some oil to be brought to the service and either flared off or transported ashore. Ultimately, a mechanical cap was fabricated and placed on the well in July 2005 that effectively ended the discharge. However, at my direction as the National Incident Commander, the well was not declared "dead" until the relief well was completed in September and the well was sealed.

The second phase was to contain as much oil as possible at the well and on the surface in the vicinity of the well where response techniques could be most effective. This effort was directed at the largest quantities of oil to prevent them from reaching shore. This included use of dispersants, in situ burning of the oil, and mechanical skimming. The aggregate amount of oil removed by these methods was constrained by sea and weather conditions that disaggregated the oil into hundreds of thousands of small slicks. The response was further complicated by environmental concerns related to the response methods and public discussion on the fate of the discharged oil in the water.

The third and final segment was to manage the consequences of oil reaching the shore with an emphasis on defending environmentally sensitive areas.

[70] Ibid.

This response was very difficult and resource intensive. In addition, it necessarily involved numerous state and local entities and contentious discussions regarding response priorities.

Throughout the process, the law required that BP and other involved companies fund all response costs, legitimate damage claims, and natural resource damages. The law in effect mandated co-production of the response under the authority and supervision of the Federal government, a structure created in the Oil Pollution Act of 1990[71] following the Exxon Valdez spill. The role of the response plan was not a concept easily grasped at all levels of government or by the public. There was a continual challenge to inform, explain, and, in some cases, defend the structure of the response.

Preparing for the future

There is no simple formula for building personal and organizational competency to address complex problems and manage co-produced outcomes. Each problem is unique and requires some level of subject matter expertise and management skill to solve. That said, I believe the key is and always will be creating better leaders who have the traits and skills to be effective in complex situations. Long ago I stopped engaging in discussions about whether leaders are made or born and whether leadership can be learned. Anyone can be a better leader. My two key lessons learned from a lifetime of leading and managing complex problems are the need to engage in lifelong learning and become more emotionally intelligent.

Senior government leaders must make a personal commitment to lifelong learning and continual intellectual refreshment. Embedded in this concept is the understanding that position descriptions, goals, and objectives for senior leaders are not the ends to be achieved. In fact, they are only table stakes, an "ante" to act in a larger role in government. Those who seek promotions as their sole goal diminish themselves and their potential to serve. To remain relevant and effective, leaders must actively seek knowledge and become competent in the use of new and evolving tools and technologies. Such a competency also increases a leader's capacity to address the growth of public participation via social and other media, as discussed at the outset.

Knowledgeable, well-informed leaders must also be grounded emotionally and capable of leading when complexity begins to introduce risk and attendant human responses. During the Deepwater Horizon oil spill response, BP Chief Executive Officer Tony Hayward made international headlines and negatively galvanized public opinion when he said he "wanted his life back."[72] What he said was actually true. There were tens of thousands of

---

[71] Oil Pollution Act of 1990, 33 U.S.C. § 2701 et seq. (1990).
[72] Johnson, B. [climatebrad]. (2010, May 31). BP CEO Tony Hayward: *"I'd like my life back."* [Video File]. Retrieved from https://www.youtube.com/watch?v=MTdKa9eWNFw

people involved in the response who wanted their lives back, including me. The problem was that it was not an appropriate statement by a leader in a senior consequential position, and it inferred a lack of empathy or personal commitment to a very complex problem. Hayward did not demonstrate emotional intelligence—generally the ability to recognize feelings and take them into account in thinking and acting.

There is a body of research that suggests that emotional intelligence enhances leadership capability. My personal journey has involved a deeper understanding of my own emotions and how I manage my feelings in times of stress and make decisions in compressed timeframes with incomplete information. Emotional intelligence is a source of calm and patience that allows for personal reflection in confronting complex situations, even urgent situations. During my interaction with the media and political leaders during the hurricane and oil spill responses, my credibility, honesty, and integrity were questioned, sometimes on live television. In those situations, it is important to focus on being clear, honest, and transparent. That is difficult to do if you cannot separate your emotions (which may be completely valid) from the task at hand, keeping your head.

As we seek to define the role of senior executives in a radically changing, fast world, it is critical that new leaders treat their profession as a trade or craft to be advanced and matured over a career and lifetime. If complexity and the need to co-produce outcomes are today's challenges for government leaders, lifelong learning and emotional intelligence are the building blocks of competency, insight, and responsible leadership. Warren Bennis, the distinguished thinker on leadership, once said, "Managers do things right, leaders do the right thing."[73] In a fast world, leaders have little choice. They must do both: the right things in the right way.

[73] Bennis, W. G., & Nanus, B. (1985). *Leaders: The strategies for taking charge.* New York, NY: Harper & Row.

Crisis and Transformation

By the Honorable Charles Rossotti, former Commissioner,
U.S. Internal Revenue Service

Introduction: Crisis and reform

I became IRS Commissioner in 1997, when the IRS was deep into one of its periodic volcanic eruptions. For 2 years the IRS was the subject of unrelenting reports of failures and abuses. A massive technology project was canceled and labeled a multibillion-dollar disaster. Millions of taxpayers' calls for assistance went unanswered. In fact, taxpayers complained so frequently of abuse and mistreatment that some congressional offices had a full-time person on staff just to handle the complaints. The IRS' bookkeeping was said to be so bad that it would not pass its own tests for taxpayers. The firestorm reached a peak in 3 days of sensational televised Senate hearings in which taxpayers cried on camera and whistleblowing IRS employees testified behind screens to hide their identities.

The kind of crisis the IRS faced in 1997 erupts periodically, often unexpectedly, at many sensitive agencies. For example, we've since had another crisis at the IRS concerning the alleged targeting of certain political groups, and an even more massive upheaval at the VA over delayed care and falsified statistics. FEMA had a major crisis over its handling of Hurricane Katrina, as did the Securities and Exchange Commission (SEC) over questionable enforcement actions. The list is long. When the issues rise to the level of nonstop TV coverage, they can raise serious issues for the management of an agency, often revealing long-standing underlying problems that appointed political leaders and SES executives must confront and solve together.

In my case, I had my confirmation hearing to become IRS Commissioner 2 weeks after the incendiary Senate hearings. However, in the 5 months that preceded the hearing, while waiting to be confirmed, I did my best to prepare for the challenge by talking to as many people as possible who, unlike me, knew something about the IRS.

Almost universally, I was advised by people outside the IRS that my biggest and most insurmountable problem would be the stubborn resistance I would encounter from the entrenched internal leadership of the Agency. Unlike most other agencies, at the IRS only the Commissioner and the General Counsel are political appointees. Everyone else in a leadership role is a senior career executive. So I was told that the principal source of the Agency's major problems, and the roadblock to solving them, was its SES cadre.

The myth and the reality of the IRS executive corps

The contrast between those comments and my conversations with IRS senior executives themselves was stark. True, some executives were in denial and blamed the critics for exaggerating the Agency's problems. But most of those I spoke with knew the IRS was in serious trouble and the problems were real. While their proposed solutions were not always clear or consistent, most knew that some big changes were needed, and they wanted to be part of the change. And I knew that there was no way on God's earth that we could execute any major improvements without the skills and institutional knowledge that these executives, most with literally a lifetime of service in the IRS, could bring to bear.

So the biggest thing I needed to do to succeed at leading the Agency to a better place was to find those IRS executives who could (and would) lead this massive transformational change. I also needed to recruit some executives from outside the Agency to obtain a mix of inside and outside perspectives. The situation didn't require a wholesale replacement of the Agency's corps of senior executives, as some observers were suggesting.

Over the course of the next 5 years, the IRS did transform almost every aspect of the Agency, all under the umbrella of what we chose to call "modernization" to provide a positive moniker for what we were doing. It was also an accurate moniker because in fact many of the problems confronting the IRS stemmed from its failure to adapt to new ways of doing business, including the Agency's failures to improve its information technology (IT) systems. In fact, those previous system failures were primarily caused by attempting to graft new technology onto obsolete business practices and organizational models. For example, the IRS was so fragmented into geographically stovepiped operating units, each with its own way of doing things and often with its own autonomous IT department, that no enterprise-wide systems could be deployed effectively.

In point of fact—and contrary to popular misconception—IRS career executives provided most of the leadership for this modernization program, which ultimately created a vastly different agency. We did supplement their leadership with a limited number of executives recruited from outside the IRS, including some from the private sector. We did this to provide some experience and skills that were not available internally, especially since much of what the IRS does is similar to work done in the private sector: auditing financial data, collecting money, answering phones. People who had spent their careers in large accounting firms and leading corporations could bring best practices to life in the IRS.

I don't have any reliable way of knowing the degree to which the antiquated structures and systems at the IRS were representative of those in other Federal agencies, nor do I have much current knowledge of how things have changed since I left the Agency (and government) after my 5-year term expired in 2002. But I can make some observations about what was good about the career members of the SES whom I saw in action at the IRS, as well as what was needed.

Notwithstanding the genuine problems that had accumulated at the IRS over many years, it was still remarkable just how much complicated and essential work this oft-criticized agency did every year. Considering that the Commissioner was one of only two political appointees in the entire IRS, and that this person was occupied with many external responsibilities, it fell heavily to the Agency's SES leadership to ensure all the essential jobs got done. And they did. It does not happen by accident that $2 trillion per year is accurately and honestly collected from 175 million people and 6 million businesses. And this is done in the context of ever-changing tax laws and regulations, all of which are mind-numbingly complex.

The SES leadership of the IRS made this work happen through a combination of strong institutional knowledge, highly effective informal networks that overcame the lack of effective official communications, and, most importantly, the dedication of the Agency's senior executives, who were committed to doing the essential work everyone knew had to get done. In so doing, these leaders took smart risks to foster innovation.

Considering the vast scale of many Federal agencies, the rapid turnover and lengthy vacancies of many politically appointed positions, and the often confusing signals that come to an agency from Congress, other executive branch agencies, and outside groups, it is clear to me that the SES cadre—at the IRS and government-wide—shows great strength in somehow getting the most essential jobs done when it comes to managing existing programs. So whatever changes may come to the SES, it is paramount that this core capability—getting the practical, day-to-day, operational work of government done—be maintained. The government, and the nation, literally cannot function without it.

Evolutionary versus revolutionary change

However, developing and implementing new programs or modernizing (transforming) old ones is a different matter. While the IRS experience shows that senior career executives can be extraordinarily effective in leading major changes—even those that drastically transform or eliminate old ways of doing things—this does not happen automatically, nor do all senior executives function equally well in this role. For new or modernized programs to succeed, two elements are necessary.

First, there must be strong leadership from the political head of an agency to define, organize, and drive the change, particularly in the face of outside political obstacles. It is unrealistic to expect career executives, no matter how talented and dedicated, to initiate and lead major changes in large government programs on their own. This is perhaps obvious, but what may be less obvious is the second key element…that is, to find and select those extraordinary career executives who are able to work on the appointee's side of the table to help him or her drive the transformation.

At the IRS, we initially handpicked a small core of executives who seemed equipped and eager to step out and lead the change. Later—in a move that remains unprecedented—we redefined every one of our senior executive and senior manager positions (more than 1,000 of them altogether) to reflect the changes in structure and culture we wanted to effect. We then made incumbents and other eligible internal candidates actually recompete for them so executives and managers could self-select themselves into (and in many cases out of) the new roles.

It has been my experience at the IRS and other organizations that people at all levels, including senior executives, broadly fall along a spectrum concerning proposed changes in their workplace: from diehards opposing any changes at all to those willing to embrace and lead change (research by Harvard University Kennedy School Professor Steve Kelman on how to change government also supports the idea that this spectrum of attitudes tends to exist in most organizations).[74]

At one end, there are those who unequivocally oppose the change and cannot be persuaded otherwise. It is easy to underestimate how large this group is. Early on in the IRS modernization effort, a few executives tried to use their connections with staffers on Capitol Hill to get me fired on the grounds that I was gutting the ability of the Agency to enforce the tax laws. It didn't surprise me, and it didn't work.

In the middle, the largest group, are those who will wait and see. At the other end are those who welcome the change and have the skills to help lead it. Some of these executives may have already seen the need for transformational change and tried to do what they could to propose or effect it. Others may see it as an opportunity to advance themselves and are willing to take the risk to try. It is extremely important to correctly identify this group of change enablers, especially at the beginning of the transformation effort, and coopt them to help lead the effort.

In thinking about the SES of the future, I think it is important to try to develop as large a cadre as possible of senior career executives who have the attitudes

---

[74] Mader, D., Kelman, S., & Myers, J. (2014). *What it takes to change government: Successfully executing ambitious strategies*. McLean, VA: Booz Allen Hamilton. Retrieved from http://mena. boozallen.com/content/dam/MENA/PDF/what-it-takes-to-change-government.pdf

(like the courage to take risks) and the capacity to lead truly transformational change, especially in the midst of what may be an existential crisis for their agency. Realistically, even though all executives are supposed to have the capacity to "lead change" (according to the ECQs), not all executives have these characteristics. But having a reasonable fraction of senior career executives with transformational leadership capacity is very important. I think this distribution of attitudes and skills is normal in any executive group. It doesn't imply a need for more than one SES, but it does imply that we need to develop some subset of career executives with these higher order capabilities.

Most likely, the best way to develop this capacity to lead transformational change in some reasonable fraction of senior career executives is to make it a significant part of the Leading Change criteria in selecting new executives—not just leading change, but leading change that is truly transformational. By the time someone is ready to be selected to the SES, they have either shown some initiative in doing so or not. Note that I think leaders can exhibit these characteristics at almost any level of responsibility. I would guess that probing this characteristic in the practical past experience of SES candidates would best help predict what they will do in the future.

Refreshing the senior executive corps with private sector experience

Finally, as to what is often lacking in the SES of today and needed in the SES of the future, I strongly believe it is actual experience with how things are done elsewhere, within but especially outside the Federal government, namely in the private sector. No matter how talented someone is and how much training and education they have, they are the product of their actual experience. For example, as I noted, most of the activities the IRS performs are very similar to activities done broadly in the private economy; yet, when I came to the Agency, almost none of its career executives had had any experience outside the IRS, much less outside government. Although there are differences, the similarities are very important. Having executives with experience in these activities elsewhere is extremely important in bringing *government* practice up to best practice.

I am aware that various programs have been tried to allow SES executives to rotate into private sector organizations for a tour of duty, but I don't believe these have been very successful or very extensive to date. Concerns about conflicts of interest and possibly other factors have been barriers. If there are ways to overcome these barriers so senior executives could serve in meaningful roles in private organizations for a period of time, this would be extremely useful. Another approach, one that may be more practical, is to recruit some fraction of new SES candidates directly from the private sector. Notwithstanding pay differentials and other barriers, I believe this is entirely possible to do, and we were largely successful when we tried to do it at the IRS. My experience there indicated to me that there are a reasonable number of people with great credentials who would be interested in working in important roles in the Federal government—either as a permanent career change or for a limited-term appointment—if for no other reason than to give back to the nation. For example, at the IRS we attracted people who had been senior partners in large accounting firms and senior executives in charge of customer service in the nation's most successful large corporations.

In summary, I think the SES of today is an indispensable asset for the Federal government and for our country. The SES keeps the trains running in government, often overcoming remarkable challenges to do so. Whatever we do, we have to maintain this capacity. At the same time, the SES can be made better by finding ways to both appoint more people with the skills and attitudes necessary to lead large-scale, transformational change and attract people with meaningful private sector experience into the SES.

Political appointees accepting leadership positions in agencies will do well to get to know their senior executives and determine how to tap their potential to help define and lead the major changes that are necessary in every agency. I believe this is an indispensable ingredient for the success of every political appointee and essential to the long-term effectiveness of the Federal government.

Courage and Character in Executive Decision Making

By Professor Steven Kelman, Harvard University Kennedy School of Government, and Dr. Ronald P. Sanders, Vice President and Fellow, Booz Allen Hamilton

Introduction: Making hard choices

What makes for an effective senior executive in government? There is no shortage of hypotheses in that regard, with policymakers, practitioners, and academics proffering a whole host of theories, but most of them focus on largely observable leadership behaviors and competencies that purport to describe a good (or at least competent) public sector executive. We decided to take a different approach, setting out to examine *how* government executives go about making difficult decisions—typically defined in the research litera-ture as those that are technically and informationally complex, fraught with uncertainty, and ultimately involving hard tradeoffs among conflicting values or interests—to see if outstanding executives did so differently. However, in the course of our examination, we discovered something that surprised us: the importance of courage and character in decision making, two exceedingly intangible but no less critical qualities of an effective government executive.

Making difficult decisions in government can be challenging under almost any circumstances. Cognitive limitations preclude decision makers from fully considering all relevant information, and cognitive biases can also interfere with their information gathering and analysis. The executive can compensate for such individual limits by seeking out advisors and other sources of input. However, the literature on groupthink also highlights the limitations of group-informed decision making. Out of these two areas of decision research has emerged an approach that Irving Janis calls "vigilant problem solving," a process in which the decision maker solicits input from advisors who are deliberately selected for their diverse knowledge and opinions[75] and in which the leader actively seeks out dissenting views, critically examines the costs and risks of the preferred (and other) choices, and demonstrates a willingness to revise his or her initial predispositions in response to the deliberations.

---

[75] Janis, I. L. (1989). *Crucial decisions: Leadership in policymaking and crisis management.* New York, NY: The Free Press.

Vigilant decision making

Vigilant problem solving is widely seen as the most effective process for making complex, difficult decisions. To examine whether that approach was more prevalent among outstanding government executives (compared to a randomly selected sample of their peers), we interviewed 20 heads of sub-cabinet-level organizations in the Federal government. All of those executives served during the Obama administration, with 10 nominated by "good-government" experts as ones who had done an outstanding job and 10 chosen at random from a listing of all Federal sub-cabinet and equivalent positions. We asked each the same set of questions about how they made important decisions, with the objective of determining whether and to what extent executives in the two categories used a "vigilant" process when making difficult decisions.

When we asked both sets of executives about their most difficult decisions, most of them (including 9 of 10 of the outstanding ones) did not identify those that were technically complex. Rather, the vast majority described their most difficult decisions as ones that were unpopular or that involved significant personal, political, or organizational risk. In other words, their most difficult decisions required courage and character to make, in part because the executives who made them had to not only decide the right thing to do but also muster the will to do it. This became the central focus jof our research, as we sought to examine the distinctions between decisions involving courage and those involving complexity.

The literature on effective decision making notes that to make a rational, value-maximizing decision, one would need to list all alternative strategies; determine all of the consequences of those alternatives; comparatively evaluate the costs, benefits, and risks of those consequences; and select the alternative that is most consistent with the organization's priorities. However, as critics have noted, it is impossible to realize this ideal because of cognitive limitations and biases.

As noted, Janis offers an alternative: a vigilant decision-making model designed to overcome both individual cognitive limitations and the well-known pathology of groupthink.[76] This model posits that a decision maker can make more effective decisions by seeking information and input from a group of advisors carefully selected for their diversity of experience, knowledge, and points of view and by actively soliciting these advisors' dissenting views, considering new information, challenging initial assumptions, and critically examining costs and risks of preferred and alternative choices. Vigilant decision making is specifically designed to avoid too much agreement and too quick a rush to judgment by a group. Its prescription is "more is better"—more information, more discussion, and more opportunities for debate and dissent.

[76] Ibid.

This model has found significant support among researchers, and it has instinctive appeal to practitioners. Thus, the research question we originally sought to examine was whether senior U.S. Federal executives (in this case, at the sub-cabinet level) generally employed a vigilant decision-making process when faced with hard choices. We also wanted to examine whether outstanding executives were more likely to rely on that approach than their peers—hypothesizing this as one reason they were more successful. However, some of the findings from our interviews led us to examine decision making when the choices were not complex but rather when they required courage to make.

Complexity, courage, and character

For our study, we interviewed 10 outstanding Federal sub-cabinet executives and a comparison group of 10 randomly chosen peers of comparable rank and responsibility. To identify those outstanding executives, we used a "reputational approach," soliciting nominations from experts on the Federal government, including the 677 peer-elected Fellows of the National Academy of Public Administration (the Academy), as well as the Partnership for Public Service's 74 Strategic Advisors to Government Executives (SAGE), a peer-elected group of former senior Federal officials in IT, acquisition, financial management, and human capital management.[77] We also solicited nominations from a group of 16 current and former senior government officials and experts from OMB, the Government Accountability Office (GAO), professional staff of the Senate Committee on Homeland Security and Governmental Affairs and House Committee on Oversight and Government Reform, former members of Congress, and a senior journalist from a media outlet that specializes in covering government management.

Those executives who received multiple nominations from these experts were identified as "outstanding." And for our comparison group, we randomly selected incumbents of rank-equivalent positions listed the most recent *Plum Book*, which is published every 4 years by the Senate Committee on Homeland Security and Governmental Affairs.[78] We conducted interviews of all 20 executives during the last year of the first term of the Obama administration, as well as the first year of the second Obama term. Each respondent was interviewed in person, generally for 2 to 4 hours; interviews were recorded and then transcribed verbatim, resulting in over 2,000 pages of transcript. Interviews followed a standard format, consisting primarily of open-ended questions. Among other things, we asked about each respondent's approach to decision making, including their typical sources of information and advice, their techniques for encouraging discussion and dissent, and examples of

---

[77] Wolfinger, R. E. (1960). Reputation and reality in the study of "community power." *American Sociological Review,* 25(5), 636–644.
[78] United States Government Policy and Supporting Positions (Plum Book). (2008). Washington, DC: U.S. Government Publishing Office.

situations in which they had changed their original predisposition to the decision.

The last question in the decision-making part of our interview protocol was, "Please think about the single most difficult major decision you have made on this job. What was the decision? Why was it difficult? How did you go about making the decision?" This line of inquiry was intended to elicit more detailed information about our original research focus on vigilant decision making. In keeping with the literature regarding what makes decisions difficult, we expected the respondents to describe those that were cognitively complex. However, as noted above, that did not turn out to be the case.

When we asked respondents why their most difficult decision was so difficult, only 1 of the 10 outstanding executives (and 5 of the 10 in the comparison group) cited complexity as the reason for the difficulty of their decision. The others said it was because the decision was unpopular; was emotionally wrenching; or went against the counsel of their advisors, hierarchical superiors, or powerful external organizations…in other words, because the decision required courage to make. The most difficult decisions included standing up to pressure from organizations like OMB and GAO or the executive's own organizational superiors. Other decisions concerned such things as canceling major IT systems over the strong objections of organizational stakeholders, terminating individual longtime career managers, and downsizing or significantly restructuring the executive's organization and staff. All of these decisions had a common theme: They were all widely unpopular, likely to encounter stiff resistance, and emotionally wrenching for the executive involved.

All of those executives—outstanding and comparison group alike—used strikingly similar words when describing their courageous decisions. For example, one stated that "ultimately, I had to make a decision that we weren't going to yield on the requirement, that doing the right thing long term was more important to the long-term viability of the program." Another told us, "I finally concluded [the program] could not be made to work…and I was not willing to implement a public program I believe is flawed." A third stated, "Well, there were certainly a lot of people that thought we should continue [the program] but, in the end, I mean, it was my call because the leader of that organization was looking to me to make that recommendation, right?"

The executives who made these decisions knew the right thing to do (of course, given that many of these decisions were unpopular, others would almost certainly disagree with them). However, they also knew that doing the right thing would be exceedingly difficult. The conflict they faced was between taking the easy way out—and thus avoiding adverse personal consequences—and acting courageously despite such consequences. In all the cases we examined, the executive made the decision they regarded as right, those adverse consequences notwithstanding.

A contingency approach to courage and complexity

As we noted above, our initial research sought to examine the extent to which senior executives used a vigilant decision-making process. And for those decisions we classified as technically complex, we found that to be true—both outstanding and comparison executives consulted multiple advisors, gathered additional information from a variety of sources, encouraged dissent, and deliberately avoided rushing to judgment. But little of that vigilance was present when they discussed decisions that we classified as courageous. Only three of the nine outstanding executives who made courageous decisions reported that they gathered significant new information to help them do so. For the rest, information gathering was minimal. Thus, instead of consulting a wide variety of advisors to get diverse opinions, our courageous executives tended to employ a more solitary decision-making process. Indeed, six of the nine outstanding executives essentially made the decision by themselves, choosing not to involve others after their initial information-gathering efforts.

As the literature suggests, Janis' vigilant decision-making model was specifically developed for decisions that are technically complex. However, as noted, those respondents who made courageous decisions did not employ this model. Rather, their courageous decisions were more likely to involve reflection and introspection, with consultation, if any, limited to a small group of trusted advisors. Thus, we posit that while vigilant decision making makes sense when faced with complexity (including complex decisions involving difficult ethical dilemmas), it is less relevant when decisions require courage. In the spirit of Tom Petty's song, those decisions require someone who "won't back down" from doing the right thing. And doing so requires character and courage.

What underlies courageous decisions? The literature in this area is sparse, especially compared to the research on decisions involving complexity. Some authors suggest that certain people have a strong sense of their own "moral identity" that may ultimately cause them to do the right thing.[79] Others posit that the decision maker must have a "self-efficacy" or self-confidence that makes them feel their decisions can make a difference.[80] But even for a self-confident executive, making a courageous decision is hard. The easy way out is to avoid an unpopular decision, and "courage in organizations is likely to be unpopular."[81] All of the decisions we classified as courageous shared this common denominator.

---

[79] Aquino, K., & Reed, A. (2002). The self-importance of moral identity. *Journal of Personality and Social Psychology, 83(6)*, 1423–1440.
[80] For example, Hannah, S. T., & Avolio, B. J. (2010). Ready or not: How do we accelerate the developmental readiness of leaders? *Journal of Organizational Behavior, 31*(8), 1181–1187.
[81] Worline, M. C., & Quinn, R. W. (2003). Courageous principled action. In K. S. Cameron, J. E. Dutton, & R. E. Quinn (Eds.), *Positive organizational scholarship: Foundations of a new discipline* (pp. 138–157). San Francisco, CA: Berrett-Koehler.

A central implication of our research is that the literature on complex decisions and the literature on decisions involving courage may provide different prescriptions for the executive faced with a difficult decision. And the extensive information gathering, diverse sources of advice and input, and discussion and debate inherent in vigilant decision making may actually serve to undermine a decision maker's intention to act courageously. Thus, while one can imagine a situation in which support from a large, diverse group of advisors might steel the executive's resolve, we believe the opposite is far more likely to be true—that is, large groups might actually tend to undermine courageous individual behavior by absolving members from accepting personal responsibility for the group's consensus. In the colorful words of Margaret Thatcher, more vigilance may induce an executive to "go wobbly."

Thus, when an executive is contemplating a decision that requires courage, self-reflection—looking inside oneself—may be more effective than relying on a group of advisors. Indeed, if deciding courageously is hard, it would seem the last thing the executive needs in such a situation is a large number of advisors debating the wisdom of the executive's decision. Support from a small group of trusted individuals whose ethical identity the executive respects may be more helpful.

In any event, our research suggests the need for a contingency model—one that advocates a different decision-making process, depending on whether the decision itself involves complexity or courage. For decisions that are technically complex, the vigilant process recommended by the literature remains optimal. But courageous decisions may require a different approach, one in which introspection—perhaps shared with a small group of trusted, supportive confidants, perhaps based on intuition—replaces more information gathering, debate, and dissent. Hence the two contingent approaches to decision making. And of course, while we have characterized these contingencies as the opposite ends of a theoretical courage-complexity continuum, we acknowledge that real-world choices are never so clear, and that a decision that first appears to be a matter of solving for complexity can easily morph into one that requires courage.

To borrow a term from organizational design theory, we believe that successful executives must be able to be *ambidextrous* in the way they approach decision making. On one hand, the executive should be able to use a vigilant approach for the run of technically complex decisions; on the other hand, he or she should also be prepared to turn inward and reflective when it becomes apparent that he or she is faced with a decision that demands courage and character.[82] Hence ambidexterity: the ability to use either decision-making model, depending on the circumstances. Interestingly, our findings also suggest that the same model may be applied to the executive's most trusted advisors as well—they too should learn to discern when their leader's

[82] O'Reilly, C. A., & Tushman, M. L. (2008). Ambidexterity as a dynamic capability: Resolving the innovator's dilemma. *Research in Organizational Behavior*, 28, 185–206.

decision demands discussion, debate, and dissent and when their moral support is the order of the day. However, it is clear that we need more research on whether, and how, successful—that is, ambidextrous—executives are able to switch styles.

Implications for the executive decision maker

The literature on decision making generally focuses on complex decisions that entail extensive information gathering and detailed cost-benefit analyses, but we believe insufficient attention has been paid to decisions involving courage, especially those made by senior government executives in the day-to-day course of their public duties. And by bringing together two important bodies of practice and research—vigilant decision making on one hand and the relatively sparse literature on organizational courage on the other—we believe we have made a contribution to decision-making theory by proffering a differentiated, contingent model for making decisions that range from complexity to courage.

Admittedly, our model is based on what can be characterized as exploratory research and theory building. We urge our colleagues, both academics and practitioners, to build upon it—and to pay as much attention to public sector executive decisions that involve courage as our profession has to those involving complexity—so government officials who are faced with difficult choices can more effectively make them. While most executives may not be called upon to make courageous, won't back down decisions very often, they are likely to face such defining moments at some time in their career; when they do, the decisions they make will likely have significant organizational, professional, and personal consequences. In other words, what they decide will matter, most especially to the individuals and agencies involved. We hope our research will help better prepare public executives to act accordingly when that time comes.

CHAPTER 3.4:

Transformational Competencies for the Next Generation of SES

By the Honorable David M. Walker, former U.S. Comptroller General

Introduction

The SES was established by the CSRA of 1978, in part to promote the "continuing transformation of government." As a person who has led three Federal agencies spanning both the executive and legislative branches of the Federal government, to me transformation in the Federal sector can be defined as follows: taking major steps to change the structure, policies, operational practices, and/or culture of an organization to improve performance, ensure sustainability, and promote continuous improvement for both today and tomorrow. This can include addressing what is done, how it is done, where it is done, and who does it.

Throughout the course of my career in government I saw members of the SES play key roles in a number of organizational transformations. I believe this is the most effective type of leadership a senior executive can provide. Indeed, the transformation of dated practices, processes, and policies is sorely needed in most Federal agencies, as many of my fellow authors attest in this anthology, and it's what we need most from the SES as a collection of individuals who are bound together by an institutional purpose. To develop senior executives with the necessary leadership skills to lead transformations we need to reconsider and refine the current OPM competencies used to evaluate these executives. The rubric we use to select and develop senior executives will determine whether or not they are genuinely equipped to lead transformations, which is no easy feat. Moreover, we need to ensure agency performance management processes actually do evaluate senior executives against the critical competencies and not some other measures. Finally, we need to clarify and strengthen the role of the most senior of all career executives, those who serve as agency COOs and chief management officers (CMO), who must be the linchpin of transformation efforts.

My personal experiences with the SES and government transformation

I have had the privilege of serving in two non-career SES positions, in three Presidential Appointment with Senate Confirmation (PAS) positions, as head of two executive branch agencies (Acting Executive Director of the Pension Benefit Guaranty Corporation and Assistant Secretary of Labor for the Employee Benefit Security Administration [EBSA] within the U.S. Department of Labor), and as head of one legislative branch agency (GAO). I have also had the good fortune of working with some of the best professional services firms in the world: PwC and Arthur Andersen.

Contrary to assertions by some, I have found that the quality of most career SES members is just as good as the private sector. When I was at GAO, contrary to past history and the Agency's culture, I made a special effort to open up GAO's SES Candidate Development Program competition to individuals from other executive branch agencies and to key congressional staff and private sector executives. We hired a number of them, a vast majority of whom were very successful after adapting to GAO's way of doing business. We also developed a lot of top career SES talent within the GAO, and many of them eventually assumed high-level positions in various public and private sector organizations. These individuals demonstrated in their new positions the quality, professionalism, and commitment of GAO's executive corps. We also increased accountability with the SES. Senior executive members were expected to lead by example and practice what they preached. They were also expected to be supportive of our overall agency transformation effort.

I have also found that most senior executives are totally committed to the mission of their department or agency. They have valuable institutional knowledge that can be extremely helpful to presidential appointees and non-career SES officials. It would be a tremendous mistake for political appointees to fail to capitalize on the talent, commitment, and institutional knowledge possessed by career SES members. Most have chosen a career of public service and should be commended for doing so.

At the same time, the government is a monopoly and does not face the same type of competition and requirements to innovate that the private sector does. This leads to inertia. Senior government executives also face constant scrutiny from a cross-section of stakeholders, including taxpayers, Congress, the White House, OMB, auditing agencies, inspectors general, the news media, unions, and their own employees. Criticism, founded or not, lurks around every corner. Naturally, the result is that most agencies tend to be risk averse, and this aversion extends to the kinds of innovation and evolution that any organization must embrace to remain relevant and avoid stagnation. Over time, this risk aversion leads many government agencies to become calcified and ineffective, which in turn requires transformations to force modernization upon them. With those considerations in mind, I took special efforts to promote innovation and risk management in the three Federal agencies I led, and I relied on senior executives at every turn to help drive those necessary transformations.

Key executive competencies for driving transformation

Since the SES system was intended to focus more on leadership and transformation within government than day-to-day management, the types of competencies senior executives should possess and be evaluated on should be restructured accordingly.

While reasonable people can differ in their opinions of which competencies should be used to evaluate senior executives, my experience as head of GAO and with PwC can be instructive. At GAO, we engaged in a number of transformational reforms, including human capital functions. One of these reforms included adopting a competency-based system for training, development, performance assessment, and feedback. After full implementation, we also used the system as input for compensation adjustments and promotions. The GAO system focused on a dozen competencies and involved a recalibration of performance expectations. On reflection, it is appropriate to add a risk management competency for SES members.

GAO Competencies

- Developing People
- Thinking Critically
- Improving Professional Competence
- Collaborating with Others
- Presenting Information Orally
- Presenting Information in Writing
- Facilitating and Implementing Change
- Representing GAO
- Investing Resources
- Leading Others

Government tends to be too process oriented and risk averse. Executives need to be innovative and results oriented while managing risks. You can't maximize value by minimizing risk!

At PwC, we adopted a competency-based model in 2014 that parallels GAO's approach in many ways but with a focus on a smaller number of competencies, more akin to OPM's Executive Core Qualifications, which are actually categories of competencies. I think some of the more interesting PwC competencies, and ones that are highly applicable to Federal senior executives for leading transformation, include Whole Leadership and Global Acumen. PwC's Whole Leadership competency concerns the personal quality of authenticity and the action of inspiring others. Our Global Acumen competency has much in common with what Thad Allen describes as "confronting complexity" with "unity of effort" and "co-produced outcomes." These qualities and behaviors aren't currently reflected in the OPM ECQs but should be.

It is clear that embracing change and taking measured risks are also necessary qualities for senior executives who will drive innovation and continuous improvement. Accordingly, the ECQs need updating to put more emphasis on intellectual agility for senior executives, along with promoting more candid and constructive conversations with senior leadership (non-career appointees), especially in situations when there is a need to "speak truth to power," as Steve Kelman and Ron Sanders have described.

Finally, I think that to promote innovation, change management, and transformation, senior executives need to lead by example. We hear this term in many contexts; here's an example of what I mean. One concept I adopted as head of the GAO and the EBSA was to elevate the most capable career SES official to the position of COO or CMO. In the case of the EBSA, that career COO, Alan Leibowitz, was elevated to the Deputy Assistant Secretary level on par with the political and non-career SES Deputy Assistant Secretary. The career SES official focused on internal issues, operations, and enforcement matters. The non-career SES official focused on policy and external issues. At GAO, the person whom I elevated to the COO position, Gene Dodaro, was a full partner with me, and along with other key career SES executives we transformed the GAO in ways that generated real and lasting results and considerable external acclaim. Gene succeeded me as U.S. Comptroller General. His elevation was well deserved, and he is the first career SES professional to be nominated and confirmed in the important position of Comptroller General of the United States.

COOs and CMOs

To date, there have only been eight Comptroller Generals since 1921. The success story of Gene Dodaro underscores the value and need to provide more opportunity and upward mobility for senior executives within government. While political appointees come and go and the priorities and policies of various administrations change, many challenges facing government are long-standing, and it is skilled career senior executives who can offer us the best opportunity to drive transformation within the Federal government. It is clear to me from my experience that to maximize the prospects of facilitating transformation, it would be highly beneficial for every large (or challenged) Federal agency to consider designating a career senior executive to serve as a COO or CMO.

The agency COO role was officially established through the Government Performance and Results Modernization Act of 2010.[83] This was a critical first step but the legislation left the role and the requirements ill defined. Important questions remain to be answered. For those 25 chief financial officer (CFO) agencies that are mandated to have a COO, what are the expected duties of the COO? And what type of executive should be designated as COO? Currently, most departments and agencies with designated COOs have made this a titular function of the Deputy Secretary without creating a new position or establishing a new and clear sphere of influence and decision rights for the COO. I believe the position should also be mandated for bureaus

---

[83] GPRA Modernization Act of 2010, Pub. L. No. 111-352, 124 Stat. 3866 (2011)

and small agencies, better defined, and, in many cases, filled by career senior executives, ideally ones who thoroughly understand the history and culture of their agency or department. Most importantly, these senior executives should have a proven demonstration of the competencies required to drive transformational change.

The United Kingdom (UK) has the position of Secretary General for all major ministries. The Secretary General is the COO/CMO who focuses on how to improve the economy, efficiency, and effectiveness of the government and address its "high-risk" areas. An equivalent COO/CMO position in the U.S. could do the same irrespective of which party or person occupies the White House and key political appointee positions.

Secretaries General in the UK have a 5-year performance-based contract that can only be extended once. In my view, this concept has merit in the U.S. government. The parallel COO position could be filled by career (preferably) or non-career SES-level professionals or presidential appointees, ideally on a competitive basis.

Adoption of the COO/CMO concept in the Federal government will be particularly important in the case of the DOD. DOD is a very large, important, diverse, and complex entity with a strong culture. It also has seven management issues that have made the GAO's High-Risk List,[84] shares two of the government-wide High-Risk areas, and is the tail wagging the dog in achieving a "clean" opinion on its financial statements. Having a Deputy Secretary-level COO/CMO in the DOD, but in a role separate from the current Deputy Secretary, would create a more reasonable division of responsibilities and span of control immediately below the Secretary level. The current Deputy would be policy oriented and externally focused, while the COO/CMO would be internally focused on management of operations—the ideal position from which to lead transformations. The new COO/CMO should be a term appointment (e.g., 5 years) with a performance contract. All internal management functions and business transformation efforts should report to this position.

In addition to the department-level COO/CMO, each of the military services and major defense agencies (what DOD calls its Fourth Estate) should also have COOs/CMOs with term appointments and performance contracts. Optimally, these officers would have dual reporting lines to the department COO/CMO and the head of their service or Fourth Estate entity. All COO/CMO candidates would have to meet an appropriate set of qualification requirements to be appointed. This approach would serve to improve the quality, consistency, and continuity within these critical positions and, most importantly, establish a nexus for innovation and transformation.

---

[84] U.S. Government Accountability Office. (2015). High-risk list. Retrieved from http://www.gao.gov/highrisk/overview

In my view, all COO/CMO positions in the U.S. government should be filled by individuals who meet specific statutory qualification requirements. These requirements should include significant leadership and operational management experience spanning a number of functional areas. They should also include a demonstrated ability to achieve transformational change and deliver positive outcomes. Ideally, COO/CMO candidates would have both public and private sector experience. And as recommended for DOD, civilian COOs/CMOs should be appointed for a period of at least 5 years and should be covered by a performance contract. This approach would significantly improve the consistency and continuity of key operational transformations in government. It would also significantly improve the efficiency, effectiveness, and credibility of the Federal government compared to the status quo.

From a personal perspective, I am pleased to say that a vast majority of the transformational changes made at the GAO during my tenure are still in place. The true test of a successful transformation is whether the changes are still in place and whether they have been institutionalized 5–10 years after the leader who promoted them left. That is what real transformation is all about.

Employee Engagement Through Collaborative Leadership

By Robert Tobias, former President, National Treasury Employees Union

Introduction

Collaborative labor-management relations are critical to obtaining the employee engagement necessary to increase productivity in the Federal government. When President Obama issued Executive Order (EO) 13522, *Creating Labor-Management Forums to Improve Delivery of Government Services*, he recognized that the engagement of employees through their unions "will improve the productivity and effectiveness of the Federal Government," and he wanted "managers and employees to collaborate in continuing to deliver the highest quality services to the American people."[85]

Recognizing that employee engagement had declined since 2010, in October 2014, the administration—in the form of the OMB's Deputy Director for Management, the Director of OPM, and the Deputy Director of the White House Office of Personnel—issued a memorandum to all heads of executive departments and agencies entitled *Strengthening Employee Engagement and Organizational Performance*.[86] The memorandum acknowledged the relationship between employee engagement and increased "mission success," mandated development of agency-wide engagement strategies, and, in so doing, specifically noted the role that collaborative labor-management relations can play in "gaining employee commitment and input."[87]

Unfortunately, despite the obvious importance to employee engagement, those responsible for implementing the collaborative labor-management program—primarily members of the SES—have not received sustained policy support or the necessary leadership development support to be successful.

---

[85] Exec. Order No. 13522, Creating labor-management forums to improve delivery of government services. (2009, December 9). Retrieved from https://www.whitehouse.gov/the-press-office/executive-order-creating-labor-management-forums-improve-delivery-government-servic

[86] Donovan, S. (2014, December 23). *Strengthening employee engagement and organizational performance* [Memorandum]. Washington, DC: U.S. Office of Personnel Management. Retrieved from https://www.whitehouse.gov/sites/default/files/omb/memoranda/2015/m-15-04.pdf

[87] Ibid., p. 2.

A brief history of Federal labor relations

Federal sector labor-management relations can be traced to 1962, when President John F. Kennedy issued EO 10988, *Employee-Management Cooperation in the Federal Service*. This EO first established the right of Federal employees to organize and join unions and, through them, collectively bargain over terms and conditions of employment. Those rights have since been codified in law; today, approximately 63 percent of the total Federal workforce (and 80 percent of those eligible for union representation) have elected a labor union to represent their interests. From that beginning until today, relations between agency executives and their union representatives have been adversarial despite the growing evidence that adversarial relationships and employee engagement are antithetical.

There have been two notable exceptions to this adversarial relationship. Shortly after taking office in 1993, President Clinton issued EO 12871, *Labor-Management Partnerships*, mandating agencies to transform the adversarial relationships that had been in existence since 1962 to collaborative relationships through a "partnership" with unions, on the theory that this would contribute to providing "the highest quality services to the American people."[88] In 2009, after the swinging policy pendulum returned to adversarial relationships under President Bush, the policy swung back once again when President Obama issued the same mandate as President Clinton through EO 13522, charging his cabinet and agency heads—and those executives who worked for them—to once again take a collaborative approach to labor-management relationships.[89]

Unfortunately, the results of those mandates have been unproven and underwhelming. Managers and union leader partners implementing EO 12871 self-reported broad creation of labor-management partnerships, improved organizational results, and improved employee engagement. However, there were few quantifiable results and no employee engagement data because OPM had not yet initiated the FEVS.[90]

Notwithstanding the fact that the National Council on Labor-Management Relations mandated that all labor-management efforts be measured against (1) mission accomplishment and service quality, (2) employee satisfaction and engagement, and (3) labor-management relations pursuant to EO 13522,

---

[88] Exec. Order No. 12871, Labor-management partnerships. (1993, October 1). Retrieved from http://govinfo.library.unt.edu/npr/library/direct/orders/24ea.html
[89] Exec. Order No. 13522.
[90] Masters, M. F., Merchant, C. S., & Tobias, R. (2010). *Engaging Federal employees through their union representatives to improve agency performance*. Retrieved from http://www.govexec.com/pdfs/021010ar1.pdf; White Paper Presented to the National Council on Federal Labor-Management Relations; Defense Partnership Council Meeting, 64 Fed. Reg. 3685 (1999, January 25). Retrieved from https://www.gpo.gov/fdsys/granule/FR-1999-01-25/99-1564; U.S. Government Accountability Office. (2001). High-risk series: An update. Retrieved from http://www.gao.gov/products/GAO-01-263

the impact has been limited.[91] There is little evidence of increased organizational results. The FEVS Employee Engagement Index (EEI) measures the intensity of the positive relationship between leaders and their followers, and each of the three elements of the FEVS EEI—Leaders Lead, Supervisors, and Intrinsic Work Experience—was lower or equal in 2015 versus 2010.[92]

	2010	2011	2012	2013	2014	2015
Leaders Lead	55%	56%	54%	53%	50%	51%
Supervisors	71%	72%	70%	70%	71%	71%
Intrinsic Work Experience	72%	72%	71%	69%	68%	69%
Government-wide Index Score	66%	67%	65%	64%	63%	64%

Source: OPM FEVS[93]

How can these results be true? Those SES members all met OPM's ECQs. As we know, those ECQs, first established in 1997, are required for entry into the SES. However, in my view, those ECQs did not (and still do not) sufficiently take into account the need for career executives to lead collaboratively and create collaborative cultures, especially when it comes to their dealings with employee unions. I believe the ECQs should go further than they do currently, to require authenticity, a high degree of emotional intelligence, and the ability to create a culture of collaboration. These are the leadership qualities that are necessary to lead effectively in today's complex Federal environment, particularly when it comes to transforming agency cultures from those characterized by adversarial labor-management relationships to ones that are collaborative. And without that sort of culture change, a truly engaged workforce will remain elusive for most agencies.

Easier mandated than done

However, as in so many things, this has been easier said than done. The Federal government's culture—that is, "the way we do things around here"—has long encouraged and supported adversarial labor-management relationships. There are many reasons for the adversarial mindset. For

[91] Ibid.
[92] U.S. Office of Personnel Management. (2014). *Labor-management relations in the executive branch.* Washington, DC: Office of Personnel Management. Retrieved from https://www.opm.gov/policy-data-oversight/labor-management-relations/reports/labor-management-relations-in-the-executive-branch-2014.pdf
[93] 9696 U.S. Office of Personnel Management. (2015, October 6). *OPM releases complete 2015 Federal Employee Viewpoint Survey results* [Press release]. Retrieved from https://www.opm.gov/news/releases/2015/10/opm-releases-complete-2015-Federal-employee-viewpoint-survey-results

example, union-organizing drives often include rhetoric that vilifies agency managers (something managers don't forget), while promising benefits through collective bargaining that simply cannot be fulfilled. So campaign promises become litigation, in part because unions have no other way to make the workplace more efficient and effective, and in part to prove to their constituents that that they are "fighting" on their behalf. This further entrenches adversarial feelings, and, presidential mandates notwithstanding, the vicious "I win, you lose" circle continues.

This adversarial culture is consistent with the command-and-control organizational structure in the Federal government. And because there can be no guarantee that if labor and management give up their adversarial "arms" they would achieve better results for their respective constituents, there is little cultural incentive to change. This is despite the fact that there is both qualitative and some quantitative evidence that a collaborative approach to labor relations does seem to increase agency productivity, decrease time spent bargaining, and reduce dollars spent litigating grievances and unfair labor practice charges. Moreover, there is plenty of compelling evidence from the FEVS to support the idea that the failure to create a more collaborative labor-management culture has contributed to declining employee engagement.

As noted above, the Leaders Lead element of the EEI, which is directly relevant to the connection between members of the SES and those they lead, dropped from 55% in 2010 to 51% in 2015.[94]

And of the five questions in the Leaders Lead index, the two most relevant to leading collaboratively—the ability to generate high levels of commitment and motivation, and respect for senior leadership—also declined significantly, from 45% to 39% (13 percent) and 56% to 51% (9 percent), respectively, from 2010 to 2015.[95]

These data explain the difficulty of creating a collaborative labor-management relationship. For example, because senior executives do not trust union leaders enough to share information, lines of communication to and from employees dry up, and employees may be reluctant to share information that may be essential to improving efficiency and effectiveness. Even worse, there is little incentive for workers to provide any of their discretionary energy—that is, the willingness to go above and beyond their assigned duties—to accomplish organization goals. For their part, union leaders do not want to risk appearing "weak" by behaving collaboratively if they do not trust that management will reciprocate.

[94] Ibid.
[95] Ibid.

What does collaborative leadership look like?

Collaborative leaders exhibit a mindset. They demonstrate values and assumptions that drive collaborative behavior and use of a collaborative problem-solving process that leads to outcomes that are different and better than any party envisioned when they began to address the problem.

The behaviors of a collaborative leader include authenticity; the ability to be aware of one's own strengths and weaknesses; an understanding of the impact of behavior on others; the ability to identify "core values, identity, emotions, motives and goals";[96] the willingness to be relationally transparent by "sharing their core feelings, motives, and inclinations with others, and showing both positive and negative aspects of themselves to others";[97] compassion; curiosity; the willingness to hold oneself accountable for one's behavior rather than blaming others;[98] and a focus on creating the trust necessary for the participants to feel sufficiently safe to offer their ideas, insights, and possible solutions into the mix.

A collaborative leader is willing to use an interest-based problem-solving process to stimulate the identification of interests, which creates a broader base for reaching resolution rather than fighting narrowly over positions and creating winners and losers. A collaborative SES leader recognizes that it may take longer to reach a decision using an interest-based problem-solving process, but implementation is faster because the interests of all parties have been met, and all parties are collaborating to implement the final decision.

Collaborative SES leaders are not born, they are developed. There are now Federal sector data to support such a provocative finding.[99] For example, J. Peter Leeds identified members of the SES who had participated in the highest number of leadership development opportunities and discovered that those agencies also had the highest employee engagement scores.[100]

Similarly, the Merit Systems Protection Board in a recently released study, *Training and Development for the Senior Executive Service: A Necessary Investment*, observed that "while training is essential for individuals across all grade levels, it is arguably most important that those at the highest levels

[96] Northouse, P. G. (2016). *Leadership. Theory and practice.* Thousand Oaks, CA: Sage Publications. Neck, C. P., Manz, C. C., & Houghton, J. D. (2016). *Self-leadership. The definitive guide to personal excellence.* Thousand Oaks, CA: Sage Publications.

[97] Ibid., p. 203.

[98] Schwarz, R. (2013). *Smart leaders, smarter teams: How you and your team get unstuck to achieve results.* San Francisco, CA: Jossey-Bass.

[99] Goleman, D., Boyatzis, R., McKee, A. (2002). Primal leadership: Realizing the power of emotional intelligence—Tapping into your team's emotional intelligence. Retrieved from http://hbswk.hbs.edu/archive/2875.html

[100] Leeds, J. P. (2015, November 24). Investment in senior executive training pays off. Government Executive. Retrieved from http://www.govexec.com/management/2015/11/investment-senior-executive-training-pays/123956

[senior executives] get the support they need to effectively carry out their roles and responsibilities."[101] Yet only half of the members of the SES complete the annually required Employee Development Plans.[102]

The necessary development includes the willingness to engage in the self-reflection necessary to identify one's assumptions and values in order to understand what drives our behavior and consider whether what drives our current behavior should be changed. To actually stop, reflect, make a choice to change, and truly change, successful SES leaders need the emotional intelligence of self-awareness to recognize their emotions, self-management to "stop" rather than act automatically in the face of often strong emotions, social awareness to understand the impact of their behavior on others, and relationship management to be able to create and maintain the relationships necessary for success.[103]

How do career leaders develop a collaborative organizational culture?

Personal leader behavior change to a collaborative mindset is the necessary interrelated action to creating an organizational culture that behaves collaboratively. As stated by McGuire and Rhodes in *Transforming Your Leadership Culture*: "Culture change is a show up, stand-up, participative, put-yourself-on-the-line personal process. Culture isn't an object or system out there. It's internal. You are in the culture, and the culture is in you."[104]

McGuire and Rhodes describe three levels of organizational culture:[105]

- **Dependent-Conformer:** Authority and control are held at the top, success depends on obedience to authority and honoring the code, mistakes are treated as weakness, and feedback is not valued.[106]

- **Independent-Achiever:** Authority and control are distributed through the ranks, success means mastery of systems that produce results, mistakes are opportunities to learn, and feedback is valued as a means to enhance advancement.[107]

- **Interdependent-Collaborator:** Authority and control are shared based on strategic competence for the whole organization, success means collaboration across all systems for shared results, mistakes are embraced

---

[101] U.S. Merit Systems Protection Board. (2015). *Training and development for the Senior Executive Service: A necessary investment.* Washington, DC: U.S. Merit Systems Protection Board. Retrieved from http://www.mspb.gov/netsearch/viewdocs.aspx?docnumber=1253299&version=1258322&application=ACROBAT
[102] Ibid., p. 17.
[103] Goleman, D. Primal leadership.
[104] McGuire, J. B., & Rhodes, G. B. (2009). *Transforming your leadership culture.* San Francisco, CA: Jossey-Bass.
[105] Ibid., p. 297.
[106] Ibid.
[107] Ibid

as opportunities for organizational learning, and feedback is valued as essential for collective success.[108]

According to McGuire and Rhodes, it is difficult for senior leaders to move themselves and those they lead from one level to another. That movement requires the willingness to accept that there may be different ways of doing things, as well as different ways of making sense of the world. Furthermore, a successful leader must have a willingness to challenge old ideas and test new ones. And after such testing, the leader must be willing to implement the new ideas until they replace the old.

Thus, if a president—or a senior executive—wants to establish a collaborative labor-management relationship, they must challenge themselves and their organizations to transform from a culture of Independent-Achievers to one of Interdependent-Collaborators.

Although the October 2014 memorandum increased the government-wide EEI goal from 63 in 2014 to 67 in 2017 and mandated the creation of processes to achieve it, neither OMB nor OPM mandated that government SES leaders be provided the necessary leader development opportunities to achieve the employee engagement goal.[109] Nor did the memorandum mandate that union leaders receive leadership development opportunities. A mandate to "partner" assumes that a union "partner" exists. Providing leadership development training to union leaders is necessary to support changing behavior from solely adversarial to adversarial and collaborative.

Conclusion

Goals cannot be achieved without providing those mandated to achieve the goals with the tools they need to be successful. The personal and organizational change necessary to create collaborative labor-management relationships has not occurred in part because of a lack of leadership competencies.

The need for SES leaders to develop themselves,[110] develop self-awareness,[111] develop necessary social and emotional intelligence,[112] and become authentic is clear. It is unfair to mandate new goals that require changed behavior to create the collaborative environment necessary for employee engagement without providing members of the SES the opportunity to learn what new behavior is needed and support them as they develop the new behaviors necessary for success.

---

[108] Ibid.
[109] Donovan, S. *Strengthening employee engagement.*
[110] McGuire, J. B. *Transforming your leadership culture,* p. 20.
[111] Kegan, R. (1994). *In over our heads: The mental demands of modern life.* Cambridge, MA: Harvard University Press.
[112] Goleman, D. *Primal leadership.*

Concluding Commentary and Recommendations

Introduction: Competencies both enduring and emergent

Managing complexity and crisis. Driving through the turbulence of transformation. Acting courageously. Leading collaboratively. Mobilizing for a unified, whole-of-government effort. Our contributors—all very successful senior government leaders—are unanimous in suggesting that in order for 21st century senior executives to effectively navigate the kinds of complex challenges they will face, they must be able to rapidly develop and demonstrate these and other emerging senior leadership competencies.

Significantly, none of these emerging qualities is part of OPM's current leadership competency model, or as yet under consideration for it. Nor are these qualities part of the ECQs derived from that model. That's problematic, since those ECQs serve as the admission test for the SES. Given that the ECQs and their constituent competencies drive executive development, selection, and now (with OPM's common ECQ-based SES performance management framework) even performance in the Federal government, we may be preparing the 21st century SES to lead last century's government.

In addition, those 20th century ECQs have become generic and purely instrumental; they could apply to any leader anywhere. They no longer take into account the unique leadership qualities required of a senior career executive in the Federal government…qualities that stem from the institutional roles that we expect that executive to play, as well as the values that undergird them.

This is not to say the ECQs should be so narrowly government-centric as to preclude executives from the private sector and NGOs from qualifying for the SES. Far from it. But those executives need to come equipped with—or very quickly develop—what I would argue are the unique leadership qualities necessary to succeed in the upper echelons of government service.

Not that the ECQs and their constituent competencies are obsolete. Many of the leadership competencies that compose the OPM model are enduring, as relevant to leaders today as they were as much as a millennium ago. But it does mean that those competencies, both emerging and enduring, must be refreshed frequently enough to keep up with the dizzying pace of change.

RECOMMENDATION 3.1: PUT 'PUBLIC SERVICE' BACK IN THE ECQs

Introduction: *Ethos* as a Core Qualification

Today's ECQs are, at their root, *instrumental* in nature. That is, they represent generic means to equally generic ends. In so doing, they ignore (at some peril, I think) the essential public-ness of the SES. Indeed, on close examination, they could be written for any organization, public or private. That is not, in my view, a good thing, given the unique institutional roles SES members play in our system of government. Senior executives are in the public service after all; they are called upon to do and decide things that senior executives in the private and nonprofit sectors are not, yet their ability to do those things is not evaluated as part of their admission to the SES.

Moreover, while *instrumental* leadership qualifications may vary—by mission, function, or operation—those that are *institutional* in nature may not. They represent (and operationalize) the common values and ethos of senior public service, regardless of where and how it is practiced, and they should be etched in marble…and required of anyone who aspires to serve in that senior capacity. Thus, OPM should reengineer its ECQs and, in so doing, modernize how it assesses and qualifies members of the SES. In that regard, those ECQs must reflect a common set of core institutional qualifications (where today they do not), coupled with a variable set of instrumental ones that reflect the variegated nature of today's senior service and that may differ over time, as well as by agency, mission, and function.

A more variegated senior service

When it comes to ECQs, one size may no longer fit all—especially because the SES is not the mobile monolith it was originally envisioned to be. As we have seen, there are a number of specialized agency—and mission-specific senior services in agencies like the Central Intelligence Agency, the Federal Bureau of Investigation, FAA, and the SEC—and there may be as many as three or four distinctly different (albeit informal) "clans" in the title 5 version of the SES: those who lead technical and functional staffs like IT and HR; those who manage agency-specific operations; and those who lead at a government-wide, enterprise level.

Thus, while it is imperative that a single set of core institutional qualifications binds together all career executives, it is hard to imagine that a single set of instrumental qualifications can suffice to identify and differentiate those who are worthy SES candidates. Yet, that is exactly what we have today.

The fact is that senior technical and functional executives may be required to lead in different ways than their "line" colleagues who are in charge of major organizations or programs. Indeed, by law and administrative custom, many of those senior technical and professional executives are not even considered part of the SES, despite the executive-level impact of their decisions and actions.

Take the case of functional leadership—as demonstrated by a chief scientist or laboratory director, for example, or even a senior legal or legislative affairs executive. By definition, their authority is based far more on functional knowledge and expertise than on hierarchical position or staff size.

However, the ECQs treat them all alike. For example, when an OPM qualifications review board (QRB) considers an SES candidate's ability to lead people, it typically looks for evidence of head count; that is, the number of people that the candidate has supervised. And candidates are often remanded or even rejected by a QRB because they haven't presided over a bureaucratic pyramid of sufficient size. But just how much is enough? 10 people? 50? 100? And what if that candidate led lots of people but not particularly well?

It gets even trickier for senior technical and professional leaders, many of whom are not even eligible to be members of the SES. Relegated to a parallel universe complete with its own alphabetic designations—STs for senior scientific and technical leaders, SLs for senior-level professionals—they are often seen as second-class cousins of "real" senior executives. After all, they can't possibly meet the same ECQs.

However, while a senior scientist in a government laboratory may not manage hundreds (or even dozens) of people, he or she may have an even greater impact on our lives, exercising leadership that is based not on hierarchical position but on technical knowledge and influence. The behaviors and competencies associated with that kind of knowledge-based leadership are likely far different than those associated with the traditional "hard power" of positional authority.

This is not to suggest that a single set of ECQs should be abandoned. The importance of the "C" in the ECQs cannot be overstated. There are clearly some common, core leadership attributes that every senior career leader should be able to demonstrate, regardless of their agency mission, functional clan, or technical field. But, in my view, these have far more to do with the common values and *ethos* of senior public service—the seminal institutional roles we described in our previous section—than the more instrumental competencies that predominate the OPM competency model and the ECQs.

The same may be said of those who lead in other nontraditional ways. What about the leader who is responsible for overseeing contracts covering millions of procurement dollars and thousands of contractor employees? Because that leader isn't managing civil servants, he or she doesn't get any credit for leading people, despite the fact that in today's co-produced government, that specialist may have far more responsibility—and impact—than his or her classic counterpart in charge of a large program unit. Or what about the leader who is responsible for driving a Cross-Agency Priority Goal under the Government Performance and Results Act[113] and is accountable for achieving interagency

[113] Government Performance and Results Act of 1993, Pub. L. No. 103-62, 107 Stat. 285 (1993).

unity of effort but without any formal chain-of-command authority over those agencies?

A menu of instrumental ECQs

The ECQs should be re-engineered to accommodate both of these dimensions: on one hand, a set of core qualifications that are institutional and enduring in nature, and would thus be required of anyone who aspires to admission in any one of the Federal government's several senior services; and on the other, a menu of additional core qualifications that are more emergent, representing more generic, instrumental leadership competencies—including those that could apply to any leader anywhere—with agencies permitted some flexibility in choosing among them. Note that these instrumental qualifications would *not* be technical in nature but would be additions to a new ECQ framework.

In that regard, I would argue that when it comes to defining what it takes to be a senior executive, today's ECQs (and many of their constituent competencies) are based on an industrial-age model that is implicitly biased toward the "hard" or positional power of hierarchical leadership. The model discounts other emerging information-age leadership models that are more reflective of today's (and tomorrow's) co-produced, connected, chaotically complex, and collaborative Federal enterprise that Thad Allen and Bob Tobias describe. By focusing on classic industrial-age managerial competencies, the current model excludes those others kinds of senior leaders whose impact may be far greater than that of those at the top of an organizational pyramid.

RECOMMENDATION 3.2: CONSTANTLY MODERNIZE THE ECQ FRAMEWORK

Introduction: Leading last century's government

In 21st century government, the implicit bias in the ECQs (not to mention the statutory definition of the SES itself!) creates arbitrary, outmoded, and ultimately dysfunctional distinctions between classes and clans of senior leaders, some in and some excluded from the SES. In my view, a senior leader is a senior leader is a senior leader—whether he or she leads through hierarchical authority or the "soft" power of expert technical or functional acumen. When those increasingly artificial distinctions become barriers to a whole-of-government senior leadership corps, government performance suffers.

A few far-sighted agencies have realized that these 20th-century distinctions are obsolete and have taken a more ecumenical approach to their senior services. For instance, the CIA's Senior Intelligence Service includes spies, analysts, scientists and engineers, and mission support staff, and the Agency has become quite adept at moving its senior officers among the various "tribes" to match talent to mission. As Pat Kennedy notes in his chapter, the Senior Foreign Service is similarly fungible, with broad "cones" of career specialization linked together by common mission and *ethos*.

Regrettably, OPM has taken the position that executives in those (and other) non-title 5 senior services do not automatically qualify for the original SES. This is despite the fact that they lead—and lead successfully—some of the most complex and dangerous tasks that government undertakes.

Industrial versus information-age leadership

The current set of ECQs implicitly assumes that leadership occurs in a hierarchy, characterized by formal position-based authority and classic bureaucratic power relationships, and QRBs assess ECQs according to this lens, emphasizing layers and levels and numbers of subordinates. Moreover, the current system takes for granted that the executive is bounded by superiors above and subordinates below, and and that even peer-to-peer relationships occur in that bounded chain-of-command context.

Thus, today's industrial-age model of executive leadership is assumed to occur *within* the hierarchical confines and contours of a particular agency, with everything else treated as part of the external environment—to be scanned, sensed, navigated, manipulated, or even dominated.[114]

Yet as Thad Allen notes, today's senior executives more and more often find themselves having to lead others outside their department or agency—and outside the comfort and convenience of their chain of command. For example, as our Section 1 contributors so emphatically note, much of what challenges government today occurs in an interagency or intergovernmental or even international context where, as a practical matter, there is no one in charge to decide a particular course of action or adjudicate conflicting interests.

In my view, the ability to lead without resorting to formal authority is one of the most compelling 21st century senior executive competencies, but there are others associated with that sort of extra-organizational leadership challenge.

The conversation with Michèle Flournoy, recounted in Section 1, offers a striking analogy. Former Secretary Flournoy talks about the need for nation-states to employ a combination of "hard" (that is, military) and "soft" power —economic, diplomatic, informational, etc.—to protect or project national interests. It strikes me that tomorrow's senior executives will need a similar set of tools…not just the hard power of position and hierarchy (even implicitly or benignly applied) but also the soft power derived from leveraging relationships, networks, interests, and values across government hierarchies and stovepipes.

The same can be said about the ECQs. Even while some of the competencies that compose them have changed, the ECQs themselves have remained static, the same today as in the last century[115]—established in an era when the

---

[114] Sanders, R. P. *Tackling wicked government problems.*
[115] U.S. Office of Personnel Management. Senior Executive Service executive core qualifications. Retrieved from https://www.opm.gov/policy-data-oversight/senior-executive-service/execu-tive-core-qualifications

world and our government were all much simpler. There was a time not so very long ago when bureaucracy wasn't the pejorative that it is today, and where executives could survive and thrive in their own organizational and functional stovepipes, relying on the hard power of formal authority and all of the classic leadership competencies that underlie it to get things done. That is less the case today, and it certainly will not be so tomorrow when the soft power of engagement and collaboration so artfully articulated by Bob Tobias may determine the success or failure of a senior executive.

To be sure, the ECQs use words that could be construed to encompass 21st century competencies. For example, the fifth ECQ, Building Coalitions, talks about developing networks and building alliances, collaborating across boundaries to build strategic relationships and achieve common goals, and gaining consensus through persuasion and negotiation. One could read this as applying to either inter- and intra-organizational experiences, but the SES selectee who demonstrates them in that latter, purely internal context—as the vast majority do—would most assuredly pass QRB review.

Skating to where the puck is going to be

Part of this is due to methodological inertia. The best leaders and organizations—in government or otherwise—rarely succeed by looking in the rearview mirror; however, that is precisely how OPM's current competency model is constructed. This is less a matter of policy than methodology, which holds that to be valid, a particular competency must be thoroughly (and empirically) documented in today's successful leaders. Thus, when OPM validates a particular leadership competency, its focus is squarely on those qualities that have made *current* senior executives successful, rather than those attributes and abilities that may be required by their successors *in the future*.

Yet, it is clear that there are leadership competencies—such as those described by our contributing authors—that will emerge as quickly as that future, and they too must be identified, validated, and, more importantly, deliberately developed in the next generation of senior executives (we'll examine ways to do that in Section 4).

OPM has updated its leadership competency model from time to time, adding some competencies and eliminating others, but even in such instances, the process OPM employs in that regard is classic, and classically ensconced in the past and present tense. It focuses on what is—and not what *will be*— required of senior leaders. The same may be said for the ECQs; they too are rooted firmly in a leader's past and present, not his or her future.

In other words, the ECQs and the competencies that compose them assume that the past is prologue. That's all well and good; as noted, there are clearly institutional qualities (and some instrumental ones) that are potentially timeless. But given the many myriad challenges facing our nation and our Federal government, one must question whether a model that defaults to what made executives successful today will suffice for their successors. Indeed, as Bob Tobias suggests, it may very well be that we're rewarding current members of the SES—and developing those who aspire to it—to lead in ways that are already obsolete or even dysfunctional, or that may be in the near future.

Bottom line: As I noted in the Section 3 Introduction, hockey superstar Wayne Gretzky once said that the secret to his success was that he learned to skate where the puck was going to be rather than where it was at any given instant…and those who did the latter were always a step or two behind. The same holds true for leadership competencies. If they are developed through the rearview mirror, we'll never see what's coming at us. Fortunately, there are professionally accepted ways to identify and validate those emerging leadership competencies that will be required in the future. OPM needs to adopt them and develop a process to regularly refresh its model and the ECQs.

RECOMMENDATION 3.3: ESTABLISH AN ENTERPRISE LEADERSHIP ECQ

Introduction: A new normal for Federal executives?

As many have noted, the original architects of the SES envisioned a mobile corps of seasoned career executives who could be plugged in to almost any leadership challenge wherever it emerged and successfully take it on. And while that founding vision has yet to be fully realized, we have argued that the institutional roles it proffered may be more relevant today than at any time since the birth of the SES.

In that regard, the nature of today's virtual, interconnected, and "Webbed" world has forced us to rethink some of our fundamental assumptions about leadership in general and, in our case, in the Federal government—and the competencies that have come to define it. For example, as Thad Allen and others (including myself) have argued, much of what government does today is collaboratively co-produced with a whole constellation of public and private entities, from other agencies and levels of government to NGOs and even other countries and international bodies. As Jackson Nickerson and I have suggested, this is the Federal government's "new normal."[116] From the short-term dramas of hurricanes and oil well disasters to the decades-long fights against cancer, poverty, and terrorism, government challenges are becoming far more complex, not only involving multiple agencies but also spanning well beyond the Federal government's boundaries. They require collaborative, integrated responses from the complex network of co-producers who share any given mission space. And they require senior executives who can lead those networks.

---

[116] Sanders, R. P. *Tackling wicked government problems.*

These *extra-organizational* challenges share two common denominators. First, as we have noted, effective responses require a leader who can mobilize multiple agencies and organizations—each with their own agendas, interests, cultures, and politics—to work together, which is often a mission impossible in today's functionally stove-piped Federal government. Second, I would contend that to do so, executives require a whole new set of leadership competencies…competencies that, with some exception, have not been deliberately or formally developed. As a consequence, many SES members are ill-equipped to deal with them.[117]

While it may not use those terms, the U.S. military recognized the need for this kind of integrated, "enterprise" leadership over 30 years ago, when a few visionaries realized (after some painful lessons on an island named Grenada) that to effectively fight—and more importantly, win—the wars of the 21st century, our armed forces needed to do so in a far more integrated way. In response, they made "joint-ness" part of our commissioned officer corps' genetic code. Tragically, that painful lesson had to be re-learned by the Intelligence Community (IC) on 9/11, and, as a consequence, the 2004 Intelligence Reform and Terrorism Prevention Act[118] mandated a similar approach to developing senior civilian "enterprise" leaders in the IC.

To provide an empirical foundation for that mandate, IC leaders (I was among them) set about to identify the leadership competencies that would be essential to the IC's future success, rather than its past. And we found them—and were able to validate them in the formal sense of that word—by seeking out and studying those executive role models who had successfully led the Intelligence Enterprise before and immediately after the attacks. In other words, we looked at those leaders who had managed to operate effectively across the many stovepipes that had impeded pre-9/11 integration and information sharing.

Developing enterprise leaders: The case of the IC[119]

Among other things, we found that those role models were *systems thinkers;* that is, they could see and connect the dots associated with complex, multidimensional challenges. They could also *take an extra-organizational, enterprise-wide perspective,* demonstrating the courage to eschew narrow, parochial (typically organizational) interests in favor of those that furthered the larger enterprise of organizations bound together by common mission goals. And finally, they had the *ability to build complex, boundary-spanning collaborative networks* and then to employ these networks to collect and share information and intelligence, gain insight, exercise non-hierarchical influence, and, above all, get things done across the IC.

---

[117] Ibid.
[118] Intelligence Reform and Terrorism Prevention Act of 2004, Pub. L. No. 108-458, 118 Stat. 3638 (2004).
[119] Sanders, R. P. *Tackling wicked government problems.*

With those results in hand, we published a directive establishing those competencies—clustered and collectively labeled *Leading the Intelligence Enterprise* —as a sixth ECQ that would be required for promotion into any of the several SES (including the original title 5 SES) that covered senior civilian leaders in the IC.[120] As part of that ECQ, we also established a mandatory mobility requirement—defined as at least one interagency assignment—as a prerequisite to promotion to senior rank. And because most IC executives were unable to meet those new requirements (they were simply not brought up that way), we phased them in over 3 years, from 2007 through 2009.[121]

The IC isn't the only part of the Federal government to recognize these emerging competencies. More or less contemporaneously, the DOD validated a similar set for its SES members, collectively labeled *Leading the Defense Enterprise*. Because it lacked a legislative mandate comparable to Goldwater-Nichols[122] or the IC's Intelligence Reform Act,[123] the Department chose not to establish that competency cluster as an ECQ (although it could have done so administratively). However, DOD officials did make a mobility assignment *after* an individual's initial SES selection a mandatory prerequisite for SES salary increases above a certain level.[124]

We also saw the need for similar enterprise leadership competencies during and immediately after Hurricane Katrina, when unconnected Federal, state, and local relief efforts made a horrendous natural disaster even worse. However, there was a silver lining of sorts. The Federal government's after-action review of the disaster led to the issuance of EO 13434, *National Security Professional Development*, establishing the National Security Professional Development (NSPD) program. Taking a page from similar efforts (and antecedents!) in DOD and the IC, NSPD was specifically designed to develop the very same enterprise leadership competencies across the agencies that made up the U.S. national security community. In so doing, it sought to produce enterprise leaders who could successfully lead a whole-of-government/ whole-of-nation response to the next Katrina.[125]

---

[120] Office of the Director of National Intelligence. (2010). Intelligence Community Directive No. 610, Competency Directories for the Intelligence Community Workforce. Retrieved from https://www.dni.gov/files/documents/ICD/ICD_610.pdf
[121] 124124 Office of the Director of National Intelligence. (2013). Intelligence Community Directive No. 660, Intelligence Community Civilian Joint Duty Program. Retrieved from https://fas.org/irp/dni/icd/icd-660.pdf
[122] 125125 Goldwater-Nichols Department of Defense Reorganization Act of 1986, Pub. L. No. 99-433 (1986).
[123] Intelligence Reform and Terrorism Prevention Act.
[124] 127127 U.S. Department of Defense Directive No. 1400.25, Vol. 1403 (1996), DoD Civilian Personnel Management System.
[125] Exec. Order No. 13434, National security professional development (2007, May 17). Retrieved from https://www.gpo.gov/fdsys/pkg/WCPD-2007-05-21/pdf/WCPD-2007-05-21-Pg650.pdf

Learning to lead the whole-of-government *before* a crisis

Unfortunately, that never happened. For years, the NSPD program atrophied from benign neglect (that has changed recently, at least somewhat; see Section 4), but that should not diminish the painful lessons that engendered it. And while those lessons were all learned *in extremis*, they may be applied to the many other Category 5 challenges our nation faces today, like global economic recovery, climate change, healthcare reform, globalization and international trade, and cybersecurity. What is their common denominator? These challenges are all "inter" in nature—interagency, intergovernmental, international—and they demand no less than leaders who can leverage an integrated, enterprise-wide effort to be successful.

For example, enterprise leaders must have an intimate understanding of the structures and cultures of various agencies and organizations that must work together as an enterprise to confront any whole-of-government challenge, yet the vast majority of senior executives have little or no experience outside their home agency. Similarly, enterprise leaders must be able to exercise influence without formal authority (soft power); yet, as we have argued, most current executives have learned to lead through the hard power of formal authority.

As Michèle Flournoy suggests, we need senior career executives who can leverage both hard and soft power to devise and execute whole-of-government and whole-of-nation solutions—in other words, enterprise leaders who can understand, build, and leverage a network of critical organizational and individual actors to achieve results that are impossible when those organizations and individuals act alone. And the competencies required to do so are neither formally recognized nor deliberately developed as part of the ECQs.

They need to be. These competencies are not new. Effective enterprise leaders like Beth McGrath, Thad Allen, Mike Hayden, and former Director of National Intelligence Mike McConnell[126] have learned to look (and lead) beyond the confines of their immediate organizations. The problem is that with few exceptions—the U.S. military and, more recently, the IC—these enterprise leaders have not been deliberately developed (Beth McGrath's more or less accidental journey, as recounted in her chapter in Section 2, is a case in point). That clearly must change if our government is to successfully confront those great "inter" challenges it faces now and in the future.

Establishing a sixth "super" ECQ

It is clear that at least for some senior executive positions—perhaps those at the very top of the bureaucratic pyramid that have cross-cutting, enterprise-wide responsibilities—a super ECQ may be needed...something like *Leading the Federal Enterprise*, similar to the one adopted by the IC and DOD. This

---

[126] Jackson, N. and Sanders, R. P. *Tackling wicked government problems.*

ECQ would require fundamentally different experiences (and the competencies that come with them) from those needed to lead an agency. And even though the competencies would use many of the same words as those in some of today's ECQs, they could only be demonstrated in an interagency (or intergovernmental, international, etc.) context.

And while one could argue that these competencies need not (and thus should not) be required of all career executives, especially at the entry level of the SES, it is clear that they are undoubtedly a prerequisite for a select subset of the government's most senior career executive positions. For my part, I would contend that every member of the SES needs to acquire, continuously develop, and demonstrate these competencies. Others may disagree, but more about that in our next section.

RECOMMENDATION 3.4: REQUIRE DUE DILIGENCE TO ASSESS AN EXECUTIVE'S CHARACTER

Introduction: Character matters

Most would agree that character is an essential attribute of a successful senior leader, perhaps even the most important of all leadership qualities. I would argue that this is especially the case in government. Indeed, in the chapter Steve Kelman and I contributed to this anthology, our research suggested that character may be one of the keys to a senior government official's success. In the case of the executives we studied, we saw it as the courage and intestinal fortitude to do the right thing, even when doing so placed those executives at some professional or organizational risk. However, while almost everyone would agree that it is the *sine qua non* of leadership, each of us likely has our own personal definition of it. It's one of those instinctive "I'll know it when I see it" qualities.

We certainly know when it's lacking, especially in the public sector. Just think about some of the more notable lapses in character we have witnessed at senior levels of government—procurement scandals, sexual harassment and misconduct, cover-ups, and whistleblower retaliation. And when the scandal involves a member of the SES, its institutional cost is incalculable—not just on the already-tenuous image of senior public servants in general but also in the administrative or legislative backlash that often comes along with it. Take the case of the recent scandal in VA, where a number of career executives were accused of essentially "cooking the books" to show fictitiously low patient wait times. As bad as the publicity surrounding those cases has been, it pales in comparison to the reaction by Congress, which passed legislation intended to make it easier to fire VA executives and, in at least one other bill, *all* career executives.

The cost of character

Given the cost of a lapse in character, even in a single career executive, wouldn't it be preferable to screen for that quality (or lack thereof) before one is even admitted into the SES…or periodically thereafter, to remain a member of it? Interestingly, integrity used to be an OPM leadership competency, but it has since been dropped in favor of the various instrumental skills that compose today's ECQs. And even when it used to be part of the model, it had little apparent bearing. Having observed, participated in, and presided over hundreds of SES QRBs when integrity was included, I can tell you that it was never specifically mentioned in the proceedings, much less examined in any depth.

Even if it had been, it may not have gone far enough. I would argue that it's not integrity but the broader concept of character—which certainly encompasses integrity, as well as other intangible qualities like courage, public service, duty, and honor—that should stand as its own ECQ, a fundamental in-or-out requirement for admission to, and/or retention in, the SES.

After all, Federal executives, both career and political, swear (literally!) that they will demonstrate character when they take the oath of office, something we have in common with those who wear the uniforms of our armed forces and, as we discussed in the preceding section, something that sets SES members apart from leaders outside of government. To the vast majority of them, that oath is not just a bunch of words recited to check an administrative box. It represents the *ethos* of senior public service, as reflected in the enduring, institutional roles (maybe duty is a better word) of the senior executive. And as such, it should be part of the SES admissions process.

It takes character to faithfully fulfill those institutional roles…to speak truth to power, to serve the government of the day without compromising the public interest, and to make tough choices between conflicting values. Yet these are the things we ask—indeed, the things we expect—members of the SES to do. As noted, we certainly know when an executive falls short of this fundamental expectation. Subordinates and peers know when a leader hedges on the truth, plays favorites when it comes to people or programs, or crosses ethical lines to get things done. When those intangible transgressions reach a certain point, we read about it in the *Washington Post*.

Thus, while the vast majority of career executives have the character it takes to lead in government, those few who don't cast a pall on the rest. And if character is what we expect, shouldn't it be a condition precedent to entry? However, as in many things, it is easier said than done. It is hard enough to define character, much less measure it. After all, whether one has character or not can be very subjective.

Due diligence to assess character

Many non-Federal organizations subject executive candidates to a rigorous due diligence process—typically accomplished by a trained, independent internal assessor—to determine whether they should be promoted to senior executive ranks. For Federal senior executive candidates, this due diligence could be conducted by a current SES member in good standing, drawn from outside the executive's immediate chain of command and charged with gathering 360-degree feedback on the candidate's fitness of character. And that confidential feedback (from a candidate's subordinates, peers, customers, and superiors) could be reported to an independent review board of the organization's most senior leaders, who would then pass judgment on the candidate's promotion.

To be sure, one could argue that allowing employees, customers, and colleagues to provide "make-or-break" feedback on an executive's character, could potentially cue all the wrong behaviors. For example, an executive-in-waiting may shy away from making the tough calls that come with being a leader, opting instead for the more popular or least contentious, even if the easier course doesn't necessarily serve an organization's best interests. We've all been tempted to take the line of least resistance, and if someone knows that his or her promotion to SES ranks is based on the wisdom of the crowd, that temptation could become even greater. Thad Allen talks about this in his chapter, as does Mike Hayden in his, and they both assert that it is up to the most senior leaders like themselves to ensure career executives resist this temptation and do the right thing.

However, with a near-peer conducting the 360-degree review, executive candidates would know—and could take some comfort in the fact—that feedback on their leadership qualities is being gathered by someone who is likely to have made similar tough, controversial calls. By definition, peer assessors know what it takes to lead an organization in challenging times, and they know when to discount the polls and give credit to a leader who has had to make an unpopular but ultimately necessary decision. In my experience, due diligence assessors take their responsibility very seriously as part of the rite of passage into the ranks of senior leadership.[127]

Character is important enough—and its absence consequential enough—to warrant establishing it as a separate ECQ, or at least as a supplemental part of the SES admissions process. Clearly, it would need to be defined more precisely and in behavioral terms that can be observed and assessed. But if we are going to demand character and courage of senior career executives, we must be willing to test for it, whether via the due diligence of peer review or some other means.

---

[127] Note that as a general matter, this due diligence process does not focus on the executive candidate's technical or managerial qualifications; candidates who have reached this stage should have already passed their instrumental ECQs.

Admittedly, such an intensive approach takes time and effort, so it may not be feasible (or appropriate) as a test for *initial* selection...especially for candidates who come from outside the Federal government. However, it could easily be incorporated into the later stages of a senior executive's first-year probationary period, after he or she has had some run time as a member of the SES but before being granted what amounts to tenure.

Although that probationary period is considered an extension of the examination process, agencies rarely take it seriously today; few freshman executives are screened out in their first year (while most agencies have demanding selection protocols, none are so good as to bat a thousand). Requiring a due diligence review before the probationary period expires would add a degree of rigor that is sorely lacking today.

Whether character is assessed before selection or during probation, I believe it's worth it—a classic case of pay me now or pay me later. To be sure, there is no guarantee that such a process would detect every potential miscreant (although the assessment itself would shape behavior...and perhaps deter the worst of it). Without it, the oath may just be an empty promise.

Developing the Next Generation of the SES

Closing The Leadership Gap

Preparing the 'next generation' for our next government. If there is one thing that the previous sections make clear, it is that an effective 21st century government will depend on the quality and commitment of those who will actually lead its various departments and agencies. That's where the rubber meets the road, and, in that regard, the old adage is true: Good, well-prepared leaders can make even the most dysfunctional systems and structures work...and poor (or poorly prepared) ones can undermine even the very best.[128] Thus, there can be no doubt that *ensuring leadership excellence* is a condition precedent to successful, smart 21st century government.

That's especially the case given the many challenges facing the SES corps that we have cataloged so far in this anthology. But the demographic challenges we described at the outset—a high percentage of retirement-eligible executives, a disaffected succession pool, frustrated minority and female candidates, and attrition driven by a presidential transition—suggest a looming leadership gap. And there are a number of systemic issues that make that gap even more ominous and its closing even more important.

First, it is fair to say that the way the Federal government has gone about identifying, preparing, and selecting its leaders—from top to bottom—is in need of substantial reform. For example, when it comes to promotions up through the ranks, current civil service rules favor tangible technical expertise over something as subjective as leadership ability. The result: on the one hand, individuals with narrow functional skills tend to get promoted up to and through executive ranks, with their leadership aptitude and abilities often an afterthought. And, on the flip side, the system practically forces top-of-their-game technical professionals to become supervisors and managers (but not necessarily *leaders*) if they want to be promoted...whether they like to or want to lead, or whether they are any good at it.

Second, the Federal government has traditionally underinvested in leadership and management development—especially in tough fiscal times, when it is very difficult to justify spending scarce resources on something so intangible. It's no wonder that results of the latest Federal Employee Viewpoint Survey

---

[128] Partnership for Public Service & Booz Allen Hamilton. (2014). *Building the enterprise: A new civil service framework.* Washington, DC: Partnership for Public Service.

(FEVS) suggest that as far as front-line civil servants are concerned, good leaders, especially good senior leaders, are in short supply.[129] However, in my view, a substantial part of the responsibility for those disappointing survey results lies with the government's "system" (such as it is) for identifying and developing senior executives, which is the focus of this section.

As an aside, I myself am a product of that leadership development system, and I personally can attest to how haphazard and under-resourced it is— especially when you compare it to how much and how long our armed forces spend developing military leaders, commissioned and otherwise, worthy of leading our troops. I spent almost 40 years in Federal service (21 as a senior executive), and I can count the time I spent in formal leadership development activities—schools, formal courses, official coaching and mentoring sessions, and the like—in *days and weeks*…and I was fortunate to work for agencies that believed in developing their civilian leaders. Colleagues in uniform can count the time they spend learning about leading and preparing to lead in *months and years*.

A problematic pipeline

For something as difficult and important as leading a government organization, with thousands of employees and millions of dollars in budget all intended to serve the public interest, this lack of leadership development is unconscionable. The government has struggled in this regard…and the results of the FEVS show it in hard, statistical terms. So the pipeline is problematic. Thus, there is the potential for a growing (and alarming) leadership gap, especially at the Federal government's most senior levels. And if one or more of the challenges outlined at the beginning of this book come to pass, that gap will increase exponentially, in both quantitative and qualitative terms— but more on that in our Concluding Commentary and Recommendations.

Clearly, it will take a substantial, sustained investment— in time, effort, and funding —to close the gap. The good news/bad news is that this is a long lead-time effort; it takes years to develop a Federal senior executive. So for the immediate future, the SES pipeline is what it is. However, it's not too late to begin that effort. If we start now, an improved development pipeline can begin to produce results (that is, better leaders!) in just a few years.

Unfortunately, we are seeing the opposite occur: Agencies are cutting back, or in many cases, canceling leadership development programs. And those that survive simply may not have the capacity to meet the demands of today, much less tomorrow. Nevertheless, at least some of the looming leadership gap posited here, especially at the agency level, can be closed with the commitment of senior agency leaders, both career and political, who are willing to do so. Once again, our contributors serve as role models in that regard.

---

[129] U.S. Office of Personnel Management. *2015 Federal Employee Viewpoint Survey* results.

- Letitia Long is a decorated intelligence officer and executive who ended her career as the Director of the National Geospatial-Intelligence Agency (NGA), the first woman to ever head one of the "big six" three-letter agencies in the U.S. Intelligence Community. Her path to that post personifies exactly what Congress had in mind when it mandated a version of the military's joint duty for senior IC executives, with stops in the Office of the Secretary of Defense (OSD), the Central Intelligence Agency (CIA), and the Defense Intelligence Agency (DIA). And she brought that same enterprise perspective to NGA, where—in addition to her focus on the mission at hand (we were at war during her tenure there, after all)—she also gave priority to the development of NGA's next generation of career leaders, knowing that they were just as important to the Agency's mission success as the latest technology.

- Dr. Reggie Wells is the long-serving Chief Human Capital Officer (CHCO) for the Social Security Administration (SSA). As the current "dean" of the Federal CHCO Council, Reggie has been a leader in the human capital community for many years and is one of its most respected members. And for good reason. Many of his agency's human capital programs are best in class; thanks to Dr. Wells' leadership, SSA's SES Candidate Development Program (CDP) is one of them. Inextricably linked to SSA's strategic succession plan, it stands out in comparison to other agency CDPs in that it actually produces graduates who become senior executives! Reggie discusses the major elements of the program and shares the secrets of its success, including the close involvement of SSA's Commissioner and senior leadership team.

- Bob Corsi, a former SES member who last served as Assistant Deputy Chief of Staff of the Air Force for Manpower, Personnel, and Services (and also a retired Air Force officer), describes how his agency has prepared military officers for senior leadership positions and, more importantly, how it has adapted that proven approach to the development of senior career executives. As he points out, the two systems cannot be mirror images of one another—the differences are just too substantial. However, he contends that an adaptation of that military model is not only possible but essential if agencies are to field an effective cadre of civilian executives.

- Dr. Suzanne Logan is the Director of the Federal Executive Institute (FEI), and she came to that position after a distinguished career as an academician, most recently as Academic Dean at the Air Force's Air University. Like Bob Corsi, Dr. Logan has had a chance to see (and shape) the U.S. military's leader development model firsthand, and she's led the adaptation of that model to FEI and its core mission of developing senior civilian managers and executives. In that regard, Suzanne argues that it requires a continuum of leadership learning over the course of an entire career to develop an effective senior leader, in uniform or otherwise, and she lays out a possible roadmap for doing so, from front-line supervisor to senior career executive.

- The Honorable Edward De Seve is an Executive in Residence with Brookings Executive Education and co-chair of the National Academy of Public Administration's *Presidential Transition 2016* project. As the U.S. Office of Management and Budget's Controller, as well as its Acting Deputy Director for Management, he also served Special Advisor to the President for oversight of the American Recovery and Reinvestment Act (ARRA).[130] In those capacities, Ed had ample opportunity to observe the interactions of career senior executives and political appointees, and he offers a new approach for accelerating the development of collaborative relationships between them, especially during the early days of a new Presidential administration, by leveraging an agency's strategic planning process as a catalyst for joint organizational development activities.

Together, these contributors offer a number of recommendations to address the leadership gap, most dealing with developmental strategies that are outside the classroom. The Concluding Commentary and Recommendations follow suit—they too emphasize on-the-job learning through such activities as rotational assignments.

And with Executive Order 13714 in hand,[131] OPM has also taken a number of positive steps to close the gap. For example, from a process standpoint, OPM is attempting to make recruiting and selecting senior executives easier, encouraging agencies to abandon the requirement for lengthy ECQ essays in SES applications in favor of more traditional resumes,[132] and it is also piloting alternatives to qualifications review boards (QRBs) as the final step in that application process. These initiatives certainly promise to make the application process far less onerous on both agencies and applicants, which hopefully will attract more top-quality candidates.

Similarly, OPM's new yearlong executive onboarding framework, which includes not one but a series of orientations and other activities all designed to help new SES members understand and succeed in their new role, is to be applauded. Most importantly, it finally begins to treat (and shape) new SES members as the whole-of-government cadre they were originally meant to be. However, it too could be improved, first by spending more time focusing on the institutional roles of the SES; and secondly, by leveraging that yearlong process—which neatly corresponds to the probationary period for new SES members—to help agencies determine if they made the right selections in the first place.

---

[130] American Recovery and Reinvestment Act of 2009, Pub. L. No. 111-5, 123 Stat. 115 (2009).
[131] Exec. Order No. 13714, Strengthening the Senior Executive Service. (2015, December 15). Retrieved from https://www.whitehouse.gov/the-press-office/2015/12/15/executive-order-strengthening-senior-executive-service.
[132] Partnership for Public Service & McKinsey and Company. (2016). *A pivotal moment for the Senior Executive Service: Measures, aspirational practices and stories of success.* Washington, DC: Partnership for Public Service.

CHAPTER 4.1:

Developing 21ˢᵗ Century Senior Intelligence Executives

*By Letitia Long, former Director of the U.S. National Geospatial
Intelligence Agency*

Introduction

For far too long, the Federal government in general and the Intelligence
Community (IC) in particular have promoted individuals with outstanding
technical expertise to the ranks of the SES with little to no regard for their
abilities to lead.

I am a recently retired 35-year career employee, with 20 years in the SES in
the U.S. Department of Defense (DOD) and the IC. I observed many well-
intentioned employees who were brilliant in their technical or analytic fields
become senior executives and then do an abysmal job. Once upon a time, the
only way to get promoted to a senior position was to become a supervisor.
While that has changed and there is now a dual track so technical experts can
continue to advance without carrying major management responsibilities, we
still have a tendency to promote those who have excelled in their technical
fields to the SES. At the same time, we are not equipping them with the tools
necessary to succeed as leaders.

I contend that LDPs, as preparation for the SES, should start on day 1 of an
employee's career. Someone told me early in my career that the military had
the corner on leadership and the civilians had the corner on management. What
I learned along the way was that the military actually taught leadership skills
—and infused them throughout all of its training curricula—and the civilian
side of the house needed to do the same. Once I was in a position to do so, I set
out to do just that. Everyone is a leader, and leader development is everyone's
responsibility. It is not limited by pay band or General Schedule (GS) level,
formal position, years of service, or those you know. Once this perspective is
embraced, we can get on with the business of developing leaders.

Background: Leading the Defense Intelligence Enterprise

When I was the Deputy Director of the DIA, I established a cohesive LDP. There were a number of leadership classes being offered at the time, but there was not a comprehensive program that developed our employees throughout their careers, adding to their knowledge base as they progressed through their careers. So we developed offerings for entry-level, mid-career, journeyman, and senior executives.

I was delivering a speech one day at DIA and was asked whether there are truly natural-born leaders or whether leadership is a learned skill. My answer was "yes." While there are those who seem to have a talent for leadership, even natural-born leaders can and should further develop their skills. I am a proponent of lifelong learning and career development. No matter how experienced we are, no matter where we are in our lives or careers, we can and should continue to learn and develop our skill sets and our personal selves—including our leadership skills.

As the Deputy Director, I attended the pilot offering of "Great Leaders, Great Culture," the leadership class for the senior executives. I thought it important that I lead by example by attending that first offering of the seminar. If it was going to be mandatory for all seniors, even I was not exempt. I remember thinking on the first day that I could have used this knowledge much earlier in my career. It was actually the first formal leadership training I had ever attended and here I was, the number two in the Agency! I was a prime example that the military had the corner on leadership and civilians on management. I vowed then to do all I could to ensure the program was spared from budget cuts. In fact, we increased the budget every year I was there from 2006 until 2010.

When I became the Director of NGA in 2010, I reviewed the LDP there (I had modeled the DIA program after NGA's, which was—in my view—best of breed at the time) and learned it was ready to be refreshed. Based on what I had learned at DIA, I realized the program needed to be much more than a series of LDPs at multiple points throughout an employee's career. In order to prepare our civilians for future leadership opportunities and challenges, we needed a holistic approach that incorporated all aspects of our talent management program.

NGA's Leader Development Initiative

Underpinning all of this was the Leader Development Initiative (LDI). As we developed our strategic plan for the core mission of NGA, LDI was the foundation for all of our initiatives. LDI was so important that I selected a top executive to lead the initiative, Mike Rodrigue. (Mike would go on to be the NGA Deputy Director.) This was a deliberate signal to the Agency of just how important the initiative was. One of the first things Mike did was to develop a framework for effective servant leadership. He outlined a set of leader competencies that we felt were necessary to be a top leader in NGA and the IC. This competency model was the thread to be used to develop leaders from new hires to senior leadership. He developed the competencies through focus groups, where participants discussed the attributes and behaviors associated with our core values. While there were 17 competencies in the overall framework, we focused on five for the senior executives: Motivating Others, Peer Relationships, Timely Decision Making, Integrity and Trust, and Courage.

I personally added courage to this list. This is an attribute that I could write a book on…something that I believe is so important for all senior executives and those who aspire to be. The attributes were also adapted and cascaded down to the lower pay band levels. We then used those attributes in position descriptions as needed attributes, in our performance appraisal process, and in our career service and succession management plans. We used them to develop a strong leadership culture at all levels to effectively lead and execute NGA's mission and vision.

Agency-wide talent management

Talent management begins with recruiting, and recruiting begins with knowing what talent already exists within your organization and what talent will be necessary in the future to optimally perform and grow your mission. This is a partnership between your human resources (HR) organization and your functional (line) offices. HR can do the recruiting, but they need to know the skills they are looking for. Our best recruitment was done with integrated teams comprising recruiters and subject matter experts. We also completely revamped our recruiting materials. We hired a professional firm to work on our branding efforts along with our Office of Communications. We redesigned our recruiting center to streamline the application process and marry it with the security clearance process.

New employee orientation and first impressions

Once an individual is hired, employee engagement starts on the first day. (Employee engagement actually starts with the first contact during the hiring process, and we worked hard to make that a positive experience.) At NGA, I would kick off the New Employee Orientation Seminar by welcoming the cohort of new employees. I talked about the LDI and the opportunities afforded to them. I talked with them about our leader attributes, their relationship to our core values of EARTH—Excellence, Accountability, Respect, Teamwork, and Honesty—and their importance to mission success. I walked them through the Agency's vision and strategy to make it real for them and ended with administering the oath of office.

I also talked about the oath, the legacy we inherit as public servants, and the importance of public service and it being a sacred public trust that we must never break. If I was not available to do this (I actually planned my travel and meeting schedule around these seminars), the Deputy Director or Chief

Operating Officer (COO) filled in. I felt it was extremely important that one of the top three engage with our new employees on their first day. It was a great investment of 30 minutes of my time every other week. Throughout my 4 years as Director, many employees provided feedback about the impression it made that the Director (or Deputy or COO) spent time with them on their first day at NGA.

Functional career services to drive career development

Another aspect of talent management is career development. While career development is ultimately the responsibility of the individual, a framework is necessary so employees know what is expected of them and what they need to learn and demonstrate to progress to the next level. The framework NGA developed was career services. Every position was covered by one of nine career services, including geospatial intelligence operations, research and development, financial management, and human capital. Career services were led by senior leaders who were responsible for the strategic management and development of professionals within that career service, integrating talent management functions including career development, certification, promotion, and workforce planning.

This was not to absolve front-line supervisors of their responsibility for developing their employees. Career services defined standards to ensure consistency across the Agency, as well as transparency into the various talent management processes. Supervisors were still responsible for assessing their employees against competencies, experiences, and core qualifications; rating their subject matter expertise and performance—including how well they exhibited the leader attributes; determining and supporting their education and training needs; and assessing their potential for increased responsibilities based on mission requirements and needs.

One of the biggest challenges we faced was with our supervisors. They were often the central link—especially first-line supervisors—to employee engagement and satisfaction. If a supervisor understood their role was to develop their employees and ensure their employees' success, then they would be successful also. This of course was a real shift for the first-time supervisor: moving from being a doer to an overseer, from being developed to being the developer, from being the follower to the leader of followers. This was why the LDI was so important.

Interagency mobility—voluntary versus mandatory

Another tool in the IC to develop our people and ensure readiness for senior executive positions is the joint duty assignment (JDA). A tenet for the Federal SES, when it was established, was that its members would move from agency to agency, bringing their expertise and strategic thinking to solve hard problems.

Another tenet was that the cadre would operate under a uniform performance-based system. The IC joint duty program was designed to develop a workforce able to lead with a community perspective and strategic outlook. It was originally established in 1997 by the Community Management Staff (CMS), which was the predecessor organization to the Office of the Director of National Intelligence (ODNI). (I was the CMS Staff Director at the time and very involved in the development of the program.) It was named the Intelligence Community Officer Program,[133] and there were two parts to it: a JDA in another element of the IC, DOD, Federal government, academia, or industry; and a community training program.

Participation was mandatory under an IC policy, but there were no repercussions if the policy was not followed. One of the lessons learned from the 9/11 Commission[134] was that we were not acting like—or performing as—a community. The Intelligence Reform and Terrorism Prevention Act of 2004 (IRTPA)[135] mandated the development of a joint duty program. The law made participation a requirement for advancement to the senior ranks—à la Goldwater-Nichols[136] and promotion to general officer for the uniformed services. A decade plus later, if one looks at the Directors and Deputy Directors across the community, they have all had multiple JDAs. I held 10 different jobs in 6 different agencies as a senior executive. I dare say I would not have been the first civilian director (with no prior military experience) of one of our major intelligence agencies without those experiences.

That said, it continues to be a challenge to manage the joint duty program. Ensuring that folks are taken care of from a home agency administrative standpoint while they are on rotation, that they have meaningful assignments when they are detailed to another organization, and that there is a seamless reintegration program when they return are just a few of those challenges. Additionally, while there are full-time program management offices in each organization to administer the program, each agency manages the program differently.

One of the complications of the program is filling behind individuals when they are out on assignment. For that reason, it is not unusual to have managers who will not allow their folks to apply for positions if their management gives them no backfill. The workload is not diminished, and deliverables must still be completed on time with one less person. To handle this, the ODNI has mandated that all positions be reimbursable so offices can hire contract talent for the duration of the absence. However, this is not always easy to do given some of the expertise requirements of the IC.

[133] Director of Central Intelligence Directive No. 1/4, Intelligence community officer programs. (2000, February 4). Retrieved from http://www.fas.org/irp/offdocs/dcid1-4.htm
[134] National Commission on Terrorist Attacks upon the United States (2004). The *9/11 Commission Report*. Washington, DC: U.S. Government Publishing Office. Retrieved from https://9-11commission.gov/report
[135] Intelligence Reform and Terrorism Prevention Act.
[136] Goldwater-Nichols Act.

For the joint duty program to be successful, it will require continued focused leadership from across the IC at the senior level. One of the more successful initiatives in this regard, early in the program's tenure, was a 2-day offsite led by the ODNI and attended by most of the IC Deputy Directors. (I was Deputy Director of DIA at the time.) We all arrived with our 4-inch-thick binder of open IC position descriptions, along with our agency lists and resumes of high-performing GS-13s, 14s, and 15s who needed joint duty experience. We rolled up our sleeves and matched over 100 folks the first day and 100 more the second day. It was a manually intensive process, but we made some really good placements and built more trust during those 2 days than we probably had at a dozen previous Deputy Committee meetings.

Something that often lurked in the background was whether an agency was trying to offload a poor performer—even though everyone had access to performance information of those seeking a joint duty position. By sitting down face to face, we voiced and addressed those concerns by putting our personal stamps of approval or backing behind every individual. Did all assignments work out perfectly as a result? No. Did most of them work out good enough? Yes. And we placed more individuals during that 2-day session than we had during all previous open seasons combined. One unique twist to the JDA program was rotations to industry. Those counted as joint duty credit, but it was a sticky issue for the lawyers. When I left NGA in October 2014, we had two employees with the private industry and one with a nonprofit, but the notion of education with industry remained nascent.

As the IC joint duty program percolated along, we implemented an internal rotational program at NGA to broaden our officers so they understood all—or more—aspects of the NGA mission set. Interestingly, some of the same challenges existed with our internal program as with the community program. Even with our internal program, we had to encourage supervisors to endorse their folks to participate, and we had to implement mechanisms to ensure folks who did participate were not out of sight, out of mind when it came to appraisals, bonuses, and training and education opportunities. Likewise, we had some of the same challenges reintegrating employees into their next jobs. As with the IC program, we wanted to take advantage of new skills learned, not simply put folks back in their old jobs. It always came back to leadership and the supervisor's ability to see beyond themselves.

Performance management with consequences

Unique to NGA (in the IC) is the agency-wide pay-for-performance appraisal and compensation program. NGA conducted a pilot program in 2000, and it is still going strong. Pay for performance is a movement away from entitlements. There are no pay increases based on longevity—rather, pay increases are all performance based. The system is similar to the certified performance-based systems for senior executives across the Federal government. Employees are rated against their performance elements and then rank ordered against their peers. The size of individuals' pay adjustments—or raises—is determined by where they fall on the 1-N list. This system ensures top performers are recognized for their contributions. We set individual, team, and agency-wide goals to encourage the team behavior we wanted.

This program was also a retention tool. During the 3 years that there were no pay increases due to the budget downturn, NGA was able to increase pay based on a certified pay-for-performance system. We may not have stock options in the government, but being able to increase the pay of your folks when no one else across the government is able to do so is powerful motivation. The system, however, is not a panacea; one must set achievable, measurable goals and have the courage to give honest, critical feedback. And that takes leadership. Equitable treatment, not equal treatment, is mandatory. Training for managers to ensure consistency across the organization is key, and mechanisms to check that consistency are crucial also.

Rank in person versus rank in position

Coupled with a pay-for-performance system is a modern promotion program. In 2013 NGA moved from a rank-in-position promotion system to a rank-in-person promotion system. A rank-in-position system requires a specific advertised vacant position, and individuals apply for that specific position. Everyone's application is reviewed, and the most qualified person is selected. In contrast, a rank-in-person system promotes employees based on a competitive evaluation of a peer group against corporate promotion criteria. The latter supports the selection of those who demonstrate the behaviors or attributes that are consistent with the values and tenets of the organization. Based on merit principles, those who meet the highest standards of professional achievement, executive qualifications, managerial competence, and, most importantly, executive leadership and potential are selected. They are then moved to positions commensurate with their skill sets and potential.

Real succession management

Workforce planning includes recruiting, which we have already briefly discussed, as well as succession management. Succession management in the IC should be a means of developing corporate officers as both agency-wide and IC professionals. It is a future-focused strategic approach to identifying and developing agency leaders considering past and current performance, future potential, and readiness for a new challenge. Succession management's development focus is on preparing for possible future assignments for which an individual may be ready now or in the future. It is to identify talent an organization already has that is ready today, or will be in the near term, and determine where that talent can be applied within the organization. (Also, there are from time to time calls for nominations for community positions.)

A succession management program asks the critical questions necessary to develop talent toward specific purposes. The process should result in a development plan for each person that focuses on needed experience, exposure, and education for potential future assignments. In kind, these development plans are to ensure a strong pipeline for the Agency's executive positions. This was implemented at NGA in 2012 with the senior executives and then cascaded down to the rest of NGA. It is an outstanding tool that lets individuals know what their leadership believes they are ready to do now and where they need to focus in their self-development for future assignments. This was also done at the IC level for a few years under former Director of National Intelligence (DNI) Mike McConnell. This is an area that needs further effort at the IC level to ensure a pipeline of officers ready to serve in the seniormost positions across the IC.

Conclusion

Development of talent is a key strategy for mission accomplishment. However, a talent management plan is not an end unto itself and must be linked to your organization's overall management framework—from the strategic plan to the employee engagement plan, the performance appraisal system, and the career development plan. The better these are synchronized, the better your chances of achieving your mission goals and objectives. And underpinning it all is strong leadership.

CHAPTER 4.2:
Reinventing SES Candidate Development Programs

By Dr. Reginald Wells, Chief Human Capital Officer,
U.S. Social Security Administration

Introduction

The Federal government has experienced a sea change that commands our attention as executives and human capitalists. Shrinking resources, increasing demands for service, and hostile social and physical environments challenge our conventional strategies and tactics. Our citizens demand change, our leaders demand innovation and austerity, and those of us who work in HR respond by devising and executing ways to guide our organizations through turbulent times to greater opportunity and effectiveness. We have truly entered an era of great volatility, uncertainty, complexity, and ambiguity (VUCA).

Our responsibility to grow and maintain a productive, engaged, and creative workforce requires our full attention and careful analysis of the impact of these changes on Federal, national, and international spaces. Our response to the new normal must be as adaptively successful as possible because failure is not an option. We need executive leaders and a Federal workforce that are transformative and able to lead effectively in a world increasingly characterized by VUCA.

There are more questions than answers about the best ways to transform the Federal workforce and workplace to adapt to the sea change. None of us should pretend to have all of the answers or to know the one definitive way to go. Instead, it will take a collective effort to find the most promising approaches. By sharing our collective wisdom and demonstrating what is and is not working, and under what circumstances, we may be able to achieve a sustainable path for preparing the Federal workforce, including the SES.

Senior executives are responsible for leading the way and coming up with solutions to the most challenging wicked problems facing our nation. It is crucial to prepare those aspiring to these leadership roles for the worst case scenarios and hope that their integrity, resilience, and commitment to excellence are up to the challenges we face today and into the future.

On two separate occasions, I have addressed Congress on the subject of diversity in the Federal government's SES. The first time in October 2003, I was very new to my responsibilities as CHCO. I agonized over the wording of my formal statement and the prospect of answering probing questions from lawmakers who were passionate about the subject and looking to take agencies to task on why they had not yet achieved better numbers with minority candidates and women in their search for senior executives. I considered our numbers to be respectable but far from ideal given the agency demographic profile overall.

During the course of this congressional hearing, my anxiety over our imperfect profile gave way to a sense of confidence. It became increasingly clear that the SSA was doing many of the right things to achieve a proportionately higher yield of minority and female executives in comparison to other agencies represented on the panel.

As I walked from the hearing room unscathed and feeling relief that my mother—a retiree of the Internal Revenue Service (IRS) after 45 years—would not experience the embarrassment of watching her son bomb before the highest legislature in the land, I made a commitment to deliver a more favorable diversity and inclusion profile for SSA's SES next time around. After all, I felt we dodged a bullet. I just knew we would have something more impressive to report when Congress called us back to report progress next time. Looking back, how naïve of me.

Fast-forward to May 2007. I was back offering testimony about our SES diversity and progress since 2003. This time, I expected to receive kudos for being an agency committed to workforce diversity. This time, I had a much better sense of how SSA compared to other Federal agencies, especially those of comparable size and complexity of mission and structure. However, this time, while I was able to report some modest gains in the advancement of women to our senior executive ranks, I found myself unable to show a demonstrable increase in the number of senior executives representing protected ethnic or racial minority groups.

The truth is that diversifying the Federal SES requires more than a sustained, concerted effort by HR or CHCOs and HR directors as agents of change. If the Federal government is to achieve diversity in the senior executive corps, the sustained, unwavering commitment of top leaders is essential. Diversifying the SES is critical to the effectiveness of the Federal workforce to deliver service at home and abroad. Many have argued the case for a diverse workforce and diverse leadership. In spite of those cogent arguments and rational voices, many believe the diversity of the SES will fall short in 2030 and beyond. That projection is both disturbing and disappointing as we enter fiscal year (FY) 2016. Agency leaders and human capitalists generally agree and assert that the diversification of the SES should be a standard feature of workforce planning and talent management. What are the barriers to diversification of the senior executive corps and what deliberate actions can government leaders take to carry out promising practices that demonstrate successful diversification of emerging leader groups?

Some assert that the ever-growing complexity of the problems demanding Federal government attention requires complex enterprise-wide solutions that are unlikely to be adequately achieved given the inadequacies of the current senior executive corps. With these assertions comes a cynicism that today's senior executive corps is too complacent and ill equipped to respond with the complex array of solutions necessary to survive and thrive in an increasingly VUCA world.

Whether you agree with the criticism or consider it overly harsh, there is consensus that it is crucial to groom a new generation of individuals to fill the ranks of the SES seamlessly as current executives retire or otherwise leave the Federal service. There is also consensus that deficient and/or unavailable executive training for members of the senior executive corps will impair their ability to address new and emerging challenges facing the nation and the world community.

While there is a fair amount of consensus about the ways in which the original vision of the SES went astray, there are many credible views and perspectives about the best ways to go about producing the leaders we need now and in the future. SSA's approach to talent management and leadership development offers a credible solution for attracting, acquiring, and retaining a talented and diverse workforce, including the resilient and resourceful leaders we need now and into the future.

The mission of SSA requires attention to workforce diversity and inclusion; SSA's leaders had the foresight to make it a priority from the beginning. Throughout the history of SSA, executive branch leadership and lawmakers appreciated the importance of having service-oriented people at the helm of the Agency. In their commitment to customer service, they demanded a certain degree of cultural and ethnic parity between the workforce and the communities they served. These service-oriented leaders instituted data-driven workforce management strategies that resulted in recruiting, hiring, and training generations of employees who reflected the characteristics of their public. The careful attention to this balance within the Agency—reinforced by an active network of affinity groups—allows SSA to enjoy one of the most diverse workforces in government today. Today we readily practice our HR mantra: recruit for diversity. Hire for talent. The result is a highly talented, highly fungible workforce that responds well to the VUCA realities of modern day.

The establishment of a Diversity and Inclusion Council pursuant to President Obama's EO 13583 has solidified our recent activities and has contributed mightily to ensuring our employee pipeline remains diverse and supplies agency leadership with viable internal candidates for all levels of leadership, including the SES. Our agency-wide mentoring program is one of the initiatives we believe will advance our workforce and leadership development agenda, especially diversity and inclusion objectives.

With a keen eye on the coming retirement tsunami, SSA's talent management strategies became a top priority just before the turn of the century; as a result, three national leadership programs were born—the Leadership Development Program, the Advanced Leadership Development Program (ALP), and the SES CDP. These three national programs complement an array of similar leadership programs offered throughout the Agency by the various lines of business (e.g., budget, finance and management, HR, operations, communications) in Headquarters and throughout SSA's regional network. All three of these programs are competitive and open to all current employees who meet the eligibility criteria (e.g., grade, permanent status in the competitive and excepted service). Employees selected into the program are relieved of their regular duties and allowed to enter a program of rotational assignments over a period of 12 to 24 months depending on the program and the candidate's individual profile as a leader. These cascading developmental programs groom talent for SSA between grades GS-9 and GS-15.

A number of SSA's current senior executives are graduates from one or more of these leadership programs. However, each program is self-contained and aimed at enhancing the leadership competencies necessary to perform effectively at the next higher grade or leadership level.

SSA's SES CDP develops high-potential individuals who have demonstrated an interest and a capacity to lead at the executive level and who possess proficiency in the ECQs and associated competencies necessary to transition from management to executive leadership. The program is open to all current, permanent GS-14 and GS-15 employees in competitive service and excepted service positions, including external applicants. The developmental experiences required to complete the program are purposely challenging, robust, stretch experiences meant to take candidates out of their comfort zones. Candidates are required to step outside their areas of technical expertise, thereby forcing them to rely much more heavily on their leadership abilities in leading and driving substantive programmatic results in their rotational assignments. The uncertainty and ambiguity triggered by venturing outside the comfort zone of familiar organizational areas challenge candidates in a way that simulates the VUCA reality.

The Executive Resources Board (ERB) closely monitors each candidate's progress in the program to ensure the candidate is adjusting well to the stretch experience and utilizing various resources available to ensure successful completion of the program and certification by OPM. To graduate from the program, the ERB must approve each candidate's certification. The ERB may determine that a candidate needs additional development before moving forward with certification. A candidate can step out of the program voluntarily or be encouraged to withdraw from the program under certain circumstances.

After a rigorous competition for selection into the SES CDP, including a formal assessment center process and interviews with members of the ERB, candidates receive a formal orientation and a 4-week residential executive training program. Using assessment results and under the guidance of their assigned mentor, candidates prepare individual development plans aimed at enhancing strengths and constricting skill gaps. ERB members do check-in interviews with the SES CDP candidates, their mentors, and their rotational assignment supervisors, who are also senior executives. During those interviews, ERB members document candidate progress, attempt to detect any developmental challenges early, and ensure the candidates are having robust leadership experiences allowing them to fulfill personal leadership aspirations and agency expectations.

Moving high-potential individuals around as well as in and out of an agency with the geographical footprint of SSA is complicated and requires support. The intricacies of executive training and development sometimes require elaborate travel planning, individual candidate needs for concierge-type services, and assignments and schedules that offer some semblance of work-life balance. Having a competent team of executive service personnel is a foundational and essential ingredient in the success of the SES CDP. If there are issues, executive service staff work through them with the candidate, mentor, assignment supervisor, ERB, and other organizational components, as appropriate.

Upon successful completion of all program requirements, candidates must have their ECQs certified by an independent QRB at the OPM. While there is no guarantee of an SES appointment upon completion of the program, once certified by OPM, each candidate is eligible for appointment to a senior executive position without further competition.

Since 1998 SSA has graduated six SES CDP classes, ranging in size from 15 to 45 individuals. We consider it a success that 84 percent of those who graduated from the program and received OPM certification assumed senior executive positions.

We believe this placement rate is healthy and a good return on investment (ROI) given all of the factors and circumstances that go into succession planning and the process of filling executive positions. We anticipate that the ROI will only improve as additional graduates from our former classes receive executive placements. The SES CDP has been essential to our succession management strategy and planning. More than 50 percent of our current career senior executives participated in or completed an SES CDP.

In the interest of continuous improvement, we encourage senior executives to offer detailed feedback on their SES CDP experience. In addition, the ERB reviews each program offering and recommends substantive modifications to the SES CDP when and where appropriate. The robust post-program evaluation has resulted in the identification of a number of important changes in program features, rules of thumb, and lessons learned. For instance, we recognized that our SES CDP could be a valuable conduit for external talent infusion. That revelation affected our program design, and our experience resulted in a couple of noteworthy changes. For instance, when we select external candidates, we offer them permanent appointments as opposed to temporary appointments that could require them to seek employment elsewhere at the conclusion of the program or return to their previous agency if not offered an executive position with us.

Our SES CDP goes beyond the minimum regulatory requirements established by the OPM. We consider OPM's regulatory requirements to be a floor instead of a ceiling for the design of our agency program. We invest in our aspiring executives in a way that sends a clear message about how much we value leadership. Our decision to design a more robust program—where candidates rotate full-time through multiple meaningful leadership assignments for 4 to 6 months each—results in graduates who are better prepared for future VUCA challenges.

To ensure assignments are meaningful, our SES CDP candidates serve in bona fide vacant SES positions. Pursuant to our program guidelines, candidates rotate through functional areas requiring them to rely far more on their leadership abilities than their technical credentials, backgrounds, and competencies. Honing leadership skills ensures candidates are more inclined to shift from the manager to the leader mindset. The requirement to leave comfort zones allows candidates to realize leadership growth spurts unlikely to occur if allowed to remain on organizational "home soil." Furthermore, the requirement to move to unfamiliar areas of the organization reinforces other basic tenets and characteristics of executive leadership in Federal service, such as organizational and geographic mobility. We believe our graduates are more fungible for having gone through this particular design feature of our SES CDP.

After almost two decades, we have learned many valuable lessons; we expect our current class (Class VII) to yield further gems of wisdom about cultivating executive leadership talent in public sector spaces. Most notable among our lessons learned are the following:

- **Leadership matters.** The most salient lesson learned is that your SES CDP is DOA ("dead on arrival") if you have not obtained the unwavering support of your top leaders. The investment, if done right, is substantial; like many things, you get what you pay for. If you have the commitment of senior leaders to fund the most essential features of your program, then your executive service team can operate with confidence and assurance that the program will hold up under scrutiny from oversight agencies.

- **ERB oversight is essential.** Close oversight from the ERB goes hand in hand with the importance of top leadership support. Be sure to choose your ERB members carefully to underscore the values you wish to emphasize. Ensure your ERB is diverse. Once ERB members are in place and clear on their charges and responsibilities, empower them to take on activities that enhance the accountability and efficacy of your CDP.

We have found the ERB to be crucial to the SES CDP communication strategy, including communication with candidates, their mentors, and the assignment supervisors who are integral to assessing candidates' progress and readiness to lead. With the able support of your executive service staff, the ERB must be able to maintain start-to-finish oversight of the program and its processes. Placement rates and placement success will depend on how well your ERB does its job.

- **The proof of the pudding is in the eating.** CDPs should offer a realistic way to grow and groom new executives for your agency. Anyone aspiring to executive leadership today should understand that success now and in the future hinges, in large part, on the ability to tolerate and thrive along a path riddled with VUCA obstacles threatening mission and core business.

We have found that by holding particular executive vacancies open for use as CDP rotational destinations, we are able to "road test" high-potential individuals and prepare them for executive leadership at a very high level of VUCA tolerance. As the candidates perform in a real leadership position that is vacant due to the recent loss of an executive, the ERB and other executives obtain keen insight into the character and capability of the candidates under real "road conditions." The assignment supervisor, who may be unfamiliar with the candidate personally, is free and more likely to offer an honest assessment since he or she has skin in the game. The assignment supervisor's overall performance is partially dependent on the performance of the candidate for the duration of the rotational assignment in this scenario.

- **Size matters.** SSA has experimented with large and small cohorts of SES CDP candidates. We are generally of the opinion that smaller is better. If we can accomplish our succession planning objectives while preserving the quality enhancements that a smaller cohort allows, we consider it ideal. As our World War II and baby boom generation executives move on to well-deserved retirement, we have no shortage of vacant executive positions to hold aside for rotational assignments. As generations X and Y move into contention for executive leadership positions and possibly drive down the average age of ascension to the SES, we will likely experience fewer vacancies during future SES CDP offerings. If we elect to run larger SES CDP classes in the future, we will do so understanding that there is a smaller supply of challenging assignments available for rotational placements. If we continue to run smaller cohorts, our smaller supply of assignments should be sufficient. The value of quality assignments for the candidates cannot be overstated. As with precision automobiles, the more realistic the road test, the greater the assurance of the car handling severe road conditions.

We have found that program timing and frequency are important also. When programs are too close together, placement rates tend to suffer because of the glut of certified candidates available for assignment. In our experience, certified candidates tend to be incredibly anxious to take on their first command before or at the completion of the program. Sometimes their morale suffers until they get that first executive assignment. Running classes and cohorts too closely together can leave you with an unhealthy ratio of too few appointments for newly minted executives, as well as too few quality assignments for the next cohort.

- **Familiarity can breed contempt.** If your executives are exclusively homegrown, you run the risk of groupthink and diminished creativity. External assignments are extremely valuable because they offer diversity of experience. The value and importance of external assignments as a mandatory or discretionary feature of the CDP has become a source of robust debate over the years. I come down on the side of at least one required external assignment as a feature of the program. SSA has a fine tradition of home-growing executive talent. It is a definite contributor to SSA's ability to achieve mission. Those elevated to the executive level know the agency business from bottom to top and are deeply committed to public service. However, the constant pattern of home-growing executive talent can result in executives who see the world in a prescribed way and see challenges facing the Agency from an insular perspective. The executive cadre's ability to innovate and react with agility may suffer or be lost altogether.

- **You get what you pay for.** Running an SES CDP economically is essential. However, try not to operate so economically that you fail to produce the leaders you need. If you attempt to do it on the cheap, be prepared to get what you pay for. Committing to a discipline of continuous improvement and robust evaluation of results will enhance your success; self-evaluation will allow oversight agencies to find things consistent with your stated expectations when they do their review.

We credit our talent management strategy with our ability to navigate the sea changes and VUCA circumstances that challenge SSA's mission attainment. We consider diversity and inclusion crucial to mission and our leadership development strategy. These are essential to our competitive advantage as an agency that serves the public directly, and demographic projections suggest they will become even more imperative in the out-years.

To prepare for the VUCA world, commit your agency workforce to rigorous talent management practices and development, and manage a healthy flow of external talent to complement your homegrown talent. It is important to link diversity and inclusion to your service mission because achieving a diverse workforce requires constant effort and vigilance. Failure to follow through on promises to women and minority employees in your agency and leadership pipelines regarding equal opportunity, diversity, and inclusion undermines the engagement of your workforce and your agency mission. We attribute much of our success at SSA to our competent, diverse workforce and find that our inclusive workplace stimulates creativity, fosters enhanced team-work and collaboration, and maximizes the creative tension and innovative value of our diverse workforce. Our talent management strategies, especially our three career development programs, deliver where we need it the most—producing exceptional employees and exceptional leaders who are empowered, knowledgeable, compassionate, engaged, and equipped to face the VUCA world with courage and resilience.

Adapting the Military Model to Develop the Next Generation of Career Executives

By Robert Corsi, SES, former Assistant Deputy Chief of Staff of the Air Force for Manpower, Personnel, and Services (and U.S. Air Force, retired)

Introduction

In this chapter, I share a development construct based on years of experience dealing with the challenges of simultaneously developing both a military and civilian workforce and an agency that values the same military-type experiences in civilian senior leadership positions. While retiring military have a distinct advantage in competing for the SES based on their progressive leadership opportunities, many of our career civilians have not in the past had those same experiences. Whether competing at the GS-14–15 grade levels or the SES level, our career civilians have coined a phrase—"no colonel left behind"—to demonstrate their frustration and inability to compete on a level playing field. Furthermore, when capitalizing on the retired military population, we end up with a senior civilian workforce that is far from diverse.

The subject of developing the next generation of leaders is hugely complex in our dynamic Federal environment, and it is important to understand our challenges compared to the private sector. To build the way ahead, I discuss some of the critical foundational elements for any development model. Finally, after building on the military model, I offer a development construct that is within every agency's ability to implement.

While critics of the SES point to lack of diversity, stagnation of the SES in their original positions, and lack of any talent management, it all starts with how we grow the talent in the first place and what the organization values in its development model. As this chapter demonstrates, it will take the collective involvement of all agency leadership to develop the next generation of leaders —nothing less.

Foundational elements

Mentoring aspiring leaders

Whether active or passive mentoring is practiced in an organization, nothing is more important to aspiring leaders in their development. Becoming a senior executive brings with it a host of new responsibilities, not the least of which is to set the right example and understand the immense responsibility of grooming the next generation of leaders. Organization heads must take the time to communicate their expectations to new senior executives, either directly or indirectly, regarding their new roles; this goes well beyond their specific job responsibilities. Clearly, new senior executives can feel over-whelmed in their jobs—and that is expected.

But mentoring should not be new to new senior executives if the organization has embraced its importance and relayed it as a necessary expectation in leaders' careers leading up to the SES. Most organizations have no policy at all when it comes to mentoring; others require, to their credit, that a new senior executive not only find a mentor but also become a mentor. Too many times, we hear that new senior executives essentially become lost patrols with no safety net to help them navigate in their new leadership role. In these instances, they not only choose to not mentor but also become less than ideal role models for their workforce.

Ideally, senior mentors should not be in the formal reporting chain for their mentees and should encourage aspiring leaders to seek mentors outside of their chain so they can obtain different perspectives on leadership develop-ment paths. Supervisors are a good source of advice on technical development but, depending on agency dynamics, may not have the knowledge of or exposure to meaningful leadership development. If we don't understand generational dynamics, we can easily lose promising leaders when they can't see a path forward or they feel stagnated based on lack of any agency leadership focus. Good mentors can help bridge the gap when agencies lack a development model and may be the only stopgap to prevent talent loss.

Mobility

Mobility is an integral part of the military leadership development model, and the Air Force believes it should also apply to civilian executives. How-ever, that can polarize aspiring civilian leaders. If mobility is that important, why do we make it a major consideration for the first time when it comes to developing current senior executives? It makes little sense to value mobility to develop current senior executives when we have grown a generation of senior executives who were selected to the SES without having been mobile. While job mobility had to be a major consideration to be selected to build leadership competencies, geographic mobility or cross-agency emphasis was never a consideration for selection. Essentially, we are changing the rules in the 9th inning and attempting to mandate mobility across the entire Federal workforce for current senior executives.

A majority of current senior executives have never been geographically or cross-agency mobile in their entire careers; yet, now there is an emphasis to drive mobility to build leadership breadth in our senior leaders. It is driving current senior executives who are retirement eligible to say enough is enough. In addition, members of the workforce are confused by the ongoing dialogue because they may not have considered mobility in their career plans and must now adjust career expectations. Mobility, both geographically and cross-agency, has a place in civilian development, but it must be part of a well-orchestrated development model that is *totally transparent* and *clearly* communicated to the workforce—especially those employees who aspire to senior leadership positions.

Personal buy-in can in fact be family buy-in when a development program requires either job or geographic mobility—or both—during the program. The personal dynamic cannot be underestimated in any development program and can change for very good reason over time. Given personal dynamics, programs must be flexible to ensure high-potential candidates are not left on the sidelines. The ability to be mobile can be very situational and often is a timing issue. While individuals may be very mobile earlier in their careers, family dynamics may require some stability for a period, and then those individuals may be able to get back on the development train when the family situation allows.

If individuals are deeply committed to leadership development, agency flexibility is incredibly important. Agencies must weigh all the professional and personal dynamics when considering aspiring leaders. Lack of mobility should never be a disqualifier if it is temporary or situational.

What's wrong with SES CDPs

There are significant challenges in advertised candidate programs for the program owners when their candidates are not selected. Whether targeting placement in the current agency or, even more challenging, placement in other agencies, the culture of the organization doing the hiring is often not considered. In many organizations, technical competency is paramount in the selection of new senior executives—and it should be. Most, if not all, SES positions use the demonstration of technical expertise as the first gate for consideration of an SES candidate. For all new senior executives, that strong technical foundation gives them credibility in representing their organization. And, just as important, it demonstrates to subordinates that they have a credible leader in charge of their function.

Most candidate programs fail to recognize the importance of technical competence, placing more emphasis on leadership competencies through building breadth and exposure to cross-functional opportunities. Candidates whose primary strength is technical competence are instead viewed with skepticism and rarely trusted with significant leadership challenges. When individuals graduate from these programs, they often find that while they were increasing their leadership skills (at least on paper), their technical value in their primary specialty degraded. Failure to demonstrate technical competence at an executive level is the overriding factor in why candidate programs rarely produce viable SES candidates. Well-orchestrated LDPs that have buy-in across an agency offer the best opportunity for individuals to be competitive for SES consideration without being labeled "candidate development."

Whether agencies advertise their own SES candidate programs or an incoming administration sees them as a panacea for growing future leaders, experience would indicate that these programs tend to build unrealistic expectations, and candidates end up frustrated about not being selected for SES upon completion. Further causing frustration is that OPM, in some instances, qualifies individuals based on their paper ECQs. Some candidates presume this to mean they are ready for the next available SES position. In reality, certification of ECQs is just one step—an important one—in the process.

Without an explanation that candidates are qualified to compete when OPM certifies their ECQs—even though they may not be best qualified (BQ)—or that a CDP does not eliminate the need to compete, candidates can't understand why they continue to be passed over in the SES selection process. We clearly applaud well-thought-out LDPs that communicate what it takes, both personally and professionally, to be competitive. But the title "Candidate Development Program" does a tremendous disservice to the participants and also the members at large who may feel they have no chance of competing. Worst yet, if they feel they are not one of the chosen few destined to fill their agency's senior leader positions, they may choose to leave the organization or, in an extreme case, Federal service altogether.

Adopting the military model to develop promising leaders

The model offered herein builds on many of the foundational aspects regarding how the military builds its general officers. Yet it adjusts to the dynamics that, unlike the military, we are not dealing with an up-or-out promotion system or mandatory moves to meet mission requirements. In addition, while civilians can "opt in" for development consideration, there are prescribed development milestones for the military, including holding critical, progressive command positions to successfully compete for promotion to the general officer/flag levels. As a general rule, some components in DOD (in particular the Air Force) have a very structured process where talented civilians compete for and attend the same professional development opportunities as their military counterparts who have also competed with their peers for these same opportunities.

Talented civilians are offered career broadening opportunities to build breadth at every level in the Air Force, Joint Staff, and other OSD-level offices to share the same leadership opportunities as their military counterparts. The DOD looks for its senior executives to be able to share the leadership mantle with their military general/flag officer counterparts and values that its career civilians have shared the same development experiences, including progressive leadership (command-like) positions. For high-potential military officers, mentoring from senior leaders is a critical enabler to guide development throughout an officer's career.

Agency head responsibility

Developing the workforce and grooming future leaders is an agency head responsibility. There is nothing more important, and it makes everything else possible concerning agency performance. In many instances, CHCOs are held accountable for developing the workforce. While CHCOs play an important role in recommending development models, senior leaders across the agency must buy in and communicate their support to the agency head. In most cases, CHCOs execute hiring decisions made by organization leadership; they don't (or should not) make the hiring decisions. CHCOs are the keepers of the hiring process and play an incredibly important role as the face of the agency in ensuring it has a transparent hiring process. Below is a framework (or model) for how an agency head could approach deliberate civilian workforce development, but it would never work without the complete support of leadership throughout the agency.

Importance of identifying key career positions

As challenging as this may be, agencies must analyze all of their professional positions, make a concerted effort to identify positions (i.e., key career positions) that will be great tests for aspiring leaders, and clearly communicate expectations for the incumbents. Typically, these positions should start at the GS-13 (or equivalent) level and progress through GS-15. Only seasoned GS-13s would be expected to compete for these positions. This will allow time for individuals to focus on building their technical expertise before competing for these positions. The key positions should be carefully selected with the support of the owning organization to ensure the incumbents can build the necessary competencies to be competitive for senior leader positions.

As a general guide, these key career positions should be in the range of 5–10 percent of the total professional positions in the agency (closer to 5 percent would be suggested initially) and corporately managed within the agency. Depending on the size of the agency, these positions should span all the major job specialties requiring SES leadership. Senior leader champions should be appointed to oversee the execution of these key positions, supported in large measure by the CHCOs. These positions should have tour limits, as they are developmental opportunities. Position duration should be in the 3- to 4-year range to allow senior leadership time to gauge development progress. Outplacement from these positions must be corporately managed with management authority to reassign individuals. In some cases, individuals may be required to sign mobility agreements to facilitate outplacement, which must be communicated very early in the process so there are no surprises at the time of outplacement. These positions should be competitive to allow for full transparency across the agency.

Filling key positions at the lower grade is no guarantor of success for filling positions at the higher level. BQ will be the determining factor in all competitions. There is no intent for supervisors of key positions to be on the sidelines;

they are the selecting authorities and, more importantly, should have been part of the decision to identify the position as key career. At no time should these positions be considered candidate programs; every level is competed. However, successful completion at the GS-15 level communicates that the individual has the necessary competencies to be competitive for the SES. Incumbents of these positions should be given priority on educational opportunities that will hone their professional skills as a way of showing the agency's commitment to leadership development. As agencies mature using this approach, it will be possible to build slates of candidates who could be management reassigned to fill these positions. This process will take at least 3–5 years to build and start the rotations if an agency is aggressive.

While some may say this model is not doable, I offer what we've done in the Air Force to implement such a model. Was it easy? Absolutely not! Did it take leadership at every level to buy into it? Absolutely! Air Force has been on a journey for the last 2 years to establish over 800 key career positions that span every functional community and are at every organizational level both in the continental United States and overseas, including our joint combatant commands where Air Force is the Executive Agent. To put the 800 in perspective, they account for 0.6 percent of our total permanent civilian population and 3 percent of our centrally managed professional positions. These positions are at the GS-13–15 levels and are only to be filled by internal candidates who are current DOD civilian employees; no external candidates are permitted.

These positions are owned by their parent organizations, and the Air Force senior functional leadership (i.e., job series owners responsible for development) partners with these organizations to identify high-potential candidates when these positions become vacant. Since we cannot force current incumbents who were not selected under the key career position rules to vacate these positions, the process will take time before all of the positions have individuals selected under the new process. Program rules regarding tour agreements, mobility, professional development opportunities, and centrally provided monies are all included. Individuals self-nominate to compete at every grade level, and a slate of individuals is provided to the supervisor of the position, who must select off of the slate or provide justification regarding why the slate does not meet the position requirement. As stated above, this is not easy, and constant communication with the workforce and military and civilian leaders is absolutely essential to reinforce at every opportunity.

When are aspiring leaders ready?

Regardless of the development model, deciding when an individual is ready for the SES may not be the right question unless we are asking when the individual is qualified to compete. Individuals can complete the most rigorous development programs and still not be selected for the SES. They may be ready to compete for SES, but it is still a BQ competitive process, and the number of SES allocations is incredibly small—just a fraction of a percentage of the civilian population in most agencies. This is no different than the military model where we have over 3,000 full colonels competing for less than 300 general officer positions in the Air Force.

In any LDP, there are *no guarantees* an individual will be selected, and that should be communicated from day 1. Yet, participants in a development program tend to be more competitive than individuals who chose not to compete for leadership development opportunities. They could have made significant personal and family sacrifices to be competitive, but they went into it with their eyes open and with full disclosure of all the challenges. Agencies could lose some of these trained leaders because of their SES vetting processes, and they could be competitive and selected for the SES in other agencies. Good agencies will applaud their trained leaders being selected, even if not by their own agency. Building enterprise government leaders is what it is all about!

A Continuum of Leadership Learning for the SES

By Dr. Suzanne Logan, Director of the Federal Executive Institute, U.S. Office of Personnel Management

Introduction

By definition, visionary leaders are ones who exhibit the qualities of openness, imagination, persistence, and conviction. While similar to transformational leaders, visionary leaders focus on the future, and they use their vision to inspire, motivate, and lead others. Transformational leaders leverage their passion and charisma to motivate others in building effective teams that work toward a common goal. Now more than ever, our country needs visionary leaders to guide our Federal government through times of growth, change, and transformation.

The problem is that we cannot wait for visionary leaders to emerge in service to our country; we must proactively develop today's workforce in a systematic and rigorous way. Requirements for professional leadership development of Federal civilian employees exist. Agencies in the executive branch have a requirement to develop future and current leaders capable of leading and transforming government. Title 5 in the Code of Federal Regulations requires all agencies to provide for the professional development of current and future executives.[137] In other words, agencies are instructed to provide a continuum of leadership development even though no government-wide sanctioned continuum for career civilians exists. Additionally, a continuum of leadership development is found in President Obama's EO, *Strengthening the Senior Executive Service*, issued on December 15, 2015.[138] This EO supports the recruitment and development of career senior executives to build a world-class Federal management team through professional leadership development for those in the SES.

To bolster a world-class Federal workforce prescribed in Title 5 and envisioned in EO 13714, career-long leadership development must be provided to the entire Federal workforce. Action must be taken now to put policy and processes in place to fully prepare Federal senior leaders for their first leadership roles and the leadership responsibilities they will assume during the

---

[137] Development for and Within the Senior Executive Service, 5 U.S.C. § 3396 (2001).
[138] Exec. Order No. 13714, Strengthening the Senior Executive Service. (2015, December 15). Retrieved from https://www.whitehouse.gov/the-press-office/2015/12/15/executive-order-strengthening-senior-executive-service

remainder of their Federal careers. I believe this can be accomplished through a well-designed continuum of leadership development put in policy by the OPM and adopted throughout the Federal government.

Career-long Federal leadership development

Most of my professional career has been spent as a teacher and leader in the discipline of continuing professional education and development. For many years, I was responsible for continuing professional education at a public university; subsequently, I spent a number of years as a USAF civilian leader in joint professional military education before assuming responsibility for interagency civilian leadership and professional development programs within the OPM in the executive branch of the Federal government.

While serving at the university in the role as an associate vice provost and faculty member in the graduate school, I observed the logical progression of learning that occurs in an academic setting. Not only do students learn from core courses within their major beside others who are pursuing the same field of study, but also they learn by taking elective courses from other academic disciplines that broaden their perspectives and world views. Similar to the workplace, university campuses serve as the backdrop for students to learn academic and interpersonal skills through their social interactions and extracurricular activities. These interactions help build personal networks and provide opportunities for professional growth while meeting the needs each individual identifies as his or her personal developmental goals.

During my time as the Chief Academic Executive for Officer Education within the USAF, I worked with the DOD Joint Staff using a curriculum continuum required for all officers' professional military education. The curriculum addresses the deficiencies identified in the Goldwater-Nichols Department of Defense Reorganization Act of 1986 (P.L. 99-433)[139] and includes a jointly designed and accredited officer professional military education continuum of learning, codified in the Chairman of the Joint Chiefs of Staff Instruction (CJCSI) 1800.01E, *Officer Professional Military Education Policy* (OPMEP).[140]

The OPMEP identifies multiple levels of education required by the Chairman of the Joint Chiefs of Staff that can be broadly categorized as Preparatory, Phase I, Phase II and/or single-phase programs offered at select institutions, and a General/Field Officer course. Completion of each phase is required before advancing to the next level and before rising to a higher rank. It defines the focus of each level and creates a continuum of learning linking the levels so that they build on the knowledge and values gained from the previous levels. This continuum of learning not only prepares officers for promotion to greater responsibilities but also serves as a pipeline for succession planning.

---

[139] Goldwater-Nichols Act.
[140] Chairman of the Joint Chiefs of Staff Instruction (CJCSI) No. 1800.01E, Officer Professional Military Education Policy. (2015, May 29). Retrieved from http://www.dtic.mil/cjcs_directives/cdata/unlimit/1800_01a.pdf

The outcomes required in the OPMEP are designed to produce strategically minded, agile, and adaptive leaders who are prepared to make use of the instruments of national power for their decision-making processes. These officers must be confident in their ability and training to operate effectively in a joint military environment and lead others in a multisector or international force. Complementing the military officers' continuum of leadership development, the DOD offers a series of programs designed for civilian leadership development. Neither codified nor required, these programs create the basis of a continuum of leadership development for civilians and include DOD-wide development opportunities that, like their military counterparts, build on the knowledge and values gained from prior training.

The programs include the Defense Civilian Emerging Leader Program targeted for DOD civilians in GS-7–11, the Executive Leadership Development Program targeted for DOD civilians in GS-12–15, and the Senior Leader Development Program targeted for DOD civilians in GS-14–15. Additionally, a number of programs are available specifically for DOD leaders that are open to both general officers and senior civilian executives. While programs such as these are more relevant now than ever because of the current focus of government agencies on improving the leadership of the Federal workforce, they are not part of a required continuum of professional Federal career leadership development.

Today, as an OPM Deputy Associate Director, I am responsible for the Center for Leadership Development. My interest in increasing the value of professional development programs led me to a review of what has been occurring for decades in the professional development of health providers. I discovered that many health professions have established professional development requirements that incorporate the use of inter-professional development (shared learning experiences of professionals from two or more professions who may in the future or routinely work together to achieve a common goal) to enhance on-the-job learning and required professional development designed for their specific health specialization.

Inter-professional development has resulted in deeper insights, shared lessons learned, and increased trust and collaboration across professional specialties, in addition to increased knowledge and skills for all participants. This "joint" professional development can meet requirements not met in professional development programs designed to only enhance medical competence in medical knowledge and skills. Inter-professional development programs improve healthcare professionals' abilities in areas such as management, team building, professionalism, interpersonal communications, patient care, ethical practice, and accountability. Learning to work more efficiently and effectively with healthcare professionals across the healthcare professions results in behavioral changes in medical practice overall. As a result, improved healthcare is achieved along with measurable outcomes, including shared trust, better decision making, and improved patient care.

As the models I have referenced demonstrate, there are existing examples of structured continua of professional development. These include learning specific to the individual (networking with others, sharing knowledge, or assessing one's strengths), intra-agency leadership development (learning within one's major department at a university, within a service, or within a healthcare specialization), and inter-professional leadership development (learning from elective courses at a university, joint military learning, or healthcare's inter-professional development).

Reflecting on the commonalities and successes of the university degree program model, the DOD model, and the healthcare professions' model, I found that the best professional education and development for a well-prepared Federal workforce from entry level through senior executive level stems from a career-long development plan. This plan has a three-pronged structure comprising (1) individual development designed to meet one's specific professional development needs, (2) formal development within the professional discipline or within one's own organization, and (3) inter-professional development across disciplines in a joint nature that builds shared competencies and interpersonal networks across professions.

Each of the aforementioned models was developed to resolve workforce gaps that existed in professionals' abilities to lead—to understand others, to work together collaboratively, and to meet the high demands of clients. University graduates must have a broader understanding or knowledge base than that provided by only understanding a chosen academic discipline. Military officers and Federal civilians must be able to lead people during peacetime operations and times of conflict when the nation is called upon to bear all instruments of power and protect our homeland. Healthcare professionals must be able to work collaboratively and simultaneously with others to heal patients when a time-sensitive approach is critical. With increasing challenges requiring Federal leaders to work across boundaries and an increasing focus on the need to better prepare our Federal workers for leadership, we must draw from these models to create a common baseline of leadership development across professions, as well as across the Federal landscape.

An evidence-based model for a leadership development continuum

Today, the Federal civil service has a few requirements for continued learning and professional development. Supervisors and managers in the civil service must meet a limited number of professional development requirements to progress up the Federal career ladder and receive recognition and recompense for their work (e.g., OPM Federal Supervisory and Management Frameworks and Guidance[141]). There are requirements that an SES candidate must demonstrate proficiency and mastery of each of OPM's five ECQs before being

---

[141] U.S. Office of Personnel Management. Training and development policy wiki, supervisory leadership development. Retrieved from https://www.opm.gov/WIKI/training/Supervisory-Leadership-Development.ashx

appointed to a SES position. And there are now requirements for development once appointed to the SES.

However, a well-structured career-long continuum of leadership development, such as the one existing within the OPMEP or one structured to include the breadth of healthcare professions, does not exist to develop Federal civilian leaders who must also be able to work together effectively when tackling the critical challenges faced by our country. There is no requirement for a three-pronged approach of development (individual, intra-agency, and interagency or inter-professional) to prepare Federal leaders for the important work for which they are held responsible. The December 2015 EO is a step in the right direction; however, improving leadership education and development once a person is a senior leader may be too little, too late.

The pieces for a strong professional development foundation exist and must be brought into a unified leadership continuum for current and future Federal civilian employees. By incorporating the DOD model of officer leader development and the construct of professional development seen in the healthcare professions that includes opportunities to develop individual strengths, development within one's own discipline and one's organization, and inter-professional and cross-organization development, an exceptional model can be conceived for Federal civilians that would provide leadership development throughout one's professional career. A government-wide continuum of leadership development can be designed that includes four specific developmental levels (supervisors, managers, executives, and senior executives) and the three realms of development (individual, intra-agency or intra-professional, and interagency or inter-professional).

Within a matrix of these categories would be specific leadership development requirements recognized and supported across Federal agencies that would significantly increase the preparation and readiness of Federal leadership for moving into each identified level of leadership. Additionally, unique individual development, profession or agency development, and inter-professional or interagency development would all be incorporated to create a comprehensive plan for each individual's leadership development, thereby satisfying individual developmental needs, agency leadership needs, and interagency needs. The result would be a more prepared, efficient, and effective Federal workforce government-wide.

Toward an "enterprise" leadership development continuum

In the book *Tackling Wicked Government Problems*,[142] Jackson Nickerson and Ronald Sanders argue that "... developing the skills, networks, reputation and trust needed for interagency leadership success takes many years and experiences and accumulates over a career." At each phase of development,

---

[142] Sanders, R. P. *Tackling wicked government problems*, p. 177.

maturing cultural awareness; leading change; making ethical decisions; thinking critically, strategically, and creatively; strategically communicating; and building coalitions must be taught along with individual and agency-specific developmental requirements.

Already existing and available to support the development of a continuum of Federal professional leadership are the ECQs. Based on attributes of successful executives in both the private and public sectors, the ECQs have been verified by organizational psychologists, HR professionals, and senior executives. The ECQs (Leading Change, Leading People, Results Driven, Business Acumen, and Building Coalitions) and their 28 supporting competencies are designed to build a Federal corporate culture that drives results, serves customers, and builds successful teams and coalitions within and outside the organization. To master these requirements, a continuum of leadership development for the Federal workforce must be designed for four levels of leadership.

Each level of professional leadership development must be designed to incorporate formal instruction for foundational knowledge, experiential activities that provide action learning, developmental relationships such as coaching and mentoring, individual assessment and feedback that provides self-reflection, and self-development that allows one to pursue areas of personal interest and individual strength. None of this developmental work should be isolated from one's own work assignments. Individuals should be able to immediately apply the lessons learned to their own challenges. However, the intent of leadership development would be not only to improve each individual's leadership but also to improve the overall leadership of our Federal agencies and the U.S. government.

Beginning with preparation to move into a supervisory role and basing professional development on the competencies needed at that level of leadership, the Federal civilian must be firmly grounded in an understanding of his or her own agency—the policies, culture, and processes necessary to be successful within that agency. In addition, the emerging leader must develop the methods and skills of supervision in an interagency or inter-professional manner. That development would focus on learning to lead people, making sound and ethical decisions, leading change, and communicating with clarity and precision whether the communication is verbal or written. This developmental program would be supplemented by the OPM-required supervisory training required now for all new Federal supervisors (see the OPM Federal Supervisory and Management Framework[143]). Supervisors preparing to move into managerial roles must build on the leadership lessons learned in their supervisory development program by further developing their ability to lead people, learning how to lead complex change and organizational transformation, and developing their analytic capabilities and creative thought processes.

[143] U.S. Office of Personnel Management. Training and development policy wiki.

Preparation for a manager's position would include studying critical thinking supported by examining strategic decisions made by executive leaders to develop lessons learned on how to operate in a VUCA environment, anticipate the need for change, and respond to uncertainty. These supervisors would also develop a strategic understanding of managing human, financial, and information resources to meet organizational goals and customer expectations through the work of their teams (see the OPM Federal Supervisory and Management Framework[144]).

Managers desiring to move into the executive level of leadership within the Federal government must learn how to be strategic leaders. The focus of their study would once again build on what was learned as a manager with an added focus on working across agencies, responding to Congress, communicating to the media, and leading in intergovernmental and multinational efforts. They would be prepared to achieve results by building coalitions internally and with other Federal agencies, state and local governments, nonprofit and private sector organizations, foreign governments, and/or international organizations to achieve common goals. It is also at this level that managers must be able to demonstrate that they have developed a mastery of the five ECQs.

Having achieved the executive's level, Federal leaders would be asked to further develop their skills and business acumen to be prepared for positions of whole-of-government or enterprise-wide leadership. They would apply what they have learned in order to successfully work across Federal government agencies, interact with Congress and the media, and assume intergovernmental and multinational roles. Support for this development exists in the fact that by law (5 United States Code 3396),[145] OPM is required to establish programs for the systematic development of candidates for the SES. In doing so OPM can develop programs that provide for the continuing development of senior executives, or it can require agencies to establish programs for the continuing development of their senior executives that meet criteria prescribed by OPM.

Analysis, critical examination, and creativity are required skills to be developed to lead at the senior executive level, along with development of attributes and behaviors necessary to effectively lead across an agency or agencies. Executives must learn to assess and evaluate the critical strategic thinking, decision making, and communication of other strategic leaders. They must learn to create innovative organizations capable of operating in dynamic complex and uncertain environments, to anticipate change, and to respond to uncertainty. Perfecting one's ability to communicate a vision; challenge assumptions; and anticipate, plan, implement, and lead strategic change in a complex organization is necessary at the senior executive level of leadership, as is the ability to foster responsibility, accountability, and trust within an organization.

---

[144] Ibid.
[145] Development for and Within the Senior Executive Service, 5 U.S.C. § 3396.

Of paramount importance for the executive's development is the need to learn to establish and sustain a performance-driven, accountable, and ethical climate throughout one's span of control, as well as to lead at the interagency level. At the interagency level, the executive may have no actual control but rather must lead using his or her span of influence.

At the pinnacle of the continuum of Federal leadership development, senior executives must stay abreast of strategies to lead high-level interagency, intergovernmental, and multinational leadership requirements; manage congressional agency relations; and lead Cross-Agency Priority Goals, projects, and programs requiring interagency, intergovernmental, and multinational collaboration to achieve U.S. national interests and objectives. Even as developmental requirements are mastered at each level of leadership, leadership development is never complete—career-long learning is a must.

Reprise: Leadership learning that exceeds the pace of change

In today's VUCA environment, the rate of workforce learning must exceed the rate of change in the environment. Continuous career-long learning is essential for all individuals at all levels to remain relevant in today's fast-paced environment. Our world keeps changing exponentially; new challenges are repeatedly presented, technologies and social media continue to transform the way we manage our data and communicate with others, and our shrinking world brings us closer to other cultures and nations. Our perspectives must continue to evolve, making each individual's leadership development critical and career-long development mandatory.

The Federal government sits at a similar crossroad to the services before the Goldwater-Nichols Act.[146] A leadership crisis will occur if the Federal government continues to allow a fragmented and marginalized system of civilian leadership development. Each agency is developing its leaders, but a Federal government-wide continuum of professional leadership development does not exist that will standardize leadership development, ensure a pipeline for succession planning, and provide measurable preparation for civilian leadership advancement. To make progress in responding to and resolving current and future challenges that span the Federal government, collaboration, coordination, and synchronization within and across Federal agencies are needed.

A government-wide requirement for agencies to adopt an OPM-provided continuum of professional leadership development for advancement at all levels of leadership would ensure each agency's succession plan includes visionary leaders who have mastered required leadership competencies and are prepared to fill leadership roles for our Federal government. A differentiated set of measurable learning outcomes evolving from the ECQs and their supporting competencies would define the required competencies that all

---

[146] Goldwater-Nichols Act.

Federal leaders are required to master before advancing. Such a continuum of professional leadership development would maximize enterprise-wide executive leadership effectiveness and potential as it significantly strengthens the ability of Federal agencies to meet their missions and tackle the future challenges of our country. A government-wide continuum of leadership development would ensure Federal leaders are systematically prepared to remain ahead of the rate of change in our world.

Ultimately, developing quality program models that are sustainable will depend on a long-term policy that supports standardization and incorporation of innovative programs as foundational features of the leadership development landscape. The way ahead is not difficult. OPM has the authority to develop policies for Federal civilians' developmental needs. The development of a policy that would be a civilian version of the OPMEP, which draws from the lessons learned by universities, the military, healthcare professions, and even OPM itself, would make the required continuum of leadership development achievable and measurable.

OPM can also lead the process of ensuring policy development that defines the continuum of leadership development. OPM could take on a role comparable to the role of the J7 staff for monitoring and accrediting the providers (either public or private) of the prescribed leadership development. All agencies would then have dependable and achievable guidance to ensure the Federal government has visionary leaders in place to meet future challenges. Practice areas within the OPM could follow the model of DOD to oversee this regulatory requirement with minimal costs. The resulting critical mass of successful visionary leaders would produce crucial, enduring, fundamental changes as the Federal government prepares to meet the demands of the ever-increasingly diverse workforce of the 21st century in a VUCA environment.

A dependable and achievable government-wide plan for leadership development is required for Federal leaders to stay ahead of the rate of change in the environment. The lack of a common requirement has resulted in inconsistent leadership development within agencies and has increased the cost of the development that does occur. Recent attempts to transform leadership development have fallen well short. The Federal government must operationalize its best efforts to institutionalize a leadership development continuum that focuses on developing common competencies that all Federal leaders must have to be effective in this ever-changing environment. A continuum of leadership development focused on developing visionary leaders and transforming the Federal government will provide a robust, resilient succession pipeline for the future that ensures the necessary skills are inculcated in all government leaders, adequately preparing them to lead the Federal workforce today while strengthening our Federal government for future generations. The time to act is now.

CHAPTER 4.5:
Creating Common Cause through Joint Executive Development

By the Honorable G. Edward DeSeve, former Deputy Director for Management, U.S. Office of Management and Budget

Introduction

As appointed and career leaders are thrown together—whether at the beginning of an administration or as vacancies occur during its course—they are challenged to reconcile their respective interests, objectives, and working styles, and they often start at opposite ends of the spectrum. Career executives believe they represent continuity in government, its "permanent" leadership cadre, whereas presidential appointees, as missionaries for the policies and priorities of a new president, see themselves as energizing change agents. Getting the two groups to collaborate to achieve agency goals can be problematic.

New political appointees often come to the job with a sense of urgency, and their common refrain is, "I can't get the bureaucracy to work with me." The response from career civil servants is often, "These people just don't get it." Reconciling these positions is essential if the organizational goals both seek are to be reached. I have written elsewhere about the need for collaboration between career executives and political appointees,[147] and since then, I have become more convinced that both groups need a common developmental framework for achieving their common purpose. While we may not want to call this *executive (or organizational) development*, there is a need for both groups to come together to understand the common challenges they face, the results they seek, the risks that are ahead, and how they can demonstrate resilience when problems do arise. This can best be done in an environment of joint development that, at the core, is rooted in collaboration to achieve common goals.

Continually during a president's term, he or she appoints the literally thousands of senior political executives in Federal departments and agencies. The number of presidential appointments available at all levels is approximately 8,000 (including various boards and commissions), and these are in constant flux.

[147] DeSeve, G. E. (2008). *Presidential appointee's handbook.* Washington, DC: Brookings Institution Press.

Those appointed executives must interact with the more than 9,000 career executives and military officers of equivalent (that is, flag) rank, many of whom are in place when those appointees arrive...and when they leave.

Presidential appointees come in many varieties. Some are policy wonks intent on passing legislation or regulations that will advance a cause, and they may have little experience or interest in managing the organizations they oversee. Others come from the private sector and have management backgrounds... but not necessarily ones that have equipped them to deal with the complex nuances associated with managing a government organization. Still others come from the public or nonprofit sector and may not be familiar with the procedures and frustrations that come with working in government generally, much less the Federal government.

What we know for sure is that career executives and presidential appointees must function together smoothly if the work of the Federal government is to get done. One way to jump-start that cooperation is through joint executive development activities among SES members and the presidential appointees for whom they work—as the foundation for greater collaboration between the two. Wouldn't joint executive development provide a common language and an opportunity for a common understanding of the challenges facing a department or agency?

Improving the quality of collaboration between career SES members and presidential appointees may be the key difference maker in either achieving the agency's mission or not. Indeed, one could argue that collaboration is the connective tissue that underpins all of OPM's ECQs and the fundamental competencies that compose them. Joint executive development focused on those competencies could provide an opportunity for agency leaders to ac-quire skills in political-career collaboration, especially when they focus on mastering those competencies *together*.

Leading change through strategic alignment

For example, the first of OPM's ECQs focuses on leading change to meet or-ganizational goals. Inherent in this ECQ is the ability to work collaboratively with other leaders to establish an organizational vision and to implement it in a continuously changing environment. However, leading change, in itself, is necessary but insufficient; getting strategic alignment between career exec-utives and appointees is an essential antecedent to any change effort.

An agency's own strategic plan should serve as a starting point. It should provide a comprehensive look at the work of the agency and should outline the specific performance goals to which it is committed; it is almost a given that sometime during the tenure of the agency's appointed leadership, that strategic plan will need to be updated. This time provides the perfect opportunity to achieve strategic alignment. Apropos of their institutional role, career executives can provide the rationale behind the existing plan, with appointed leaders collaboratively setting the direction of its update, and with the plan serving as the neutral ground that allows both the career and appointed leaders to see where the other is coming from.

Further, that new strategic plan—or for that matter, any significant change to be undertaken by a new administration—should be structured carefully and rooted in an understanding of the history and culture of the organization… an understanding that can only come from that agency's career executives and middle managers. Thus, political appointees and career executives need to create a collaborative network that enables them to develop and manage the change. This is best done by fostering a common language and common goals through common developmental experiences at the outset of the appointee's tenure. In so doing, the individual and collective qualities of resilience, strategic thinking, and visioning, as well as flexibility and decisiveness, can all be learned (or re-learned) by both groups collectively.

Case study: The American Recovery and Reinvestment Act[148]

The ARRA provided an opportunity to test the approach described above. The program's purpose and goals were specified in the legislation, but translating these into an organizational vision that would actually achieve them required the creation of a complex, interdependent network of committed political and career officials that included the White House, Federal agencies, grantees (particularly state and local governments), oversight agencies like the Government Accountability Office, the 15 Inspectors General of the Recovery and Transparency Board, and Congress. Continual communication among the parties and continual reinforcement of the need for speed in achieving the purposes of the Act served to create a common basis for action.

The Act included more than 200 separate appropriation items across more than 20 departments and agencies, and it also involved every state and territory. This kind of complexity and the speed at which the Act needed to be executed if it was to be effective meant that top-down, hierarchical, authoritarian leadership was unlikely to work. Instead, the agencies were formed into a network of networks that communicated with the Recovery Improvement Office, or RIO (which I led), continuously and with each other in twice-a-week conference calls. The financial staffs of the agencies had the challenge of weekly financial reporting. The appointees and program staff had to get the money announced quickly, get it under contract, develop an oversight and reporting infrastructure, produce results, and maintain public support.

---

[148] American Recovery and Reinvestment Act of 2009.

In each agency, senior appointees—typically the Deputy Secretary or agency COO—worked side by side with the senior executives who headed the programs that received funds. Early on, senior political appointees (represented by Rahm Emanuel, the President's Chief of Staff; Ron Klain, the Vice President's Chief of Staff; and Rob Nabors, the Deputy Director of OMB) and their career SES counterparts realized that ARRA could not be managed top down. External networks were required as well. The Vice President coordinated the work of the cabinet heads and led the outreach effort to state and local governments. In each state government, there was a single responsible official who was tightly connected to the RIO and who could be quickly mobilized to take rapid action if a problem occurred. Similarly, there were single responsible individuals in agencies.

Here's how it worked. When a sequencing problem arose between a highway project and an Environmental Protection Agency (EPA) project, I was able to invoke—at the Vice President's urging—the network of relationships that existed between the U.S. Department of Transportation's Deputy Secretary, the EPA Deputy Administrator, state-level environment and transportation secretaries, and other responsible state officials, and we resolved the problem within 24 hours—to the amazement of congressional observers.

While interactions among those in this network may not have seemed like executive and organizational development in the classic sense, there was a very real component of joint learning involved. This individual and group/team development occurred more on the job than in the classroom, but the principles of network management—commitment to common purpose, trust, governance structure and enabling technology, leadership, and access to authority and resources—served as the framework and foundation for joint learning.

Institutionalizing joint executive development

Accordingly, at the executive branch level, I believe that before, during, and after the formal presidential transition process, the incoming administration should develop and execute a continuous formal leadership and organizational development process for its appointees that focuses, among other things, on the leadership and management competencies embedded in OPM's ECQs. That process should include relevant agency SES members to provide insight into how the two groups—political appointees and career executives—can work together. And at the agency level, each agency should provide common leadership and organizational development programs that mix the two groups, using the development (or update) of the agency's strategic plan as a means of bringing about their strategic alignment with the results both are committed to achieving, the risks they will face, and a plan for ensuring resilience when the agency is faced with adversity—anticipated or unanticipated.

The senior leadership of the organization, both political and career, must share a common commitment, must be credible in expressing this commitment, and must communicate their commitment throughout the organization. However, it is not unusual for some senior political executives to come to their jobs without significant leadership or managerial experience, and any presidential appointee who arrives at his or her post and immediately b egins giving orders runs the risk of alienating those most important to the implementation of the agency's work—the career executives, managers, and front-line employees who actually perform the agency's mission.

Joint development of collaboration skills will foster a culture that is focused on solving problems, not protecting turf. And as a byproduct, that joint development will also help organizational leaders build and leverage a network of networks that is both internal and external to the organization. This network does not replace the formal organizational structure of the agency; rather, it augments that structure and further enables appointees and SES members to do their jobs effectively. Thus, a new approach to joint leader development would go a long way to ensuring the success of agencies in developing and implementing policies that are valued by the American people and create value for the nation as a whole.

Concluding Commentary and Recommendations

Introduction: Supply versus demand, quality versus quantity

As we noted at the outset, the Federal government's senior executive corps has a supply and demand problem. On the demand side, record numbers of career executives—the Partnership for Public Service estimates as much as 85 percent of the corps[149]—will be eligible to retire over the next decade. While we do not project a retirement tsunami, those seasoned executives will leave government eventually, perhaps sooner than later given the challenges discussed in previous sections. So there will be lots of promotion opportunities, but will there be enough high-quality successors to fill them?

As we have discussed, among members of the most obvious internal succession pool—current Federal managers at the GS-14 and GS-15 grade levels—it is just not clear that the SES has the appeal it once did. Many look at the arguably well-intentioned but ill-conceived attempts at SES reform (for example, in the U.S. Department of Veterans Affairs), severe salary compression, pay and bonus freezes and pay caps, and potential job rotations mandated by EO 13714, plus all the other added headaches—all for little or no additional reward—and they may conclude that they're better off just where they are.

To be sure, some will argue that there is no supply-demand gap, inasmuch as there will always be plenty of candidates (both internal and external) in line for the next senior executive vacancy. But will they be prepared to lead 21st century government? Will they have the requisite leadership skills and experiences to succeed in tomorrow's SES? That's the question…and the answer is uncertain.

Closing the gap…

Part of that uncertainty has to do with lead time. If past career patterns are any guide, it used to take at least two decades for an entry-level GS-7 to make his or her way up into the career SES; even if you assume an accelerated learning curve and/or lateral entry can cut that gestation time in half, we're

---

[149] Partnership for Public Service & McKinsey and Company. (2016). *A pivotal moment for the Senior Executive Service: Measures, aspirational practices and stories of success.* Washington, DC: Partnership for Public Service.

still looking at a minimum of a decade of hopefully deliberate leadership development (whether inside or outside government) to prepare someone to be a senior career executive. Even then, given the documented impatience of millennials, it's not clear they will wait that long. So if an agency's executive succession plan (presuming it has one) isn't looking out at least a decade—in terms of both numbers and competencies—it runs the considerable risk of having a pool of SES candidates who, at best, are ready to lead today's government, but not necessarily tomorrow's.

The key, of course, is a deliberate, long-term, whole-of-government leadership development strategy that complements today's largely agency-centric ones, so that together, agencies and the Federal government as a whole are capable of building an SES succession pool of sufficient size *and* skill to meet the projected demand for new career executives. However, it is not clear that the Federal government as a whole has such a strategy, and without one, the nation risks a career senior leadership gap of critical proportions. It is also not clear that the nation cares, but that is another matter—those who contributed to this volume do, and what follow are some recommendations to close that gap.

RECOMMENDATION 4.1: BUILD A WHOLE-OF-GOVERNMENT EXECUTIVE SUCCESSION PLAN

Introduction: Planning for the future

If we assume it takes no less than 10–15 years to develop a senior executive, the Federal government is already behind the curve, especially with the potential gap between the supply and demand for top-notch senior executive candidates with the skills required for 21st century government.

It doesn't take a rocket scientist to figure out how to get ahead of that curve: deliberate succession planning and execution. However, while OPM several years ago required agencies to develop SES succession plans,[150] many agencies haven't bothered—or if they did, it was largely ineffectual, as agencies were fearful that such an exercise may be perceived as pre-selection and thus a violation of merit system principles (it is not!).[151] In addition, notwithstanding the long lead times associated with executive development, those agencies that do have succession plans tend to focus on the sufficiency of the immediate succession pool—that is, those GS-15s and equivalents who are either ready now to assume an SES position or who can be prepared to do so in

---

[150] Berry, J. (2010, August 3). *Guidance on freeze on discretionary awards, bonuses, and similar payments for Federal employees serving under political appointments* (OPM CPM 2010-14). Washington, DC: U.S. Office of Personnel Management. Retrieved from https://www.chcoc.gov/content/guidance-freeze-discretionary-awards-bonuses-and-similar-payments-Federal-employees-serving
[151] Partnership for Public Service & Booz Allen Hamilton. (2011). *Preparing the people pipeline. A Federal succession planning primer.* McLean, VA: Booz Allen Hamilton. Retrieved from https://www.boozallen.com/content/dam/boozallen/media/file/PARTNERSHIP FOR PUBLIC SERVICE-PeoplePipeline-2011.pdf

12–24 months. The extended leadership development pipeline, stretching over as much as 5–7 years, is rarely considered except in the most general sense.

However, perhaps more importantly, those succession planning efforts, such as they are, are exclusively agency-centric, focusing solely on the pipeline *within* an agency, despite the fact that the SES is supposed to be a corporate resource. This isn't really a surprise. As we have noted, the SES and its progeny have been insular since their inception.

Start with an enterprise SES database

Given the boundary-spanning challenges facing 21st century government, the SES must become what it has always aspired to be: a government-wide resource. First, OPM (or even better, the President's Management Council) needs to build a comprehensive inventory of current executives, as well as those in the senior leadership pipeline—including Presidential Management Fellows, Senior Presidential Management Fellows,[152] and SES Candidate Development Program participants and graduates—so it can begin to get a sense of their capabilities and competencies. And I don't mean a basic demographic analysis…that's easy. Rather, we need an inventory of the specific capabilities of the SES population and its pipeline—their skills, experience, education, and expertise, preferably all in a searchable database—so OPM can begin to apply big data analytics to model the dynamics of the executive corps.

That sounds relatively straightforward—every large multinational company has one, as does our military—but unfortunately, it's another case of easier said than done. When I was at OPM, we attempted to create such an SES database, only to meet with severe opposition from several agencies, most notably DOD. Their argument: Their executives belonged to them…they were agency assets, not to be shared, and by making information about their capabilities known to other agencies, the fear was that they would be vulnerable to poaching.

However, it's time to revisit and force the issue. Simply put, OMB should require that agencies (and/or agency executives themselves) provide detailed information on their executives, as well as those who are considered to be potential successors. And OPM should be instructed to build a searchable database—with appropriate information security—of that executive inventory. To be sure, that information will initially have gaps, but it's at least a start. And with it, bodies like the President's Management Council (PMC)—or the Enterprise Executive Resources Board that we recommend in Section 5—can begin to formulate a *whole-of-government* succession plan.

---

[152] Authorized by Executive Order 13318 renaming the President's Management Fellows but never implemented.

Building a multiagency succession model

A government-wide executive succession plan is something that's never even been attempted. However, I would argue that given the risks to the viability of the senior executive corps, it is sorely needed. And the good news is that a model exists. As recounted by Tish Long in her chapter, the 17 agencies and 6 cabinet departments that compose the Intelligence Community (IC) developed and executed a multiagency succession plan in 2009. And with over 2,000 SES and equivalent positions (in five different senior services across the IC) to consider, that plan was of sufficient scale to serve as a model for the whole-of-government effort advocate here.

To be sure, the IC's departments and agencies started with the same "for internal use only" mindset as every other Federal agency. However, the painful lessons of 9/11, the Intelligence Reform Act's mandate[153] for greater interagency collaboration, and the commitment of senior leaders like Tish Long and her fellow agency directors and deputies (the IC's equivalent of the PMC) helped turn that mindset around.

And the forcing function? The IC's then-new requirement that all succession candidates for its agencies' top senior executive positions—including the most senior career positions in those agencies—had to have completed at least one interagency assignment to even be eligible for consideration.[154] So when Tish and our colleagues realized that many of the most likely executive succession candidates could not (yet) meet that requirement, they knew they had to take affirmative action as a *group* to rectify the situation.

A risk-based approach to succession management

Here is what we did. First, we identified the 60–70 top career executive positions across all 17 intelligence agencies—typically those that had a direct reporting relationship to an agency head—and then assessed the attrition risk of their incumbents by looking at such things as their retirement eligibility (as well as the retirement propensity of current and prior incumbents), historical turnover patterns, and external market demand for their skills. We identified those that were likely to become vacant over the next 12 months as posing the highest attrition risk, those likely to turn over in the next 2 to 3 years as moderate risk, and those expected to become vacant over the ensuing 3 to 5 years as low risk.

---

[153] Intelligence Reform and Terrorism Prevention Act of 2004, Pub. L. No. 108-458, 118 Stat. 3638 (2004).
[154] Office of the Director of National Intelligence. (2013). Intelligence Community Directive No. 660, Intelligence Community Civilian Joint Duty Program. Retrieved from https://fas.org/irp/dni/icd/icd-660.pdf

The resulting risk categories represented the demand side of the equation.[155] We then focused on the supply side, examining the succession pools for each of the top positions in each agency, including potential candidates from all across the IC. The sufficiency of each succession pool was evaluated in terms of a number of predetermined, objective criteria: Did everyone in the succession pool possess the requisite leadership competencies and technical skills for the position in question? Had potential successors all completed at least one interagency mobility assignment (as noted, a condition for promotion to senior executive rank in the IC)? Was the candidate pool sufficiently diverse?

A succession pool was deemed sufficient (coded as green) if it had at least three candidates who met all of the criteria and were thus "ready now" to fill behind the incumbent of that position; positions with an insufficient number of ready-now candidates were identified as having unacceptably high succession risk (coded as "red"). We also identified and pooled candidates who could be readied—that is, deliberately developed—for the particular position in 2 to 3 years.

In so doing, the IC's senior leadership found that a considerable number of their key career executive positions across the IC had both a high attrition risk and a high succession risk. In other words, the various agencies anticipated a number of key senior leadership vacancies in the ensuing 12 months, but both individually and collectively, those agencies had an insufficient number of highly qualified executive candidates ready to fill those vacancies. And the most glaring deficiencies in those candidate pools? Many of the individual candidates lacked the prerequisite interagency mobility assignment, and, in the aggregate, most of the pools lacked diversity.

Those findings spurred Tish and her colleagues—leaders like CIA Deputy Director Michael Morell and Federal Bureau of Investigation (FBI) Associate Deputy Director Bob Ford—into action, collectively developing individual executive development plans (including a number of interagency executive exchanges to meet the mandatory mobility requirement) to mitigate the most mission-critical succession risks.

Two things to note. First, we focused on the sufficiency of the succession pools for a relatively small number of key career executive positions, and not so much on the individuals in those pools. To be sure, we evaluated the characteristics of each of those candidates against a set of objective succession criteria, including the degree of their *individual* readiness. However, in every case, the bar was set even higher: every succession *pool* also had to have at least three candidates who met all of the criteria...this to avoid any hint of pre-selection.

---

[155] Note that OPM has since adopted this risk-based nomenclature but has recommended it for agency use only; see U.S. Office of Personnel Management. (2009). *A guide to the Strategic Leadership Succession Management Model.* Washington, DC: U.S. Office of Personnel Management. Retrieved from www.opm.gov/hcaaf_resource_center/assets/Lead_Guide.pdf

Second, in no case did participating agencies give up their ultimate selection authority. Thus, while everyone in the multiagency succession pool was highly qualified to fill the anticipated vacancy, the agency with the vacancy reserved the right to choose any one of those candidates for the position.

Taking it to government-wide scale

So it's possible to develop a true whole-of-government succession plan, at least for those top career executive positions in the various executive departments and agencies that are fungible—like the various Chief Officers. And if the predicted leadership gap is even close to real, there is clearly a need to do so. After all, if OPM can declare that information technology (IT), HR, and acquisition jobs are mission critical and thus bear special attention, the same status should be afforded SES positions. As a general matter, there are enough retirement-eligible SES incumbents to qualify their positions as having some attrition risk, especially those that by definition have enterprise responsibilities, and there are enough questions about the sufficiency of their succession pools (if nothing else, with regard to their diversity) to warrant it.

As suggested above, I would start with the various Chief Officer (CXO) positions like CIO, CFO, and CHCO, inasmuch as candidates for these positions can come from across the Federal government. They represent a relatively manageable number, and I would charge the respective CXO councils—the Chief Financial Officers Council, the CHCO Council, the Chief Information Officers Council, etc.—to conduct the initial attrition/succession risk analysis, with the PMC (or the Enterprise ERB we recommend in Section 5) as the final customer of the results.

Given that its members will likely be the selecting officials for CXO vacancies, the various councils could provide the PMC or EERB slates of interested, highly qualified candidates, both internal and external, much as DOD does for its internal SES vacancies. President Obama's Executive Order 13714 singled out this DOD best practice, and it is relatively easy to take to scale.

As noted, this effort would require a comprehensive inventory of executive experience and expertise—a true executive talent management system. Some agencies, most notably DOD, already have one (again, truth in advertising… my Booz Allen team helped build it),[156] and any one system could be easily adapted for government-wide use. Most importantly, none of this requires any additional statutory authority. Like most of our recommendations, a whole-of-government succession plan, supported by a far more robust enterprise executive information system, is entirely within the administrative authority of OPM and OMB. It's just a matter of will.

---

[156] U.S. Department of Defense Directive No. 1400.25, Vol. 1403 (1996), DoD Civilian Personnel Management System.

RECOMMENDATION 4.2: MAKE INTERAGENCY MOBILITY A PREREQUISITE FOR SES PROMOTION

Introduction: Mobility as key to 21st century executive development

If a whole-of-government succession plan is a matter of will, so too is more executive mobility. However, with the exception of accountability and pay, few other SES issues generate more controversy. Should some sort of interagency (or equivalent) experience be a prerequisite to SES selection…if not for all SES positions, at least for those that entail some whole-of-government responsibilities? As rare as that interagency experience may be—as we have noted, statistics indicate that more than 80 percent of current SES members have spent their entire government careers in their home agency[157]—this remains one of the key executive development issues for a 21st century SES, just as it was for career executives in the Senior Foreign Service (SFS) and the five senior services in the IC.

In this day and age, cross-cutting, boundary-spanning problems are the norm; as a consequence, the case for interagency mobility assignments as a way of developing SES candidates (and deploying SES members) for a whole-of-government role is even more compelling than it was in 1979. As Beth Cobert and our other contributors assert, 21st century government demands leaders who are able to see the big picture, take an enterprise point of view, employ certain *enterprise* leadership competencies to overcome agency-centric stovepipes—their own as well as those of other agencies—and achieve the kind of interagency unity of effort that Thad Allen talks about in his chapter.

Indeed, one could assert that mobility is the only effective way to develop those competencies. Certainly all of our contributors take this view, and many of those who came up through the ranks of career executives to take a political appointment, like Beth McGrath and Pat Kennedy, embody it.

There is also ample anecdotal evidence to support this point of view. One need only look at the number of challenges facing our nation that require whole-of-government leadership—the kind originally envisioned for the SES—to realize they require a whole new set of leadership competencies, most of which can only be developed through deliberate, managed mobility. While there may be exceptions, it just seems to strain common sense to suggest that an executive can acquire an enterprise perspective from the vantage of a single agency.

It would seem the most effective way to develop that perspective is via a series of increasingly responsible interagency assignments, starting well before an individual becomes an executive—just as the U.S. military, the SFS, and the IC do. But if it is to work, enabling mechanisms must be put in place.

---

[157] Partnership for Public Service & McKinsey and Company. *A pivotal moment.*

Lessons learned: The case of the IC[158]

The IC offers a contemporary case in point. Beginning in 2005, the Office of the Director of National Intelligence (ODNI) led an unprecedented effort to design and implement an interagency mobility assignment system specifically intended to develop enterprise-focused leaders across the IC. Officially designated as the IC civilian joint duty program (after the military term of art), its development and implementation offer insights into the many organizational and administrative lessons learned along the way.[159]

The effort was prompted by the 9/11 Commission, which found among other things that the intelligence failures that led to the 9/11 tragedy were caused in part by senior leaders in the IC, virtually all of them career executives, who were singularly stove-piped.[160] In other words, the U.S. faced a threat that demanded a whole-of-government response, but it was led by leaders (and organizations) that just didn't think that way. With the Commission's findings in hand, the drafters of the Intelligence Reform and Terrorism Prevention Act (IRTPA) of 2004 took a lesson from the U.S. military's legacy of joint duty—that is, the requirement to complete an assignment in one of the several inter-service combatant commands as a prerequisite to flag rank—and they directed a similar approach in the IC.

Specifically, the IRTPA mandated that the DNI "seek to duplicate joint [military] officer management policies" and authorized him to "prescribe mechanisms to facilitate the rotation of [civilian] personnel of the intelligence community through various elements of the intelligence community" and to make such assignments "a condition of promotion to (certain senior) positions within the intelligence community."[161] The program's implicit hypothesis was that over time, the IC's 17 separate agencies, spread across 6 cabinet departments, would be led exclusively by executives who had a broader, whole-of-IC mindset, just like the original vision of the SES. To be sure, most of the heads of the IC's various agencies generally supported the concept of civilian joint duty—and the development of senior leaders with an enterprise focus—on its merits. This was especially true of the heads of DOD's largest intelligence agencies (like the National Security Agency, NGA, and DIA), which were all headed by general or flag officers who themselves had had to complete one or more military joint assignments on their own way to flag rank.

[158] Adapted from my chapter (Chapter 13) in Nickerson, J. A., & Sanders, R. P. (Eds.). (2014). *Tackling wicked government problems: A practical guide for developing enterprise leaders.* Washington, DC: Brookings Institution Press.
[159] Intelligence Community Directive No. 660.
[160] National Commission on Terrorist Attacks upon the United States (2004). *The 9/11 Commission Report.* Washington, DC: U.S. Government Publishing Office. Retrieved from https://9-11commission.gov/report
[161] Intelligence Reform and Terrorism Prevention Act.

However, support for applying that same concept to civilian senior executives did not necessarily (or easily) translate into the creation of a system for developing civilian enterprise leaders in the IC. It took the IC almost 2 years of intense interagency contention and ultimately, collaboration to resolve the myriad issues underlying its design, development, and implementation.

In that regard, interagency mobility—whether before or after promotion to the SES—has always been easier said than done.[162] There are all sorts of structural and cultural reasons for this, among them the Balkanization of today's senior executive corps and the fact that agencies have historically treated senior executives (as well as those who aspire to the SES) as their organizational property to be developed for their own internal use only.

However, there is also a practical reason, the first one the IC learned: For interagency mobility to have a chance, the organization(s) involved must establish administrative mechanisms to enable it. That was apparent from the few senior services in the Federal government that took interagency mobility as a given, like the U.S. Department of State and the CIA; in addition to a mobility-friendly culture, traditions, and operational necessity, they also put in place administrative policies and mechanisms that *enabled* that mobility, something the original SES sorely lacks.

Thus, exhortation by senior agency leaders notwithstanding, the IC's experience suggests that a successful interagency mobility program also has to answer these mundane but no less important questions: Who funds the mobility assignment, and who gets selected for it, especially if it is career-enhancing? Who evaluates and rewards the individual's performance during that interagency assignment, and what happens when the individual returns to their home agency? And, most importantly, how does that mobility assignment count in the promotion process? Is it nice to have but not essential, a square-filling yes-or-no question? Or do the quality of the assignment and the individual's performance while on it get taken into account? These are all critical questions if a developmental mobility program (interagency and otherwise) is ever to be taken to government-wide scale.[163]

What will it take to make interagency mobility work? Here are some considerations.

---

[162] Note that given the developmental focus of this section, our discussion here is limited to the question of pre-SES interagency mobility. We will save a discussion about mobility until *after* one is selected to the SES for our concluding section inasmuch as that mobility is, at least in theory, a matter of law and a condition of SES employment.

[163] Adapted from Nickerson, J. A. *Tackling wicked government problems.*

RECOMMENDATION 4.2.1: IDENTIFY ENTERPRISE EXECUTIVE POSITIONS

The first step in enabling that mobility would be to identify those senior executive positions that require some form of whole-of-government experience. Much like it does with all SES positions today, OPM could establish general, government-wide classification criteria and, with appropriate oversight and audit, empower agencies to apply that criteria subject to review and final approval during the biennial SES allocation process. The agency's recent guidance regarding the National Security Professional Development (NSPD) program, which encourages agencies to identify such positions as a technical requirement rather than a leadership one, is a step in the right direction, but it needs to go further.[164]

Given the relatively small number of enterprise executive positions (possibly in the range of 1,500 to 2,000),[165] that process would not present an undue administrative burden, but the challenge will be to overcome the likely agency bias against such a designation—with all of the strings (like some loss of control over selection) that may come with it. However, with a set of government-wide criteria and appropriate OMB or PMC oversight, that parochial bias could be overcome. And as far as the pipeline is concerned, much as Bob Corsi suggests in his chapter, agencies could, with minimal OPM oversight, identify key feeder positions at grades GS-13 through 15 and reserve them for competition among interagency mobility candidates. The incentive to do so? If an agency wants its best and brightest to be eligible for a mobility assignment in another agency, it must open its ranks to outsiders in exchange.

Of course, if an interagency mobility candidate is selected and geographic relocation is involved, costs associated with the move would have to be funded by someone other than the receiving organization—else that organization would chose a local candidate in almost every case. These expenses could be centrally funded by OPM or OMB. Or the selectee's home agency could even bear the costs if its employee is only "loaned out" to another to acquire interagency experience, with the expectation that the individual would return to the agency's ranks better prepared for a senior position. That's the way our military does it.

---

[164] Cobert, B. F. (2016, June 15). *National Security Professional Development (NSPD) Interagency Personnel Rotations Program guidance* [OPM letter]. Retrieved from https://www.chcoc.gov/content/national-security-professional-development-nspd-interagency-personnel-rotations-program-0. In its most recent NSPD guidance, OPM recommends the PMC program and encourages agencies to give those who complete its required 6-month rotational assignment "strong preference" in SES positions that require a whole-of-government perspective.
[165] Partnership for Public Service & Booz Allen Hamilton. (2014). *Building the enterprise: A new civil service framework*. Washington, DC: Partnership for Public Service.

This is all moot if *all* senior executive positions require interagency experience as a prerequisite. That would force the issue, but, as noted, that may be a bridge too far…at least to start. It would be enough to require it for certain career executive positions, especially those that are at the top of the pyramid, at Tier 3 or even the putative Tier 4 described in our final section. That would keep the numbers—and associated cots—relatively small.

RECOMMENDATION 4.2.2: CREDIT *ANY* LONG-DURATION "OUT-OF-BODY" ASSIGNMENT

If some form of pre-SES interagency mobility assignment (IC employees called it an "out of body" experience) is to be mandatory, what kinds of assignments will count? Which would most contribute to the development of enterprise leaders? The U.S. military's approach to joint duty is instructive but likely unworkable for the SES. The DOD actually maintains a list of joint military assignments that numbers almost 11,000—including tours in the Department's several combatant commands, the Office of the Secretary of Defense, or the Joint Chiefs of Staff—to fill just over 1,000 flag officer positions. Add to that centrally managed (and directed) military officer assignments, regularized rotation cycles and geographic mobility, and an up-or-out promotion system that maintains a steady flow of candidates through the system, and the system works well. Because of mandatory retirement rules, the Senior Foreign Service and the FBI and Drug Enforcement Administration's joint SES operate in similar fashion.[166]

That model was problematic for the IC, as it is for general government application. Unlike the military, there is no centralized personnel assignment system, especially one that is interagency in nature, nor are there a sufficient number of rotational assignments in the IC's relatively few joint organizations, like the National Counter Terrorism Center (NCTC) or the Office of the Director of National Intelligence itself, to fill that pipeline.

Accordingly, the IC agreed to a much simpler default approach: That is, almost any interagency assignment (for example, from one IC agency to another, or even to a position outside the IC) would suffice. After all, at its most basic level, the mobility program was intended to foster the development of executive candidates with a broad, whole-of-IC perspective. We applied a variation of that principle to external applicants; by definition, someone applying from outside the IC, or even from outside government met the interagency (or equivalent) mobility requirement.

In addition, the IC also determined that certain assignments *internal to a particular IC agency* could provide the experiential equivalent of an interagency assignment, to the extent that they involved significant responsibility for interagency, interdepartmental, or even international programs or operations—

---

[166] Adapted from Chapter 13 in Nickerson, J. A. *Tackling wicked government problems.*

for example, as an intelligence agency's liaison to one of the DOD's combatant commands, an assignment to one of the dozens of FBI-led Joint Terrorism Task Forces in major U.S. cities, or a tour with international organizations like the North Atlantic Treaty Organization.

The IC also agreed that such interagency assignments would have to be at least 1 to 3 years in duration to be credited, on the premise that anything shorter would not give individuals on civilian "joint duty" sufficient understanding of the agencies to which they were assigned, or the opportunity to learn and demonstrate some degree of mastery of that assignment.[167] Taken together, these various measures were intended to give as many IC professionals as possible the opportunity to serve in an interagency capacity and, in so doing, begin to build an "enterprise" mindset, person by person and assignment by assignment.

However, given that these rotational assignments were a prerequisite to promotion to senior ranks, the number of potential candidates who would be eligible for and interested in those assignments could potentially number in the tens of thousands. Taking a pre-SES mobility requirement to government-wide scale would potentially require even larger numbers, so crediting a wide variety of interagency (and equivalent) assignments is probably the only viable option.

Compare this to the more military-like approach to civilian executive development taken by the Air Force, as described in Bob Corsi's chapter. Under that model, his agency identified and set aside a relatively small number of corporately-managed, pre-SES positions worldwide and reserved those "key" positions for individuals who had declared their interest in a developmental track leading to an SES position…and the requisite mobility that came with it. Competition for those positions is reserved for those on that mobility track. This too could work on a government-wide scale, but only with similar limits on the number of individuals competing for those coveted mobility assignments; for example, competition could be restricted it to those in certified CDPs.

RECOMMENDATION 4.2.3: ESTABLISH A SIMPLE REIMBURSABLE FUNDING MECHANISM

The third most important question: Who pays the salary of participants while they're on mobility assignment? This answer too seems easy: Just let the employee's "home" (that is, employing) agency fund the mobility assignment. After all, it's to prepare one of its own for senior leadership. However, fiscal limits would likely restrict the size of the program…not an issue if you want the program to be elite, but it's problematic if you're trying to generate enough mobility-qualified candidates to fully fill the SES succession pool.

---

[167] Tours in combat zones counted "double." See Intelligence Community Directive No. 660.

Thus, it is one thing to absorb the cost of the salaries and expenses (including any relocation costs) associated with a few dozen SES candidates on individual mobility assignments, as well as to absorb the impact of their temporary loss (that is, the costs of backfilling them) to individual organizational units. But multiply those salaries, expenses, and replacement costs by a factor of 10, and then again by the number of departments and agencies, and the option of just eating the cost quickly becomes untenable.

A pre-SES mobility program could do what the military services do: Centrally establish and fund the salaries, expenses, and relocation costs associated with several thousand "joint" positions across government, with those positions reserved for individuals competitively selected for an interagency mobility assignment. By way of comparison, the U.S. military maintains about 10 joint billets in its uniformed developmental pipeline for each of its approximately 1,000 flag officer position. Again, multiply that by a factor of six or seven (the number of career SES positions government-wide), and one gets a sense of the resources required…an amount that may be prohibitive, not to mention a rather large, visible, and, hence, vulnerable budget line item.

As Bob Corsi notes in his chapter, the Air Force has taken this approach, setting aside a relatively small number of key pre-SES positions exclusively for mobility candidates and centrally funding any relocation costs associated with them. Corsi suggests that every agency should be willing to make such an investment, but, presumably, these could also be centrally funded by OPM and/or OMB at government-wide scale. However, there are other challenges with this approach. Unlike the military, civilian agencies would likely have to be given the opportunity to compete for the mobility assignment (see below).

With its need for a large-scale pre-SES mobility program, the IC has taken a different approach. There, interagency mobility assignments are generally treated as reimbursable details, with the *gaining* agency responsible for paying the salaries and expenses of those temporarily assigned to it and then billing those costs back to the individual's home agency.

Given that most of those interagency mobility assignments are to vacant positions that have already been funded in the gaining agency's budget, a reimbursement model can work. And when the number of interagency mobility assignments can be established in advance, the giving agency can project the amount of reimbursable funds it will receive from the gaining agency and can use those funds to hire staff in advance to replace those they send off on assignment; this was the approach perfected by the IC's National Counter Terrorism Center (NCTC) and is detailed below. There is still a time lag for reimbursed funds to transfer from the gaining agency back to the home one, but those complications are worth it—the IC's large-scale mobility program is largely cost-neutral and self-sustaining as a consequence.

RECOMMENDATION 4.2.4: SELECT MOBILITY CANDIDATES THROUGH COMPETITION

At first blush, the question of 'who gets to go?' also seems straightforward. Why not just let agencies choose who they want to send off on a mobility assignment? Again, that simplicity works for small numbers but not at scale... especially if the receiving agency has any say in the matter. Thus, if mobility becomes a mandatory prerequisite for promotion to the SES, the relatively few mobility "feeder" opportunities will likely draw a significant number of interested applicants—so many that an agency advertising such an opportunity would likely be inundated with them. Given that assumption, the IC first decided that selection for those precious few mobility assignments would be subject to two rounds of merit-based competition.

Thus, when an agency was willing to offer one of its vacant positions as a civilian joint duty opportunity, it would advertise that vacancy to other IC agencies. Those agencies would then solicit applications from their interested employees and conduct an initial first round of merit-based competition to select one or more highly qualified individuals from among those applying. Those finalists would then be nominated for consideration to the IC agency initially advertising the opportunity, and a second round of competition would ensue—this time from among the nominees of several agencies. Eventually (and I do mean eventually), the advertising agency would select the winner from among the many candidates referred to it by all of the agencies.

Needless to say, while merit principles were well served by those two rounds of competition, the time it took for them to run their course became problematic, and that fill lag was further compounded by the time it took the selectee to actually report for the mobility assignment. Add to that the time it took the receiving agency to reimburse the donor agency for the costs of the employee selected for the temporary assignment (a statutory requirement for long-term temporary assignments between agencies), and the timeline from start to finish—that is, from a joint duty vacancy announcement to an employee actually reporting for that assignment—became untenable. Agencies began to limit the number of joint duty opportunities they were willing to offer.

The National Counter Terrorism Center (NCTC) piloted an alternative that seems to overcome these various administrative delays without compromising on merit, and it could serve as a potential model for whole-of-government application.

The NCTC's several hundred funded positions are designed to be staffed primarily by personnel on 1- to 3-year rotational assignments from the various IC agencies; as a result, administrative delays could have had a significant operational impact. Accordingly, instead of an *ad hoc*, vacancy-by-vacancy approach to its staffing, the NCTC negotiated annual aggregate staffing quotas with each of the IC agencies designated to contribute employees. Each of those agencies still conducts its own independent competition to identify mobility candidates, but once they are selected, they are queued up and available for immediate assignment to the Center as vacancies occur, all without a second round of competition.

Thus, when the giving and the gaining agency—for example, the FBI and the NCTC—are able to mutually establish in *advance* the number of counterterrorism analysts the Bureau would 'owe' the Center, questions of who pays and who selects become much less problematic. To be sure, it requires both the giving and gaining agencies to centrally manage their respective personnel rotations, much as Tish Long did when she was Director of NGA. But with preset mobility quotas, standard mobility assignment tour lengths, and more predictable funding, this has proven far less complicated and far more expeditious than *an ad* hoc approach. Nevertheless, the process has not been extended beyond the NCTC to date.

A possible variation on this option would be to limit competition for mobility assignments to only those in certified SES CDPs or equivalents. That would keep competition manageable, costs down, and funding predictable but would require significant changes to CDPs (see Recommendation 4.7).

RECOMMENDATION 4.2.5: HAVE THE GAINING AGENCY EVALUATE MOBILITY DETAILEES

Who does my 'report card' when I'm on a mobility assignment? The answer to this question will have a significant impact on the pool of GS-13s, 14s, and 15s who apply for an interagency mobility program. Will the home agency continue to rate (and reward) those who go off on a mobility assignment to another agency, or will that be left to the gaining agency that provided them with a rotational assignment?

Arguably, it should be the latter, since the gaining agency would presumably be in the best position to judge the performance of an individual on mobility assignment to its ranks. The alternative—for home agencies to continue to rate mobility candidates—is problematic, in part because of the concern that the individuals being evaluated would be "out of sight, out of mind" from their rating official, and their performance appraisals would suffer as a result.

Moreover, from a developmental standpoint, an individual on mobility assignment to another agency should be fully integrated into the culture of that other agency, part of the team as it were, so it would be awkward to treat that individual differently when performance appraisal time comes around. The fact that the Federal government now has a more or less standard SES performance appraisal system (see Section 5) helps in this regard, and OPM should consider extending it to pre-SES mobility candidates.

But if the receiving agency evaluates a participant's performance, will it also be responsible for rewarding that mobility candidate with a performance bonus if he or she is judged to be outstanding? The answer has to be yes... otherwise, those high performers who regularly receive a performance bonus will shy away from even applying for a mobility assignment. Moreover, since the mobility candidate is filling a legitimate vacancy in the gaining agency, presumably his or her potential bonus has already been budgeted by that agency as part of its overall performance bonus budget.

That said, we found that performance bonus philosophies varied widely across the IC—some agencies were quite generous, others not so much—and this further complicated matters. In the end, the IC split the difference, with the gaining agency rating employees assigned to them, but leaving it to their home agency to reward them (or not) according to their specific performance bonus philosophy. Not the best solution, but given the variability across government, perhaps the only workable one.

RECOMMENDATION 4.2.6: VEST SES SELECTION WAIVERS WITH OPM OR SOME OTHER CENTRAL AUTHORITY

If an SES position in a particular agency requires interagency experience, and that agency's 'Best Qualified' internal candidate doesn't have it, can the mobility requirement be waived?

Waivers have proven to be the most controversial of all the issues that attend a mandatory interagency mobility program. In the early days of military joint duty under the Goldwater-Nichols Act,[168] all-too-frequent waivers almost killed the concept, as officers gambled that if their home service's top leadership—those who picked the admirals and generals—were familiar enough with them, they could be picked for promotion without checking the mobility box. It wasn't until waiver authority was transferred from the individual service secretaries to the Secretary of Defense that waivers suddenly became rare, and officers realized they needed a joint assignment if they ever expected to compete for flag rank.

The IC also confronted this with its civilian version of joint duty. Ideally, much like the Secretary of Defense for DOD, the Director of National Intelligence (DNI) would have sole authority to grant civilian joint duty waivers in SES (and equivalent) selections, but this was made more complicated by the fact that by law, individual cabinet secretaries had unfettered legal authority (subject to OPM QRB review, of course) to make those selections—authority that, according to their lawyers, could not be superseded by the DNI.

After much rancorous debate (and the departure of at least one strongly opposed cabinet secretary), those cabinet secretaries all agreed to voluntarily

---

[168] Goldwater-Nichols Department of Defense Reorganization Act of 1986, Pub. L. No. 99-433 (1986).

cede waiver authority to the DNI; however, that agreement rests solely on the goodwill of their successors, so it remains tenuous.

In the case of a government-wide mobility program, waivers may actually be less complicated, at least for SES positions that require it. Since OPM delegates SES selection authority to department and agency heads and ultimately approves their SES selections via the QRB process (or some variation), it could and should centrally retain the authority to waive a mobility requirement in any given case…and hopefully it would do so on only the rarest of occasions. The alternative—vesting that authority in agency heads—would, much like the early experience of our military in this regard, leave SES candidates with the perception that they could play the odds, avoid the sacrifices associated with mobility, and obtain a waiver when it came to their promotion into the SES. No, waivers must be closely controlled if prerequisite interagency mobility is to work.

Mobility as the best way to develop *enterprise* leaders

The developmental arguments in favor of pre-SES mobility are compelling, but so too are the challenges associated with effectively enabling it. Moreover, those SES members who require a whole-of-government perspective need to acquire it well before they join senior ranks, rather than after attaining SES rank; at that point, an SES member should be more focused on leading and managing the government and less on worrying about broadening his or her background. That suggests that like the IC, mobility reassignments should start as early as GS-13, more or less equivalent to the point in the career of military officers when they compete for and complete their first joint duty assignment.[169]

Still, requiring prospective SES candidates to diversify their experience should not be overdone. Depth of knowledge is also important, and, in some cases, paramount.[170] Just think of that 'branch' of the SES that is narrowly focused on the operations and missions of a particular agency…like the IRS or SSA, or even some parts of DOD.

Accordingly, given the resistance it is likely to engender, prerequisite interagency mobility for all SES positions may be a bridge too far, and it may not be warranted in the case of those SES positions (however many there may be) that remain narrowly agency-centric in focus. It may be more feasible— and more appropriate—to limit that requirement to a subset of those positions. That may also make the costs and incentives associated with such an effort easier to come by as well.

---

[169] Hale, R., & Sanders, R. (2016, January 26). Developing civilian leaders in DoD. Defense News. Retrieved from http://www.defensenews.com/story/defense/commentary/2016/01/26/developing-civilian-leaders-dod/79055042.. Note that the IC has gone even further, reducing initial eligibility for an interagency mobility assignment from GS-13 to GS-11.
[170] Ibid.

Thus, the caveat we first offered in Section 3: Given the variegated nature of the SES, it may be that only a select number of senior executive positions require a whole-of-government perspective, and therefore the prerequisite interagency mobility that could provide it. And that requirement may also vary depending on level of responsibility. In some cases, even entry-level SES positions may require it; in others, it may not be necessary until one ascends to the top tier of the organizational pyramid (but more about that in Section 5).

OPM has recognized this distinction in a laudable attempt to reinvigorate the moribund National Security Professional Development (NSPD) program engendered by EO 13434, issuing guidance in July 2016 that encourages agencies to (1) identify those select SES positions that require interagency experience as a *technical* qualification requirement; (2) use the PMC's Interagency Rotation Program and other temporary and permanent career-broadening assignments to provide such interagency experience to candidates for those SES positions; and (3) afford those SES candidates who have actually acquired such interagency experience "strong preference" when making selections for those SES positions.[171]

As I said, these are laudable steps. First begun under the leadership of Kay James in the George W. Bush Administration, they could have (and should have) been taken years ago; in that regard, former Acting OPM Director Beth Cobert deserves great credit for driving them home. But because they treat interagency mobility as something less than mandatory—and something other than *leadership*—there is no guarantee that they will ensure a senior executive corps (or even a subset of that corps) that has a whole-of-government perspective. As we discuss in Section 5, it takes a forcing function—something like making mobility a prerequisite for promotion to the SES—to ensure that perspective.

RECOMMENDATION 4.3: RAISE THE BAR FOR AGENCY CDPs[172]

Introduction: Unrealistic expectations and consolation prizes

At present, most SES vacancies are filled by candidates who compete for them as they occur, an *ad hoc* approach that often takes months, impedes any sort of succession planning, and creates a bias against external—that is, unknown and unfamiliar—applicants for SES vacancies. A much smaller number of vacancies are filled by graduates of OPM-certified agency SES CDPs, who can be noncompetitively promoted to an SES position.

In theory, relying on a CDP pipeline to ensure an adequate supply of qualified SES candidates would seem to be more strategically effective (and significantly less time consuming), but the track record of CDPs has been problematic. Studies have consistently indicated that far fewer than half of CDP graduates

---

[171] See note 160 above
[172] Adapted from Nickerson, J. A. *Tackling wicked government problems.*

are ever promoted to the SES, a sure sign that these well-intended programs are just not achieving their intended purpose. As Bob Corsi points out in his chapter, CDPs often raise unrealistic expectations on the part of their graduates; those graduates assume that completing the program actually means something, but at the end of the day, this turns out not to be the case.

There are several reasons for this poor track record. For example, when it comes to promotion to the SES, agencies have a decided bias toward candidates with specialized technical/functional skills and/or agency-specific experience (and the organizational connections that come with it) versus the typical CDP's emphasis on developing more general leadership skills. Thus, it's no wonder agencies fill most of their SES vacancies one at a time, and from a candidate pool deliberately narrowed by specialized technical and experiential requirements that are often so agency specific that they exclude external candidates...including external CDP graduates.

There are latent factors that may make it even more problematic. All too often, agencies may fill the ranks of their CDPs with unsuccessful internal SES applicants; in effect, the CDP serves as a consolation prize for non-selection. And in some cases, CDP ranks are padded with women and minorities, as if greater diversity in an agency's SES pipeline counts as much as actually translating that diversity into greater diversity in the ranks of its SES. The latter remains abysmal (see Recommendation 4.4).

A Hall of Fame batting average

There are some exceptions to the poor record of CDPs. In his chapter, Reggie Wells describes the SSA's CDP program, one of the Federal government's best. Its combination of formal courses, targeted rotational assignments, and, perhaps most importantly, senior coaches and mentors results in one of the highest SES promotion rates in government. However, the CDP placement record belongs to the IRS. Its storied XD (short for Executive Development) program has a graduate-to-SES selection "batting average"—that is, percentage SES placement rate—in the high 90s.

The IRS' secret: the link between its sophisticated succession planning system and XD. Slots in the latter are advertised only when the IRS projects actual SES vacancies, and those slots are filled only with candidates who possess the specific technical or functional qualifications required of those projected vacancies. Thus, if IRS anticipates the retirement of an IT executive, its XD announcement will advertise for that particular skill set, *in addition* to the more general ECQ-based qualifications. And when a candidate with those specific technical requirements is selected for, and eventually completes, the XD program, there's a high probability of an actual SES vacancy in the immediate offing that fits his or her technical qualifications.

In other words, IRS uses its XD program to develop the general leadership skills of candidates who already meet the technical or functional requirements of anticipated SES vacancies, so when those vacancies occur, the program's graduates can fill them without further competition. To be sure, this perpetuates the bias toward SES candidates (and CDP applicants) with specialized technical skills and agency-centric experience compared with those who are mobile, generalist leaders, so the results are mixed: an SES cadre that is highly technically competent but stove-piped and insular, and potentially lacking strong, multifaceted leadership experience. One can argue that this is contrary to the original vision of the SES and the SES CDPs intended to provide agencies with their succession pipelines. But who can argue with a CDP placement rate of above 95 percent...especially if the way to get there isn't rocket science?

CDPs: Use them or lose them

If CDPs are ever to be effective at preparing individuals for senior rank, and at ensuring an adequate SES succession pool, they must be significantly strengthened. Otherwise (again, with some exception), they are simply not worth the investment...or the disenchantment on the part of frustrated CDP graduates. For example, OPM could easily require a stronger link between an agency's succession plan and its CDP, much like the IRS model, with continued CDP certification contingent on a high placement rate...maybe not 95 percent (agencies aren't always going to guess right when it comes to projecting a particular SES vacancy, or in selecting the right CDP applicant for the ones they do predict), but high enough to force greater accountability for post-CDP placement and more attention to pre-CDP succession planning.

OPM could also raise the bar for CDP certification by establishing far more rigorous standards and, in so doing, ensuring agency SES CDPs are more likely to produce capable, executive-ready graduates. However, requiring more rigorous CDPs does little good if having one is a matter of agency discretion. Nothing today would prevent an agency from repeating history and relying on *ad hoc* selections. Accordingly, OPM could go so far as to also require that every agency develop a CDP that meets its certification standards —smaller agencies could form a consortium to achieve sufficient scale, or look to OPM to resurrect the government-wide CDP it prototyped in 2006–2007 (see Recommendation 4.5). Will that solve the problem? Not necessarily. Even if they have a certified, top-of-the-line CDP, there's nothing to stop agencies from continuing to ignore CDP graduates.

There's always the blunt instrument approach in this regard. OPM could go so far as to require that, as a general rule, agencies can only fill their SES vacancies from the ranks of CDP graduates. That would certainly ensure a high SES placement rate and thus a high return on an agency's CDP investment, but what if an agency guesses wrong in its succession plan and finds it doesn't have a technically qualified CDP graduate in the queue to fill a critical SES vacancy? Given the imprecise nature of succession plans generally—and merit-based government succession plans in particular—this is inevitable.

However, so long as there is a provision for OPM to waive the requirement and/or mandate that every new SES selectee—especially those from outside government—complete a CDP equivalent during his or her first-year SES probationary period, the CDP-only rule could work. Indeed, that's just a slight variation on OPM's new SES onboarding requirement. Thus, that bar is not unreasonably high, and by raising it, agencies would have every incentive to improve their succession plans, as well as their CDPs.

RECOMMENDATION 4.4: BUILD AN INTERNAL HEADHUNTING CAPABILITY FOR SES JOBS

Introduction: Playing the SES lottery

There's an old adage among executive headhunters that says the candidates you want are not the ones searching for a new job; the best candidates are quite successful just where they are and rarely spend their time perusing executive "want ads" for a new position.[173] To be sure, there are some exceptions to this adage; some of the most successful executives get bored and look elsewhere for a new challenge. But as a general matter, the best executive talent isn't searching—they need to be found and recruited.

This is especially the case with diversity candidates; talented women and minorities who are interested in competing for an SES appointment are stuck with two choices. Today, the only way for those outstanding candidates to find the right SES position is to wait and hope one opens up in their own backyard, where they're already known, or to find one via the BWOM method (a technical HR term meaning "by word of mouth").

Alternatively, they can start applying to SES vacancy announcements on USA Jobs. Sadly, many executive candidates refer to the latter as the "SES lottery," as they try to guess which of the literally hundreds of senior executive vacancies posted there are real and which are *pro forma*, already slotted for an internal heir apparent. The net result is that after a few unsuccessful attempts, many talented candidates don't bother to apply to most SES vacancies.

Needless to say, none of these approaches are very effective; they all represent long odds, especially when every SES vacancy announcement attracts hundreds of resumes (many from push-button online candidates who are barely interested), and agencies are left to sort through them by blunt instrument paper reviews and panel interviews. This makes the prospect of improving diversity even more daunting.

If you want to improve the odds for those candidates—that is, match them to real openings that best fit their skill sets—you have to go out and search for them, recruit them, and then get the best of them in front of selecting

[173] Sanders, R. (2015, February 26). Probing the details of the president's new SES program. *Federal Times*. Retrieved from https://www.Federaltimes.com/story/government/management/blog/2015/02/26/white-house-leadership-development/24049835

officials. Imagine if you were an agency head looking for a new CIO, and a skilled headhunter presented you with a slate of diverse, ready-right-now CIO candidates—especially women and minorities—who had already been pre-vetted, perhaps even pre-assessed...candidates you likely would never see because they would never bother to apply if you just relied on USA Jobs.

An internal headhunting capability

Bottom line: The best SES candidates have to be found and recruited, especially for opportunities in another agency. So one of the things OPM could do is establish an internal fee-for-service headhunting operation to find, recruit, and match outstanding SES candidates, especially women and minorities, to SES vacancies. That's how the rest of the planet fills key executive jobs, and while I'm not suggesting the Federal government stop announcing SES vacancies for free and open competition, I am arguing that that passive approach should be supplemented by a more proactive, precision-guided, on-demand headhunting operation run out of OPM, at least for select SES vacancies.

Here's how it could work. An agency with an SES vacancy—maybe it's one in the C-suite, where the internal candidate pool lacks real depth or diversity—would go to an OPM executive search specialist, who would go find talent the new-fashioned way: by tapping into a social media database of diverse, high-performing/high-potential candidates, as well as the network of senior career executives, functional or industry experts, and others who may have a read on them. That search specialist would identify those who may fit the bill; vet them as discreetly as necessary with their subordinates, peers, and superiors; evaluate them against the job's qualifications; and then reach out and actually *recruit* those who may offer the best fit.

Pre-recruit does *not* mean pre-select. The agency would still have to advertise the vacancy, and those pre-recruited candidates would still have to apply and compete for it along with everyone else. But the point is to go find them and convince them to apply. To get the operation jump-started, OPM could limit the initial search pattern to the literally hundreds of CDP grads already in waiting out there—if just one of those grads is identified as Best Qualified, she or he could be selected without further competition, just like that!

This scenario would also help improve the diversity of the senior executive corps, which too is certainly a worthy goal—not only because its members should collectively look like America from a demographic and public policy standpoint but also because of the significant advantages that such diversity can bring from a cognitive one. However, this has proved particularly intractable. Despite years of exhortation by administrations both Democratic and Republican, the needle has yet to really jump.

That's partly the result of low SES turnover—it's hard to move that needle if there are relatively few opportunities to change the complexion of the corps—

but this may be changing. As noted at the outset, there's evidence that SES retirements are increasing, so there may be an opening, pun intended, to see some real progress. However, it will take more than further exhortation. As with mobility, if the Federal government is to make a dent in SES diversity, it needs to establish enabling administrative mechanisms to do so.

RECOMMENDATION 4.5: RESURRECT THE GOVERNMENT-WIDE CDP[174]

Introduction: An alternative to agency-centric CDPs

Agency CDPs only have so much capacity, and, as noted, their track record is generally poor. In many cases, participation is offered as a consolation prize to unsuccessful internal SES applicants; in other cases, they simply formalize 'good-old-boy' succession plans that perpetuate the lack of diversity in the senior executive corps. To ensure talented individuals, especially women and minorities, have every opportunity to make their way into executive ranks, OPM could also revive the government-wide SES CDP that it prototyped in 2004.

That program, known as Fed CDP for short, was the result of a strategic partnership between then-OPM Director Kay Coles James and key Democratic and Republican legislators. Among other things, it was intended to help improve SES diversity by providing an alternative pathway into the SES for high-potential candidates who may not have had the career opportunities in their home agency—perhaps because their career path was blocked there or because their agency couldn't afford to have an OPM-certified CDP of its own.

Despite its lofty intentions, the program was plagued by startup difficulties (truth in lending…I had responsibility for the program), and it was reluctantly abandoned by then-OPM Director Linda Springer after just two cohorts, much to the chagrin of both its proponents and its graduates. Perhaps its greatest flaw was the open competition for its limited number of slots; that feature attracted hundreds of applicants, and it made the screening and selection of participants unduly complicated and time consuming. However, the alternative—letting participating agencies competitively select and nominate candidates—was just as problematic, insofar as that approach suffered the same deficiencies as agency CDPs, only on a government-wide basis.

Require a succession plan to participate

However, none of the Fed CDP's flaws are insurmountable, and I believe that properly retooled, it can open up new opportunities for talented SES candidates…especially interagency ones! We've also learned a lot since its initial demise, with a succession of related initiatives that could inform a second try at a government-wide CDP.

[174] Ibid.

First, when President George W. Bush issued an Executive Order in 2004 renaming the Presidential Management Intern Program to "Fellows" (for reasons that were obvious 15 years ago), he also authorized, at the urging of then-OPM Director Kay Coles James, a *Senior* Presidential Management Fellows (PMF) Program for high-potential GS-14s and 15s and their external counterparts.[175] That program, deliberately modeled after the White House Fellows Program, was to emphasize leadership experience, rather than graduate studies, and it was to feature senior-level rotational assignments. However, for reasons that remain unclear, its implementing regulations were never issued despite over a year in design and development…lost somewhere in OPM transition after the departure of Director James.

That disappointment notwithstanding, elements of that initiative re-emerged in 2011, when the PMC under President Obama established an Interagency Rotation Program for high-potential GS-13s, 14s, and 15s from across government. Designed to do exactly what its name implies—develop the *interagency* leadership competencies of participants via a 6-month developmental assignment in another agency—it can trace its lineage to the IC's civilian joint duty program; like it, the PMC's initiative helps potential SES candidates acquire more of a whole-of-government perspective.[176] Over 100 participants have completed the program to date.

Finally, in his late-2014 speech to SES members, President Obama announced a third installment of the theme, a new White House Leadership Development Program for Future Senior Career Executives. Intended to "…provide top civil servants and SES candidates with rotational assignments with leaders responsible for driving progress on Cross-Agency Priority Goals,"[177] the program complements the PMC's interagency rotational program, and it provides participants an opportunity to be exposed to the highest levels of government.[178] It welcomed its initial cohort in 2015.

All of these programs—the original Fed CDP, the Senior PMF Program, the PMC Rotation Program, and the new White House effort—have ambitious titles and ambitious goals, and all were designed to provide some sort of interagency or intergovernmental experience.

However, only the first two were expressly designed as OPM-certified CDPs, which would have permitted their graduates to be noncompetitively promoted into senior executive ranks. And without that designation, those who

---

[175] See Exec. Order 13318. I helped design the Senior Fellows program and develop its implementing regulations but left the agency for the IC before those regulations could be issued.
[176] U.S. Office of Personnel Management. Training and development: Leadership development. Retrieved from https://www.opm.gov/policy-data-oversight/training-and-development/leadership-development#url=PMC-Interagency-Rotation-Prgm
[177] U.S. Office of Personnel Management. (2015). *Congressional budget justification performance budget.* Fiscal year 2016. Washington, DC: U.S. Office of Personnel Management. Retrieved from https://www.opm.gov/about-us/budget-performance/budgets/congressional-budget-justification-fy2016.pdf
[178] Sanders, R. Probing the details.

complete either of the two more recent additions will not gain any substantive advantage in promotion to the SES, other than the prestige of participating in them.[179] While OPM's CDP certification criteria are rigorous, both the PMC and the White House programs—separately or (preferably) combined —could meet them and, in so doing, provide additional routes into the SES.

Absent that, all of these programs have characteristics that could be incorporated and integrated into a "next generation" government-wide CDP. And if you combine a revitalized, 2.0 version of the Fed CDP with an OPM headhunting capability, suddenly Federal agencies would have access to a whole new *interagency* pool of promotion-ready candidates—a pool that is (hopefully) more diverse than those primarily internal sources that agencies currently default to today, and filled with candidates who have already been vetted, affirmatively recruited, matched with the best SES vacancy, and deemed eligible for noncompetitive selection.[180]

RECOMMENDATION 4.6: DELEGATE BUT CERTIFY AGENCY SES SELECTION PROCESSES

Introduction: Balancing administrative burden and rigor

As previously noted, OPM under Beth Cobert's leadership has made a number of improvements designed to simplify and speed up the SES selection process. These include the use of resumes instead of lengthy ECQ essays to assess the qualifications of senior executive applicants, and alternatives to the paper-intensive QRB, which reviews those ECQ essays and ultimately certifies an agency's selection of a new SES member.

Both of these initiatives may ultimately accomplish their intended purpose, and both have merit. However, since ECQ essays and QRB reviews, as administratively burdensome as they are, were designed to ensure new SES members would meet the very highest standards of leadership and character, what will take their place?

About the only things you can glean from applicants' ECQ essays are their writing ability and their genuine interest in the position. The latter is a good thing, at least in theory! A well- (and personally) written set of ECQ essays is evidence that the applicant has put some skin in the game, at least in terms of time and effort. However, these days, SES candidates can go out and hire a professional to write their ECQ essays; therefore, while the ethics of that may be questionable, even the 'skin in the game' test is problematic.

---

[179] Recall that in its most recent NSPD guidance, OPM recommends the PMC program and encourages agencies to give those who compete its required 6-month rotational assignment "strong preference" in SES positions that require a whole-of-government perspective.
[180] Is this guaranteed to improve SES diversity? No, but that doesn't mean we shouldn't try. We know that there are plenty of outstanding, diverse SES candidates out there just waiting for the right opportunity, so these ideas (none of which requires significant investment in the grand scheme of things) could at least give the Federal government a fighting chance to improve its odds.

So as an initial applicant screen, ECQ essays are of questionable effectiveness. I know; I oversaw hundreds of QRBs when I was at OPM, and the vast majority were rubber stamped "approved." And since ECQs are all that QRBs examine at the end of the selection process, the Boards themselves are of questionable value...with one exception.

Every agency Chief Human Capital officer will tell you the same thing: 99 times out of 100, the QRB process is *pro forma*. But every once in a while, an SES selection is questionable—for example, if a soon-to-be-former political appointee is trying to burrow in near the end of an administration—and a back-channel call to OPM can ensure that a QRB takes a closer look. So while I am all for eliminating QRBs as a general matter, or delegating them to individual agencies, there needs to be some oversight mechanism or escape clause that subjects a particular SES selection to extraordinary review.

Are resumes better? Yes, under the right conditions. When I was OPM Associate Director, we advertised a number of very senior positions at OPM, including one that would oversee all of its products and services—everything from its various leadership development programs to expert consulting—and we were specifically looking for candidates with private sector experience in that regard. However, the Best Qualified candidates we eventually received were all current Federal employees. When we asked to see those applicants who had been screened out, we found a number who had submitted only resumes and, as a consequence, had been summarily rejected by OPM's own personnel office. Because there were no ECQ essays attached, they had been disqualified without the office even bothering to see if their resumes provided sufficient evidence of the ECQs in non-essay form.

Needless to say, we asked our personnel office to take another look, and they found that several of the resumes included more than enough detail to conclude that the applicant met the ECQs. So we got another BQ list and ended up selecting someone with on-point private sector experience from that expanded list. That said, resumes can also be deceptive, especially in this day of online vacancy announcements and push-the-button applications; a casually interested job searcher can send out dozens of mass-produced resumes at the click of a mouse. So resumes can also be of questionable value when it comes to evaluating a candidate's ECQs.

Standards and skin in the game

Are there any alternatives? I would offer three that, taken together, can provide the kind of quality control originally envisioned for the QRBs without engendering additional administrative burden. First, while resumes are fine as an initial showing of an applicant's interest in a particular SES vacancy, I would add a step to the SES application process that requires a prospective candidate to put some skin in the game...in other words, to expend some additional *personal* effort to apply for any given SES vacancy. For example, an applicant could be required to provide a personally written supplementary narrative specifically addressing how his or her experiences meet the specific qualification requirements of the job, or perhaps sit for an initial video interview. Whatever the requirement, it should be something that makes an applicant do more than simply forward a pre-prepared resume to apply for an SES vacancy.

Second, I would give agencies wide latitude in their SES screening and selection process, under the principle that OPM should be in the business of telling agencies *what* they need to do, but not *how* they need to do it. In that regard, I would have OPM set rigorous government-wide, outcome-based standards that an agency's SES selection process must meet, much like delegated examining authority for rank-and-file civil service jobs. For example, has the agency validated any mandatory technical qualification requirements in addition to the ECQs? Or, does the agency use validated assessments, such as scored behavioral event interviews or simulations, to rate and rank SES candidates? And if an agency meets those standards, its SES selections would be allowed to forego OPM QRB certification. However, I would also include a hotline to trigger by-exception, special QRB review in sections that may appear tainted.

Finally, I would refer back to the due diligence process I recommended in Section 3 as a way to assess a candidate's character and fitness for senior executive rank. No selection process, no matter how rigorous, will be perfect. Predicting whether a selectee, especially a career executive selectee, will be successful on the job is as much art as science; even with state-of-the-art assessment instruments, individuals will be selected who do not have the leadership or technical competencies—or character—to do the job.

The problem is that you won't know that until they actually get on the job, but therein lies the solution. I would require peer-reviewed due diligence before an SES selectee has completed his or her 1-year probationary period but after having some run time actually on the job. After all, the probationary period is supposed to be part of the examination process, so why not take advantage of it and rigorously evaluate a new selectee's fitness for the SES based on actual on-the-job behavior?

In summary

I believe that, taken together, the various recommendations set forth from our contributors and those proffered in the Concluding Commentary can help the Federal government ensure the next generation of senior career executives is adequately prepared to lead 21st century government…not just from an agency standpoint but, more importantly, for the whole-of-government as well. However, these recommendations are not intended to be exhaustive in that regard.[181] There are lots of other development strategies—everything from mentoring and executive coaching programs to formal, residential executive development courses—that are also effective in this regard; largely because they are proven, I chose not to include them here.

Finally, none of this should not be taken to infer that development stops once someone is promoted to the SES. To the contrary, as Thad Allen, Suzanne Logan, and others have argued, leadership requires a commitment to lifelong learning. For example, I am an advocate of additional executive mobility assignments to prepare sitting senior executives for even higher levels of responsibility, but these are addressed elsewhere in this anthology. In addition, there are a number of post-selection developmental programs that, while not addressed here, are no less important.[182]

In that regard, it is also worth noting that OPM has resurrected a highly-regarded program known as *Leading EDGE* for continuing senior executive development; originally sponsored by the PMC and administered by VA, that program was intended to give experienced senior executives an opportunity to collaborate via a series of leadership workshops and action learning projects; at its peak in 2014, it reached over 4,000 senior executives, and I applaud its restart under the auspices of the FEI.[183]

---

[181] For a more complete discussion, see the beginning and ending chapters from Nickerson, J. A. *Tackling wicked government problems.*
[182] Ibid.
[183] Truth in lending: My team provided contract support to Leading EDGE, both its original iteration and its recent resurrection under OPM.

SECTION 5:

Revitalizing the Federal Senior Executive Corps

Reimagining a Senior Federal Service

Career leadership matters most of all. If it is to meet the ever-increasing expectations of its citizens, the 21st century Federal government will need to be well led, well managed, and well served—by the political appointees who occupy its highest ranks, the senior career executives who translate their policy decisions into action, and the literally millions of managers and front-line employees and contractors who follow their lead. Senior career executives are the engine and the drive train that run our government, and it is clear that we ignore or degrade their capacity—especially their leadership capacity—at our peril.

And, as I have argued, these are indeed extraordinarily perilous times. There are a host of external whole-of-government/whole-of-nation challenges that our country faces…from threats abroad to threats at home. Everything is connected—a global economy of haves and have-nots; rising regional, international, and transnational tensions; the explosion (pun intended) of two-edged technologies that can help us or hurt us, often at the same time; climate change and all of its adverse effects; inexorable demographic trends across the globe; the list goes on.

Add to that the trauma of Presidential Transition (any Presidential Transition), more rather than less partisan rancor across all of the branches of government, and the growing influence of social media in shaping or sabotaging an administration's agenda, and the life of a 21st century career executive is certainly going to be interesting.

Thus, it is clear the nation will need its very best and brightest at the helm, and that includes the Federal government's senior executive corps. The question is whether they'll be there when we need them, and there is some hesitation in the answer. As I noted at the beginning of this volume, the internal demographics of the Senior Executive Service (SES) are daunting: a retirement bubble on one hand; a less-than-enthusiastic succession pool on the other; and a "social contract" between the Federal government and its career leaders that has been subverted (if not severed) by pay and bonus freezes, media-fueled politicization, and plain old lack of respect and appreciation. So one must wonder, are today's (and tomorrow's) career executives up to it? If we advertise an SES vacancy, will the best candidates apply? And if they do, and we're able to hire them, can we keep them and motivate them in the face of all these challenges?

I believe at an individual level, today's senior executive corps is in the main, up to the challenge—at least up to a point. When it comes to providing technical and functional excellence, doing the right thing from an ethical standpoint, demonstrating a commitment to public service, or leading complex agency operations and programs, the individual members of the senior executive corps—to include anyone in any of the Federal government's several senior services—are at the top of their game. Notwithstanding some notable (and notorious) individual lapses in character, senior career executives go about making a hyper-complex Federal government work in a way that the vast majority of Americans take for granted—and given the range of hard and soft skills it takes to do so, that's a high compliment.

That said, is the system that produced those executives—the venerable SES (and all of its various progeny)—up to the challenge of keeping them at the top of their game, especially if the playing field has shifted from an agency to an enterprise focus? And is that system (or more accurately, what has become a loosely connected system of systems) up to recruiting and retaining top-notch replacements when they move on? Is a system that was conceived and implemented in the late 1970s and last retooled, at least legislatively, more than 10 years ago up to the challenges of government in the second and third decades of the 21st century and beyond?

The need for serious reform—statutory and administrative

I personally do not believe so. While many have argued that good leaders can make even a flawed system work for a while, it is clear that the ecosystem that is the senior *Federal* service—that is, the whole of the various systems that govern how senior career leaders are developed, selected, deployed, motivated, and, yes, held accountable—is in need of some serious reimagining. Not radical, paradigm-shifting surgery perhaps, but something bolder, something more than the administrative changes made by President Obama's recent, well-intentioned SES Executive Order.[184] As with previous sections, my Concluding Commentary provides what I believe are several viable recommendations in that regard, many of which are derived from the thoughts and ideas of the four authors who have contributed to this section.

- First, former Under Secretary of Defense Bob Hale makes the case that it will take both tangible and intangible steps to revitalize the senior executive corps. He argues that while SES pay will never match that of the private sector, it has to be more standardized and predictable; in other words, it cannot be treated as a political football, subject to the vagaries of

---

[184] Exec. Order No. 13714, Strengthening the Senior Executive Service. (2015, December 15). Retrieved from https://www.whitehouse.gov/the-press-office/2015/12/15/executive-order-strengthening-senior-executive-service

an administration or Congress. However, he also asserts that the simple things—like verbal recognition of a job well done—can provide an executive as much psychic value as a pay increase, and we need to pay more attention to those tools as well.

- Next, the Government Accountability Office's (GAO) Director of Strategic Issues, Robert Goldenkoff, looks at all of the various studies and reviews his agency has conducted that touch upon the health and vitality of the SES, and they paint a pretty problematic picture. If things like the Federal Employee Viewpoint Survey (FEVS) are any barometer, front-line employees have disturbingly little faith in their senior leaders, both political and career. However, like all good GAO officials, he has some serious, practical proposals for improvement.

- Then, the Office of Personnel Management's (OPM) Deputy Associate Director, Steve Shih, who oversees government-wide SES policy, builds on many of the initiatives outlined by his boss, former Acting OPM Director Beth Cobert, in Section 1 but with a look beyond the current administration to some of the more practical, day-to-day policy and program challenges the SES will face in the future. Clearly, these are no less important than the broader strategic issues that face the corps.

- Finally, former Office of Management and Budget (OMB) Controller and Acting Internal Revenue Service (IRS) Commissioner Danny Werfel focuses on the intangible side of the equation, recounting his efforts to bring together and build a team of senior career executives to help solve a crisis of public confidence at the IRS. In so doing, he reminds us of the promise of the SES, and of the efficacy of the Service's original vision. When he most needed senior executives—from within the IRS, as well as from all across government—to help one of our nation's most important and visible agencies, they signed up without hesitation, even without some of the enabling mechanisms I posit below.

It is clear that it will take a combination of these various initiatives—legislative and administrative, as well as cultural and institutional—to ensure that the senior *Federal* service, and all of the executives it supports, remains as viable and vital an institution as it was intended to be.

As has been my custom, following the chapters of our four contributors, I offer a number of additional recommendations, all of which are (hopefully) bold enough. However, while many of them fall within an administration's existing legal authority, this section is different in that several recommendations go beyond that red line—they would change the fundamental architecture of the SES and, as such, would require legislation. As I have acknowledged, that can be risky, but I believe the risk is warranted. The "platform is burning," and while it may just be smoldering at the moment, there is every possibility that the flames will get inexorably hotter—just ask our SES colleagues in the U.S. Department of Veterans Affairs (VA) or IRS. Thus, the time for action is now.

Sustaining the SES in Difficult Times

By the Honorable Robert F. Hale, former Comptroller and Chief Financial Officer for the U.S. Department of Defense

Introduction

While serving for more than 12 years as a political appointee in the DOD, I have worked closely with many members of the SES, both as a supervisor and colleague. Members of the SES have been enormously helpful to me in carrying out my responsibilities in the Department and, in my view, have contributed substantially to maintaining our national security. Sustaining a strong senior executive corps is key to maintaining an effective government.

Today's senior executive corps faces problems, including problems getting good people to join the SES ranks. This chapter argues that we can help sustain a strong senior executive corps by reforming rules for the civil servants they supervise, especially speeding hiring and making it easier to terminate poor performers. In my experience, SES members spend too much time handling the relatively small numbers of poor performers. We also need to encourage SES members to maintain their in-depth technical skills while also broadening their backgrounds. In a recent EO, President Obama took a step toward requiring broadening, though I believe some of the provisions in the EO need to be altered. Finally, we need to increase the incentives to join the SES. While large pay increases seem highly unlikely anytime soon, Congress and the next administration might be able to agree to expand merit-based pay, perhaps going beyond the first steps in the recent EO. We can also help make SES service rewarding by doing a better job of telling SES members that, in many cases, they are doing excellent work.

Introduction: Why we need a strong senior executive corps

I recall numerous times when SES members were helpful, but one event stands out. In 2013, the law imposed substantial budget cuts (known as "sequestration") on the DOD and many other Federal agencies. Because the cuts occurred mid-year, and because of issues related to funding for wartime needs, DOD faced a 30-percent reduction in its non-war operating funds during the second half of fiscal year (FY) 2013. Departmental leaders, including many senior executives, scrambled to come up with plans to meet the legally required cuts while minimizing harm to national security.

As DOD's Comptroller, I coordinated much of the Department's efforts, and one of my senior executives took the lead in coordinating our response with senior personnel throughout DOD. The Department's response included unpaid furloughs for DOD civilians, including many of the SES members who were working to accommodate these extraordinary cuts. Even while being "rewarded" with unpaid furloughs, SES members worked tirelessly and successfully to accomplish the required cuts while minimizing mission degradation.

No sooner had the government completed accommodating the 2013 sequester than lack of agreement on the budget for FY 2014 forced a 16-day shutdown of government operations, beginning on October 1, 2013. Again, many senior executives and civil servants trudged home on furloughs. And, again, members of the SES (including a number on my staff) led efforts to maintain critical aspects of the Department's activities when they were permitted to work. Without their help, I couldn't have carried out my responsibilities to coordinate the shutdown activities.

Critical though they are to the functioning of government, the SES today faces serious challenges. Some members of Congress castigate civil servants and the SES, seemingly treating them not as valued employees but as symbols of a government they believe is too large. SES members themselves are becoming frustrated with budget limits that do not permit them the staff or the budgetary stability needed to meet mission needs. Perhaps of greatest concern, anecdotal evidence suggests that some of the best senior civil servants are not interested in serving in the SES.

If government is to meet national needs effectively, we must sustain a capable senior executive corps. This chapter offers three examples of important and much-needed changes.

Reform the civil service to help the SES

While this book focuses on the SES, it must do so in context. SES members manage the civil service. Based on my experience, improved accountability and flexibility in the civil service, as well as streamlined hiring, would reduce the time SES members spend on hiring and firing. This would allow them more time to focus on improving government, which should both help improve government and assist in sustaining the SES.

Accountability and flexibility

Compared to the civil service as a whole, SES members can more readily be held accountable for their actions. At a minimum, managers have the authority to transfer senior executives to new jobs without extensive paperwork, hearings, or appeals.

Unfortunately, that level of accountability and flexibility often does not extend to civil servants below the SES level. At levels below the SES, the best solution for sustained poor performance may be termination of the employee. That gives the employee a chance to start over in a new environment, and the government can hire someone who can perform more capably.

But experts agree that firing a civil service employee is difficult.[185] The poor performance must be extensively documented. The employee has the right to appeal any termination decision, which results in still more workload for the supervisor. Termination actions can sometimes morph into accusations of favoritism and violation of equal opportunity laws, which engenders still more paperwork and angst. I found that my SES members spent an inordinate amount of their time handling poor performers, who often were the same employees who filed equal opportunity or other complaints.

Congress recently took some incremental actions to allow the DOD to hold employees more accountable. In the National Defense Authorization Act for Fiscal Year 2016,[186] Congress extended the probationary period for new DOD employees from 1 to 2 years. Congress also required that DOD take performance into account when accommodating reduction-in-force actions.

The government should go further and institute regular review points throughout a career, where performance is assessed and managers have greater flexibility to terminate poor performers. At these review points, termination would primarily be a management determination, with appeals limited to demonstrable bias in the formulation of personnel reviews along with discriminatory or political motivations. The presence of clear review points might provide more incentives to managers to document poor performance, which does not always occur today. The right for appeal on selected grounds would help maintain the apolitical nature of the civil service.

Greater flexibility to terminate poor performers would help SES members who must manage personnel and attend to the always-difficult problem of handling poor performers. Improved flexibility would also help the Federal civil service as a whole.

Hiring

Changes that streamline civil service hiring practices, including sharp reductions in the time required to hire, would help nurture and sustain the SES as well as aid the civil service as a whole. Improvements in hiring practices have been discussed for years. Nevertheless, in a 2014 statement, the Director of OPM noted that there was still a need to untie the knots in the Federal hiring process.[187]

[185] Holan, A. D. (2007, September 5). Firing Federal workers is difficult. *PolitiFact*. Retrieved from http://www.politifact.com/truth-o-meter/article/2007/sep/05/mcain-Federal
[186] National Defense Authorization Act for Fiscal Year 2016, H.R. 1735, 114th Cong. (2015).
[187] Metzenbaum, S. H. (2014, May 29). Untying the knots in the Federal hiring process [Web log post]. Retrieved from https://www.volckeralliance.org/blog/2016/jun/untying-knots-Federal-hiring-process

My experience as the DOD's Comptroller made me aware of the problems with Federal hiring. As Comptroller, I oversaw two large defense agencies, both of which hire many new college graduates. One of these agencies, the Defense Contract Audit Agency (DCAA), hires several hundred college graduates annually. Many are accounting majors, who are in demand in the private sector. By 2014 the civil service had gone 3 years without a pay raise, the government had experienced the turmoil of sequester cuts and shut-down, and Congress continued to criticize the Federal civil service.

I recall asking the DCAA Director whether he was still able to hire high-quality graduates in view of all these problems. He reported that he generally could and that pay and budgetary turmoil did not seem to be discouraging high-performing college graduates from considering service with DCAA. The time required to complete the hiring process, however, was a problem. Private companies would often hire within weeks, whereas government hiring often required months. Sometimes promising graduates were simply not able or willing to wait.

OPM has made efforts to improve Federal hiring, but more needs to be done. Improvement could include better use of fellow and intern programs, more short-term hires from outside government, and the sharing of promising candidates among Federal agencies. Improvements would help the SES and government as a whole.

Increase SES breadth of experience while maintaining depth

Today's Federal government increasingly faces challenges that require intera-gency solutions. For example, cyber issues are on everyone's mind in the Federal government, particularly after the serious breach at OPM. Some agencies, including the DOD and the U.S. Department of Homeland Security (DHS), have special expertise that can be useful in meeting cyber challenges. Tapping this expertise requires interagency leadership and management.

There are many other issues that demand interagency efforts. Examples in-clude integration of diplomatic and military initiatives involving the DOD and the U.S. Department of State (DOS), integration of healthcare between the DOD and the VA, and creation of shared approaches to reduce costs for services such as payroll.

To be effective at leading and managing interagency issues, SES members need breadth of experience as well as the inclination to manage on an intera-gency basis. Yet a 2014 study by the Partnership for Public Service and Booz Allen indicated that more than 80 percent of those promoted to the SES came from within their own agency and only 8 percent moved to a different agency once in the SES.[188] The study recommends creation of a corps of "enterprise executives" who have the inclination and breadth of experience

---

[188] Partnership for Public Service & Booz Allen Hamilton. (2014). *Building the enterprise: A new civil service framework.* Washington, DC: Partnership for Public Service.

to lead and manage interagency issues effectively. Service in multiple Federal agencies, and in the private sector, would be one criterion for entrance to this enterprise corps. This proposal makes sense to me as a way to improve the management of critical interagency issues.

However, there is also an important role for SES members who have depth of knowledge in functional areas, coupled with the skill and stature necessary to lead. For example, there are thousands of rules governing the use of appropriated funds that are codified in financial management regulations. Violation of these rules can cause employees to run afoul of the Anti-Deficiency Act.[189] Willful violations of this act can result in criminal penalties; even inadvertent violations often lead to administrative penalties that damage careers.

For me the dark days of the 2013 government shutdown underscored the importance of SES members who know the fiscal laws and the rules that derive from those laws. During a government shutdown, employees are prohibited from engaging in any activities other than those required to ensure safety of life and protection of property. Conducting any other activities while the government is shut down, even including handling emails other than those related to life and property, may violate the Anti-Deficiency Act.

During the 16-day government shutdown in 2013, and in my coordinator role, I chaired regular late-afternoon meetings of senior defense leaders (including many senior executives) to review the detailed implementation of the shutdown in order to steer clear of legal violations while also minimizing harm to the Department's mission. We dealt with a wide variety of issues, many that were of great concern to military and civilian leaders. Issues included what to do during the shutdown regarding personnel away from home on training (most had to come home and then go back), how to handle military academic athletic events that contributed to morale and training (most had to be canceled but some were funded by nongovernmental groups and could continue), and whether to continue military funerals (they continued, but it was a close legal call that engendered considerable discussion).

During these afternoon debates, I was grateful for the senior executives who participated—especially the lawyers, personnel experts, and financial managers. They knew the rules, which was critical to keeping the Department (and me) out of legal trouble. But they also understood what actions would most harm the DOD's mission. And they knew how to make decisions and make sure they were carried out. Finally, they had the stature to get quick access to their own most senior leaders to keep them informed and bring their views back to the group.

The events of the 2013 shutdown are seared in my memory, but there are many other issues that demand a combination of technical skill and ability to lead and manage. These include managing complex acquisitions, handling complex contracts, and dealing with financial and program audits.

[189] Anti-Deficiency Act, 31 U.S.C. § 1341 et seq.

Senior executives with technical and leadership skills may be especially important in the DOD. Military officers fill many leadership roles in the Department, often serving as acquisition program managers and financial leaders at military bases and echelons above them. But these military officers rotate frequently—2 years is a common tenure for military in senior positions. Their successor in a particular job may have breadth of experience, but he or she usually lacks knowledge of what has been done in the past and how well it worked. Senior executives, who often act as deputies to military officers or lead in related functional areas, usually stay longer in a job and can provide much-needed corporate memory.

For all these reasons, I believe that a substantial portion of the SES should combine leadership with in-depth technical knowledge. They should remain in jobs long enough to provide corporate memory. The Partnership for Public Service study agrees that some SES members should move among agencies, although it is not clear how many senior executives the study would recommend as functional leaders.

Identifying SES members with strong technical skills, and permitting them to remain in jobs for significant periods, does not mean that breadth of experience is unimportant. All SES members should have some diversity during their careers. As a senior manager in the Office of the Secretary of Defense, which had oversight of activities in the military services and defense agencies, I found that senior executives who had worked in the military services or defense agencies provided better advice. They had "walked in the moccasins" of the organizations they oversaw and understood how to provide useful guidance and make it stick.

In a 2015 EO, President Obama sought to increase breadth of experience.[190] The EO requires that some senior executives rotate for a minimum of 120 days to different departments, agencies, subcomponents, functional areas, or non-Federal partners. Agencies were required to put a plan in place by May 31, 2016, that establishes a goal of rotating 15 percent of their senior executives in FY 2017.

While the intent of this EO is good, timing is a key problem.[191] By the time individuals become members of the SES, they should be leading and managing the government rather than broadening their backgrounds. Federal agencies should encourage prospective members of the SES to broaden their backgrounds earlier in their careers—probably starting when they are serving as GS-13s.

The length of rotations is also problematic. Rotations of 120 days are not likely to result in valuable work or meaningful learning experiences. But a

---

[190] Exec. Order 13714.
[191] For more discussion of this and subsequent points, see Hale, R., & Sanders, R. (2016, January 26). Developing civilian leaders in DoD. *Defense News*. Retrieved from http://www.defense-news.com/story/defense/commentary/2016/01/26/developing-civilian-leaders-dod/79055042

120-day rotation may be long enough to disrupt the employee's current work, especially if his or her position is backfilled during the rotation by someone equally out of place. However well intended, short rotations may result in performance issues—both individual and organizational. In my view, individuals who aspire to the SES should hold one or more assignment(s), each of approximately 1 year in length, leading to diversity of experience while also allowing them to contribute in their new roles. Consistent with the approach in the EO, many types of assignments should qualify as broadening experiences.

Given the importance of broad experience within the SES ranks, Congress should consider requiring rotations as a prerequisite for service in the SES. There is precedent for such a requirement. In the 1980s, Congress felt that military officers lacked needed experience in joint (that is, multiservice) positions. Yet military officers, especially the best officers, saw little career benefit in serving in joint positions because this duty took them away from the service that controlled their promotions. So, in the Goldwater-Nichols legislation passed in 1986,[192] legislators required military officers to have a multiservice tour in order to be eligible for promotion to general or admiral. This provision has significantly increased interest in joint duty among fast-track military officers.

Congress took similar action in the U.S. Intelligence Community (IC) following the 9/11 terrorist attacks. Noting the failure of intelligence leaders to "connect the dots," Congress required the Office of the Director of National Intelligence (ODNI) to implement a requirement for joint duty as a precondition for promotion of any civilian to senior executive rank in the IC.

My bottom line: Senior executives should have both depth of knowledge and breadth of experience. The White House has raised the right issue with regard to experience, and Congress may want to require diversity of experience as an additional prerequisite for promotion to SES. But civil servants should meet the prerequisite *prior* to becoming members of the SES.

Provide more incentives to join and remain in the SES

Anecdotal evidence suggests that some of the best employees do not want to join the SES. During my tenure as Defense Comptroller, a person I thought was highly qualified chose not to apply for a vacant SES position on several occasions. The individual cited the desire to avoid personnel management issues and increased stress.

Many factors contribute to this troublesome trend, but there are also a number of changes that might help reverse the trend. I offer two examples—one requires legislation, one does not.

---

[192] Goldwater-Nichols Department of Defense Reorganization Act of 1986, Pub. L. No. 99-433 (1986).

Lessen pay compression

Today, a person at the top of the General Schedule (GS) may well earn the same or even more than members of the SES. GS personnel receive locality pay allowances. In the area including Washington, DC, where many senior civil servants work, a GS employee at the top of the scale (GS-15 at pay step 10) earns $160,300 a year as of January 2016 when locality pay is included. Annual pay at the top step exceeds $150,000 in most locations. Under the January 2016 scale, and prior to the 2015 EO, SES pay ranged from $123,000 to $185,000. It was difficult just to match the pay for someone who accepted a promotion to the SES, let alone offer a substantial increase in salary.

The obvious solution is to restructure SES salaries so that they are significantly higher—perhaps starting at the current ceiling of $180,000 and going up. This would not seem out of line with senior management salaries in major private sector companies. Upward restructuring should be kept in mind when there is a major overhaul in the civil service system. Such an overhaul might create a political environment more conducive to permitting significant pay increases.

Currently, however, a significant upward restructuring of SES pay seems highly unlikely. Especially during a period when anti-government sentiment abounds in Congress and the country, Congress almost surely would not support big salary increases for members of the SES. Moreover, a major increase would put many SES salaries above those for most members of Congress ($174,000 in 2016).

While fundamental restructuring that increases SES pay seems unlikely, first steps can be taken. The President's 2015 EO took such a step. The EO directs agencies to ensure that senior executives earn salaries at least equal to the salaries, including locality pay, of the GS employees they supervise. So now an SES in the Washington, DC, area would earn a minimum of $160,300. But a top-level GS employee might still receive no raise, or only a small raise, when he or she becomes a member of the SES, even though responsibilities increase substantially.

Merit pay offers another option for improving incentives. The 2015 EO took an important step in that direction, telling agencies to increase the maximum amounts available for SES bonuses from about 5 percent today to as much as 7.5 percent. So more SES bonuses may be available or they may become larger.

Congress and the administration could go further, increasing bonuses substantially for the most capable SES members by increasing the number who are eligible for presidential rank awards. Today, members of the SES are eligible for prestigious presidential rank awards either at the meritorious level (a one-time cash payment equal to 20 percent of salary, with up to 5 percent of all SES eligible) or at the distinguished level (one-time cash payment equal to 35 percent of salary, with up to 1 percent of all SES eligible).[193] Congress might be willing to increase merit pay for SES members, perhaps making 10 percent of all SES eligible for the meritorious rank award and 2 percent eligible for the distinguished rank award. This action would provide sizable monetary awards for the most capable members of the SES.

Harness the power of praise

Many of this chapter's proposals for sustaining the SES would require legislation. But one important initiative would not require any new laws.

Everyone, including members of the SES, appreciates being praised for good work, so long as the praise is warranted and appropriate. There are already many programs and initiatives designed to recognize SES accomplishments. These include the presidential rank awards mentioned above as well as the "Sammie" awards presented annually by the Partnership for Public Service (the Sammies recognize both SES and civil service achievements).

However, in my experience at the DOD, senior managers (myself included) did not always do as much as they could to note the accomplishments of the SES and all civil servants. The Department does an excellent job commending military members for their service to the nation. That praise is well deserved and should continue. However, as the furloughs associated with the 2013 sequestration and shutdown made clear, the military cannot fight effectively without the support of the Department's civil servants. Whenever the Department thanks the military for their service, I hope they will also thank the SES and civil servants who support them. In the wake of many negative events, this small step may help reassure civilians about their worth to the government.

Over a career spent largely in Federal service, including 12 years in senior positions in the DOD, I have found the SES to be invaluable in meeting government needs. To maintain an effective government, we must take steps to sustain the SES. I hope that the suggestions in this chapter will help move us in that direction.

---

[193] Note that in recent years, because of concerns about providing large cash awards during tight budget times, the administration has not even made the maximum number of presidential rank awards permitted by current law.

CHAPTER 5.2:
Surfing the Churn: The Opportunities and Challenges of SES Attrition

By Robert Goldenkoff, Director of Strategic Issues, U.S. Government Accountability Office

Introduction

While the long-forecast tsunami of executive retirements has so far been more of a steady drizzle than a cataclysmic deluge, the fact remains that the senior executive corps is a workforce at risk. For one thing, executives are aging. Nearly half of all senior executives are age 55 or older, and almost a quarter are over age 60. Add to that morale busters such as fiscal pressures that have made it difficult for agencies to carry out their vital missions, periodic bureaucrat bashing that is sometimes aimed at executives, pay compression, and legislative proposals that would make it easier for agencies to fire senior executives, and the potential for higher rates of attrition—along with the leadership continuity, institutional knowledge, and expertise that each go out the door with it—is a very real concern.

The demographic and other challenges facing the SES underscore the importance of succession planning. The Obama administration and many agencies have launched efforts to better motivate, engage, and retain executives. While these are all important steps in the right direction, the GAO's research over more than 20 years involving the government as a whole, individual agencies in the U.S. and abroad, and specific occupations has identified an important ingredient for success: High-performing organizations do far more than simply retain executives for the sake of retention, as this may only serve to perpetuate an agency poorly positioned to meet current or emerging needs. Instead of a position-based approach to succession planning, they use a more strategic, scenario-based approach that emphasizes strengthening both current and future organizational capacity, focusing on the skills and competencies necessary to carry out today's mission and over-the-horizon requirements.

Going forward, job #1 for agency heads is to plan for and manage executive turnover by developing policies, programs, and cultures aimed at retaining high-performing leaders while simultaneously using the churn to make space for new talent to transform the organization's culture, improve diversity, and ensure it has the skills and competencies needed to meet ever-evolving missions. To be sure, strategic succession planning is an ongoing, long-term investment with the following key ingredients: (1) workforce analytics, (2) strategic planning and organizational reexamination, (3) meaningful performance management, and (4) a robust action plan. The active support of top-level leadership is a must.

Use workforce analytics to assess vulnerabilities and target remedial efforts

A key first step in retaining senior executives is to gain visibility over the dynamics of the executive workforce, including data that inform attrition-related questions. What's going to happen? When and where will it happen? To whom might it happen? What are the risks to the organization? The goal is to help agencies forecast, with greater precision, areas in the organization at risk for skill gaps that could affect mission accomplishment and other strategic goals, and inform decisions on how to address them.

Government-wide, approximately 50 percent of all career senior executives who were onboard at the end of 2014 will be eligible to retire by the end of 2019. This compares to approximately 32 percent for the Federal workforce as a whole. However, retirement eligibility varies across agencies. Similar variation likely exists within agencies, components, various occupations, locations, etc., so obtaining full visibility over an agency's retirement profile—including those eligible for early retirement—will require data broken out by a number of different variables. As part of this effort, agencies should look at the demographic characteristics of those at, or nearing, retirement eligibility, as turnover enables agencies to make progress on their diversity goals.

Importantly, retirement eligibility does not necessarily equate with actual retirements, and, in fact, many employees continue to work beyond when they are first eligible to retire, in some cases for a number of years. Many variables influence executives' employment decisions, including an individual's financial and health status, the employment status of a spouse, and the availability of post-Federal employment opportunities. Consequently, agencies also need to obtain data on historical retirement trends. The results of OPM's FEVS can also be mined for this purpose. The FEVS asks employees about their retirement plans (for the record, the results of the 2015 FEVS show that among all Federal employees, 25 percent said they would retire within 1 to 5 years).

Once an agency knows more about its retirement trends, a key next step is determining the risks to the agency if and when those losses occur. In considering these risks, the various roles of an executive need to be taken into account. These roles include, among others, program execution, talent management, and communication.

The most obvious risk is to program execution. Executives provide the overall vision for the program as well as day-to-day leadership. They are the subject matter experts, possess the institutional knowledge, drive continuous improvement, and are thus the ones to turn to in both routine and crisis situations. Senior executives are also critical for managing and integrating a multisector, multigenerational workforce, bringing together networks of actors with various expertise and skills. Although relatively few in number at most agencies, senior executives' loss can profoundly affect mission accomplishment. For example, the Inspectors General at both the IRS and the VA cited executive turnover as one of several factors contributing to management challenges within key programs at those agencies.

Risks to talent management should be considered as well. Executives play a critical role in coaching, mentoring, and developing employees, strengthening the overall capacity and performance of an organization. As one example, senior executives can help boost employee engagement by leading, supporting, and holding supervisors accountable for such engagement drivers as performance conversations with staff, career development and training, work-life balance, an inclusive work environment, and employee involvement. Perhaps it is not surprising, then, that the DHS, an agency that consistently has among the lowest employee engagement scores of all large agencies, has a history of high levels of executive vacancies.

Another risk involves internal communications and information flows, both downward and upward. Executives can communicate to staff the policy and vision of agency heads, providing the line of sight linking employees' daily work with an agency's strategic organizational goals and mission. They also play an important role in implementing organizational transformations, helping line employees become more accepting of change. With respect to upward communication flows, senior executives play an important role in relaying information from line managers to senior agency officials and can be the critical link in ensuring bad news gets delivered.

If done fairly and honestly, agencies may find that the enterprise risks associated with the departure of one executive may differ substantially from that of another executive. For example, how has the executive performed against an agency's expectations and standards? Is the executive a leader or a controller? Is he or she open to innovation and new ways of thinking? Does he or she have effective interpersonal skills? Is he or she supportive of the agency's goals and objectives? Does he or she actively support and encourage engagement, diversity, and inclusiveness?

Additional organizational objectives should be considered as well, such as increasing diversity in the senior ranks and bringing in new skills and perspectives. Available data from OPM suggest that the SES cadre could benefit from both. Indeed, as of September 2014, around two-thirds of senior executives were male, 79.4 percent were White, 11 percent were African American, 4.4 percent were Hispanic or Latino, and 3.2 percent were Asian. Moreover, in 2014, almost 90 percent of executives joined the SES at the same agency in which they were working prior to becoming an executive. While internal promotions are important for upward mobility, they limit the amount of fresh thinking that is brought into an organization.

These are all difficult and sometimes uncomfortable questions for an organization's senior leadership team to address, but their answers can help inform where to target retention efforts and when to let natural attrition take its course.

Link workforce analytics to strategic planning and organizational reexamination

Workforce planning is a necessary but insufficient condition for effective succession management. Agencies must also ask such questions as, what are the strategic goals of the organization, and how can executives' knowledge and experience contribute to them? In this way, succession planning is a tool that helps agencies achieve longer term mission outcomes.

High-performing organizations begin this process by reexamining the status quo. Many Federal programs, policies, functions, and activities were designed years ago to address earlier challenges with the technology that was available at that time. It is not uncommon for agencies to think that changes and innovations to a program are prohibited by law, regulation, or policy but, when they dig a little deeper, find no such constraint to innovation exists. In other cases, agencies do what they do because, well, they have always done it that way. As one example, agencies frequently complain about the difficulties they encounter when trying to hire employees who are a good fit for the agency. They may say things like, "We're having trouble filling a position—none of the candidates have the right skills." In many cases, the issue is not with the applicants, it's with the position description—it was written decades earlier, and agencies have simply neglected to update it!

GAO has noted the importance of reexamining the base of all major Federal programs, policies, functions, and activities by reviewing their results and ensuring they are still relevant.[194] Key to the exercise is asking such fundamental question as:

- Why was a program initiated—what was the intended goal?

- Are outcome-based measures available to assess progress in meeting its intended goals?

- Is it properly targeted to areas where needs are greatest?

- Is it using the most cost-effective approaches when compared to other tools and program designs?

- Does it use prevailing leading practices?

[194] U.S. Government Accountability Office. (2005). *21st Century challenges: Reexamining the base of the Federal government* (Report No. GAO-05-325SP). Washington, DC: U.S. Government Accountability Office. Retrieved from http://www.gao.gov/assets/160/157585.pdf

One agency that has conducted this type of reexamination and linked succession planning with the forward-looking process of strategic planning is the U.S. Census Bureau. In an effort to strengthen its current and future organizational capacity to carry out its mission in the face of such challenges as budget reductions, rising enumeration costs, rapidly changing technology, and its own outmoded business processes, the Bureau began a reexamination and succession planning and management effort in the years following the 2000 Census that continues to this day. Among other things, the Bureau recognized it needed to reengineer its approach to taking the Decennial Census, including doing a better job of planning strategically, setting goals, working across silos, and leveraging technology.

These changes had implications for the skills and competencies of the Bureau's workforce, including its executives. For example, the Bureau's FY 2013–2017 Strategic Plan notes that its managers "need to...provide opportunities for professional development, be more tolerant of failure to reach goals or bring innovative products to fruition, and encourage and reward innovation and creative thinking."

Although the effectiveness of the Bureau's reexamination efforts won't be known until cost and quality measures on the 2020 Census are published, the Bureau's efforts highlight the importance of including organizational reexamination in any long-term workforce planning effort. Doing so will help ensure the skills and competencies of the executive corps and other employees will align with future mission needs.

Conduct meaningful performance management

Credible and effective performance management helps create a line of sight showing how executive, unit, and team performance can contribute to the achievement of organizational outcomes. When implemented well, performance management is not a report card, and it is certainly much more than the once- or twice-a-year ratings process to which many Federal employees have grown accustomed. Instead, leading organizations use their performance management systems to drive internal change and achieve results through a process that includes planning work, setting expectations, monitoring performance, providing regular feedback and coaching, and offering incentives. In this way, effective performance management is critical to executive succession planning because it helps executives see the extent to which their leadership efforts align with mission accomplishment and the steps they need to take to continually improve.

However, agencies often stumble when it comes to developing effective performance management systems. Nonperforming leaders, though few, are rarely removed; marginal leaders seldom get the training and feedback they need to improve; good leaders don't usually get the coaching to become great; and great leaders hardly get sufficient rewards and recognition to keep them inspired and motivated.

There are many reasons agencies don't use their performance management systems to more strategically manage employee performance. In some cases, the processes are seen as time consuming to implement or distracting from mission-oriented functions. The goal, then, is to not simply "do" performance management but instead create an organizational culture of high performance. Such organizations have flatter hierarchies and are less process oriented, more externally focused, and heavily focused on results.

In 2003, Congress revamped the pay system for executives by requiring agencies to provide more rigorous and realistic ratings of their executives, most of whom at that time were rated in the top two performance categories. Agencies are allowed to raise SES basic pay and total compensation caps if OPM certifies, and OMB concurs, that agencies' executive performance appraisal systems, in their design and application, make meaningful distinctions based on relative performance.

Meaningful distinctions in ratings are important for several reasons. First, they provide transparency to the senior executive. At many organizations, leaders make assignment, bonus, and other decisions based on an executive's performance. The leaders know how well that person performs, but, without meaningful distinctions, the only person who is unaware of his or her performance is the executive. Likewise, meaningful distinctions are the starting point for performance conversations. If an agency's modal rating for its executives is at the outstanding level, it's hard for the executive to own the feedback, assuming it's provided at all. After all, why work on improving when your rating says you're already the best?

As GAO pointed out in its 2015 report, the lack of performance distinctions is still problematic, as more than 85 percent of career executives were rated in the top two of five rating levels for FY 2010–2013.[195] A key issue is cultural in that even though a rating level of three represents fully successful performance in a position where the bar is already high, it is perceived by employees as average or ordinary.

Going forward, it will be important for agencies to use their SES performance management system as a strategic tool in the succession planning process. Effective performance management and the open, honest feedback it should generate help hold leaders accountable for results and drive the internal change needed to be more effective.

Develop an action plan

Workforce analytics, organizational reexamination, and performance management collectively help agencies identify what their workforce and mission will look like in the future and what is expected of executives to achieve that

---

[195] U.S. Government Accountability Office. (2015, January 22). Results-oriented management: OPM needs to do more to ensure meaningful distinctions are made in SES ratings and performance awards. Retrieved from http://www.gao.gov/products/GAO-15-189

mission. But arguably the most difficult job is how best to act on the results of those activities, namely actively managing executive attrition to produce a leadership corps with the skills and competencies needed to meet current and emerging mission requirements. A key first step is to develop a thoughtful action plan that, among other things, identifies and reinforces factors that affect executives' decisions to stay and addresses the factors that cause executives to retire. While varying government-wide, agency-specific, and personal issues influence executives' decisions, the results of recent surveys provide some clues.

Perhaps the most interesting and recent data come from OPM's 2016 SES Exit Survey,[196] which highlights the "regrettable losses" occurring in the ranks of the government's top leaders. Of the 162 executives who reported they are retiring or resigning voluntarily, 56% said they intended to work for pay after leaving their agency or planned to look for employment in the near future. According to the study, the departing executives were leaving with the intent to continue working, in most cases for higher pay.

The OPM study also found that "agencies can influence whether or not executives stay in the organization." Although 70 percent of the respondents said that no effort was made to encourage them to stay, many of the respondents said that some verbal encouragement or other form of agency recognition could have changed their decisions, including an increase in pay (37 percent), verbal encouragement to stay based on their value to the organization (24 percent), or an award (24 percent).

These results are regrettable because the outcomes seem so avoidable. Many of the departing senior executives plan to continue working, and some might have stayed had their agencies provided an encouraging word, perhaps even a simple "thank you" for their efforts.

According to OPM, the factors most often cited in contributing to executives' decisions to leave include work environment issues such as:

- The political environment (42 percent)

- Senior leadership (38 percent)

- The organizational culture (38 percent)

- A desire to enjoy life without work commitments (38 percent).

Other factors were the opposite of the reasons to stay in an organization, including lack of recognition for accomplishments (34 percent) and insufficient pay (29 percent). Stress on the job was also a factor (30 percent).

---

[196] Senior Executive Service Exit Survey Results, Spring 2016 (https://www.chcoc.gov/content /release-2016-governmentwide-ses-exit-survey-report)

The good news here is that even though the SES workforce is aging and becoming increasingly retirement eligible, turnover is not an inevitable outcome and, in some cases, can be managed with agency interventions. The results of OPM's study and similar research highlight the need for agencies to understand and monitor the job satisfaction and other factors that affect the employment decisions of senior executives. The FEVS, an annual OPM survey that asks Federal employees about their work experiences, their agencies, and their leaders, is a starting point. This information needs to be supplemented with micro-level data collected by individual agencies, such as pulse surveys, exit surveys, and exit interviews.

Once patterns are identified, agencies can then develop action plans with appropriate retention strategies. While Federal agencies don't have the same tools the private sector has to retain top talent, such as the ability to offer higher pay, there are still a number of actions agencies can take. In any case, pay is not always a primary issue with executives, especially among those already working in public service. Various studies of both private and public sector organizations have noted the impact that nonfinancial incentives can have on retention, including:

- New challenges and responsibilities

- Greater verbal recognition and encouragement for results achieved

- Opportunities to make a difference

- Better work-life balance

- New skills and self-development

- Rotational assignments

- Opportunities to train, coach, and mentor others.

Several of these strategies directly or indirectly align with the stay/leave decisions made by SES members as cited in OPM's exit survey, such as greater recognition and better work-life balance. Importantly, and not surprisingly, agencies should tailor their retention approaches to the needs of the individual. Generic retention efforts have limited effectiveness in a diverse workforce, which is why agencies should explore a menu of options for their executives.

As the number of SES retirements is likely to increase in the years ahead, agencies should change their views of the risks posed by the potential turnover: Not all retention is necessarily good and not all turnover is necessarily bad. If managed well, agencies can "surf the churn," building their capacity to meet current and ever-evolving mission requirements.

Retaining, Motivating, and Recruiting the Senior Executive Corps

By Stephen Shih, Deputy Associate Director for Senior Executive Services and Performance Management, U.S. Office of Personnel Management

Introduction

During the 21st century, the Federal government will face serious challenges that are likely to significantly affect the quality, depth, and effectiveness of the senior executive corps. Federal agencies will experience the strong generational changes currently reshaping the demographics of our nation's population and labor force. Specifically, the aging of a substantial segment of the United States population will lead to a vast increase in retirements and other workplace departures, vacancies in critical jobs, and a shortage of available workers —including senior executives. These dynamics will cause heightened multisector competition for a smaller pool of talent.

Compounding these problems are a number of conditions in recent years that have further impeded Federal agencies' efforts to successfully recruit and retain talent: severe budget constraints, congressional efforts to speed the removal of Federal employees without adequate concern for appropriate legal procedures, and a frequent lack of recognition and appreciation for Federal service. Moreover, the modern era continuously presents wicked problems of unprecedented complexity and scale, requiring the attention of senior leaders with modern competencies and global perspectives to address. In this environment, Federal agencies may encounter significant obstacles competing against multisector employers for limited SES and other talent.

Getting real: The challenge of sustaining a strong senior executive corps

First, Federal agencies (and other employers in our country) are at strong risk of losing a sizable proportion of their workforce, including the SES, without a proportional source of replacement workers. Approximately 64 percent of the current SES workforce will be eligible to retire in the year 2017, and 85 percent will be eligible to retire in the next 10 years;[197] this means Federal agencies will be vying against other motivated Federal and non-Federal employers to replace departing SES leaders with qualified leaders from a significantly smaller national talent pool. This dynamic will occur due to the retirements and other departures of increasing numbers of workers across our nation from the baby boom generation (often described as those born during the massive increase in births in the mid-1940s to the mid-1960s, who began to reach the general retirement age of 65 in the year 2011).

As the baby boom generation departs the national workforce, far fewer potential replacement workers will be available due to the significantly declined birth rates in subsequent generations. As a result, Federal agencies are likely to experience broad and deep critical difficulties in both successfully retaining a larger group of SES leaders eligible for retirement and replacing departing SES leaders from a significantly smaller supply of workers from subsequent generations. The available talent pools will be not only smaller in size but also of increasing attractiveness to other Federal agencies and non-Federal organizations experiencing similar talent shortages and needs. In sum, competition for talent will greatly increase as the demand for talent increases and the supply of talent decreases.

Furthermore, the presence and availability of seasoned SES talent will likely precipitously decline. Our data show the large majority of current SES employees are either already eligible or will soon be eligible for retirement (a fact that is unsurprising due to the experience and qualifications required of SES jobs), and survey data indicate significant numbers of SES actually do intend to leave the workforce in the very near future. Although agencies are actively engaged in developing other Federal employees who could succeed to these positions and pipelines of talent in other sectors through succession planning efforts, filling so many positions over a short period will still be a significant challenge.

Next, Federal agencies have recently operated in a climate not well-suited to mission accomplishment or the recruitment and retention of top talent, including SES. Federal agencies have suffered impacts on operations and personnel management due to frequent budgetary challenges arising from economic factors, uncertainty in the appropriations process, and a shutdown of the Federal government. In addition, although relatively few ethics problems have occurred in the career workforce in recent years, some individual employees have been involved in high-profile incidents involving misconduct, inefficient management, and unlawful operation of programs entrusted to them; these incidents have negatively affected the standing and reputation of the Federal government.

Although these incidents have involved a limited number of agencies and a small set of specific individuals and issues, Federal agencies as a whole have

---

[197] Partnership for Public Service & McKinsey and Company. (2016). *A pivotal moment for the Senior Executive Service: Measures, aspirational practices and stories of success.* Washington, DC: Partnership for Public Service.

ultimately suffered from the ensuing fallout—damaging the public's perception of the Federal government's credibility and prestige, drawing particular congressional attention and legislative proposals for removing Federal senior executives in new ways that give short shrift to appropriate process, and ultimately negatively affecting the attractiveness of the Federal government as an employer. In recent years, numerous observers have noted that the Federal workforce has not enjoyed a level of support, resources, recognition, appreciation, or prestige that would position the government to tout Federal service as a job of choice for prospective workers.

Furthermore, the modern era has introduced our nation to a time of significant complexity and scale (e.g., economic and national security challenges involving greater interdependencies of nations around the world; new and more specialized issues resulting from technological advances), demanding the best talent, including senior executives, with modern leadership skills. Federal SES leaders, in particular, will need to restore faith in the Federal government and successfully drive appropriate accountability for results in a resource-constrained environment by serving as responsible stewards of public investments.

In addition, SES leaders will need to possess heightened people skills to manage and influence a multigenerational workforce and diverse multisector groups of national and often international stakeholders. Federal agencies and other organizations will no longer succeed with only a local or even regional focus, nor can they be led only by senior leaders with conventional competencies involving traditional top-down project management approaches confined to local silos and narrowly confined operational responsibilities. Rather, modern SES and other senior leaders must possess a rare combination of skills, including a base level of technical proficiency, an ability to lead large enterprise coordination and collaboration efforts, an ability to innovate and also achieve results, an ability to strategically communicate, and emotional intelligence (including its application). These competencies are reflected in the Executive Core Qualifications (ECQ) validated by OPM against which SES candidates are assessed, and agencies should tailor their job requirements and assessments to emphasize these specific leadership competencies when hiring SES leaders.

Most importantly, to surmount the challenges created by the aging of the baby boom generation and the environment in which agencies are operating, Federal agencies and their leaders will need to attain a model status as employers and organizations to hire and keep top talent and to achieve mission success. For model employer status, Federal agencies must ensure efficient and effective hiring, strong employee engagement, and effective retention and succession management. Conversely, for model organization status, Federal agencies must hire and empower senior leaders and other personnel with modern competencies necessary to enable agencies to achieve operational efficiency, innovation, accountability, results, positive stakeholder engagement, and strong people management; this will enable agencies to accomplish their missions in the 21st century environment and enhance credibility and support from the public and other stakeholders.

Looking forward: Improving recruitment, performance management, employee engagement, and succession management

In my current position at OPM, I am leading several efforts to improve Federal employment of SES personnel—informed by data and a whole-of-government enterprise perspective, as well as my own experience as an operational SES leader in a cabinet-level department. For example, OPM is helping Federal agencies more successfully compete for SES talent by designing and administering efficient and effective hiring processes. Such processes must include the hiring, training, and management of high-quality human resources staff, as well as the accompanying commitment of SES hiring managers to work with human resources staff early and throughout the hiring process to ensure the hiring stages and actions (including application and assessment) are appropriate and successful.

These hiring processes must involve continual engagement with candidates to help identify, bring, and keep top candidates in the hiring process until onboarding. Under my leadership, OPM has developed and partnered with other agencies to test a number of SES hiring innovations, including a resume-based hiring method and the development of structured interview questions that have helped achieve improvements in both the speed and quality of SES hiring at some agencies. OPM is continuing to work with more agencies to adopt these hiring tools, as appropriate, and jointly develop additional innovations (e.g., cutting-edge simulation and video-based leadership assessments) that will position agencies to have the best hiring processes.

In addition, OPM is working with Federal agencies to improve performance management and employee engagement. This effort is based on our understanding that agencies more successfully attract and motivate top SES talent when agencies have a strong track record of and reputation for enabling high employee performance and growth and where employees achieve that performance and growth. At OPM, I led an interagency effort a few years ago to design a government-wide SES performance appraisal system. This system has now been voluntarily adopted by approximately 94 percent of Federal agencies (and soon all cabinet-level departments), enabling the Federal government to improve the quality, consistency, equity, and transferability of SES performance management with an emphasis on both results and leadership. Although the media has recently devoted some attention to organizations interested in abandoning performance appraisal systems, the Federal government is required by law to maintain objective communication and measurement systems to evaluate its employees in order to drive high performance and help the Federal government remain accountable to its citizens.

In addition, because we know the effectiveness of a system or tool is only as good as its implementation, OPM is working with agencies to emphasize execution, not just adoption of systems. Specifically, I am currently leading an effort to help agencies prioritize and implement a philosophy known as "Performance Management Plus," where the "Plus" refers to the emphasis on employee engagement to further supplement traditional performance management processes—serving as a key to unlock employees' high performance and commitment to their organizations. Similarly, many of the non-Federal organizations currently experimenting with performance management alternatives are in fact simply emphasizing employee engagement, including frequent and high-quality communication between supervisors and their employees, as well as supervisors' commitment to the needs and interests of their employees.

From our examination of data, research, and multisector benchmarking, we know Federal agencies and their leaders may achieve a high-performance culture by prioritizing the engagement of their senior executives and other staff. Successful engagement results in high individual performance and retention of personnel and is empowered by continued supervisory attention to employees' training and development needs, professional advancement goals, and work-life integration priorities. I am currently leading efforts at OPM to support agencies in each of these areas, including through the issuance of policies and products on employee engagement action planning and execution, leadership development, and work-life and wellness programs.

From data gathered through OPM surveys, we have identified numerous areas where Federal agencies can better engage their SES leaders. For example, a number of our recent general SES surveys revealed opportunities for Federal agencies to improve their performance management communication and recognition of SES leaders and continue emphasizing assessment and support for their SES leaders' developmental needs.

Data from our recent SES Exit Survey indicate a number of key engagement opportunities for agencies to better retain and manage their SES leaders, including the following findings:

- Almost half of SES respondents indicated they will continue working after retiring or resigning from their agency, in most cases for higher pay.

- A majority of SES respondents reported their agency made no effort to encourage them to stay.

- A large percentage of this group (70 percent) indicated one or more of the following—they might have decided to stay if they had received an increase in pay (37 percent), verbal encouragement to stay (24 percent), or an award recognizing their performance (24 percent).

- Respondents cited their work environment (including such factors as political environment, their own senior leadership, organizational culture, and work-life balance) as the biggest factor contributing to their decision to leave.[198]

[198] U.S. Office of Personnel Management. (2015). *Senior Executive Service exit survey results: April 2015*. Washington, DC: Office of Personnel Management. Retrieved from https://www.opm.gov/policy-data-oversight/senior-executive-service/reference-materials/ses-exit-survey-result-spdf.pdf

OPM also annually administers the government-wide FEVS that obtains engagement information from Federal employees, and OPM recently developed an employee engagement dashboard that provides Federal leaders with data on the engagement levels of their workforce (available at www. UnlockTalent.gov). Recently, the Federal government reversed a multiyear trend of decreases in employee engagement scores across agencies, and this positive direction must be continued to position the Federal government to successfully attract and retain top talent.

Federal agencies must emphasize and devote continual attention to strategic succession management so they are prepared to replace departing SES personnel—from both internal pools of employees prepared for succession and external talent brought into agencies through leading recruitment and hiring programs. Agencies need to regularly conduct workforce analyses, including engaging SES personnel on their career goals and needs, to identify separation risk and prepare succession plans. In developing succession plans, agencies should identify potential internal successors and commit to training and development to maintain a deep succession pipeline.

Particularly in a budget-constrained environment, agencies should partner with each other to share training solutions. My organization at OPM has developed a comprehensive suite of leadership development tools, available through our online "Manager's Corner" learning portal. OPM has made our own tools available, and obtained such tools from other agencies, through a website (www.hru.gov) that enables agencies to access tools developed by other agencies at no cost. In addition, OPM provides a broad range of even more extensive leadership training solutions, available to agencies on a reimbursable basis, as described on OPM's website (www.opm.gov). Soon, OPM will gather and share best practices for talent and succession management and will offer agencies a shared technological solution to support such programs.

Next, to achieve a competitive advantage for top talent, Federal agencies must establish a reputation as model employers and organizations. Having served as a senior leader in several agencies, I am acutely aware of the challenges, but also the tremendous opportunities available, for Federal agencies to succeed in the modern environment. For example, in an Acting Assistant Secretary position at the DHS, I served on a senior leadership team that provided direction within DHS and also across the national security enterprise in the United States to plan for, prepare for, prevent, and respond to—with limited authorities and resources—significant emergencies involving extraordinarily complex natural disasters and manmade threats.

In this capacity, I helped provide enterprise leadership and coordination across national sectors and international borders, including for the following extraordinarily broad and complex challenges that occurred during a 6-month period: November 5, 2009, Fort Hood shootings in Killeen, Texas; December 25, 2009, attempted underwear bombing of Northwest Airlines Flight 253;

January 12, 2010, Haiti earthquake; April 20, 2010, Deepwater Horizon oil spill in the Gulf of Mexico; and May 1, 2010, attempted bombing in Times Square in New York.

Each of these crises required me and my senior executive colleagues to demonstrate 21st century leadership skills, including basic technical proficiency (e.g., experience and knowledge of homeland security policies, methods, best practices, and solutions); large enterprise coordination (many of these incidents required international partnering and collaboration); innovation (to identify new solutions and resources for new situations in a resource-constrained environment); results orientation (to demonstrate measurable success and accountability to the public); strategic communication (to manage public messaging and positively engage stakeholders); and emotional intelligence (to successfully influence diverse partners and stakeholders and manage a diverse workforce in an environment involving funding and asset limitations).

And although each of these crises was far too complex and broad for any one leader, organization, or even country to singlehandedly address, each provided an opportunity for the coordination and unity of more powerful multination and multisector solutions. To succeed under these conditions, SES leaders must have modern leadership competencies enabling them to influence, unify, and leverage the combined support, authorities, capabilities, and resources from organizations and countries to assemble and apply effective solutions normally beyond the reach of an individual leader.

Finally, to acquire SES leaders with the modern leadership competencies required to succeed in the 21st century, Federal agencies will again need to succeed in hiring, development, and succession management. Federal agencies will successfully attract top SES talent from other agencies and other sectors by following first-class recruitment and hiring programs and by being model employers and organizations. Federal agencies will also succeed in retaining and developing internal successors for SES positions by operating strong workforce and succession management programs to identify succession risks and opportunities and ensure preparation of internal successors through development and employee engagement.

The current improvement efforts I am leading at OPM include initiatives to modernize and improve SES development and succession management. With respect to development, my organization has recently produced a number of government-wide solutions to help agencies develop their current and future SES leaders in a high-quality and consistent manner (many of them available through the OPM SES webpage [www.opm.gov/ses], Manager's Corner [www.hru.gov], or OPM's Training and Development Wiki [http://www.opm.gov/WIKI/training/Index.aspx]), including:

- Managerial and Supervisory Development Framework and Guide;

- ECQ Learning Interventions Study;

- Federal Coaching Network Program;

- Situational Mentoring Program;

- The President's Management Council Interagency Rotations Program;

- Model SES Onboarding Program.

We have also developed online and classroom courses on various leadership topics, including strategic leadership, employee engagement, generational diversity, executive excellence and wellness through strategic leadership, and application of ECQs for enterprise leadership. As part of a larger reform effort, OPM is also helping agencies design talent management and succession planning programs for SES.

In sum, Federal agencies will need to prioritize a number of strategies to hire, manage, and retain a successful senior executive corps in the 21st century. Agencies will need to achieve a competitive hiring advantage as model employers and organizations. Agencies will also need to strategically commit to operating best-in-class human capital management programs involving workforce analysis, succession planning, performance management, development, and employee engagement to achieve a high-performance culture. In this way, agencies will best position the Federal government to maintain a senior executive corps with the top talent for the modern era.

CHAPTER 5.4:

Through the Storm: Navigating the IRS through Crisis to Recovery

By the Honorable Daniel Werfel, former U.S. Office of Management and Budge Controller and Acting Commissioner of the U.S. Internal Revenue Service

Introduction

The President's Chief of Staff looked directly at me from over his desk. "We need you to be the Acting Commissioner of the IRS," he said.

Twenty minutes earlier I had come out of a meeting in the Eisenhower Executive Office Building and was immediately informed by my assistant that I needed to head to the West Wing. The Chief of Staff had dropped in at my office at the OMB and was looking for me. Surprise visits from the President's right-hand man were not exactly routine and, as a result, my mind was filled with questions and curiosity as I walked briskly past the cars parked on West Executive Avenue and into the White House.

As I made my way up the stairs to the main floor of the West Wing on this warm and clear mid-May afternoon in 2013, the IRS was not front and center in my thoughts. Serving as the Controller of OMB and also having taken on the responsibilities of the Deputy Director for Management, I was consumed at the time with the day-to-day issues surrounding the budget sequester, which had been in effect for 2 months. And while I had briefly read about a troubling report issued the previous day by the Treasury Inspector General for Tax Administration (TIGTA), I was busy with a long to-do list of other urgent matters. Thus, the IRS was the furthest thing from my mind when I walked into Denis McDonough's office and took a seat across from him.

"We need you to be the Acting Commissioner of the IRS"

In the moment after he spoke those words, various thoughts and emotions hit me simultaneously:

- This is the biggest, most challenging and important assignment that has ever been asked of me.

- I am humbled by the confidence that he and the Treasury Secretary have in me.

- I need to talk through this with my wife.

- I hope my nearly 10 years as an SES leader in government have prepared me for this.

- I hope I don't let anyone down, including the American people, as well as the tens of thousands of civil servants working at the IRS.

As these thoughts were swirling in my head, Denis and I spoke about the assignment for a few minutes. It was a significant management and leadership challenge to be sure. The TIGTA report indicated that the IRS was using an inappropriate flagging mechanism to determine which social welfare organizations would receive tax-exempt status, resulting in conservative group applications receiving more scrutiny than others. The implication of political bias in IRS operations directly undercuts citizen trust—a trust that is absolutely critical to the successful administration of our tax system. Therefore, the public trust needed to be rebuilt quickly.

The current leader had announced his resignation, with other senior personnel departures expected. Myriad investigations were being launched, including multiple committees across Congress and the U.S. Department of Justice (DOJ). The media coverage was intensifying with each day and was unsurprisingly very negative. There would be multiple congressional hearings as well as public protest demonstrations outside IRS facilities. Morale among IRS employees, not just in the Tax Exempt Division but throughout the whole organization, was taking a big hit.

Sequestration had further cut the resource base on which IRS operates, so the agency was facing acute budget challenges. The October 2013 launch of the Affordable Care Act[199] was growing closer in time and, while the U.S. Department of Health and Human Services had the brunt of the responsibility, the IRS had several very significant, critical system and process deployments that needed to be effectively executed. Crisis or no crisis, the IRS has an ongoing responsibility to run and manage the nation's tax system, which was becoming increasingly complex with emerging threats to program integrity, such as identify theft.

As I stood up to leave Denis' office, I told him how honored I was to be asked and that I needed to discuss the potential assignment with my wife. In the pit of my stomach, a new level of nervousness I had never previously experienced began to take hold as I knew with each passing moment that I would ultimately say yes.

Why me?

Upon reflection, there are several reasons why I was a logical choice to assume the reins at IRS in the wake of the crisis that had emerged. I had served in SES leadership positions at OMB in the administrations of both Presidents

[199] Patient Protection and Affordable Care Act, Pub. L. No. 111-148 (2010).

Bush and Obama. Despite being appointed to act or serve in "political" positions during this period, I had always maintained my status as a career civil servant SES. And as the *Wall Street Journal* had described me in a piece written on the Sequester in March 2013, I was a "green shade" management geek, with a passion for the nuts and bolts of government operations.

My green shade reputation—a reference to the traditional view of bean counting accountants wearing green-shaded visors as they hovered over old-fashioned adding machines—was earned over the previous 6 years serving as the leader of the government-wide Chief Financial Officers Council. In this post, I was surrounded by the nation's top public finance executives, as we set requirements for government accountants, determined the form and content of government financial reports, and explored best practices in areas such as risk management, improved integrity of Federal spending, and internal controls.

Together, we drove reform initiatives to improve the management of Federal real estate, eliminate fraud and error, and deal with acute challenges such as standing up the budget and reporting infrastructure to implement the American Recovery and Reinvestment Act of 2009.[200] These disciplines and activities justifiably screamed more bureaucrat than political operative. In the wake of a crisis triggered by implications of potential political bias, who better to step in and lead than an SES civil servant who, like so many other civil servants, had a proven track record of pursuing government improvements and program integrity with the same energy and enthusiasm regardless of the President in office?

Moreover, these various experiences had provided me the right training on and knowledge of how to work collaboratively with various stakeholders in the Federal community to diagnose the root cause of management weakness, design and implement the appropriate interventions, and stay grounded in the substantive tasks at hand rather than being unnecessarily deterred by political objectives or distractions. Perhaps most importantly, my experience working to tackle the toughest financial management challenges put me side by side for many years with the CFOs of all the major Federal agencies.

You are not alone

Soon after my discussion with the White House Chief of Staff, I was on my way home to discuss this remarkable turn of events with my wife when my cell phone buzzed. It was Jeff Zients, the former Acting Director of OMB who had been my boss and mentor since 2009. He immediately told me he was aware of the assignment I was offered and even seemed to sense that I was en route to discuss the matter with my family. He had very specific advice for me. It was the first in a series of key pieces of advice that I received that helped shape my journey and approach at the IRS. Jeff wisely counseled me on that phone call that my success or failure in taking on the job of Acting IRS Chief had less to do with my own skills, experience, and approach and much more to do with

---

[200] American Recovery and Reinvestment Act of 2009, Pub. L. No. 111-5, 123 Stat. 115 (2009).

the people with whom I surrounded myself. Whether bringing in outside support and expertise from other government agencies or the private sector or leveraging the talent from within the IRS, I would need a strong team. And identifying that team, Jeff urged, should be my top and most urgent priority.

Jeff has a knack for pointing out extremely important and logical truths that can change your perspective on something in an enormously positive way and leave you wondering how the thought had somehow alluded you until he mentioned it. Again, my mind started to flood with various thoughts all at once. How would I build this team overnight? Who would I ask to join me? And perhaps more daunting, who could I *convince* to join me?

A SWAT team of agency CFOs

On May 22, 2013, I arrived at the IRS for my first day on the job. I did not arrive alone. I spent the previous several days winding down my responsibilities at OMB, reading as much as I could about the IRS and its responsibilities, and making phone calls...lots of phone calls. I had taken Jeff's counsel to heart and I was actively building a team to help me run the IRS at a time of great turbulence and complexity.

Where better to start my search for willing and able professionals to help take on the immense challenge at hand than agency CFOs? Federal CFOs are apolitical. They spend their days and nights focused not on policy formulation, but on how to make the engine of their agencies hum. Many of them have been in seat for years and have seen just about every management-related curve ball that the government could throw at them. I remember each phone call to my CFO colleagues vividly and was moved (but not surprised) by how rapidly they said the words I was hoping to hear: "Danny, I'm in."

When all was said and done, I brought four different agency CFOs to the IRS in 2013. Todd Grams, the CFO of the VA, joined as my Chief of Staff. David Fisher, the CFO of the GAO, joined as the IRS' first Chief Risk Officer. Peggy Sherry, the CFO of the DHS, joined as the Deputy Commissioner for Operations and Support. Jim Taylor, the CFO of the U.S. Department of Labor (DOL), joined as the IRS lead on the Affordable Care Act.[201]

It is worth noting that all four of them were career civil servants, serving in the government for multiple decades. Each had played a major role helping me solve a management challenge at some point earlier in my career; in addition, each of them came with a different but complementary set of experiences in public sector management. Although I brought in several additional talented individuals to assist,[202] most of the key players who helped me on my journey

---

[201] Patient Protection and Affordable Care Act.

[202] Most significant in supporting me were Jen O'Conner, who joined the Counsel's office and provided invaluable experience helping with the IRS response to ongoing investigations, and Dave Vorhaus, who served as my special assistant and was instrumental in helping me coordinate the first 30 days of my tenure there.

did not come from elsewhere in the Federal government. They were waiting for us when we arrived.

The men and women of the IRS

On my first day on the job, the first thing on my agenda was a meeting with IRS' Senior Executive Team, otherwise known as the SET. Made up of roughly 50 senior executives, these individuals together lead roughly 90,000 Federal employees in running the nation's tax system. The dynamic at our first meeting was, in a word, complex. The group had been through a lot over the previous few weeks, losing their former leader and watching as the organization they called home was thrust into the national spotlight, accused of violating its solemn duty to administer the tax code without bias.

Concerns and stress among the IRS leaders took many shapes and forms. There was immense frustration that a problem area in one relatively small part of the organization was painting the entire organization in a negative light. There was a growing and unsettling sense that a lot of what the organization had been working toward over the years and so many of its recent successes would be wiped away by this one event—this one significant management failure, the causes of which remained murky at that point in time. There was concern about employee morale, the growing presence of media and cameras at IRS locations, and the safety of employees due to growing expressions of anger from the public. And of course, there was the nervous uncertainty of participating in the very first meeting with their new leadership team. It was the feeling you have at the start of what you know will be a long and tough journey, but you don't know how long and you can only imagine how tough.

My message that morning and throughout my time at the IRS came from an extremely honest and sincere place. I was a career civil servant with deep respect for the work and mission of Federal employees. That respect extended to the men and women of the IRS, an organization I had long admired. I was aware of and appreciated their work, success, challenges, and deep sense of disappointment and frustration at the current circumstances. I wanted and expected their direct involvement and support in the journey we were about to take. I had no monopoly on the right answer, I told them, and while I would ultimately make and own the tough decisions that were ahead, I wanted their help in thinking through each of them.

At some points across my years of Federal service, I had unfortunately seen what happens when a new leader starts with an inherent distrust of the existing workforce and is not inclined to actively include them in the leadership of the organization from day 1. I would not make that mistake.

We were going to move forward with a new era of transparency. We were going to bend over backward to meet the requests of all the entities conducting investigations. We were going to fix what TIGTA said needed to be fixed, but we would also seek out other improvements to go above and beyond the TIGTA recommendations. And in each of these endeavors to rebuild the public trust, we were going to do it to the maximum extent practical as a team.

What I quickly learned during and in the immediate aftermath of that meeting was that the IRS leaders were ready to roll up their sleeves and begin rebuilding the public trust. Critical to our approach was redefining what *leadership engagement* should mean for the IRS going forward. To reassure the American people of the integrity of the nation's tax system, leadership engagement would need to go well beyond symbolic support and well-articulated intentions. It would require robust priority setting along with persistent realignment of resources and barrier removal to ensure success.

For example, discussions emerged regarding where talented people in the organization could be moved to higher priority assignments. Suggestions started coming in about where we could update or streamline standard operating procedures in a manner that would remove obstacles to enable a smarter way of doing business. With a new sense of empowerment and flexibility to realign, accelerate, and advance, the long and tough journey had begun in earnest.

"Here's what's keeping me up at night"

While many of the investigations are now complete and many of the final investigative reports have now been written, it is not clear whether there will ever be consensus on the root causes of the events leading up to the TIGTA report in May 2013. What is clear, and what was immediately apparent in the early days of my IRS journey, was that poor communication within the organization, both vertically and horizontally, had directly contributed to the underlying problem.

Thus, a critical guiding principle to our road ahead was to avoid insularity and establish new operating norms related to communication and collaboration across business units. As a result, the new leaders whom I brought into the IRS shared a common objective with me: Integrate long-standing IRS leaders into the decision-making process. To ensure diverse perspectives, we needed a new framework for surfacing and discussing emerging challenges—both within the IRS and, to the extent appropriate and allowable by law, with external stakeholders.

This new framework involved various pieces, most significant of which was standing up an enterprise-wide risk management (ERM) program. However, a new ERM does not break down information silos overnight. Thus, one step we took to accelerate improved communication was the creation of an integrated "problem solving" group that met with me once a week. Invitees included representatives from various parts of the organization as well as the new leaders brought in from the outside. The meeting began with me sitting down at one end of a conference room table and stating to the assembled group, "Here's what's keeping me up at night," before introducing the thorniest management challenge of the week. I then asked the group to brainstorm with me on what steps we could take to solve it.

The problem-solving group had many benefits. It symbolized and reflected our intent to manage the organization through this crisis as an integrated team and drive meaningful discussion across separate business units. I benefited immensely from the collective input of long-standing IRS leaders.

For example, in an early problem-solving session, I posed the question of how we could rapidly reduce the long-standing backlog of social welfare organizations with pending applications for tax-exempt status. This backlog and the aggrieved taxpaying entities waiting for review were a central concern highlighted in the May 2013 TIGTA report. There were many dimensions to the challenge of the ongoing backlog. In response to TIGTA, new procedures were in an early phase of deployment. In addition, given the public uproar over the review process itself, employees involved in the review were in a highly risk-averse state of mind, concerned that a decision on any application, no matter how substantive, objective, and proper, would draw considerable scrutiny.

This problem-solving group—made up mostly of personnel outside the Tax Exempt Division—calmly and professionally analyzed the problem and formulated an idea for a new self-certification program that would enable applicants in our backlog to forgo review if they would be willing to certify that they meet the legal requirements for 501I(4) status. This self-certification process was one of the key drivers in reducing the backlog, ending the long wait for approval by many tax-exempt applicants.

IRS "in their veins"

Another critical part of my journey was traveling to the regional offices to speak directly with the IRS workforce. Through these visits, my understanding of how the IRS operates increased exponentially. For example, I saw for myself how budget cuts were leading to understaffing in taxpayer assistance walk-in centers, which in turn led to crowded waiting rooms and long lines.

Also, these visits enabled me to hear directly from IRS professionals, a significant majority of whom work in the field and not at headquarters. What were their frustrations, concerns, and hopes for the future? In one meeting in the field, I asked the group what I could do during my time as Acting Commissioner to help. A longtime IRS employee stood up and shared his thoughts that the position of Deputy Commissioner for Services and Enforcement, which was vacant at the time, was a critically important leadership position. The right person in that job, he stated, would make a tremendous difference in building a connection between the leaders in Washington and the people in the field. He shared that he understood my decision to bring in IRS outsiders to fill other key positions, such as Deputy Commissioner for Operations

Support. But he strongly suggested I hire someone with the IRS "in their veins" for the Services and Enforcement slot—someone who grew up in the organization and had walked in the shoes of the thousands of other IRS employees who had begun and would likely end their careers as IRS employees.

It was a suggestion that immediately resonated with me. And while we did not specifically exclude any qualified candidates from the job search, I reached out to John Dalrymple, a respected and retired IRS executive with 30-plus years of experience in the organization. I convinced him to apply for the job and he ultimately joined the team as Deputy Commissioner for Services and Enforcement.

True north

I mentioned earlier that the Jeff Zients phone call I received on the way to talk to my wife was the first in a series of moments where I received sage advice during my journey with the IRS. Another came the night before my first hearing as Acting Commissioner. That evening, which was roughly 2 weeks after I arrived at the IRS, I was dealing with a self-confidence crisis. In the midst of a media and public firestorm over the matter, the hearing the next day presented my first opportunity to speak publicly as the new IRS Chief and to answer all the tough questions on how I would proceed.

I knew the media coverage of the hearing would be intense. And I knew that my words, my demeanor, and my approach would be closely scrutinized and commented upon. Also something that was weighing on me was that I knew that this first public appearance would be very closely watched by the roughly 90,000 people that make up the IRS workforce.

Facing this reality, I had doubts that I could find the right voice in the midst of all of the complicated dynamics that were emerging at that time. So with my confidence not where it needed to be, at about 9 pm the night before the hearing, I phoned a friend. That friend was Dan Tangherlini, who a year earlier had stepped into a similar situation at the General Services Administration (GSA). The GSA Administrator had resigned over the scandal of an expensive Las Vegas conference, and the White House Chief of Staff at the time had asked Dan to step in at a moment's notice and lead the organization through its crisis. Dan was the perfect person for me to talk to in that moment because not only had he walked in my shoes but also he had done it with grace and effectiveness.

Dan's advice that evening perfectly encapsulates the role of a civil servant SES in the U.S. government. Dan told me that no matter what happens during the hearing, no matter how sharp the rhetoric, how much of a circus atmosphere it becomes, no matter the sound bites, the talking points, and the various political narratives being laid out before you, remember who you are and what your job is.

You are a public sector management expert, he told me. You are a substantive, thoughtful, and patient presence in the middle of everything that might be going on around you. You are an expert being brought in, like you have many times in your career before, to tackle a public sector management challenge. You need to do what you always do and what you were trained to do—roll up your sleeves and objectively and analytically assess the management challenges that exist, rely on credible evidence in drawing your conclusions, thoughtfully construct an action plan to address the management weaknesses you find, and drive a robust process for implementing your plan.

What he was describing was the core role of a career SES. And he was reminding me that my approach in doing the job, and therefore my voice in the hearing, should reflect that role.

Whenever political distractions (and there were many) added complexity to the situation I was facing, I attempted to filter them through this lens: What is the right thing to do to fix the problem I was asked to fix? To embody this mindset, my leadership team and I developed a question that we would ask ourselves whenever we felt there was a risk that we may be swerving off course on our primary role and mission. And that question was, are we following "our true north"? Our true north became the phrase that symbolized for us our effort to keep with the identity and role that Dan Tangherlini had so aptly framed out for me on that phone call. It is the core question that SES leaders and other civil servants ask themselves every day as they carry out their indispensable role in making the government work and finding ways to make it work better.

EDITOR'S
Concluding Commentary and Recommendations

Introduction: A smoldering platform

So let us reconsider our opening question: Can the Federal government recruit, retain, motivate, and deploy a career senior executive corps—to include the venerable SES and all of its various progeny—that is up to the kinds of whole-of-government challenges that have been documented throughout this volume?

By now, that question must seem rhetorical...and the answer somewhat paradoxical. Almost without exception, our contributors agree that change is necessary—systemic and structural as well as cultural and organizational —if the senior executive corps is to be able to attract and retain the kind of leadership talent necessary. But at the same time, there is also unanimous agreement that some aspects of our senior service(s)—for example, the core values and common *ethos* that ground their members, as implicit as they may be—should remain exactly as envisioned at the inception of the SES. Hence, the paradox: Change, even transformational change, may be necessary, but it must not come at the expense of the SES' original vision.

To be sure, the SES has not been static. It has undergone some changes. But even when those changes have spun off another new look-alike senior service, they have largely been incremental in nature. For example, President Obama's recent SES EO is largely limited to a series of incremental administrative initiatives—most notably, rotational assignment targets—that are worthwhile, but it implicitly concedes that any sort of significant legislative reform is beyond the pale.

There are some exceptions to be sure, most notably in lesser known spinoffs of the SES. The compensation flexibilities afforded the Securities and Exchange Commission (SEC) and the other FIRREA[203] agencies come to mind, as well as those provided VA under its title 38 authorities, all driven by the need to improve senior executive (and senior professional) pay in order to better compete in their respective labor markets. But for the most part, our various senior services have all been variations on the central theme, their creation seemingly spurred more by the need for greater independence from OPM

---

[203] Financial Institutions Reform, Recovery, and Enforcement Act of 1989, Pub. L. No. 101-73 (1989).

than any great structural or systemic leap forward; as a consequence, there has been no real impetus for more sweeping, systemic reforms.

Then VA's wait-time scandal erupted, and, for better or worse, the whiff of statutory change was in the air—and, with it, an opportunity for the 45th President.

Whole-of-government challenges require whole-of-government solutions

If there is a priority in this regard, I would argue that it should not be agency-centric, but rather at the government-wide, enterprise level. When it comes to the complexity of taking on whole-of-government and whole-of-nation missions, the senior services generally fall short in preparing their denizens for the challenges that those missions entail…again, with some of the notable exceptions we have examined in this section.

The reality is that, notwithstanding those exceptions, senior executives (SES members and otherwise) are almost exclusively agency-centric in skill set and mindset, as functionally and organizationally stove-piped as the government itself. Most have remained in the same agency for their entire careers,[204] often promoted for their technical skills and never venturing across (much less out of) the Federal enterprise to broaden their experience or their expertise. The result: Few are equipped to lead the whole-of-government enterprise.

This is largely through no fault of individual executives. As the Partnership for Public Service and Booz Allen observed in our 2009 report, *Reimagining the Senior Executive Service*, senior executive development and selection have historically been decentralized, left to individual agencies to execute, with uneven results.[205] And things like interagency mobility—pre-executive and executive alike—have become virtually nonexistent without policies and administrative mechanisms specifically designed to enable them.

As noted, there are some exceptions; the IC and the DOD have each taken aggressive steps to manage their executive corps more corporately, and President Obama's EO seems to mandate as much. But, for most senior executives, the prospect of leading an interagency enterprise is daunting indeed.

This must change, and not just to realize the original vision of the SES. In addition to learning the tradecraft associated with their particular functional, technical, or organizational domains, senior career executives must be developed as leaders with an enterprise perspective, and this development must begin well before they even compete for senior executive rank.

---

[204] Partnership for Public Service & McKinsey and Company. (2016). *A pivotal moment for the Senior Executive Service: Measures, aspirational practices and stories of success.* Washington, DC: Partnership for Public Service.
[205] Partnership for Public Service & Booz Allen Hamilton. (2009). *Unrealized vision: Reimagining the Senior Executive Service.* McLean, VA: Booz Allen Hamilton. Retrieved from https://www.boozallen.com/content/dam/boozallen/media/file/reimagining-the-senior-executive-service-2009.pdf

In that regard, the establishment of a sixth ECQ called *Leading the Federal Enterprise*—one that makes one or more mobility assignments a condition of SES promotion—must also be considered…if not for all senior executive positions, at least for those that demand whole-of-government leadership expertise. This change is critically important, but only one of several I believe necessary to revitalize a senior Federal service.

Previous sections have already addressed some of those changes—for example, ways to more quickly identify, validate, and develop emerging leadership competencies, as well as measures to ensure new SES entrants understand their institutional obligations and have the courage and character it may take to fulfill them—but those changes were more focused on an individual dimension of a 21st century SES. In this Concluding Commentary, I proffer some of the more systemic, strategic changes that need to occur if the senior Federal service is to remain vital and viable. Given that those changes will ultimately require legislation, I also proffer a strategy to achieve that seemingly impossible mission…if not this year or next, then eventually, as this system of systems reaches middle age and begins to show it.

RECOMMENDATION 5.1: ESTABLISH A FEDERATED WHOLE-OF-GOVERNMENT SES FRAMEWORK

Introduction: A collection of systems…by default

In considering whether and how to retool the SES, we need to acknowledge that it no longer covers all of the Federal government's senior career executives. As I have pointed out in earlier sections, a number of "alternative" senior services have emerged since the inception of the SES in 1979, and they now cover a significant percentage of the senior executive corps. While these systems have separate bases in law, they are more like the original SES than they are different. For example, most use the same or some variation of the ECQs, most are bounded by the same Executive Level (EX) II salary cap, and most are implicitly grounded in the same institutional *ethos* as their Title 5 progenitor. And perhaps most importantly, several of them include features that are closer to the original vision of the SES than the SES itself—features that could serve as models for reform.

Administrative control versus mission flexibility

One thing that most of these systems share is some degree of independence from OPM's administrative control. Thus, notwithstanding all of the notable improvements cited by former Acting OPM Director Cobert in Section 1, as well as Steve Shih in this section, those agencies that have separate spinoff systems still fear a one-size-fits-all model centrally regulated by OPM, one that would hypothetically impede their ability to tailor their senior systems to meet their particular mission needs.

For example, OPM controls the number of SES allocations and doles them out every 2 years. As you can imagine, the process has become a numbers game, with agencies typically wanting more allocations on one hand, and OPM (with an assist from OMB) holding the line on the other. But agencies that have their own systems are not subject to this process. That is not to say they are without restraint—most are subject to congressional oversight, but by committees that may be more familiar with (and sympathetic to) the needs of their mission. However, the fact of the matter is that legitimate or not, many agencies bristle under OPM's thumb and, if and when they can, they try to make their "separate peace" with the Hill.

The irony, of course, is that while many have managed to secede from the original SES, most haven't radically departed from its basic tenets. Bottom line: These separate senior systems are more alike than different, their familial resemblance born more out of institutional necessity (or inertia?) than legal mandate. And where they differ from the original SES, usually at the margins, those differences are based on mission imperatives—imperatives they fear OPM will not respect. Hence the Balkanization we see today.

I've seen both sides. I've been an agency CHCO, responsible for managing a separate slice of the SES corps, and I've served as Associate Director of OPM, where, among other things, I had responsibility for SES policy. In that capacity, I helped engineer its last major legislative overhaul: the "grand bargain" that raised the SES salary cap from EX III to EX II in exchange for greater rigor and discipline in SES performance management. At least, that was the theory. But, in my view, the reality of implementation took a different path.

Thus, while that bargain's enabling legislation mandated a much stronger link between organizational performance (to include such things as customer and employee satisfaction) and individual senior executive performance ratings, I believe OPM ended up translating that mandate into a by-the-numbers, one-size-fits-all checklist. Coupled with the creep of salary compression at EX II, it has become clear that that *quid pro quo* has fallen short of its original purpose.

It is no surprise, then, that a number of agencies have sought their independence from this model, cutting their own deals with Congress to establish separate senior services. For instance, there's the Senior Foreign Service (SFS), established by the State Department just 1 year after the SES. Similarly, the Central Intelligence Agency (CIA) used its almost unlimited personnel authorities to establish its own Senior Intelligence Service (SIS) shortly thereafter. DOD's own intelligence agencies followed suit, acquiring legislative authority in the early 1990s to establish a separate Defense Intelligence Senior Executive Service (as well as its own Defense Intelligence Senior Level System) to parallel the SIS and the original Title 5 senior service.

The Federal Bureau of Investigation (FBI) and Drug Enforcement Administration (DEA) followed with their own SES, as did the Federal Aviation

Administration (FAA), Transportation Security Administration, and banking and financial regulators under FIRREA, the latter with extraordinary authority to set pay well above the current EX II cap. And most recently, Congress even gave DHS the authority to create its own Senior Cyber Service, "notwithstanding any other provision of law."

Thus, the SES is anything but monolithic; as I have noted, it is variegated and gerrymandered like congressional districts, in part to preserve agency mission focus and independence, and in part to recognize that the executive talent market is no more monolithic than the senior executive corps. And all of these systems have one thing in common: They are largely beyond the reach of OPM and its title 5 authorities.

As noted, these separate senior services all have to answer to their congressional committees, and that doesn't mean the committees are any easier on those agencies than OPM. But this is not a good thing from a whole-of-government perspective, as each senior service exists as an island, with executive movement and mobility between them made even more difficult by the lack of an OPM-approved interchange agreement that could open the door, literally and figuratively, to far more mobility amongst them (see Recommendation 5.2).

Unity without uniformity: The Senior National Intelligence Service

Is this gerrymandered model inevitable or irrevocable? In my view, there is a middle ground somewhere between one monolithic system and a Balkanized set of separate senior services. We explored that middle ground with the ODNI as part of the implementation of the Intelligence Reform Act[206] and its mandate to better integrate the 17 separate agencies that compose the IC.

As we knew all too well, the IC's agencies had a history of relative independence and, in some extreme cases, even rivalry. That independence can be traced in part to the fact that 15 of those agencies are organizationally "owned" by one of six cabinet departments (the remaining two agencies, ODNI and CIA, are independent executive agencies unto themselves). Furthermore, the thousands of civilians employed by those departments and agencies are governed by five different statutory personnel systems, each of which includes its own senior executive service. Indeed, the 'regular' SES is the smallest component of the IC's large executive population, with most of the IC's many hundreds of senior positions outside the purview of title 5 and OPM.[207]

How does one achieve greater unity of effort, given that crazy quilt of personnel systems and separate senior services, without mandating lockstep

[206] Intelligence Reform and Terrorism Prevention Act of 2004, Pub. L. No. 108-458, 118 Stat. 3638 (2004).
[207] For example, the Senior National Intelligence Service (covering ODNI executives), CIA's Senior Intelligence Service, the original SES, the FBI and DEA's separate SES, DOD's Intelligence Senior Executive Service, and the SFS, among others. https://seniorexecs.org/images/documents /Fragmentation_of_the_Senior Executive_Service.pdf

uniformity? One way to bring about greater integration was the IC's civilian joint duty program, something already discussed at some length in Sections 3 and 4, which was designed to develop a cadre of enterprise leaders. That program made interagency mobility assignments (and the enterprise perspective that came with them) a prerequisite for promotion to senior executive rank.

But after promotion, all of the integrative effects of a pre-promotion interagency assignment would atrophy if IC senior executives simply reverted to their separate stove-piped senior services. So we concluded that as a complement to mandatory mobility, the IC needed an overarching framework that better integrated those senior services. The result was something called the Senior National Intelligence Service, or SNIS.

While one could argue that this was yet another case of creating yet another independent senior service, the SNIS was supposed to be different. It was deliberately designed as a "federated" system; that is, an overarching system of systems intended to promote interagency unity without requiring one-size-fits-all interagency uniformity.[208] In this case, the SNIS encompassed the IC's five senior services, establishing common policies and practices where it made sense but also respecting the authority of the individual departments and agencies who "owned" those senior services and who needed the flexibility to tailor them to meet their own unique mission requirements.

Balancing cohesion and independence

Perhaps most importantly, those common policies were established not by regulatory decree (it was not clear the DNI had the legal authority to do so) but by mutual agreement amongst the agencies involved—we referred to those administrative agreements as our "treaties"—to avoid trespassing on the otherwise sacrosanct statutory authorities of those signatory agencies. In effect, the heads of the IC's various departments and agencies all agreed to voluntarily exercise their separate authorities according to those common consensus policies. For example, all of the departments and agencies agreed to employ a common, three-tiered rank structure for their respective senior services, each with a corresponding common salary band, to ensure interagency pay equity and, more importantly, facilitate lateral interagency executive reassignments and the mission interoperability that came with them.[209]

Other common features of this federated framework included the voluntary adoption of OPM's five ECQs as an "admissions test" for the separate senior services (most had administratively defaulted to those ECQs already), plus

---

[208] Thompson, J. R., & Seidner, R. (2009). *Federated human resource management in the Federal government: The Intelligence Community Model.* Washington, DC: IBM Center for the Business of Government. Retrieved from http://www.businessofgovernment.org/report/federated-human-resource-management-Federal-government-intelligence-community-model

[209] Office of the Director of National Intelligence. (2009). Intelligence Community Directive No. 612, Intelligence Community Core Contract Personnel. Retrieved from https://fas.org/irp/dni/icd/icd-612.pdf

a sixth ECQ that focused on leading the Intelligence Enterprise.[210] In addition, we identified—and validated—a common set of leadership competencies to support that sixth ECQ, as well as a common set of executive performance standards to be incorporated in every IC senior executive's performance plan regardless of the senior system that covered the executive.[211] However, those common standards could be supplemented by department- and agency-specific ones, and almost all of the departments and agencies did so. Indeed, in most cases, the IC's framework was plugged in to a department's existing SES performance appraisal system.

These standards were the foundation for another critical component of the SNIS: a common senior executive performance management system that established (again, by mutual agreement) a single performance evaluation cycle, as well as a single five-level rating system, complete with common rating-level definitions.[212]

However, as noted, we did not (and could not) force each department to conform to the IC's framework, as each retained the statutory authority to set up its own SES appraisal system; they each had to agree to incorporate our requirements into theirs…and only for a subset of their respective executive cadres. To their great credit, they all did, although they retained the right to waive those common IC-wide elements with advance notice to ODNI, an escape clause their lawyers insisted on but which (as far as I know) has never been exercised.

Thus, the SNIS was intended to establish a common baseline for all of the IC's senior executives and their parent senior services. While it may not have reached its full potential in that regard, it does offer a model for an overarching senior Federal service, one that can unify without insisting on uniformity—sort of an *e pluribus unum* ("out of many, one") approach to integrating the Federal government's senior services.

Implementation: A federated system of systems…by design

As a system of systems, the Federal government's collective senior services would not (and could not) be reduced to a one-size-fits-all set of detailed regulations that ignores legitimate differences in mission, structure, culture, talent market, and a whole host of other variables. However, at the same time, I would argue that those senior services have to be better integrated—with far more permeable, open borders with one another—if we are ever to deal with the whole-of-government and whole-of-nation challenges that we face.

---

[210] Office of the Director of National Intelligence. (2010). Intelligence Community Directive No. 610, Competency Directories for the Intelligence Community Workforce. Retrieved from https://www.dni.gov/files/documents/ICD/ICD_610.pdf
[211] Ibid.
[212] Office of the Director of National Intelligence. (2008; amended 2012). Intelligence Community Directive No. 656, Performance Management System Requirements for Intelligence Community Senior Civilian Officers. Retrieved from https://fas.org/irp/dni/icd/icd-656.pdf

Accordingly, I would submit that we need to reimagine the Federal government's various senior services as a federated system of systems, a single senior Federal service comprising not just the SES but also the alphabet soup that defines all of its progeny—the SIS, SFS, FAA Executive Service, the FIRREA senior systems, VA's title 38 system, FBI/DEA SES, Defense Intelligence SES (DISES), etc.—and encompassing all of those senior career executives that serve it. I would go even further and include those senior professionals and scientific and technical executives who provide the world-class technical leadership that is just as critical to 21st century government as the managerial kind.

This new senior *Federal* service would encompass all of them. In this federated model, I would not give OPM and/or OMB regulatory authority over these separate systems (it is not clear that the agencies that own those separate systems, and the congressional committees that authorized them, would go along with that in any event).[213] Rather, OPM and OMB could be statutorily empowered to convene the institutional owners of these systems and coordinate a common, consensus set of principles and processes to develop, assess, select, compensate, and deploy career executives across the whole-of-government. And as a *quid pro quo*, OPM would establish a master executive interchange agreement (see Recommendation 5.2) that would enable—indeed, ensure—executive mobility among the various senior services and their constituent agencies.

However, this federated model would, by law if necessary, still protect and preserve the existing statutory authority of any particular department or agency to vary from that model or, if necessary (like the SNIS model), secede from it altogether. That dynamic—agencies would cede some of their current statutory discretion in exchange for greater access to a broader, far more mobile pool of senior executives—would serve as the glue that holds the federation together.

And in so doing, it would establish a whole-of-government system that could tap top career leaders from all agencies as a government-wide resource, not just as individual agency assets. Current differences in executive compensation among Federal agencies would need to be dealt with to minimize disincentives for mobility, but these and other structural elements of this federated model are addressed below.

RECOMMENDATION 5.2: ESTABLISH A MASTER INTERCHANGE AGREEMENT TO CONNECT SENIOR SERVICES

Introduction: Connecting the executive dots

As I have noted, there are at least seven senior services in the Federal government, with a grand total of some 10,000 executives (the original title 5 SES

---

[213] President Obama's Executive Order 13714 acknowledges this by requiring those agencies that have separately established senior executive systems to follow the EO to the extent practicable.

being the largest, with about 7,500 executives), but the problem is that never the twain shall meet. Why? Because each senior service has its own slightly different appointment rules and admissions standards, and while they are all variations on the basic theme, their separate-ness in law has made the boundaries between them largely impermeable, especially when it comes to voluntary, executive-driven career mobility.

For example, if a 20-year member of the CIA's SIS wants to take a 'regular' SES position in the DOD—and the DOD desperately wants that individual—the SIS officer has to apply for the vacancy just like a GS-15 seeking his or her first SES job. Today, that means ECQ essays, a panel interview, qualifications review board (QRB) review, etc., all to determine if the individual is executive material.

That is a real case by the way; I personally helped an SIS officer navigate the labyrinthine title 5 process. And even though this was largely *pro forma*, since the individual had served in a senior executive capacity for two decades and met all the technical qualifications and then some, DOD almost lost him because of the sheer bureaucratic hassle of it. And think about all of those GS-15s who applied for that job, not knowing that DOD already had an executive it wanted to hire for it but was forced to advertise the vacancy in order to reach him.

Now, had my colleague been in the 'regular' title 5 SES, he could have accepted a voluntary reassignment from DOD. But since he was a member of a "separate but equal" senior service, he had to apply, be selected, and receive approval by an OPM QRB. This is where something called an Interchange Agreement—in this case between DOD and the CIA, or more broadly between all the agencies that have senior services—would have helped.

Thus, under Federal regulations (5 Code of Federal Regulations [CFR] §214.204):

> "...OPM and any agency with an executive personnel system essentially equivalent to the SES may, pursuant to legislative and regulatory authorities, enter into an providing for the movement of persons between the SES and the other system. The shall define the status and that the persons affected shall acquire upon the movement...(p)ersons eligible for movement must be serving in permanent, continuing positions with career or career-type appointments. They must meet the qualifications requirements of any position to which moved."

In English, that's an interchange agreement, and it means no complicated, show-me-your-papers border crossings between senior services.

A critical enabler of executive mobility

With such an interchange agreement, an executive in one senior service could move to a permanent position in another without any further competition…

just like that. Seems pretty simple and straightforward. Since both CIA and DOD (indeed, every agency with its own senior service) select their senior executives on the basis of merit, it should be easy for the two, under OPM auspices, to establish an agreement that enables that easy movement.

Alas, not so fast. Heretofore, OPM has taken the position that to qualify for an interchange agreement with the SES, an agency with its own senior service must allow "free and open competition" (in other words, it must advertise its senior positions on USA Jobs), use the ECQs to screen candidates, and provide for QRB or equivalent review of all senior selections.

The problem is that many of the government's "other" senior services choose not to meet one or more of these procedural requirements, but for perfectly legitimate reasons. For example, CIA and the various defense intelligence agencies that fall under the DISES generally do not publish public vacancy announcements, allow external applicants, or provide for open competition for positions in their senior services, for obvious reasons having to do with security and clearances. Nor do they permit OPM to review the qualifications of those selected for those positions, for the same reasons. Hence, their efforts to establish an interchange agreement with the original SES have been rebuffed by OPM...at least to date.[214]

Focusing on principles, not process

Note the implication here, that somehow a Senior Foreign Service Officer who has been named an ambassador, or who has run an embassy as second-in-command to one, is somehow not qualified to be a member of the SES. Or that executives in the FBI, DEA, CIA, FAA, or SEC are somehow not SES-worthy.

While none of them had may have had to apply for their executive position through USA Jobs, each had to vie for their promotion to executive rank via a competitive process every bit as rigorous as the 'regular' SES. They all had to demonstrate that they met some variation of the ECQs. And the fact that they had to compete against other internal candidates shouldn't be held against them. After all, you don't hire an FBI Assistant Director or a CIA Station Chief off the street. Since OPM is already looking for agencies to pilot alternatives, waiving a QRB review should not be a showstopper, and I'm certain the agencies interested in an interchange agreement could conjure up a suitable substitute that takes their particular needs (for example, greater confidentiality or clearance level) into account.

So while these agencies may not meet the letter of OPM's interchange checklist, I would argue that they meet the principle ascribed in the CFR; that is, "...in the interest of good administration and consistent with the intent of the civil service laws and any other applicable laws."[215] And so long as they continue to do so, there's no good reason for OPM not to establish one or

[214] I know because I was doing the trying when I was the IC Chief Human Capital Officer.
[215] Administrative Personnel, 5 C.F.R. § 214.204 (2013); see also Movement of Persons between the Civil Service System and Other Merit Systems, 5 C.F.R. § 6.7 (1963).

more interchange agreements between the original SES and the various other senior services, or to do it all at once with a master Executive Interchange Agreement that administratively links all of these senior services together under the single federated system I propose. The whole-of-government benefit of such an agreement is obvious.

RECOMMENDATION 5.3: ESTABLISH A NEW GOVERNMENT-WIDE SENIOR EXECUTIVE STRUCTURE

Introduction: Reflecting reality

In my view, most fundamentally, the senior Federal service needs a new architecture, one that departs from the level-free "open range" currently in place.

Recall that back in 2004, Congress (at the administration's urging)[216] adopted a decentralized architecture, eliminating the old six-level SES rank and compensation structure in favor of a single, broad salary range that potentially reached all the way to EX II. Part of the legislation's *higher pay for higher performance* bargain, the idea was to give agencies the discretion to tailor their own rank levels and salary control points within the new salary range; however, few took advantage, in part because even that expanded salary range was still relatively compressed. Those that did ended up with more or less the same three-tiered structure:[217]

- Tier 1, ranging from the minimum point in the salary range to EX III; typically reserved for front-line, entry-level senior executives who supervise senior managers at the GS-15 level.

- Tier 2, typically starting at the mid-point between EX III and EX II; reserved for senior executives below the agency or departmental level who supervise other senior executives...in effect, second- and sometimes third-level executives

- Tier 3, set at the new maximum salary cap (EX II); typically reserved for the most senior career executives in a given department or agency, including those at the upper echelons who report directly to the agency's political hierarchy.

There are a few things to note here. First, most SES members were already at the EX III salary cap when the 2004 changes occurred, given that it had been years since that cap had been raised. Second, an agency's ability to pay senior executives above EX III was and remains contingent on OPM's biennial

---

[216] Led by then-OPM Director Kay Coles James; at the time, I was Associate Director of OPM and a fervent advocate for the open, rank-less range to maximize individual agency flexibility. However, that was before my time in the IC, where the need for greater *interagency* consistency became paramount.

[217] 220220 Partnership for Public Service & Booz Allen Hamilton. (2014). *Building the enterprise: A new civil service framework.* Washington, DC: Partnership for Public Service, pp. 35–36.

certification that the agency's SES performance management system meets certain regulatory standards of rigor and realism.

In theory, that certification is not automatic; however, after more than a decade, agencies know what it takes to pass that test, so it no longer serves as one. Thus, most agencies have long since moved to something resembling this notional, three-tiered structure to be able to make salary distinctions among their executives based on relative level of responsibility and performance.

Distinctions without difference

However, this notional structure underscores just how narrow even the new, broader salary range is. With only about $14,000 separating the old EX III cap from the new EX II one, it is still difficult to make performance- and/or responsibility-based pay distinctions among executives. It hasn't helped that the new cap has been relatively static. When it has been adjusted (and there have been no guarantees there), it has been less than even the meager government-wide General Schedule (GS) increases. Thus, it's no wonder that salary compression has emerged again as an issue. And, although unintended, the President's recent EO has exacerbated that compression by effectively raising the *de facto* floor of the SES range.

The net result is that more and more senior executives find themselves at or approaching the EX II cap, and given the relatively small spread between EX III and EX II, there is not much room for significant differentiation. Couple that with controls and constraints on SES performance bonuses—when they're not banned outright by the President or Congress—and you have a senior executive compensation system that is broken.

Thus, a little more than a decade since it was codified, the higher pay for higher performance *quid pro quo* that justified raising the cap to EX II has lost much of its leverage. With OPM certification no longer the carrot (or the lever) that it once was, agencies expect to be able to raise the pay of their senior executives up to EX II, and they do so regularly.

For those reasons, most agencies have gravitated over time to this three-tiered framework, including all of DOD and the various agencies of the IC, making it the *de facto* (if not *de jure*) architecture of the SES. As a consequence, it could easily be adopted as the government-wide standard. However, while this architecture reflects today's reality, and it offers some advantages over an open salary range, it is not sufficient to sustain a viable senior executive corps in the future.

To be sure, there are other systemic problems with SES compensation. Those problems are well known and need not be detailed here, but the bottom line is that with rare exceptions like the SEC, senior executive pay (base and/or variable) will never approach comparability when it comes to labor market rates. Luckily, external equity is not what motivates most senior executives, but pay distinctions based on relative responsibility and contribution—that is, internal and performance equity, respectively—are another matter.

This is especially the case when it comes to incentivizing mobility. If those senior executives who are responsible for leading a particular department or agency are classified as Tier 3 (and paid at or near the EX II cap), how do you accommodate—much less compensate—the subset of Federal senior executives who have earned even broader, whole-of-government responsibilities?

As we have argued, those executives should be required to follow a career path that requires mobility—functional, geographic, and/or organizational—as a mandatory prerequisite to those lofty responsibilities. And as we know, that mobility comes with some cost (and risk) to one's career and family. Yet now, there is no way to acknowledge those responsibilities, or the sacrifices an executive may be asked to make in order to earn them, particularly when it comes to compensation.

Implementation: Codify three tiers and add a fourth

One option is to increase the SES pay cap to EX I, but to do so only for a relatively small number of enterprise executive positions—estimates range from 800 to 1,500[218]—that have government-wide, cabinet-level leadership responsibilities and impact. In effect, this adds a fourth tier to the de facto three-tiered structure described above.

This four-tiered structure is not new. Booz Allen and the Partnership for Public Service were among the first to advocate it in their landmark report on civil service reform.[219] As we detailed in that 2014 report, Tier 4 would be reserved for those executives who have whole-of-government responsibilities. This would typically be an agency's most senior career leaders; chief functional officers (chief information officer, chief human capital officer, CFO, etc.); chief scientists and engineers; and others whose responsibilities require them to lead across agencies, levels and jurisdictions of government, sectors, and even national borders.

This new fourth tier, along with its higher salary cap, would offer additional career progression and promotion opportunities (and rewards) for those who sign up for the mandatory mobility that has to be a prerequisite for these enterprise positions, and it would also relieve the pay compression that has simply moved from the old cap to the new over the last decade.

Some will argue that senior executives are already subject to mandatory mobility, so there is no need to 'bribe' them with more money just to do what they are legally obligated to do anyway. But as we have seen, few executives are actually willing to be mobile, and those who are often find other agencies impenetrable, whether it's on their way up through the ranks or after they've

[218] Ibid.
[219] Ibid.

entered the senior service. Couple that with the fact that forced mobility is often used to punish rather than develop an executive and it quickly becomes clear that the legal obligation, while great in theory, has never been successfully operationalized.

These changes require legislation, especially those that would increase the SES pay cap, and many would argue that this is a political impossibility. However, there is a potential way ahead…and precedent for it.

As noted, the 2004 legislation that raised the SES pay cap to EX II was part of a legislative *quid pro quo*, a political grand bargain that would give senior executives the potential for higher pay as a reward for higher performance, but in exchange for greater rigor and realism in the performance management systems that would evaluate that performance. Congress and the administration (led by then-OPM Director Kay James) agreed back then that the tradeoff was worth it, and I believe that the contours of a similar grand bargain are emerging—one that would offer some career executives the opportunity for higher pay, but in exchange for greater mobility and greater accountability that would come with a Tier 4 appointment.

But what's to stop agencies from gradually expanding the number of Tier 4 positions? And who would oversee appointments to those positions to ensure they don't become just another rung on the internal agency ladder, with "outsiders" basically barred from real consideration as in today's broken structure? The answer must be a governance structure and set of enabling mechanisms that together comprise an enterprise talent management system to manage those executives who sign up to lead the whole-of-government.

RECOMMENDATION 5.4: APPOINT AN ENTERPRISE EXECUTIVE RESOURCES BOARD TO MANAGE CAREER EXECUTIVE TALENT

Introduction: An enterprise talent management model

If it is to work, this proposed four-tiered, federated system of systems requires a new governance structure that can manage—not regulate, but *manage*—the Federal government's executive talent for the enterprise a whole.

Today, individual agency Executive Resources Boards (ERB) perform this talent management function for their own career executive cadres; each agency (at least each agency covered by the original SES) operates in more or less isolation in this regard, albeit within the parameters of common, government-wide regulations issued by OPM. Those ERBs, each chaired by a senior appointee (typically the agency's Deputy Secretary or equivalent) and comprising the agency's top political and career executives, are responsible for developing and selecting SES members and then assigning them to key leadership positions across the agency. Thus, they have an unerringly agency-centric focus.

However, when it comes to managing executive talent on an interagency, *enterprise* basis, there is no overarching enabling mechanism, no "corporate" governance structure or body to drive career executive recruiting, development, retention, and, perhaps most critically, deployment for the whole-of-government.

Is that not OPM's role? As the Federal government's central HR office, it has institutional responsibility for regulating (and policing) the government-wide terms and conditions of employment for SES members. But aside from retaining authority to approve certain executive personnel decisions—such as individual SES selections through the QRB process—OPM leaves the day-to-day decision-making of executive talent management to individual agencies, and the net result is that career executives remain "for internal use only."

Thus, while most Federal agencies and their senior executives are bound by OPM's regulations, those agencies have substantial discretion when it comes to key executive decisions, such as who gets developed, who gets promoted, and who get reassigned. That discretion is appropriate, at least up to a point, but I believe it comes at a cost: Agencies (and agency ERBs) will tend to make executive talent management decisions that are in their individual interests, and not necessarily in the interests of the broader enterprise.

Nowhere is this more apparent than with respect to mobility. In my view, if there is a single compelling justification for a whole-of-government executive talent management system, it has to do with mobility. If one buys the premise that mobility is an essential chapter in the development and deployment of a 21st century senior career executive, the simple truth is that no amount of exhortation will make that mobility a reality, even if that exhortation comes from a body like the President's Management Council (PMC) or even the President.

As I have argued, it also takes enabling mechanisms to facilitate that mobility, and given that we're talking about *interagency* mobility, those mechanisms have to be institutional, as opposed to departmental in nature.

A "Super" Executive Resources Board

In that regard, perhaps the most important of these enabling mechanisms is the establishment of an Enterprise Executive Resources Board (EERB) to manage the development and deployment of a select number of career executives and candidates. This, too, was a key recommendation of the 2014 Partnership for Public Service report on civil service reform,[220] so it is not new. But as the best platform for truly managing interagency mobility—for the development of senior executive candidates before promotion to the SES, as well as for their deployment afterwards—it is nonetheless integral to a 21st century senior Federal service.

---

[220] Ibid.

As we have noted, senior executives today are agency-centric in orientation; most of them (and their agencies) do not view themselves as government-wide assets, nor are they developed and managed accordingly. Recent data, for example, show that 81 percent of career executives are promoted from within, that is, from the agency in which they had been working prior to promotion to the SES.[221] And only 8 percent have moved to a different agency *after* their promotion to the SES.[222]

We saw this firsthand in the Intelligence Community (IC). Twice before the 2004 Intelligence Reform Act,[223] the heads of the IC agencies, including the Director of Central Intelligence (the nominal head of the IC before the creation of the Director of National Intelligence), all declared mobility to be important, but to no avail.

To be sure, senior leadership commitment is a necessary element of mobility, but it is not sufficient. But it also takes a forcing function—like making mobility as a prerequisite to promotion to and retention in the SES—as well as the administrative infrastructure to enable that mobility. Prior sections have already considered some of those administrative details necessary for pre-SES (that is, developmental) mobility to work, but what about post-promotion? How can individual executives be *deployed* as enterprise assets in a federated senior Federal service?

As previously noted, there are at least two examples of a more corporate approach to executive talent management, and these may serve as models. For one, the DOD largely manages its SES members as a single cadre via something called the Defense Executive Advisory Board (DEAB). Established by DOD Directive[224] and nominally chaired by the Deputy Secretary, the DEAB conducts regular executive talent reviews, recommending decisions about selection, development, and deployment across the agency that the chair ultimately approves.

However, the DOD model tends to focus more on its top career civilians (Tiers 2 and 3 of its three-tiered structure) in the Office of the Secretary of Defense and the constellation of defense agencies, leaving the military services to manage their own executive cadres under the aegis of the Department's overarching policy directive. In that regard, while it resembles a federated model, President Obama's EO cited DOD's approach as the basis for its SES talent management mandate (see Section 1). We've also seen some very successful products of that model, most notably in Beth McGrath's chapter. She attributes her own enterprise perspective to this sort of deliberate development, and although the model is clearly DOD-centric, that's a very big enterprise in and of itself, so it counts.

---

[221] Partnership for Public Service & McKinsey and Company. *A pivotal moment.*
[222] Ibid.
[223] Intelligence Reform and Terrorism Prevention Act.
[224] U.S. Department of Defense Directive No. 1400.25, Vol. 1403 (1996), DoD Civilian Personnel Management System.

The other example is in the IC, a federated executive talent management model in the extreme.[225] Each of the six cabinet departments that "own" IC senior executives have their own independent ERB (as do the two independent agencies, CIA and ODNI); however, the larger subcomponents of those departments—like Tish Long's NGA, the National Security Agency, Defense Intelligence Agency, and the FBI also have separate ERBs. All told, the IC had as many as a dozen of them, each managing its agency's own executive talent.

As we have already discussed at length, the Intelligence Reform Act[226] forced the IC to break down those executive stovepipes; however, in so doing, we chose *not* to establish a stand-alone, ERB-like body to manage executive talent at the enterprise level, opting instead to use the standing committee of agency deputy directors—the so-called DEXCOM—to assume this responsibility along with its other IC management functions. Tish Long describes its operation in her chapter, as well as the key leadership role she played in it, and it may serve as a potential model for the rest of government.

Taking senior executive talent management to scale

These models and mechanisms can be applied at the whole-of-government level. The President by Executive Order, or OPM by regulation, could establish a new *Enterprise* ERB (EERB) to manage select senior career executive talent, with particular attention to those select SES positions that have whole-of-government responsibilities; alternatively, Congress could pass legislation to do so, along with the establishment of a new Tier 4 salary cap.

This EERB would be responsible for managing the select number of career executive positions identified by the departments and agencies (or perhaps OPM and OMB) as having whole-of-government impact. Co-chaired by OMB's Deputy Director for Management, it would most certainly comprise select PMC members and OPM's Director, but, for its own credibility, it could not be composed exclusively of political appointees.

Rather, because it would consider the development, selection, deployment, and retention of the nation's most senior career executives, I would contend that the EERB must also include an equal number of the Federal government's most respected current and former career executives, with a co-chair drawn from their ranks. This ensures that there is no hint or perception of partisan politics in its processes or its deliberations. To that end, career members of the EERB should all be appointed by the President for 5-year terms, so they are not beholden to any particular administration.

The EERB's job would be to identify, select, evaluate, and assign a select number of career SES members drawn from agency ranks to meet *enterprise* executive requirements. Such positions might include agency chief operating officers (COOs) and other chief officers, deputies to those cabinet or sub-cabinet

---

[225] Thompson, J. R. *Federated human resource management.*
[226] Intelligence Reform and Terrorism Prevention Act.

officers serving as Cross-Agency Priority Goal leaders, or even serving as those CAP leaders in their own right. It could also be responsible for making (or validating) other "benchmark" executive decisions—for example, the number executive billets or, as recommended below, critical pay requests.

Thus, not every SES member would be subject to EERB's coverage nor eligible for the benefits that accrue from it. The EERB would manage an elite pool of career executives: those with interagency experience acquired via one or more mobility assignments and/or demonstrated or developing enterprise leadership skills—in other words, those who can meet a sixth *Leading the Federal Enterprise* ECQ and be eligible to compete for prestigious Tier 4 enterprise leadership positions. In addition, executives competing for a Tier 4 position would have to pass a full due diligence review to assess their character and fit for these most senior career positions (see Section 3).

And to guard against creating what amounts to a permanent senior bureaucracy, appointments to these enterprise executive positions would be subject to a 5-year renewable limit, contingent upon successfully meeting the terms of annual performance contracts with the Chair of the EERB.[227] At the conclusion of their term, enterprise executives with career SES status could continue for an additional term in their current enterprise executive position, be assigned to another such position, or return "without prejudice" to a career SES position in their home or some other agency.

All of these actions would be overseen by the EERB but administered by OPM Executive Resources staff. The EERB would also monitor the pipeline of enterprise-qualified senior executive candidates (for example, those who may encumber key mobility-track positions at the GS-13, 14, or 15 level), oversee internal executive searches, and market and match enterprise executive opportunities to highly qualified candidates to ensure that there is an adequate bench of talent to fill those positions as they turn over.

There are other enabling mechanisms that are critical to an enterprise executive talent management model, many of which were discussed in preceding sections of this anthology. These include:

- The proposed four-tiered architecture that decompresses salary and provides real incentives for executive mobility;

- A common, consensus-based policy framework that unifies the Federal senior executive corps without lockstep uniformity;

- A master executive interchange agreement that enables mobility among those senior services;

- An internal OPM headhunting capability to facilitate that mobility for both developmental and deployment purposes;

[227] Partnership for Public Service & Booz Allen Hamilton. *Building the enterprise.*

- A government-wide Candidate Development Program (CDP), perhaps modeled after the White House Leadership Development Program or the now-defunct Fed CDP; and

- A Federal Executive Institute focused on developing whole-of-government leadership skills, among other things.

All of these are elements of a 21st century SES, and the good news is that the Obama administration and OPM have started the Federal government down this path. For example, President Obama's EO 13714 is a start, and former Acting OPM Director Beth Cobert has done much to implement it. These and other OPM and agency-level efforts will all facilitate a true whole-of-government senior executive corps.

However, more needs to be done. The development of true enterprise executives, developed with an emphasis on varied multiagency and multisector experience, must be woven into the fabric of the 21st century SES, starting early as potential candidates move up the ranks and continuing throughout their careers. And that won't happen without a whole-of-government talent management system to support it.

RECOMMENDATION 5.5: MAKE INCREMENTAL FIXES TO SES COMPENSATION

Introduction: A broken promise

No discussion about the SES can be complete without some attention to pay and performance accountability…and the risks and rewards that are supposed to come with it. After all, that was the supposed "deal" with the SES, a social contract between senior executives and their government that put more of their pay at risk to incentivize, (or differentiate) high performance—a common practice in the private sector, but before 1978 largely untested in the Federal government.

This was a nascent, early version of a 'total compensation' strategy that deliberately changed the traditional mix between base salary and bonus, with the latter potentially increased to as much as 20 percent of an executive's base pay (or more, under certain circumstances).[228] That's important. Under this new social contract, the *eligibility* for a bonus was part of the compensation package, and while no *individual* executive was ever to be guaranteed a bonus, the *eligibility for one* was supposed to be.

However, as noted, in the years since 1979, pay compression became acute; most executives eventually capped out in terms of their base salary, and promotions in the old six-level SES rank system became meaningless. How do you keep an executive happy under those circumstances?

---

[228] For example, with a presidential rank award.

Agencies were left with only two tools—performance ratings and performance bonuses—giving rise to all sorts of games. I know; I've seen and played most of them. For example, performance ratings became like Lake Woebegone, with almost every executive rated as outstanding, with severe ratings inflation the result. And bonuses were either rotated among seniors (for example, you got one every third year and just had to wait your turn) or spread like a thin layer of peanut butter across an agency's entire executive cadre to keep as many executives (all good performers or better) as happy as possible.

A grand bargain: Higher pay for greater appraisal rigor

As we have noted, in 2004 Congress attempted to fix that with an elegant piece of legislation designed relieve pay compression, but that relief came with a *quid pro quo*.[229] The legislation raised the SES salary cap from EX III to EX II, but, as noted above, only on one condition: Before an agency could pay any of its executives up to that new cap, OPM and OMB had to certify its SES performance management system as sufficiently rigorous, which was code for ensuring the agency held the line on the number of outstanding performance ratings.

It is important to note that the design of SES performance management systems was decentralized, and the certification of those systems was agency by agency. OPM Director Kay James' hypothesis at the time was that if agencies had more of a say in those systems (albeit within a broader OPM framework, of course), they would take SES performance management more seriously, and thus we let a thousand flowers bloom!

That worked for a few years. Since agencies could only pay their executives up to EX II if their SES appraisal systems were certified, they took the certification process seriously and made substantial improvements in the way they evaluated and rewarded their career executives...so much so that the vast majority of agencies were certified the first time around. More importantly, overall ratings began to be more distributed, individual ratings became more realistic (and more closely tied to agency performance), and bigger bonuses were reserved for an agency's highest performers.

But all good things eventually come to an end, and this brief shining moment in the history of SES performance management was no different. Here, in my humble opinion, is what happened.

First, not unexpectedly, individual executive salaries began to creep upward within the salary range, in part because the SES salary range itself was never fully adjusted to reflect labor market increases. Of course, we all know the reason for that: across-the-board increases in the SES salary range were tied (at least politically if not legally) to the salary ranges of congressional members and staff, as well as senior political appointees. And as the nation confronted severe economic turbulence—beginning with something called

---

[229] Truth in advertising: I helped write it.

the Great Recession of 2008—no one was in the mood to raise their pay, least of all for themselves!

Performance bonuses: Theory versus political reality

So history once again repeated itself. With overall SES salary levels frozen and capped, agencies began to gradually increase individual executive salaries within that range (this despite the best efforts of a succession of OPM Directors, including Linda Springer and John Berry), essentially foregoing any pretense of salary management discipline, until many of them maxed out again…albeit at the higher EX II. That's still not comparable to many private sector executive positions, but everything is relative, and another round of pay compression had its effect on SES morale.

However, this time, variable pay provided little or no additional relief, as the Obama administration first zeroed out and then severely reduced aggregate bonus funding as a percentage of payroll; it even canceled presidential rank awards and the financial rewards associated with them one year. The reasons were political, though no less arguable. The country was in the middle of a recession, and the optics of big bonuses for bureaucrats, no matter how extraordinary their accomplishments, were and will always be problematic.

But that doesn't help the senior executives who achieved those accomplishments. So with most other motivational tools unavailable, individual performance ratings began to creep up again, and whatever benefit that had been derived from the original grand higher-pay-for-higher-performance bargain largely evaporated.

The Obama administration has since loosened up bonus limits,[230] first allowing agency bonus pools amounting to 5 percent of their SES payroll, and then more recently 7.5 percent, but both are far below the statutory maximum of 10 percent of payroll. As a consequence, many career executives still feel the total compensation compact has been broken. And the fact that that break—in effect, an executive pay cut—came so easily has made it worse.

The net result is that without some political and/or legal guarantee that the variable pay component of the senior executive corps' total compensation package will remain intact—to include the commitment that (like the private sector) even in the worst of times, some outstanding career executives can be financially rewarded for their extraordinary efforts—it will cease to be relevant as part of the social contract for senior executives.

Now, I'm not naïve. The odds of achieving such a guarantee are probably somewhere between slim and none. And I do not mean to suggest that

[230] Metzenbaum, S. H. (2014, May 29). Untying the knots in the Federal hiring process [Web log post]. Retrieved from https://www.volckeralliance.org/blog/2016/jun/untying-knots-Federal-hiring-process

without that guarantee, the Federal government should stop awarding performance bonuses (especially substantial ones) for extraordinary executive performance. But I do believe that without some more institutional predictability and stability, senior executives will be less inclined to consider bonuses part of their compensation compact, and potential SES candidates less likely to consider it a selling point.

Base pay: Give the EERB case-by-case critical pay authority

Base pay is the other component of the senior executive's compensation compact, and that too is in need of repair. We have already argued for a structural adjustment much like the one that occurred in 2004, in this case legislation establishing a fourth executive tier (and salary band) that ranges from EX II to EX I, but reserved for those mobile executives with whole-of-government responsibilities.

That is a start, but it will not fix the system. We already know that compensation for some critical senior executive positions lags the private sector. As a consequence, Congress has seen fit to give some agencies the authority to substantially raise the pay of their senior executives to maintain some parity with their private sector competition for senior talent.

For example, the FIRREA agencies like SEC and the Federal Deposit Insurance Corporation have to pay well above EX I to compete for Wall Street talent; similarly, VA has special title 38 United States Code pay-setting authority so it can pay physicians and other clinicians well above $300,000 per annum (it should also be noted that those substantially higher executive salaries also come with fewer traditional civil service protections, a point we explore in Recommendation 5.6).[231]

Those extraordinary, agency-specific salary levels have been warranted— and largely accepted—because of the realities of their particular talent markets, but there is virtually no chance of making them more generally applicable to other senior executives.

The best the Federal government has been able to do is establish so-called critical pay authority[232] that, in theory, lets OPM and OMB approve salaries for certain positions up to the Vice President's salary level, and even higher with approval from the President. However, just describing that critical pay authority gives one a sense of how high the bar is, and how bureaucratically difficult it is to justify. That's why to date, some 15 years after it was authorized, it has been approved for only a single-digit handful of cases.

---

[231] Grades and Pay Scales, 38 U.S.C. § 7404, Subchapter III (2010).
[232] Pay Authority for Critical Positions, 5 U.S.C. § 5337 (2008); see also Streamlined Critical Pay Authority, 5 U.S.C. § 9503 (2011).

Note that IRS was given streamlined critical pay authority as part of the 1998 Restructuring and Reform Act,[233] and it allowed the Commissioner (with Treasury Department oversight) to offer salaries up to the Vice President's level to as many as 50 senior executives under time-limited appointments. I can attest that we used that authority quite effectively to bring top-notch private sector talent, managerial as well as technical, to the agency, but Congress revoked it as part of its reaction to the latest round of IRS controversies, which has already led to the departure of at least two critical pay executives who had served the IRS with distinction.[234]

So what's the answer? While it is clear that many would like to see overall senior executive salary levels decoupled (legally and otherwise) from those that apply to members of Congress and senior political appointees and then raised substantially, this is not likely to happen. However, something more incremental may be possible. There are certainly individual cases that justify such levels, and I would advocate giving the EERB streamlined, IRS-like authority to approve critical pay requests up to and above the Vice President's level, as already allowed by law. This would realign authority from OPM and OMB (and the President) to a body that brings both operational and career executive perspectives to that decision.

Performance management: Contracts for performance accountability

No examination of senior executive pay, especially variable pay and performance bonuses, is complete without some discussion about how senior executives are (and should be) held accountable for results—and the rewards and consequences for the same. That means we must have a discussion about executive performance management, yet another touchy subject with plenty of options. And in considering those options, we must also take into account their impact on executive mobility, something that may not be obvious at first blush.

As recounted in Section 4, the IC discovered that one of the keys to interagency executive mobility was greater homogeneity among individual agency performance management systems. Too little similarity, and high-performing executive mobility candidates familiar with (and presumably successful in) their own agency's appraisal system would shy away from a mobility assignment in an agency with an unfamiliar one. We found that the decentralized SES performance management framework that OPM established in 2004—which encouraged each agency to do its own thing when it came to executive appraisals[235]—had the inadvertent consequence of inhibiting that mobility.

---

[233] The Internal Revenue Service Restructuring and Reform Act of 1998, also known as the Taxpayer Bill of Rights III, (Pub. L. 105–206, 112 Stat. 685, enacted July 22, 1998)
[234] Noble, Z. (2016, July 1). Milholland exits IRS. Retrieved from https://fcw.com/articles/2016/07/01/mulholland-exits-irs.aspx
[235] Those agencies with separate senior services were already doing so.

That phenomenon drove the IC to create a common set of salary bands and performance standards, common rating levels and label definitions, and even a common rating cycle, all to ensure that executives (and executives-in-development) who were considering an interagency mobility assignment would not be dissuaded by an appraisal system new to them in the gaining agency.

The good news is that perhaps in anticipation of that concern government-wide, OPM under Director John Berry followed suit in 2012, mandating a common, whole-of-government SES performance management system. And much like the IC's precursor, it features a common set of performance standards—based on the five ECQs—as well as common rating levels and labels, rating cycles, and other procedural requirements.[236]

As a result, all agency title 5 SES appraisal systems today are mirror images of one another, with little substantive variation among them. In mandating that uniformity, OPM has removed one more significant impediment to interagency executive mobility. Now, when a career executive considers a permanent SES assignment in another agency, he or she need not worry about figuring out a new, unfamiliar appraisal system. That's the good news. A standard, government-wide SES performance management system is an essential element of interagency executive mobility.

Competencies versus contracts

However, in my view, while the new system effectively enables interagency mobility, it may fall short when it comes to driving accountability for results. Thus, it is far too one-dimensional. By basing its performance elements on the five ECQs (essentially clusters of competencies), the system focuses too much on *how* an executive performs, and that may come at the expense of evaluating *what* that executive actually sets out to accomplish.

For example, at the start of the appraisal cycle, the system requires an executive to establish one or more performance objectives in each of the ECQ categories: Leading Change, Leading People, Driving Results, Business Acumen, and Building Coalitions. The problem is that real results—implementing a new policy or program, reorganizing an office, acquiring and fielding a new information technology system, etc.—require an executive to apply *all* of these core competencies together. Thus, it's problematic for a senior executive to set a tangible individual performance objective based on a single ECQ.

Conversely, it is just as problematic to focus exclusively on what an executive is held accountable for accomplishing. That's what led thousands of taxpayers to file complaints against the IRS in the late 1990s. Back then, the agency evaluated its executives and managers on how much they collected in taxes (a classic "what"), without regard to how they did so. The value proposition

---

[236] OPM memorandum, New U.S. Senior Executive Service Performance Appraisal System, January 4, 2012.

was simple: The more taxes collected, the higher the performance rating and bonus. And it's no wonder that how some of them accomplished that end crossed the line. So when we set out to design a new SES appraisal system for the IRS, we made sure it balanced and assessed both dimensions, with the "how" including behaviors associated with things like customer and employee satisfaction—behaviors IRS executives had never been held accountable for in the past.

As for the "what," each executive negotiated a performance contract with their boss (mine was with Commissioner Rossotti), each with a set of tangible, measurable program, policy, or operational objectives. The underlying assumption of this unique two-dimensional approach was that how someone accomplished those objectives—for example, in a way that satisfied customers and engaged employees—was just as important as achieving the objective itself. And ignoring the "how" could lead to problematic behavior.

Implementation: Appraisals based on *what* and *how*

That IRS executive appraisal system was recognized as best-in-class by OPM, and I believe it is still a model worth emulating. We designed a similar two-dimensional system for the IC 10 years later, with each senior executive accountable for a common set of behaviorally defined competency clusters that all had to do with leading the entire Intelligence Enterprise—in that case, things like collaboration and information sharing that were specifically designed to cure some of the dysfunctions that had contributed to 9/11— plus a set of objectives laid out in an annual performance contract. Even agency heads were required to execute annual personal performance agreements with the Director of National Intelligence that held them accountable (often in a shared way) for particular results.

In sum, both dimensions are important. What executives set out to accomplish and how they go about doing so should be given roughly equal weight, and evaluating one without the other can be problematic. A singular focus on results, without regard to how those results are accomplished, can lead to the sorts of "ends justify the means" abuses we saw at the IRS. But at the same time, an exclusive emphasis on competencies can vitiate the drive it takes to achieve a stretch objective. Is there tension between the two? Most definitely, but that tension is healthy, each dimension tempering the other.

The addition of an annual performance contract to today's SES performance management system would bring about a renewed emphasis on bottom-line results, but not at all costs. Rather, each executive would also be assessed against each of the ECQs to evaluate how well they went about achieving those results. Each senior executive would be required negotiate such a contract with their agency COO or equivalent, and each contract would have a set of individualized, agency-specific objectives, along with the five common ECQ-based performance standards.

And at the end of the performance cycle, each executive would be evaluated against both dimensions: whether they met or exceeded the specific objectives in their contract *and* how well they demonstrated the common, government-wide ECQs along the way. And in so doing, the system would strike a better balance between not only the "what" and "how" of the executive's performance but also government-wide uniformity on one hand and agency-level specificity on the other.

RECOMMENDATION 5.6: PROVIDE PEER REVIEW FOR GREATER SES ACCOUNTABILITY

Introduction: Accountability delayed, accountability denied[237]

As we have hinted, it may take a grand bargain to drive future SES reforms of any substance, including those described throughout this anthology. We have already described one of its main elements—the opportunity for higher pay (up to EX I) as a *quid pro quo* for more pre- and post-SES promotion mobility.

Is a mandate for more mobility enough political capital to warrant a new Tier 4 for an elite group of career executives, along with the higher salary cap that would come with it? With all due respect, I do not think that's enough. Even the fact that most career executives would not have access to that top tier may not be sufficient to overcome the likely political opposition to raising the SES salary cap. Instead, I believe the promise of higher executive pay must come with more executive accountability, which may then be sufficient for a second grand bargain of reforms.

What would greater executive accountability look like? We have already had a glimpse of it in the VA, with Congress—lately at the urging of the Department itself—acting to significantly revise the adverse action appeal rights of VA executives. That legislation was vigorously opposed by the Senior Executives Association on constitutional grounds, and although it was enacted, its long-term effect remains uncertain.

In the short term, VA exercised its authority under that legislation and proposed the removal of several senior executives; however, the Merit Systems Protection Board (MSPB) reversed those actions on appeal, notwithstanding a law that was supposed to make it easier to fire SES members. The matter was further complicated when one of the employee appeals made its way into Federal court, and the Justice Department declined to defend the government's position on the grounds that the aforementioned legislation was Constitutionally flawed.[238]

---

[237] Adapted from Sanders, R. (2016, February). Balancing Accountability and Protections: An Alternative Approach. Retrieved from http://www.Federaltimes.com/
[238] See the Attorney General's letter to the Senate Legal Counsel re: Helman v. Department of Veterans Affairs (May 31, 2016). Retrieved from http://Federalnewsradio.com/workforce-rightsgovernance/2016/06/doj-says-key-va-choice-provision-ses-appeals-unconstitutional/

Understandably, these outcomes drew the ire of the Department's senior leadership, as well as those in Congress who enacted the legislation, and in their frustration, they have already proposed additional measures that further erode SES protections.

Who can blame them? At least in theory, all that Congress and VA sought to do was make senior career executives more accountable, and, as a 20-year member of the SES, I cannot argue with that goal. Given the vital institutional role they play in our system of governance, career executives *should* be held to the very highest of standards, and they *should* be held accountable when they fail to meet them. I don't know any of my SES colleagues who would disagree, and most would concede that an appeals process that may take years and an army of lawyers to run its course is hardly conducive to that core principle.

Yet it is also clear that that same institutional role places career executives squarely at the intersection of politics and administration. As a consequence, they deserve as much protection (perhaps even more so) from arbitrary, capricious, and, above all, politically motivated actions as rank-and-file Federal employees. And I don't know any political appointees who would argue with that either.

So was MSPB wrong in thwarting the clear intent of Congress? As it turns out, no, given the law it was asked to implement. You see, while Congress legislated a drastically shortened appeal process, it left in place most of the legal standards—many based on case law developed over the past four decades, some embedded in the Constitution itself—that govern the adjudication of those appeals.

And that's the problem. When it comes to senior career executives, it should be less about legalisms and more about leadership. SES members should be judged by a higher standard, as leaders entrusted with protecting and serving the public's interest and not just as individual civil servants. And that standard should encompass such intangible qualities as judgment and character, appearance and example.

A jury of career executive peers

Who should apply such a standard? I would argue that the actions of senior career executives are best judged by other senior career executives—that is, by a jury of their peers who would judge the conduct and/or performance of a career executive in terms of his or her fitness for office—rather than an administrative law judge or a political appointee. Under this principle, Congress could establish a tribunal of senior career executives, appointed by the President and drawn from the ranks of current or former SES members, to adjudicate cases like those from the VA.

Of course, the members of such a panel would be trained in the rights and protections, both statutory and constitutional, afforded career executives; they would also be guided by legal counsel. And they would still hear and weigh evidence regarding charges levied against a career executive, with full due process rights afforded the latter. But in addition to those strict rules of due process and evidence, this senior executive accountability review board would also be empowered to judge the fitness of the senior executive to remain one against a standard that lets the board judge not just guilt or innocence, but also whether that executive has demonstrated the leadership qualities and character befitting a member of the senior Federal service.

These are intangible qualities to be sure, but they are nonetheless critical. And, in my humble opinion, only a jury of an executive's peers can reasonably judge whether that person has engaged in "conduct unbecoming a member of the senior Federal service."

There is precedent for something like this. The U.S. military judges the fitness of its general officers in much the same way, as do a number of law enforcement and intelligence agencies (most of whom are exempt from MSPB review); the latter employ administrative mechanisms like accountability boards to judge the actions of their officers against a higher standard, but in a manner that is still designed to protect them from partisan political influence. And since 1979, separate and apart from MSPB, private labor arbitrators have adjudicated thousands of adverse action appeals from unionized Federal employees, with appellate bodies granting those arbitrators almost untouchable deference.

So the creation of such a senior executive accountability review board is legally possible...indeed, as of this writing, Congress has taken up a variation of this for VA. Based on a proposal originally proffered by the Department, the legislation would extend coverage of its so-called title 38 authority—which among other things, allows VA to pay certain clinicians market-based salaries well above $300,000 per annum—to the Department's career SES members.

The *quid pro quo*? Career SES members in VA would no longer be able to appeal an adverse action (such as a demotion or removal for cause or poor performance) to the MSPB. Instead, those appeals would be heard by a professional review board, the same body that hears and adjudicates the removal of physicians. And that means that the Department has final say in the matter.

Obviously such a significant change in executive appeal rights government-wide would require a change in the law, but since both Congress and the VA are considering similar legislation as of this writing, the opportunity will likely present itself. The constitutionality questions raised by the Justice Department can be addressed as well.[239]

[239] Ibid.

The question is whether, in the name of additional accountability, that legislation ends up eroding the protections that should be afforded career executives, in VA and otherwise. The pending VA Professional Review Board legislation is flawed in that regard. In my opinion, an adverse action appeals process that ends with a political appointee, even if that appointee is a cabinet secretary, will always be viewed with suspicion by career executives. Career executives—peers of the appellant—must be the judges.

Thus, while greater accountability—in the form of revised senior executive adverse action appeal rights—could be part of the potential *quid pro quo* for higher pay, it must be in a form that is acceptable to career executives: independent, impartial, expeditious, and, above all, empathetic. Only a jury of peers meets this test.

The Way Ahead— Editor's Summary and Conclusions

A Blueprint for Reform

Let us end where we began, with our original three-part premise. First, that 21*st* century government, with all of its challenges, will require a career senior executive corps like no other before it, one whose members are capable of leading across the whole-of-government if they are to effectively address those challenges. Even those career executives who have a singular agency focus (and there will always be some) will have to be able to demonstrate the ability to lead across boundaries as the things government does become more and more interconnected, co-produced, and net-centric.

The good news is that this is exactly what the original architects of the Senior Executive Service (SES) had in mind when they conceived of it almost 40 years ago. The bad news is that we have never fully realized that vision, and, given the challenges we face, we cannot afford to wait any longer to do so.

Second, as technically capable as today's SES members may be, most of them have not been formally developed and prepared for this brave new boundary-spanning world. The government-wide regulatory framework that drives that formal development is largely agency-centric in execution, setting broad policies but devolving important day-to-day decisions—like who gets developed and promoted into the SES, how they are rewarded and deployed, etc.—to the agency level.

The Office of Personnel Management (and in some cases, OMB) provides oversight regarding those decisions, but execution of today's senior executive framework is largely decentralized. As such, it is simply not conducive to developing an executive corps with a whole-of-government perspective or the leadership experience and expertise to operationalize it.

And third, as a consequence, there is a looming leadership gap, and it is both qualitative and quantitative in nature. Quantitatively, this gap may be most acute in the short term, if the ever-expanding SES retirement bubble is burst by the trauma and drama of presidential transition; however, there is evidence of something more systemic—and potentially more worrisome—at work: that is, the alarming number of top-notch GS-14s and 15s (especially women and minorities), logical successors to today's executive cadre, who may no longer aspire to SES rank. But over the long term, the qualitative gap may be even more serious if and as our current system continues to clone career executives with an exclusively agency-centric perspective and skill set.

How does the Federal government close those gaps? Over the preceding sections, our contributors and I have offered a number of observations in that regard, and I have taken the liberty of translating them into 23 recommendations; these have been detailed at the end of each section and are summarized below. Most importantly, the vast majority of these recommendations require no special legislation…just the political and organizational will to implement them.[240]

Section 1: The Challenges of 21ˢᵗ Century Government

The challenges so well documented in Section 1 by Beth Cobert, Michèle Flournoy, Christine Fox and Emelia S. Probasco, and Robert Shea paint a daunting picture, one of a Federal government that will be exponentially harder to lead, and they make it clear that we will need a whole-of-government senior executive corps to do so. Given the agency-centric nature of today's SES, that will require a years-long transformation, perhaps even a generational one. But we must start now. Here's how we can begin to build it.

- **Recommendation 1.1: Start with a Whole-of-Government Executive Talent Management Strategy.** Such a strategy should cover every aspect of executive talent management, from development, acquisition, and compensation to retention, accountability, and deployment. And most importantly, it should do so from a whole-of-government vantage. Note that this strategy is not the same as a set of government-wide SES policies, but rather would include a set of clearly defined enterprise goals, objectives, and outcome-based performance metrics. And given its enterprise focus, this is something the President's Management Council (PMC) is best positioned to take on (with OPM technical assistance, of course). The good news here is that President Obama's SES Executive Order already vests a subset of the PMC to focus on the senior executive corps, and this group is in a strong position to begin developing a whole-of-government executive management strategy.

- **Recommendation 1.2: Establish a Permanent Mechanism to Engage Career Executives.** This too seems like a no-brainer. Career executives should have a seat at the big table where big decisions are made—indeed, I think their institutional role demands it. And in so doing, they should be engaged like they're actually part of the executive branch's leadership team, as opposed to yet another employee stakeholder group. Once again, there's good news: The SES Advisory Committee established by EO 13714

---

[240] As noted on several occasions throughout this anthology, these recommendations are mine and mine alone, not because I have any particular pride of authorship, but rather because I am not so presumptuous as to assume that any of my fellow contributors agree with them…if they do, so much the better, but I will leave that for them to say.

was a good albeit *ad hoc* start, and it could easily be institutionalized as a permanent mechanism to involve and engage the senior executive corps.

Section 2: Reexamining the Institutional Role of the SES

It is clear that the original vision of the SES—as a mobile corps of "super" public servants moving from challenge to challenge—is as much or more relevant today than it was at the SES' inception. But what about the unique institutional role for the SES implied by that vision…a role grounded in such core administrative values as the rule of law and the public interest? Is it still valid in 21st century government? The answer, at least according to our contributors, is an unequivocal yes, but it is not clear that that role is clearly understood by those who must embody it. That too must change.

- **Recommendation 2.1: Frame and Formalize the Institutional Role of the SES.** Accordingly, the critical role career executives play in our system of government needs to be further explicated, understood, and ultimately formalized in law or regulation if it is to be preserved and protected. And while there is some risk in doing so, it would be worth it if that meant elected officials (and their staffs), the media, and, most importantly, our citizens had a greater understanding of the role and just how vital it is. A bipartisan commission, perhaps comprising individuals with resumes like those of the contributors in this book (see Recommendation 5.5), could help in that regard.

- **Recommendation 2.2: Teach Career Executives What It Really Means to Really Be One**

  That institutional role not only must be described to career executives and other internal and external stakeholders, but also become part of the career executive's leadership DNA, inculcated and internalized in the senior executive corps itself. This is the job of the Federal Executive Institute (FEI). Once a prominent feature of FEI's flagship *Leadership for a Democratic Society* program for new or soon-to-be senior executives, the institutional role of the SES should take center stage again. With OPM's renewed emphasis on executive onboarding and continuing leadership education, the platform exists to make that happen.

- **Recommendation 2.3: Appoint Career Directors General as Stewards of the SES' Institutional Role.** While a government-wide policy framework already exists to regulate the senior executive corps, that framework is operationalized at the agency level. That is where senior executives face difficult "do the right thing" dilemmas every day, and as such, that is also where the executive's institutional role is potentially most at risk. Someone needs to be made officially accountable for preserving and protecting that role…not as a compliance cop, but rather as steward, mediating and moderating between appointees and careerists so that both may fulfill their institutional obligations. The Foreign Service's Director General plays such a role in the State Department, and it is worth replicating across all agencies.

Section 3: Leadership Qualities for the 21st Century

The world is changing at a dizzying pace, and today's senior executive needs to be able to demonstrate leadership qualities that we couldn't even imagine 10 or even 5 years ago—cutting-edge competencies like managing crises and complexity or achieving enterprise unity of effort without formal authority. At the same time, they must also demonstrate competencies that are as enduring as our system of government—qualities like courage and character. Both sets should be reflected in the Executive Core Qualifications (ECQ) that serve as the admissions test for the SES. Unfortunately, neither of these critical competencies is included, with implications that are subtle but important. Here's how we can fix that.

- **Recommendation 3.1: Put Public Service Back in the ECQs.** A career executive's institutional role requires a set of leadership competencies unique to public service. In that regard, most would concede that it is much harder to get things done in government, and not just in a bureaucratic sense. Career executives often work in paradoxes, striving to strike a balance between such things as the rule of law and service to the government of the day. This is deliberate (the 'intelligent design' of our Constitution clearly says as much!), yet OPM's ECQs no longer reflect that unique public-ness. Competencies that are institutional in nature and exceptional to government need to be made part of the ECQs once more.

- **Recommendation 3.2: Constantly Modernize the ECQ Framework.** While a career government executive's *institutional* role should be relatively enduring, that executive's *instrumental* skills must also be continuously refreshed to reflect rapidly emerging leadership demands. Yet the ECQs haven't changed since their inception. While OPM has made incremental (and mostly positive) changes to the two dozen or so now-exclusively instrumental competencies that currently compose the ECQs, those competencies need to be regularly and rigorously refreshed, with a particular eye toward what's on and over the horizon—what *tomorrow's* executives will need to be able to do.

- **Recommendation 3.3: Establish an Enterprise Leadership ECQ.** Today's career executive must lead in a whole-of-government world, but few have been deliberately developed and prepared to do so. This requires a set of "enterprise" leadership competencies that are arguably unique— like building and leveraging cross-agency networks or achieving unity of effort without formal authority—but the ECQs make no distinctions in that regard. If we do lead in a whole-of-government world, then the ECQs should be amended to reflect that reality, to include a sixth ECQ, perhaps entitled *Leading the Federal Enterprise*, that requires evidence of an executive's ability to do so.

- **Recommendation 3.4: Require Due Diligence to Assess an Executive's Character.** Finally, to be successful, senior leaders (especially those in government) also require character…indeed, their followers should demand it! While character has a "we'll know it when we see it" quality, we certainly see the headlines when a leader lacks it. As a consequence, it should be an integral part of SES screening, selection, and onboarding—and formally assessed as part of a comprehensive "due diligence" process during the executive's first-year probationary period—as a fundamental in-or-out requirement for retention in the SES.

Section 4: Developing the Next Generation of the SES

If 21st century government requires a mix of enduring and emerging leadership competencies, especially those associated with the ability to lead cross-agency, whole-of-government efforts, how do we go about preparing career executives to effectively demonstrate these competencies? Almost by definition, such a whole-of-government developmental model requires some form of managed mobility and the enabling policies and administrative mechanisms to make it work. This demands a whole new leadership development model—one that is far less agency-centric in nature, in which career executives (and perhaps even more importantly, their potential successors) are treated as corporate assets and prepared accordingly.

- **Recommendation 4.1: Build a Whole-of-Government Executive Succession Plan.** We know it takes deliberate, strategic succession planning and execution to prepare future leaders. While most agencies have decent succession plans today, the executives (and executive candidates) they cover are strictly "for internal use only." If we want to develop career executives with a whole-of-government skill set, the PMC needs to build a comprehensive inventory of current and prospective career executives; identify critical gaps against anticipated demand, both qualitative and quantitative; and develop a comprehensive plan to ensure the Federal enterprise has an adequate interagency pool of succession candidates, especially for those key executive positions that have whole-of-government responsibilities.

- **Recommendation 4.2: Make Interagency Mobility a Prerequisite for SES Promotion.** For the Federal government to prepare career executives to effectively address all of the critical whole-of-government and whole-of-nation challenges it faces, it should make some form of mobility a prerequisite to becoming a member of the senior executive corps—just as the U.S. military, Senior Foreign Service, and U.S. Intelligence Community (IC) do. This mandate should at least apply to those positions that entail whole-of-government responsibilities, and it should be enabled by the mundane but no less essential administrative mechanisms necessary to make mobility work.

- **Recommendation 4.3: Raise the Bar for Agency CDPs.** In theory, relying on a Candidate Development Program (CDP) pipeline to ensure an adequate supply of qualified SES successors would seem more strategically effective (and significantly less time consuming) than posting individual SES vacancies on an *ad hoc* basis. However, the effectiveness of many CDPs is questionable given that most CDP graduates are never promoted to the SES. OPM should take a lesson from those few CDPs that are effective and condition continuing CDP certification on a stronger linkage to pre-CDP succession planning, as well as to a sustained high placement rate.

- **Recommendation 4.4: Build an Internal Headhunting Capability for SES Jobs.** Something is wrong when SES candidates think their odds of winning the lottery are better than applying for SES vacancy announcements in USA Jobs. If you want to improve those odds, you have to find and match talented applicants to real openings that best fit their skill sets. That's what headhunters do—they know the best candidates aren't trolling the want ads (like USA Jobs) for their next challenge. OPM could follow suit by establishing an internal, fee-for-service executive search operation to ferret out, recruit, and match outstanding SES candidates (especially women and minorities), to SES opportunities.

- **Recommendation 4.5: Resurrect the Government-Wide CDP.** An internal headhunting capability would help, but so too would a government-wide CDP. OPM tried one once and, while it had its flaws, we've learned much since, especially from recent efforts like the PMC's Interagency Rotation Program and the White House Leadership Development Program…not to mention the stillborn *Senior* Presidential Management Fellows Program. It wouldn't take much to take the best of these programs—as well as what we've learned from those relatively few CDPs that actually work—and resurrect a government-wide CDP. It's sorely needed.

- **Recommendation 4.6: Delegate but Certify Agency SES Selection Processes.** OPM's efforts to streamline the SES application process are commendable. Resumes are fine (up to a point), as are alternatives to an OPM qualifications review board (QRB), but both have their downsides. In that regard, it's time to give agencies wider latitude in the way they search for, recruit, screen, and assess candidates. OPM should still set rigorous, outcome-based standards, much as it does with delegated examining authority for rank-and-file civil service jobs; however, it should let agencies figure out how they'll meet those standards and forego central QRB certification of their SES selections.

Section 5: Revitalizing the Federal Senior Executive Corps

It is clear the nation needs the very best and brightest senior career executives at its helm. But will they be there when we need them? And will they have the core values and competencies to lead the whole of 21st century government? Is the system—or more accurately, the systems—that produced today's executives up to the challenge of keeping them at the top of their game on into the future, especially if the focus has shifted from agency to enterprise? I would argue that the answer is no…and that the whole of the various systems that govern how senior career leaders are developed, selected, deployed, motivated, and, yes, held accountable, is in need of some serious reimagining.

- **Recommendation 5.1: Establish a *Federated* Whole-of-Government SES Framework.** While the nation requires a whole-of-government senior service—a senior *Federal* service—to lead it, more than half a dozen alternative senior services currently coexist with the SES, each of them administratively walled off from it as well as each other. The result is a Balkanized, largely immobile executive corps that remains predominantly agency-centric in both orientation and operation. These various senior services need to be unified under a federated executive talent management framework that integrates the government's senior services into a single *corpus*…bound together under an umbrella of common institutional principles that enable cross-agency development and deployment.

- **Recommendation 5.2: Establish a Master Interchange Agreement to Connect Senior Services.** A common, unifying framework is necessary to integrate the Federal government's various senior services, but it is not sufficient. In addition, the barriers between those senior services must be made more permeable. OPM can do so administratively by establishing a master Executive Interchange Agreement that links all of these senior services together, making the borders between them far more permeable. In so doing, OPM would enable an executive in one of those services to move to a permanent position in another with relative ease…and without any further competition.

- **Recommendation 5.3: Establish a New Government-Wide Senior Executive Structure.** A senior Federal service also needs a new, common architecture that departs from the level-free open range currently in place. The original idea of that open range was to give agencies the discretion to tailor their own rank levels and salary control points; however, most have ended up with more or less the same three-tiered structure. That structure should be formalized and a fourth tier added that would permit a relatively small number of enterprise executives to progress to Executive Level (EX) I. This would require legislation (one of the few recommendations herein that does), but EX I would only be for a relatively elite group of between 1,000 and 1,500 career executives that have government-wide, cabinet-level leadership responsibilities and impact.

- **Recommendation 5.4: Appoint an Enterprise Executive Resources Board to Manage Career Executive Talent.** This four-tiered, federated architecture requires a governance structure that can manage the Federal government's executive talent for the enterprise a whole. Today, individual agency Executive Resources Boards perform this talent management function for their own career executive cadres. The President or OPM could establish a new Enterprise Executive Resources Board (EERB), drawn from the PMC but co-led by an equal number of career executives, to manage select senior career executive talent...with particular attention paid to those elite Tier 4 executive positions that have whole-of-government responsibilities.

- **Recommendation 5.5: Make Incremental Fixes to SES Compensation.** Our career executive compensation system is clearly broken, and it needs more than a new pay cap at EX I. That's a start, but Congress has seen fit to authorize some agencies—like the Department of Veterans Affairs (VA) and the FIRREA[241] agencies—to raise senior executive pay substantially in order to better compete with the private sector. FIRREA-like pay levels may be a bridge too far for all senior executives, but short of that, the EERB could be given streamlined authority to approve so-called critical pay requests up to and above the Vice President's level, as already allowed by law.

- **Recommendation 5.6: Provide Peer Review for Greater SES Accountability.** Congress has sought to make career executives more accountable. That's code for making it easier to fire them. But in principle, that goal is not illegitimate. Most career executives would agree that they *should* be held to the very highest standards, and a years-long adverse action appeals process is hardly conducive to that core principle. In its stead, the adverse actions of career executives should be judged by a jury of their peers—that is, a tribunal of other career executives who would judge the conduct and/or performance of a career executive in terms of his or her fitness for office. This would require legislation, but career executives would likely find this far more acceptable than some of the legislative proposals circulating on the Hill.

When it comes to building a 21st century senior executive corps, the vast majority of the recommendations set forth above require no special legislation. However, that doesn't mean they are easy to implement. If they were, OMB or OPM would have already done so. Nor does it mean legislation wouldn't help...the few recommendations that do require an act of Congress, like raising the pay cap to EX I, are crucial to the continuing viability of the senior executive corps.

---

[241] Financial Institutions Reform, Recovery, and Enforcement Act.

Realistically, it is unlikely that the next administration and the next Congress will take steps to modernize the SES just because it's the "good government" thing to do. That's not an editorial comment, just a political reality, and it will likely take some sort of impetus—a scandal, a major management failure, some dire threat—to fuel the discussion. However, that opportunity may come sooner than later...it may even be upon us now.

RECOMMENDATION 6.1: ANOTHER GRAND BARGAIN TO REINVENT THE SES.

As problematic as some of them may be, the various legislative efforts to diminish SES appeal rights may have a silver lining. If they've done nothing else, those efforts have opened the door to additional reforms, especially as a *quid pro quo* for greater SES accountability...and as a way to get greater buy-in from an anxious executive corps. Recall that it was just such a grand bargain in 2004 that raised the SES pay cap to EX II, and there is an opportunity to follow a similar path today. Thus, if Congress attempts to go beyond the VA to "improve" the adverse action appeal process for all career executives, the administration could propose legislation to (among other things) raise the pay cap to EX I for that select group of mobile enterprise executives who have whole-of-government responsibilities.

RECOMMENDATION 6.2: APPOINT A BLUE RIBBON COMMISSION TO PROPOSE SES REFORMS.

Ideally, when it comes to SES reform, the next President and the next OPM Director would simply pick up where the current ones have left off, building on EO 13714 and making other incremental improvements. However, if that doesn't happen, a blue ribbon commission on reforming the SES could help—especially if it were drawn from the ranks of current and former senior officials like those who contributed to this book.

Now, some cynics would argue that a commission is just a politically expedient way to continue to "admire" the problems rather than solve them, but I have personally been involved in two commission-driven reform efforts—the restructuring of the Internal Revenue Service circa 1998, and the integration of the Intelligence Community circa 2004—and both were reasonably successful.

Granted, both efforts were driven by something much bigger than personnel problems (a scandal in one case, a tragedy in the other), but both included significant personnel reforms as part of the statutory solutions their commissions recommended. VA is following a similar path...indeed, to its credit, the Commission on Care focuses on leaders and leadership development as a key part of its recommendations. So commissions can work, especially if they speak with respected, bipartisan voices on issues that an administration, Congress, and the people care about.

A final word

In sum, it is clear that the SES and its sister senior services need to be transformed if their members, the Federal government, and the nation as a whole —are to meet the challenges of the 21st century. And at the risk of being a bit Pollyannaish, I believe that there is some cause for optimism in that regard.

First, whether or not one agrees with the recommendations set forth above, they demonstrate that much can be done administratively to "jump start" the transformation of the SES; to be sure, much has been done already, but I would venture that even (especially?) those who have led those changes would acknowledge that more is necessary. But the fact that much of the "more" can be done without legislation means that further progress is possible. It's just a matter of will.

In addition, there are those who have served in all branches of government and on both sides of the aisle who truly care about this issue. They want to see an SES that is up to the challenges of 21st century government. That certainly includes those who took the time and effort to contribute to this anthology, all of them highly regarded and respected in their own right… and now speaking as one. Do they represent a groundswell of support for reform? Not yet, not even close, but their voices carry disproportionate weight when it comes to matters of "good government," and that too improves the chances of success.

And success is imperative. Year in and year out, the vast majority of career executives remain as selfless and dedicated to their cause as the day they first took the oath, and they will continue to labor and lead in the trenches without worrying about the prospects for reform. The best of them can make even the most decrepit system work, but only for so long…so we owe them—and the American people, whether they know it or not—our best efforts. And our best leaders. So let's get started.

Bibliography

Administrative Personnel, 5 C.F.R. § 214.204 (2013).

American Recovery and Reinvestment Act of 2009, Pub. L. No. 111-5, 123 Stat. 115 (2009).

Anti-Deficiency Act, 31 U.S.C. § 1341 et seq.

Aquino, K., & Reed, A. (2002). The self-importance of moral identity. *Journal of Personality and Social Psychology, 83*(6), 1423–1440.

Barr, S. (1999, November 6). Improper payments cost U.S. big; GAO report cites $19.1 billion in errors at just 9 agencies. *The Washington Post.* Retrieved from https://www.highbeam.com/doc/1P2-621786.html

Bennis, W. G., & Nanus, B. (1985). *Leaders: The strategies for taking charge.* New York, NY: Harper & Row.

Berry, J. (2010, August 3). *Guidance on freeze on discretionary awards, bonuses, and similar payments for Federal employees serving under political appointments* {OPM CPM 2010-14). Washington, DC: U.S. Office of Personnel Management. Retrieved from https://www.chcoc.gov/content/guidance-freeze-discretionary -awards-bonuses-and-similar-payments-Federal-employees-serving

Berry, J., & Zients, J. (2012, January 4). *Senior Executive Service performance appraisal system* {Memorandum). Washington, DC: U.S. Office of Personnel Management. Retrieved from https://www.chcoc.gov/content/senior-executive-service-performance-appraisal-system

Budget Control Act of 2011, Pub. L. No. 112-25 § 354, 125 Stat. 240 (2011).

Carey, M. P. (2012). *The Senior Executive Service: Background and options for reform.* Washington, DC: Congressional Research Service. Retrieved from http://digitalcommons.ilr.cornell.edu/cgi/viewcontent.cgi?article=1942&context=key_workplace

Center for Effective Government. (2005, May 31). House considers CDBG but avoids attacking PART [Web log post]. Retrieved from http://www.foreffectivegov.org/node/2453

Center for Effective Government. (2006, February 6). Initial analysis of the president's 2007 budget [Web log post]. Retrieved from http://www.foreffectivegov.org/node/2769

Chairman of the Joint Chiefs of Staff Instruction (CJCSI) No. 1800.01E, Officer Professional Military Education Policy. (2015, May 29). Retrieved from http://www.dtic.mil/cjcs_directives/cdata/unlimit/1800_01a.pdf

Civil Service Reform Act of 1978, 6 Pub. L. No. 95-454 § 601 et seq. (1978).

Clark, C. S. (2016, February 23). Hoyer to union: Lawmakers shouldn't use "bureaucrat as an epithet." *Government Executive.* Retrieved from http://www.govexec.com/oversight/2016/02/hoyer-union-lawmakers-shouldnt-use-bureaucrat-epithet/126147

Cobert, B. F. (2016, June 15). *National Security Professional Development (NSPD) Interagency Personnel Rotations Program guidance* [OPM letter]. Retrieved from https://www.chcoc.gov/content/national-security-professional-development-nspd-interagency-personnel-rotations-program-0

Committee on Government Reform and Oversight, Committee on the Judiciary. (1996). *Investigation into the activities of Federal law enforcement agencies toward the Branch Davidians: Thirteenth report* (Report No. 104-749). Washington, DC: U.S. Government Publishing Office.

Defense Partnership Council Meeting, 64 Fed. Reg. 3685 (1999, January 25). Retrieved from https://www.gpo.gov/fdsys/granule/FR-1999-01-25/99-1564

DeSeve, G. E. (2008). *Presidential appointee's handbook.* Washington, DC: Brookings Institution Press.

Development for and Within the Senior Executive Service, 5 U.S.C. § 3396 (2001).

Director of Central Intelligence Directive No. 1/4, Intelligence community officer programs. (2000, February 4). Retrieved from http://www.fas.org/irp/offdocs/dcid1-4.htm

Donovan, S. (2014, December 23). *Strengthening employee engagement and organizational performance* [Memorandum]. Washington, DC: U.S. Office of Personnel Management. Retrieved from https://www.whitehouse.gov/sites/default/files/omb/memoranda/2015/m-15-04.pdf

Espionage Act of 1917, 18 U.S.C. § 792 et seq. (1917).

Exec. Order No. 12871, Labor-management partnerships. (1993, October 1). Retrieved from http://govinfo.library.unt.edu/npr/library/direct/orders/24ea.html

Exec. Order No. 13318, Presidential Management Fellows Program. (2003, November 21). Retrieved from https://www.gpo.gov/fdsys/pkg/CFR-2004-title3-vol1/pdf/CFR-2004-title3-vol1-eo13318.pdf

Exec. Order No. 13434, National security professional development (2007, May 17). Retrieved from https://www.gpo.gov/fdsys/pkg/WCPD-2007-05-21/pdf/WCPD-2007-05-21-Pg650.pdf

Exec. Order No. 13522, Creating labor-management forums to improve delivery of government services. (2009, December 9). Retrieved from https://www.whitehouse.gov/the-press-office/executive-order-creating-labor-management-forums-improve-delivery-government-servic

Exec. Order No. 13714, Strengthening the Senior Executive Service. (2015, December 15). Retrieved from https://www.whitehouse.gov/the-press-office/2015/12/15/executive-order-strengthening-senior-executive-service

Federal Daily. (2010, April 27). Senior Executive candidates worry about pay, work/family balance. FCW. Retrieved from https://fcw.com/Articles/2010/04/27/SES-survey-salary-benefits.aspx

Federal Funding Accountability and Transparency Act of 2006, Pub. L. No. 09–282, 120 Stat. 1186 (2006).

Financial Institutions Reform, Recovery, and Enforcement Act of 1989, Pub. L. No. 101-73 (1989).

Foreign Service Act of 1980, Pub. L. No. 96-465, 94 Stat. 2071 (1980).

Goldwater-Nichols Department of Defense Reorganization Act of 1986, Pub. L. No. 99-433 (1986).

Goleman, D., Boyatzis, R., McKee, A. (2002). Primal leadership: Realizing the power of emotional intelligence—Tapping into your team's emotional intelligence. Retrieved from http://hbswk.hbs.edu/archive/2875.html

Government Performance and Results Act of 1993, Pub. L. No. 103-62, 107 Stat. 285 (1993).

GPRA Modernization Act of 2010, Pub. L. No. 111-352, 124 Stat. 3866 (2011).

Grades and Pay Scales, 38 U.S.C. § 7404 (2010).

Gun Violence Epidemic, 162 Cong. Rec. H4981 (2016). Retrieved from https://www.gpo.gov/fdsys/pkg/CREC-2016-07-14/html/CREC-2016-07-14-pt1-PgH4981.htm

Hale, R., & Sanders, R. (2016, January 26). Developing civilian leaders in DoD. *Defense News*. Retrieved from http://www.defensenews.com/story/defense/commentary/2016/01/26/developing-civilian-leaders-dod/79055042

Hannah, S. T., & Avolio, B. J. (2010). Ready or not: How do we accelerate the developmental readiness of leaders? *Journal of Organizational Behavior,* 31(8), 1181–1187.

Hayden, M. V. (2016). Playing to the edge: *American intelligence in the age of terror.* New York, NY: Penguin Press.

Holan, A. D. (2007, September 5). Firing Federal workers is difficult. *PolitiFact*. Retrieved from http://www.politifact.com/truth-o-meter/article/2007/sep/05/mcain-Federal

Hughes, A., & Shull, J. R. (2005). *PART backgrounder* (OMB Watch). Washington, DC: Office of Management and Budget. Retrieved from http://www.for-effectivegov.org/sites/default/files/regs/2005/performance/PARTbackgrounder.pdf

Improper Payments Elimination and Recovery Improvement Act of 2012, Pub. L. No. 12–248, 126 Stat. 2390 (2013).

Improper Payments Information Act of 2002, Pub. L. No. 107–300, 116 Stat. 2350 (2002).

Intelligence Reform and Terrorism Prevention Act of 2004, Pub. L. No. 108-458, 118 Stat. 3638 (2004).

Internal Revenue Service Restructuring and Reform Act of 1998, Pub. L. No. 105-206, 112 Stat. 685 (1998).

Janis, I. L. (1989). *Crucial decisions: Leadership in policymaking and crisis management*. New York, NY: The Free Press.

Johnson, B. [climatebrad]. (2010, May 31). BP CEO *Tony Hayward: "I'd like my life back."* [Video File]. Retrieved from https://www.youtube.com/watch?v=MTdKa9eWNFw

Kegan, R. (1994). *In over our heads: The mental demands of modern life*. Cambridge, MA: Harvard University Press.

Kelman, S., Sanders, R., & Pandit, G. (2016, May). "Tell it like it is": Decision making, groupthink, and decisiveness among U.S. Federal subcabinet executives. Governance. doi:10.1111/gove.12200

Kim, A. (2015, April). The Federal government's worsening millennial talent gap. Retrieved from http://republic3-0.com/Federal-government-millennials-talent-gap

Leeds, J. P. (2015, November 24). Investment in senior executive training pays off. *Government Executive*. Retrieved from http://www.govexec.com/management/2015/11/investment-senior-executive-training-pays/123956

Loria, K. (2014, August 19). 6 Strange body hacks that are actually useful [Web log post]. Retrieved from http://www.businessinsider.com/strange-body-hacks-that-are-actually-useful-2014-8

Mader, D., Kelman, S., & Myers, J. (2014). *What it takes to change government: Successfully executing ambitious strategies*. McLean, VA: Booz Allen Hamilton. Retrieved from http://mena.boozallen.com/content/dam/MENA/PDF/what-it-takes-to-change-government.pdf

Marbury v. Madison, 5 U.S. 137 (1803).

Masters, M. F., Merchant, C. S., & Tobias, R. (2010). *Engaging Federal employees through their union representatives to improve agency performance.* Retrieved from http://www.govexec.com/pdfs/021010ar1.pdf

McCaleb, I. C. (1996, July 11). GOP Waco findings skewer Reno, ATF. *United Press International.* Retrieved from http://www.upi.com/Archives/1996/07/11/GOP-Waco-findings-skewer-Reno-ATF/2411837057600

McGuire, J. B., & Rhodes, G. B. (2009). *Transforming your leadership culture.* San Francisco, CA: Jossey-Bass.

Metzenbaum, S. H. (2014, May 29). Untying the knots in the Federal hiring process [Web log post]. Retrieved from https://www.volckeralliance.org/blog/2016/jun/untying-knots-Federal-hiring-process

Movement of Persons Between the Civil Service System and Other Merit Systems, 5 C.F.R. § 6.7 (1963).

National Commission on Terrorist Attacks upon the United States (2004). *The 9/11 Commission Report.* Washington, DC: U.S. Government Publishing Office. Retrieved from https://9-11commission.gov/report

National Defense Authorization Act for Fiscal Year 2016, H.R. 1735, 114th Cong. (2015).

Neck, C. P., Manz, C. C., & Houghton, J. D. (2016). *Self-leadership. The definitive guide to personal excellence.* Thousand Oaks, CA: Sage Publications.

Nickerson, J. A., & Sanders, R. P. (Eds.). (2014). *Tackling wicked government problems: A practical guide for developing enterprise leaders.* Washington, DC: Brookings Institution Press.

Noble, Z. (2016, July 1). Milholland exits IRS. FCW. Retrieved from https://fcw.com/articles/2016/07/01/mulholland-exits-irs.aspx

Northouse, P. G. (2016). *Leadership. Theory and practice.* Thousand Oaks, CA: Sage Publications.

O'Reilly, C. A., & Tushman, M. L. (2008). Ambidexterity as a dynamic capability: Resolving the innovator's dilemma. *Research in Organizational Behavior, 28,* 185–206.

Obama, B. (2014, December 9). Remarks by the president to senior leaders of the Federal workforce. Retrieved from https://votesmart.org/public-statement/941830/remarks-by-the-president-to-senior-leaders-of-the-Federal-workforce#.V_VjD-IrLIU

Office of the Attorney General (2016, May 31). Letter to P. Bryan, Senate Legal Counsel, re: Helman v. Department of Veterans Affairs. Retrieved from https://m.govexec.com/media/gbc/docs/pdfs_edit/060216kl1.pdf

Office of the Director of National Intelligence. (2010). Intelligence Community Directive No. 610, Competency Directories for the Intelligence Community Workforce. Retrieved from https://www.dni.gov/files/documents/ICD/ICD_610.pdf

Office of the Director of National Intelligence. (2009). Intelligence Community Directive No. 612, Intelligence Community Core Contract Personnel. Retrieved from https://fas.org/irp/dni/icd/icd-612.pdf

Office of the Director of National Intelligence. (2013). Intelligence Community Directive No. 660, Intelligence Community Civilian Joint Duty Program. Retrieved from https://fas.org/irp/dni/icd/icd-660.pdf

Office of the Director of National Intelligence. (2008; amended 2012). Intelligence Community Directive No. 656, Performance Management System Requirements for Intelligence Community Senior Civilian Officers. Retrieved from https://fas.org/irp/dni/icd/icd-656.pdf

Office of the Director of National Intelligence. (2016, June 10). *ODNI releases first public report on intelligence community workforce demographics, seeking diverse talent pool* [Press release]. Retrieved from https://www.dni.gov/index.php/newsroom/press-releases/215-press-releases-2016/1387-odni-releases-first-public-report-on-intelligence-community-workforce-demographics,-seeking-diverse-talent-pool

Oil Pollution Act of 1990, 33 U.S.C. § 2701 et seq. (1990).

Partnership for Public Service & Booz Allen Hamilton. (2014). *Building the enterprise: A new civil service framework.* Washington, DC: Partnership for Public Service.

Partnership for Public Service & Booz Allen Hamilton. (2011). *Preparing the people pipeline. A Federal succession planning primer.* McLean, VA: Booz Allen Hamilton. Retrieved from https://www.boozallen.com/content/dam/boozallen/media/file/PeoplePipeline-2011.pdf

Partnership for Public Service & Booz Allen Hamilton. (2009). *Unrealized Vision: Reimagining the Senior Executive Service.* McLean, VA: Booz Allen Hamilton. Retrieved from https://www.boozallen.com/content/dam/boozallen/media/file/reimagining-the-senior-executive-service-2009.pdf

Partnership for Public Service & McKinsey and Company. (2016). *A pivotal moment for the Senior Executive Service: Measures, aspirational practices and stories of success.* Washington, DC: Partnership for Public Service.

Patient Protection and Affordable Care Act, Pub. L. No. 111-148 (2010).

Pay Authority for Critical Positions, 5 U.S.C. § 5337 (2008).

Performance Appraisal, 5 U.S.C. 43 § 4301 et seq. (2006).

Pinkerton, J. P. (1995). *What comes next: The end of big government—and the new paradigm ahead.* New York, NY: Hyperion.

Reassignment and Transfer Within the Senior Executive Service, 5 U.S.C. § 3395 (e).

Risen, J. (2006). State of war: *The secret history of the CIA and the Bush administration.* New York, NY: Free Press.

Sanders, R. (2015, February 26). Probing the details of the president's new SES program. *Federal Times.* Retrieved from https://www.federaltimes.com/story/government/management/blog/2015/02/26/white-house-leadership-development/24049835

Sanders, R. (1994). Reinventing the Senior Executive Service. In P. W. Ingraham & B. S. Romzek (Eds.). *New paradigms for government: Issues for the changing public service.* San Francisco, CA: Jossey-Bass.

Sanders, R. P., & Nickerson, J. (2014). Tackling wicked government problems: A practical guide for developing enterprise leaders. Washington, DC: Brookings Institution Press.

Schwarz, R. (2013). *Smart leaders, smarter teams: How you and your team get unstuck to achieve results.* San Francisco, CA: Jossey-Bass.

Senate Select Committee on Intelligence. (2014). *Committee study of the CIA's Detention and Interrogation Program. Findings and conclusions.* Retrieved from https://web.archive.org/web/20141209165504/http://www.intelligence.senate.gov/study2014/sscistudy1.pdf

Stephens, R., & Kolodge, K. (2016). *Building consumer trust in technology.* Retrieved from http://www.jdpower.com/sites/default/files/jdp_ces_2016_final_for_distribution.pdf

Streamlined Critical Pay Authority, 5 U.S.C. § 9503 (2011).

Thompson, J. R., & Seidner, R. (2009). *Federated human resource management in the Federal government: The Intelligence Community Model.* Washington, DC: IBM Center for the Business of Government. Retrieved from http://www.businessofgovernment.org/report/federated-human-resource-management-Federal-government-intelligence-community-model

U.S. Department of Defense Directive No. 1400.25, Vol. 1403 (1996), DoD Civilian Personnel Management System.

U.S. Government Accountability Office. (2005). *21ˢᵗ Century challenges: Reexamining the base of the Federal government* (Report No. GAO-05-325SP). Washington, DC: U.S. Government Accountability Office. Retrieved from http://www.gao.gov/assets/160/157585.pdf

U.S. Government Accountability Office. *Financial management: Improper payments reported in fiscal year 1999 financial statements* (Report No. GAO/AIMD-00-261R). (2000, July 27). Washington, DC: Government Accountability Office.

U.S. Government Accountability Office. (2015). High-risk list. Retrieved from http://www.gao.gov/highrisk/overview

U.S. Government Accountability Office. (2001). High-risk series: An update. Retrieved from http://www.gao.gov/products/GAO-01-263

U.S. Government Accountability Office. (2015, January 22). Results-oriented management: OPM needs to do more to ensure meaningful distinctions are made in SES ratings and performance awards. Retrieved from http://www.gao.gov/products/GAO-15-189

U.S. Merit Systems Protection Board. (2015). *Training and development for the Senior Executive Service: A necessary investment.* Washington, DC: U.S. Merit Systems Protection Board. Retrieved from http://www.mspb.gov/netsearch/viewdocs.aspx?docnumber=1253299&version=1258322&application=ACROBAT

U.S. Office of Personnel Management. (2015). *Congressional budget justification performance budget.* Fiscal year 2016. Washington, DC: U.S. Office of Personnel Management. Retrieved from https://www.opm.gov/about-us/budget-performance/budgets/congressional-budget-justification-fy2016.pdf

U.S. Office of Personnel Management. (2009). *A guide to the Strategic Leadership Succession Management Model.* Washington, DC: U.S. Office of Personnel Management. Retrieved from www.opm.gov/hcaaf_resource_center/assets/Lead_Guide.pdf

U.S. Office of Personnel Management. (2014). *Labor-management relations in the executive branch.* Washington, DC: Office of Personnel Management. Retrieved from https://www.opm.gov/policy-data-oversight/labor-management-relations/reports/labor-management-relations-in-the-executive-branch-2014.pdf

U.S. Office of Personnel Management. (2015, October 6). *OPM releases complete 2015 Federal Employee Viewpoint Survey results* [Press release]. Retrieved from https://www.opm.gov/news/releases/2015/10/opm-releases-complete-2015-Federal-employee-viewpoint-survey-results

U.S. Office of Personnel Management. Pay & leave salaries & wages—2016 executive & senior level employee pay tables. Retrieved from https://www.opm.gov/policy-data-oversight/pay-leave/salaries-wages/2016/executive-senior-level

U.S. Office of Personnel Management. Senior Executive Service executive core qualifications. Retrieved from https://www.opm.gov/policy-data-oversight/senior-executive-service/executive-core-qualifications

U.S. Office of Personnel Management. (2015). *Senior Executive Service exit survey results: April 2015.* Washington, DC: Office of Personnel Management. Retrieved from https://www.opm.gov/policy-data-oversight/senior-executive-service/reference-materials/ses-exit-survey-resultspdf.pdf

U.S. Office of Personnel Management. Training and development: Leadership development. Retrieved from https://www.opm.gov/policy-data-oversight/training-and-development/leadership-development#url=PMC-Interagency-Rotation-Prgm

U.S. Office of Personnel Management. Training and development policy wiki, supervisory leadership development. Retrieved from https://www.opm.gov/WIKI/training/Supervisory-Leadership-Development.ashx

U.S. Office of Personnel Management, Chief Human Capital Officers Council. Senior Executive Service performance appraisal system. Retrieved from https://chcoc.gov/content/senior-executive-service-performance-appraisal-system

United States Government Policy and Supporting Positions (Plum Book). (2008). Washington, DC: U.S. Government Publishing Office.

Williamson, E. (2007, December 13). OMB offers an easy way to follow the money. *The Washington Post.* Retrieved from http://www.highbeam.com/doc/1P2-11441162.html?refid=easy_hf

Wolfinger, R. E. (1960). Reputation and reality in the study of "community power." *American Sociological Review*, 25(5), 636–644.

Worline, M. C., & Quinn, R. W. (2003). Courageous principled action. In K. S. Cameron, J. E. Dutton, & R. E. Quinn (Eds.), *Positive organizational scholarship: Foundations of a new discipline* (pp. 138–157). San Francisco, CA: Berrett-Koehler.

Index

A

Allen, Thad   *IV, IX, 111, 113, 136, 153, 156, 211, 232*

American Recovery and Reinvestment Act of 2009   *166, 202, 203, 265, 313*

Anti-Deficiency Act   *242, 313*

Archuleta, Katherine   *IV, 47*

B

Blair, Dan   *iii, IV*

Blair, Dennis   *39*

Borras, Rafael   *IV*

Budget Control Act of 2011   *18, 313*

Building the Enterprise: A New Civil Service Framework (April 2014)   *318*

Bush, President George W.   *6, 34, 39, 65, 115, 222, 228, 319*

C

Candidate Development Program   *X, 10, 43, 48, 109, 135, 165, 178, 179, 180, 181, 182, 187, 207, 222, 223, 224, 225, 226, 227, 228, 229, 290, 308*

Central Intelligence Agency   *VII, IX, 57, 60, 61, 62, 63, 64, 65, 165, 209, 213, 276, 280, 281, 319*

Character   *X, 48, 112, 127, 128, 129, 131, 132, 157, 158, 159, 181, 231, 236, 298, 307*

CHCO Council   *165, 210*

Chertoff, Michael   *116*

Civil Service Reform Act of 1978   *55, 110, 314*

Civil Service Retirement System   *39*

Clark, Tim   *IV*

Clinton, President William J. Clinton   *111, 141*

Cobert, Beth   *IV, VIII, 5, 7, 47, 55, 211, 222, 237, 290, 304*

Code of Federal Regulations   *100, 191, 280, 281, 314*

Collaboration   *7, 8, 9, 10, 30, 36, 82, 83, 85, 86, 89, 142, 145, 183, 193, 198, 200, 201, 204, 208, 213, 257, 261, 268, 296*

Cooke, David O.   *103*

Robert Corsi   *X, 184*

Courage   *IX, X, 21, 60, 61, 63, 66, 96, 112, 125, 127, 128, 129, 130, 131, 132, 133, 154, 157, 159, 169, 173, 183*

Cross-Agency Priority Goal   *289*

D

Dalrymple, John   *270*

Defense Contract Audit Agency   *241*

Defense Executive Advisory Board   *287*

Defense Finance and Accounting Service   *85*

Defense Intelligence Agency   *165, 168, 172, 212*

Defense Intelligence Senior Executive Service   *60, 275, 279, 281*

Department of Defense   *IV, IX, X, 7, 11, 17, 21, 26, 27, 57, 58, 61, 70, 73, 74, 83, 84, 85, 86, 87, 88, 90, 93, 97, 103, 105, 115, 138, 139, 155, 156, 167, 171, 187, 189, 192, 193, 194, 195, 199, 207, 210, 212, 215, 216, 220, 238, 239, 240, 241, 242, 243, 246, 273, 280, 281, 283, 287, 315, 319*

Department of Education   *8*

Department of Homeland Security   *IV, 57, 74, 111, 116, 241, 249, 260, 266, 276*

Department of Justice   *40, 115, 65, 264, 297, 299*

Department of State   *IX, 17, 58, 67, 70, 115, 213, 241*

Department of the Treasury   *8, 263, 294*

National Defense Authorization Act
for Fiscal Year 2016   240, 317

National Geospatial Intelligence Agency
VII, X, 165, 168, 169, 170, 172, 173, 174,
212

National Security Agency   VII, IX, 57, 60,
65, 66, 212, 288

National Security Council   16, 88

National Security Presidential Directive 41
(NSPD 41/HSPD 13) in 2004   115

National Treasury Employees Union
X, 112

National Aeronautics and Space
Administration   vi, IV, IX, 58, 66, 75

Neal, Jeff   76

Nickerson, Jackson   153, 195, 317, 319

National Security Professional
Development   222, 314

North Atlantic Treaty Organization   216

O

O'Conner, Jennifer   266

O'Keefe, Sean   IV, IX, 58, 75, 97

Obama, President Barack   7, 8, 9, 10, 13,
18, 34, 37, 40, 41, 42, 44, 45, 47, 50, 55, 79,
116, 118, 128, 129, 140, 141, 177, 191, 210,
228, 236, 238, 243, 247, 265, 272, 273, 287,
290, 292, 317

Office of Management and Budget   vii,
viii, IV, VII, IX, X, 5, 6, 7, 10, 32, 33, 34, 35,
48, 49, 50, 55, 58, 75, 88, 111, 129, 130, 135,
140, 146,166, 203, 210, 214, 237, 252, 263,
264, 265, 266, 275, 279, 288, 293, 303, 314,
316, 321

Office of Personnel Management   vii, IV,
VIII, XI, 5, 7, 8, 10, 12, 13, 17, 42, 43, 44,
45, 46, 47, 48, 49, 50, 55, 100, 110, 113, 134,
136, 140, 141, 142, 146, 147, 149, 152, 158,
166, 178, 179, 180, 187, 192, 193, 194, 196,
197, 198, 199, 201, 203, 206, 207, 210, 214,
220, 221, 222, 224, 225, 226, 227, 229, 232,
237, 240, 241, 248, 249, 252, 253, 254, 255,
257, 258, 259, 260, 261, 262, 272, 274, 275,
276, 277, 279, 280, 281, 283, 285, 286, 288,
289, 290, 292, 293, 294, 295, 296, 303, 306,
308, 313, 314, 320, 321

Office of Presidential Personnel   12

Office of the Director of National
Intelligence   171, 172, 215, 244, 276,
278, 318

Office of the Secretary of Defense   vi, 86,
165, 187, 215, 243

Oil Pollution Act of 1990   119, 318

OPM ECQ 1: Leading Change   86, 196,
201, 295

OPM ECQ 2: Leading People   86, 109,
196, 295

OPM ECQ 3: Results Driven   109, 196

OPM ECQ 4: Business Acumen   109, 196,
295

OPM ECQ 5: Building Coalitions   109,
152, 196, 295

OPM Qualifications Review Board   149,
152, 179, 220, 221, 229, 230, 231, 280, 281,
286, 308

OPM's Federal Executive Institute   vi, X,
42, 165, 191, 290

Organizational Boundaries   17

Organizational Culture   145, 252, 253, 259

P

Partnership for Public Service   vii, 129,
205, 241, 243, 246, 286, 318

Performance Accountability Council   88

Performance Improvement Council   88

Petty, Tom   131

Plame, Valerie   64

PMC's Interagency Rotation Program
222, 228, 308

President's Management Agenda   7

President's Management Council   vii, 10,
45, 88, 262, 286

Presidential Directive 27: Procedures for
Dealing with Non-Military Incidents
115

Presidential Rank Awards   245, 246

Presidential Transition   IX, 39, 58, 75, 97,
98, 102, 104, 166, 203, 235, 303

Probasco, Emelia S.   IX, 6, 23, 304

R

Reagan, President Ronald   *51*

Rice, Condoleezza   *65*

Risen, James   *65, 319*

Rodrigue, Michael   *168*

Rossotti, Charles   *IX, 92, 111, 112, 121*

S

Sanders, Ronald   *127, 137, 195, 315, 316, 317, 319*

Scott, Anthony   *10*

Senate Committee on Homeland Security and Governmental Affairs   *129*

Senior Executive Survey Exit Survey Results   *XI, 50, 253, 254, 259*

Senior Executives Association   *X, 40, 49, 50, 51, 70, 83, 116, 118, 175, 182, 297*

Senior Foreign Service   *VI, IX, 45, 58, 68, 69, 70, 72, 105, 211, 215, 279, 281, 307*

Senior National Intelligence Services   *277, 278, 279*

September 11, 2001 Terrorist Attack   *27, 62, 115, 154, 171, 208, 212, 244, 296, 317*

SES Accountability   *VI, X, 10, 39, 40, 41, 44, 49, 60, 62, 81, 91, 99, 109, 135, 169, 181, 193, 197, 211, 224, 239, 240, 257, 261, 285, 290, 294, 295, 297, 299, 300, 304, 297, 310, 311*

SES Advisory Committee   *50, 51*

SES Attrition   *XI, 38, 39, 40, 208, 209, 210, 247, 247, 248, 250, 253*

SES Bonuses   *19, 41, 172, 245, 283, 291, 292, 313*

SES Compensation   *11, 50, 62, 136, 172, 252, 272, 279, 283, 284, 290, 292, 293, 310*

SES Hiring   *11, 44, 258*

SES Mentoring   *69, 73, 84, 85, 103, 179, 185, 186, 254, 285*

SES Mobility   *79, 97, 216, 217*

SES Onboarding   *225, 262*

SES Performance Management   *147, 252, 258, 291, 294, 295*

SES Probationary Period   *225*

SES Promotion   *10, 41, 211, 223, 274, 297, 307*

SES Recruitment   *45, 169, 191, 256, 258, 260, 261*

SES Retention   *XI, 11, 41, 80, 94, 158, 173, 247, 250, 254, 256, 257, 259, 286, 287, 288, 304, 307*

SES Retirement   *i, III, 10, 11, 37, 38, 40, 44, 178, 181, 185, 205, 208, 210, 215, 223, 235, 248, 254, 256, 303*

SES Rotational Assignment   *44, 104, 179, 219, 272*

SES Salary Compression   *41, 205, 283*

SES Talent Management   *9, 8, 11, 12, 45, 47, 48, 168, 169, 170, 174, 176, 177, 178, 182, 183, 184, 210, 248, 249, 262, 285, 286, 287, 288, 290, 304, 309, 310*

Shea, Robert   *ii, iv, viii, IX, 6, 30, 35, 304*

Sheikh Mohammed, Khalid   *63*

Sherry, Margaret (Peggy)   *266*

Shih, Stephen   *IV, XI, 237, 255, 274*

Soft Power   *15, 151, 156*

Stovepipes   *17, 56, 151, 154, 211, 288*

Strengthening Employee Engagement and Organizational Performance   *314*

Succession Management   *11, 169, 173, 174, 179, 208, 250, 257, 258, 260, 261, 320*

Succession Planning   *10, 11, 45, 48, 51, 79, 165, 179, 181, 192, 198, 206, 207, 208, 210, 211, 222, 223, 224, 227, 247, 248, 250, 251, 252, 256, 262, 307, 318*

T

Tackling Wicked Government Problems: A Practical Guide for Developing Enterprise Leaders   *195, 317, 319*

Tangherlini, Daniel   *270, 271*

Taylor, James   *266*

The National Commission on Terrorist Attacks Upon the United States (i.e., the 9/11 Commission)   *27, 62, 115, 154, 171, 208, 212, 244, 296, 317*